Politics and Society in the South

POLITICS

AND

SOCIETY

IN THE

SOUTH

Earl Black and Merle Black

HARVARD UNIVERSITY PRESS
Cambridge, Massachusetts
London, England

Library of Congress Cataloging-in-Publication Data

Black, Earl, 1942–
  Politics and society in the South.

  Includes bibliographical references and index.
  1. Political parties—Southern States. 2. Southern
States—Politics and government—1951–
3. Political participation—Southern States.
4. Southern States—Race relations. 5. Southern
States—Social conditions. I. Black, Merle.
II. Title.
JK2295.A13B58 1987   306'.2'0975   86–18421
ISBN 0–674–68958–5 (alk. paper) cloth
ISBN 0–674–68959–3 (paper)

For our families
Sena and Stacey
Debra, Claire, and Julia

Preface

ALTHOUGH the South has experienced tremendous change in recent decades, it remains the most distinctive American region. Southern political conditions, trends, and possibilities profoundly interest many Americans within and without the region. For almost two generations, V. O. Key's *Southern Politics in State and Nation* has been the standard book on regional politics. Key's magnificent analysis remains unsurpassed in its treatment of the old southern politics, but subsequent changes have rendered it inadequate as a guide to the new southern politics.

Our study progresses from the new political sociology of the region to the most significant features of the emerging southern politics. We seek to provide an understanding of the social forces that are reshaping southern politics and are propelling the region toward party competition, as well as to explicate the South's most important political tendencies, both national and state. We identify and analyze the critical changes and continuities in the region's social order, economy, race relations, and mass public opinion, and then relate these changes and continuities to the most salient characteristics of the new southern politics.

In attempting to explain the complexities of southern political life we have explored many topics and employed a variety of research methods. Because the new southern politics cannot be fully appreciated unless it is measured against traditional southern institutions and practices, we have compared and contrasted, whenever feasible, the era of classic one-party politics (1920–1949) with the developments of the subsequent thirty-five years (1950–1985). By subjecting the occurrences of the past six decades to systematic investigation and interpretation, *Politics and Society in the South* provides a synthesis of regional trends and prospects.

We are very much aware, however, that our study tells only part of the story of regional politics. It is not about the politics of individual states, and it does not depict major regional politicians in any detail. We have sought to explain the changing milieu within which southern politicians operate, without describing the particulars of specific situations. These omissions are not due to a lack of interest in such topics. Neither time nor space permits adequate coverage of general tendencies and specific illustrations in a single book. In our judgment a broad synthesis of southern political developments is the most urgent and compelling need in the field of regional politics. We hope to write other books that will do justice to the most prominent and influential southern politicians and will compare more thoroughly the politics of the southern states.

We have used the conventional definition of the region that Key employed in *Southern Politics,* that is, the eleven former Confederate states: Alabama, Arkansas, Florida, Georgia, Louisiana, Mississippi, North Carolina, South Carolina, Tennessee, Texas, and Virginia. Our only regular departure from this convention occurs when we use the presidential election year surveys of the Center for Political Studies of the Institute for Social Research of the University of Michigan (formerly the Survey Research Center). Their representative sample of the South ("Solid South") is based on ten states, the former Confederate states minus Tennessee. The SRC-CPS election studies data were made available through the Inter-University Consortium for Political and Social Research; neither the collector of the original data nor the consortium bears any responsibility for the analyses or interpretations presented here.

We are deeply indebted to many individuals and institutions who have helped us in different ways. At Harvard University Press Aida Donald encouraged us from the beginning and provided judicious editorial advice. Dorothy Whitney edited the manuscript with exceptional diligence and imagination. Elizabeth Suttell coordinated a variety of editorial tasks, and Deborah Schneck did the artwork. For criticism and counsel, we wish to thank James L. Sundquist, William C. Havard, Dick Richardson, John Shelton Reed, George Rabinowitz, Thad Beyle, Blease Graham, Gerald C. Wright, Jr., Harold W. Stanley, Martin P. Wattenberg, David S. Broder, and the late James W. Prothro. Arlon Kemple, Don Haynes, and Anne Stubbs provided excellent research assistance. Merle Black was aided by several grants from the University Research Council of the University of North Carolina at Chapel Hill and by a one-semester Kenan Leave from the University of North Carolina at Chapel Hill. Earl Black benefited enormously from his year in residence as a fellow of the Woodrow Wilson International Center for Scholars in 1977–78 and from sabbatical leave in 1982–83 from the University of South Carolina.

Parts of the book have been adapted from material published elsewhere, and we wish to thank the relevant authorities for permission to incorporate material from Merle Black, "The Modification of a Major Cultural Belief: Declining Support for 'Strict Segregation' among White Southerners, 1961–1972," *Journal of the North Carolina Political Science Association* (now *Politics and Policy*), 1 (Summer 1979), 4–21; and from

Merle Black, "North Carolina: The 'Best' Southern State?" in Thad L. Beyle and Merle Black, eds., *Politics and Policy in North Carolina* (New York: MSS Information Corporation, 1975), pp. 13–36. Permission to quote from V. O. Key, Jr., *Southern Politics in State and Nation* (New York: Alfred A. Knopf, 1949), was generously given by Marion T. Key; and Alfred A. Knopf, Inc., kindly granted us permission to quote from W. J. Cash, *The Mind of the South* (New York: Alfred A. Knopf, 1941).

We assume responsibility for all errors of fact and interpretation.

Contents

I
The Changing South

one

Old Politics,
New People

AT MIDCENTURY V.O. Key published *Southern Politics in State and Nation,* the definitive study of the "old" southern politics. Focusing mainly on the period 1920–1949, Key critically analyzed the South's most salient political practices, including the development and maintenance of one-party political systems, highly depressed rates of white political participation, the relentless subordination and exclusion of blacks from politics, and state politics devoted principally to advancing and protecting the interests of "haves" rather than the much larger group of "have-nots." It was a portrait neither of political democracy nor of efficient governance. "When all the exceptions are considered, when all the justifications are made, and when all the invidious comparisons are drawn," Key wrote, "those of the South and those who love the South are left with the cold, hard fact that the South as a whole has developed no system or practice of political organization and leadership adequate to cope with its problems."[1]

The "Old" Southern Politics

The "old" or "classic" southern politics originated around the turn of the century and began to disintegrate about midcentury. J. Morgan Kousser convincingly demonstrated in *The Shaping of Southern Politics* how southern Democrats decimated their political opponents—blacks, white Republicans, and white Populists—in state after state during the 1890s and 1900s and thereby established one party politics.[2] Ways and means of achieving disfranchisement varied across the region, but everywhere stringent new suffrage requirements (poll taxes, literacy and "understanding" tests, secret ballots, registration and residency requirements) were enacted and enforced. When the new laws were combined with such informal means of handling despised opponents as "persuasion," verbal and economic intimidation, ballot box fraud, and selective violence (including political assassinations, burnings, and beatings), it was not difficult for conservative white Democrats to clear the electorate of former slaves, sons of slaves, and "worthless" white men.[3]

While imposing insurmountable burdens upon blacks, the new suffrage rules also severely handicapped unschooled whites, who often could not read (and thus correctly mark) the ballots, and whites with meager incomes, who could not afford to pay a poll tax. Once the disfranchising provisions were established, the southern elite could enforce its beliefs that blacks were not members of the political community and that, among whites, voting was a privilege to be earned rather than a right to be exercised. "By 1910, almost no Negroes and only about half of the whites bothered to vote in the most hotly contested elections," Kousser estimated, and "the Southern political system which was to last through mid-century had been formed."[4] As a "democracy" of white and black males gave way to a "broadly based oligarchy" of white males, "southern politics [shifted] from active competition to mandatory tranquility."[5]

With their rivals destroyed in most states and crippled elsewhere, the winning Democrats proceeded to enforce white partisan solidarity to preserve the dominant group's way of life.[6] No one has better captured the meaning of the Democratic party to these white southerners, only a generation or so removed from the Civil War and Reconstruction, than W. J. Cash:

> The world knows the story of the Democratic party in the South; how, once violence had opened the way to political action, this party became the institutionalized incarnation of the will to White Supremacy. How, indeed, it ceased to be a party *in* the South and became the party *of* the South, a kind of confraternity having in its keeping the whole corpus of Southern loyalties, and so irresistibly commanding the allegiance of faithful whites that to doubt it, to question it in any detail, was *ipso facto* to stand branded as a renegade to race, to country, to God, and to Southern Womanhood.[7]

Under these intense pressures for conformity, Jasper B. Shannon argued, "adherence to the name and symbol of Democracy became the chief article of faith in the new political creed."[8]

There was more to southern orthodoxy, of course, than enthusiasm for white supremacy, hostility to full-fledged democracy, and loyalty to the Democratic party. Most southern Democrats' core beliefs included the glorification of the Confederacy and veneration of the Lost Cause, the primacy of state's rights over rights of the national government, a constricted sphere of legitimate functions for state and local governments, minimal taxation and expenditure, an emphasis on individual rather than social responsibility for personal and family economic well-being, and the legitimacy of extralegal force (epitomized by lynching) to punish perceived violations of the region's caste system.[9] Though this creed was not entirely conservative (William C. Havard has emphasized several progressive themes, including the regulation of out-of-state corporations),[10] it was resolutely biased in favor of the economic and power interests of the more affluent whites.

The white South's main device for preventing national challenges to its racial practices, its tenacious loyalty to the Democratic party, powerfully conditioned and constrained state political activity. In Key's words, "Consistent and unquestioning attachment, by overwhelming majorities, to the Democratic party nationally has meant that the politics within southern states—the election of governors, of state legislators, and the settlement of public issues generally—has had to be conducted without benefit of political parties." When the southern states achieved regional unity in national politics, they "condemned themselves internally to a chaotic factional politics."[11]

In establishing one-party rule, southern Democratic leaders transformed general elections into empty and meaningless rituals.[12] The real political contests, those where outcomes were in doubt, concerned *which* Democrat would receive the party's nomination. Democrats had previously chosen their nominees for statewide office in party conventions, but these elitist gatherings, composed of successful local party activists, denied rank-and-file Democrats any direct voice in selecting their party's candidates. Losing candidates and their followers could always charge that the "people's choice" had been rejected by the party leadership, an increasingly troublesome accusation in political systems that failed to provide mechanisms for authentic popular choice. Astute in matters affecting their own survival, leading Democrats gradually began to understand the advantage of determining nominees in primary elections, where the final decision rested with registered white Democrats.[13]

Between 1896 and 1915 every southern state adopted some version of the direct primary system to nominate Democratic candidates.[14] In its most typical form—the dual primary system—Democratic nominees had to demonstrate wide acceptability by winning a majority, not simply a plurality, of the total vote. If no candidate secured a majority in the first primary, most southern states either required or permitted a second (runoff) primary limited to the two leading candidates from the first primary. Thus came into being the white South's most renowned institution of political choice, an electoral system whose main purpose, as Kousser has argued, was far more to forestall irreconcilable divisions and bolts among white Democrats than to provide "democracy" for whites.[15]

Shifting nominations from conventions to direct primaries changed the style of many southern politicians because it forced them to cultivate an appeal beyond local party notables. Candidates for statewide office now tried to "stand out in a crowd" through the rhetoric of exaggeration and ridicule. Reflecting upon the campaign styles of successful Democratic politicians after Republicanism had been banished, Cash detected an enhanced emphasis on "the personal and the romantic" in distinguishing rival campaigners. "Was this candidate or that one more showy and satisfying? Did Jack or Jock offer the more thrilling representation of the South in action against the Yankee and the black man? Here, and here almost alone," Cash concluded, "would there be a field for choice."[16]

Kousser argued that the transition to primary nominations facilitated "demagoguery" because "primary candidates had to lambaste their opponents publicly." Furthermore, "when the statewide primary became the only important election, candidates had to fabricate issues. Since no deep cleavages divided the voting public in the primaries, campaigns usually revolved around questions of personality, petty scandal, or charges that one or more candidates represented an evil political machine or a despised, but politically impotent group such as the Communists or the blacks. To attract attention, competitors were virtually forced to make charges they could not prove, promises they could not keep."[17] Sensational accusations might inspire a lively and close contest but normally failed to stimulate extensive popular participation. Nor did such battles produce many victories for politicians striving to represent the economic interests of the bulk of the potential electorate, the have-little and have-not whites.

Time and again Key demonstrated the triumph of the haves and the defeat of the have-nots in matters of state taxing and spending. Economic *and* racial conservatism generally predominated among the South's governors and congressional delegations, as exemplified by Richard Russell, Carter Glass, Pat Harrison, Harry Byrd, James Eastland, Walter George, John McClellan, Strom Thurmond, and John Stennis. The South's conventional wisdom was embedded even more firmly in the leadership of state legislatures, where small groups of experienced, professional politicians returned, session after session, to preserve and enhance the political and economic interests of the region's county seat elites.[18] This outcome requires explanation, for in most southern states even the shrunken electorates of the early twentieth century probably contained more have-littles and have-nots than middle-class whites simply because there were so few middle- and upper-class whites in the populations.

Although the numerical center of political gravity may have rested with nonaffluent whites, the region's haves provided most of the politicians, supplied most campaign finance, and controlled the society's wealth. Affluent whites had the most to lose from state governments bent on redistributing wealth from haves to have-nots. For politically alert haves the strategic objective was to maintain steady control over the major institutions of state government despite being—even after massive disfranchisement—still outnumbered by have-nots. It was not an insuperable problem. Close attention to the political agenda, timely use of impressive financial resources, years of experience in practical politics, continuous efforts to ensure the presence of a core of senior senators and representatives in the state legislatures and Congress, and the ability to frame issues and identify candidates who could appeal for the votes of common whites without simultaneously arousing them against the upper classes—all of these political skills and resources could be adroitly employed in order to keep critical state and national offices in safe and reliable hands.[19]

The common touch was indispensable. Colorful phrases, memorable anecdotes with well-conceived punch lines, an ability to defend one's honesty and integrity at the drop of an accusation or to attack an opponent's character, intelligence, ancestry, and morals should the occasion demand it—such attributes were all part of the paraphernalia necessary to survive in the mass political culture of the rural and small-town South in the early twentieth century. Countrified verbal slugging came naturally to many ambitious politicians (particularly to experienced damage suit lawyers) but was a necessary evil to others. Sometimes dignity was sacrificed. Former *New York Times* editor Turner Catledge, a Mississippi native, once reminisced about observing the stately and otherwise dignified Georgia Senator Walter George engage in "anti-Negro, anti-Semitic, anti-labor, and anti-Yankee" oratory, using fiery language that quickly had the crowd "on their feet, cheering wildly. Shouts of 'Go to 'em, Walter,' and 'Let 'em have it,' were punctuated by rebel yells." The conservative senator, under attack in 1938 from President Franklin Roosevelt for his lack of enthusiasm for the New Deal, easily won renomination. "George had done what he had to do," Catledge concluded. "It reminded me of what [Mississippi Senator] Pat Harrison used to say—that he could be a statesman for five years, but on the sixth—election year—he went back home to 'sling the shit.' "[20]

Conservatives thrived in the old southern politics, although they did not completely dominate electoral politics. The situation was far different for the few authentic champions of the lower orders, such politicians as Huey Long, Lister Hill, John Sparkman, James Folsom, Claude Pepper,

Estes Kefauver, Albert Gore, and Ralph Yarborough. One-party politics reduced the incentives and compounded the hazards confronting politicians who wished to win office by appealing directly to the region's have-littles and have-nots on the basis of their economic self-interest.[21] Cash attributed much of the problem to the poor whites themselves: "Bound rigidly within the single great frame by the hypnotic Negro-fixation, estopped by the necessity of unity, if the black man was to be kept in his place, from any considerable development of faction, the masses were stripped of every possibility of effectual political action for the amelioration of their estate, even . . . when they themselves should come dimly to desire it."[22]

Key viewed "the absence of organized and continuing factions with a lower-bracket orientation" as the "striking feature of the one-party system."[23] Much of the natural constituency for the provision of goods and services to the lower orders had been permanently disfranchised; others faced formidable suffrage requirements; and still others did not vote because the typical "issues of one-party politics" were not considered "matters of importance." Leadership of the rarest sort would be required to arouse nonaffluent whites effectively. A successful politician would need the ability to identify and dramatize "issues that touch people deeply," the skill to mobilize and organize the potential constituency, and the savvy to secure tangible economic benefits. Moreover, in order to challenge effectively the powers that usually dominated state politics, an optimistic and fighting champion of the underdog was required. Such activities were intrinsically risky, for they cut against the grain of the active electorate and invited the malign attention of the upper orders. Once in a blue moon such politicians did appear—Huey Long is the standard example—but campaigning as an overt friend of the have-littles and have-nots amounted to "doing it the hard way" in the old southern politics.[24]

Thus emerged the main features of traditional southern politics: a politics compressed within a single political party, where the main differences centered on the personalities and qualifications of the candidates rather than significant issues; a politics in which most adult southerners were either ineligible to vote or did not bother to participate; a politics in which policy outcomes were egregiously slanted in favor of the haves, the few white men with wealth and political influence. As H. D. Price expressed the intrinsic stagnation of one-party politics, "The politics of black belt vs. non-black belt or of agrarian protest vs. Big Mules is fascinating to behold, but essentially a merry-go-round. The most interesting thing is the campaign itself, not any substantive policy results. Such politics is cyclic, if not plain static."[25] The old southern politics went round and round in circles, seldom moving beyond the question of whether Jack or Jock would win public office. Essentially it was a politics of limited taxation, limited spending, and, above all, determined resistance to any changes in the racial status quo.

For Key (and countless other observers), the overarching explanation for the South's failure to nurture the institutions and beliefs necessary for stable democracy lay in the exigencies of white racial domination: "In its grand outlines the politics of the South revolves around the position of the Negro." Why was the preservation of white supremacy the paramount objective—the ultimate concern—of the old southern politics? Key attributed the primacy of racial politics to the values, interests, and leadership of the white politicians who lived in rural areas with substantial black populations. "It is the whites of the black belts who have the deepest and most immediate concern about the maintenance of white supremacy," he contended. "Those whites who live in counties with populations 40, 50, 60, and even 80 percent Negro share a common attitude toward the Negro."[26]

Though he sometimes used language (as in the following quotation) that appeared to blame the victims of white racism rather than the victimizers for the region's deficiencies, Key understood clearly which white southerners were the most zealous white supremacists and the most committed defenders of one-party solidarity:

> The hard core of the political South—and the backbone of southern political unity—is made up of those counties and sections of the southern states in which Negroes constitute a substantial proportion of the population. In these areas a real problem of politics, broadly considered, is the maintenance of control by a white minority. The situation resembles fundamentally that of the Dutch in the East Indies or the former position of the British in India. Here, in the southern black belts, the problem of governance is similarly one of the control by a small, white minority of a huge, retarded, colored population. And, as in the case of the colonials, that white minority can maintain its position only with the support, and by the tolerance, of those outside—in the home country or in the rest of the United States.[27]

Reducing Key's perspective to its bare essentials, the "fundamental explanation of southern politics is that the black-belt whites succeeded in imposing their will on their states and thereby presented a solid regional front in national politics on the race issue."[28]

Plantation or multi-unit agriculture commonly prevailed in the black belt counties, and the whites who controlled extensive agricultural operations wanted an ample supply of cheap, unskilled, and docile labor.[29] White authorities deliberately minimized black educational opportunities (too much education might ruin otherwise reliable and complaisant field hands), and the preposterous idea of intermingling the scions of white planters and the offspring of black tenants in schools was beyond contemplation. Genuine political democracy would have meant majority black electorates in many counties and sizable black minorities in many more counties. Motivated by complementary social, economic, and political interests to keep blacks thoroughly subordinated, many black belt whites regarded even the most trivial racial changes elsewhere in their states as dangerous precedents, for minute concessions might stimulate future demands for more substantial reforms.

White racism was by no means limited to the southern black belts. A 1940 Gallup poll reported that 98 percent of white southerners preferred segregated schools,[30] and fictional as well as nonfictional accounts of white southerners residing outside the black belts in the 1940s document extraordinarily racist attitudes and behavior.[31] In projecting a united regional viewpoint on racial questions, black belt whites could thus draw upon the consensus of the non-black belt areas that the South was a "white man's country."

But if virtually all white southerners in the 1940s were conventionally racist, Key insisted that the salience and intensity of these shared racist perspectives varied significantly within the region. Whites outside the black belts were certainly concerned about preserving the racial status quo. Working-class and poor whites could gain some sense of superiority—some satisfaction—by virtue of their race. In the words of an old East Texas working-class white, a man who had never earned more than the minimum wage in his life and who was, apart from racial matters, a thoroughly decent human being, "When they come to my house, they come to the back door."[32] Whites who hired and fired found blacks useful not only as inexpensive labor but also as a means to hold down white wages. Yet beyond the black belt counties, the region's largest minority was a local minority, and whites were less "threatened" than their counterparts in the old plantation sections by all aspects of racial change. Blacks were neither so central to the local economy nor so sizable a bloc of prospective voters in local elections. As a result, non–black belt whites were racist but comparatively less preoccupied with preserving undiluted white supremacy. Confronted by the racial conflicts of the 1950s and early 1960s, whites outside the black belts were initially defiant and hostile but later exhibited some willingness—grudging and exasperated, to be sure—to adapt to new circumstances.

In earlier times southern racial crises had usually been settled according to the repressive racial policies that were advocated most fervently by black belt whites. "Although the whites of the black belts are few in number," Key observed, "their unity and their political skill have enabled them to run a shoestring into decisive power at critical junctures in southern political history."[33] Indeed, Kousser repeatedly emphasized the crucial role of the black belt whites in creating the one-party system.[34] Black belt political influence rested not only on the widespread commitment to white supremacy of non–black belt whites, but also on alliances and understandings with large-scale industry and finance, forces that were not indifferent to or unconcerned about race relations.

When the general issue of the proper position of blacks in southern society was once again raised around midcentury—the key events were Supreme Court decisions outlawing the "white" primary in 1944 and school segregation in 1954 and the Montgomery bus boycott of 1955–56—the black belt whites united to defend their way of life. They were joined by whites outside the black belts and by much of southern industry and finance in the "massive resistance" movement, a movement that was initially successful.[35] But for a variety of reasons the black belt whites were eventually unable to sustain the segregated social order they preferred against a combined "revolt from below" and "intervention from outside" the region. As a consequence of the civil rights movement and federal penetration, many of the most transparent differences in racial practices between the South and the rest of the nation have vanished. Lest we be misunderstood, these changes do *not* mean that contemporary southern politics is completely emancipated from old-style racism or that interracial conflicts are unimportant. Yet as we shall show throughout this book, in its political life the modern South is far more similar to the non-South than ever before.

Since 1950 a host of truly momentous political developments have occurred in the South—the Supreme Court's school desegregation ruling and the massive resistance of many white southerners to that decision; the growth of a civil rights movement protesting racial discrimination and the revival of black political participation; the enactment of national legislation meant to reform the South's segregationist racial traditions; the rise and decline of George Wallace's movement; the revitalization of the Republican party and the spread of political independence among whites in a region long dominated by the Democratic party; and the election of Lyndon B. Johnson and Jimmy Carter as President. These events have obliterated many prominent characteristics of the "old" southern politics, focused renewed national attention on the region, and reemphasized the extraordinary stakes of politics in the South.

Underlying the profound political changes of the recent southern past have been equally important transformations of the region's population, economy, and social structure. Though politics broadly understood is our central concern, it would be myopic to ignore the demographic and socioeconomic changes that clearly differentiate the South of the 1980s from the South in 1950 or the South of the 1920s. As is so frequently the case, Key's insights provide an appropriate starting point. At the conclusion of *Southern Politics* Key confronted the "unfathomable maze formed by tradition, caste, race, poverty" and inquired, "Is there a way out?" His answer was simultaneously skeptical and optimistic. Ignoring or rejecting the likelihood of basic political reform emanating from either state capitols or Washington, as well as any significant rebellion by black southerners, Key emphasized instead "changes in the composition and distribution of the population and in the nature of economic organization and endeavor. These changes are altering the shape of the mold that influences, if it does not fix, the shape of southern politics." Specifically, he argued that *declines* in the relative size of the black population and *increases* in urbanization and industrialization constituted "fundamental trends" that would slowly foster political arrangements more consistent with "national ideas of constitutional morality."[36] Systematic consideration of these factors, as well as other population trends not discussed by Key, will allow us to evaluate the extent to which the old South has given way to (yet another) new South and the degree to which the South still differs from the rest of the nation.

The Changing Racial Composition of the South

Key formulated the resolution of regional peculiarities as the task of "emancipation of the white from the Negro" and suggested that black southerners were indirectly contributing to this "emancipation" by abandoning the region in search of less racial discrimination and better educational and job opportunities. In the black exodus Key discerned both a potentially major change in the structure of regional politics and the possibility of diminished white preoccupation with the political and economic subordination of blacks. "It is not to be supposed, of course, that a reduction in the Negro population ratio brings with it immediately a shift in white political attitudes," he wrote. "That change comes only gradually; an alteration of population composition, however, creates a new political setting that will eventually make itself felt."[37] Because of their obvious significance for southern politics past and present, trends in the relative size of the black population need to be examined.

Comparisons of the proportion of blacks in southern and nonsouthern populations in 1920, 1950, and 1980 show that differences between the regions have been declining (table 1.1). In 1920 the percentage of blacks among all southerners (32) exceeded the percentage of blacks among all

Table 1.1. Diminution of southern black populations: percentage of blacks in total population in 1920, 1950, and 1980, by state, subregion, region, and nation

Political unit	1920	1950	1980	Percentage change
Deep South				
Mississippi[a]	52[b]	45	35	−33[c]
South Carolina	51	39	30	−41
Louisiana	39	33	29	−24
Georgia	42	31	27	−36
Alabama	38	32	26	−33
Peripheral South				
North Carolina	30	27	22	−25
Virginia	30	22	19	−37
Arkansas	27	22	16	−40
Tennessee	19	16	16	−18
Florida	34	22	14	−59
Texas	16	13	12	−25
Deep South	44	35	29	−34
Peripheral South	24	19	15	−35
South	32	25	20	−39
United States	10	10	12	+18
Non-South	3	5	9	+193
South:non-South ratio	10.7	4.8	2.2	
Deep South:Peripheral South ratio	1.9	1.9	1.9	

Source: U.S. Census.

a. States are ranked (highest to lowest) according to the proportion of blacks in the total population in 1980.

b. Figures are rounded to the nearest whole percentage.

c. Percentage reduction or increase in the proportion of blacks in the total population between 1920 and 1980.

nonsoutherners (3) by a factor of 11. It is unlikely that any other theoretically important census variable would produce such fundamental interregional differences, differences that could not fail to be reflected in politics. Seventy-seven percent of all black Americans lived in the South in 1920; six decades later, following extensive black out-migration, the South contained only 45 percent of the nation's blacks. After also exporting whites through 1950, the region subsequently became a net importer of whites. These demographic patterns have culminated in the declining relative size of the black population in the South and small but steady increases in the relative size of the black population outside the South. Although the long-term trend in racial composition is increased similarity between the regions, even in 1980 the proportion of blacks in the South (20) was twice as great as it was in the non-South (9). Appreciable regional differences in racial composition thus persist.

Even though the regional trend of falling black populations can be traced in every southern state, the individual states diverge considerably in regard to the proportion of blacks in their populations. Since findings for the entire region may well conceal interesting differences within the South, and since it is impractical to discuss results for eleven separate states, we shall frequently report findings for two subregions, the Deep South and the Peripheral South, that are defined in terms of the relative size of the black population. Building on Key's observation that the southern states "with fewest Negroes seem most disposed toward deviation from the popular supposition of how the South behaves politically,"[38] we shall refer to the five contiguous states that have repeatedly contained the highest black populations (Mississippi, South Carolina, Louisiana, Georgia, and Alabama) as the Deep South and designate as the Peripheral South the six states with relatively smaller proportions of blacks (North Carolina, Virginia, Arkansas, Tennessee, Florida, and Texas).[39]

The proportion of blacks in the Deep South has been consistently almost twice as large as the proportion in the Peripheral South populations (table 1.1). Aside from the theoretical utility of distinguishing southern states with higher black populations from those with smaller black populations, comparing and contrasting the Deep South and the Peripheral South is necessary to avoid overestimating change within the region. Because a steadily increasing majority of southerners—rising from 58 percent in 1920 to 69 percent in 1980—reside in the six Peripheral South states, in the absence of subregional controls the more distinctively "southern" or "traditional" behavior of the Deep South may be obscured or even lost. Through subregional comparisons, findings that are genuinely characteristic of the entire region may be distinguished from regional patterns that actually disguise critical differences between the subregions. Important subregional differences, with the Deep South responding in a markedly more traditional fashion than the Peripheral South, should be anticipated whenever racial phenomena are involved.

Whether we are interested in states, subregions, or the region, there are at least two important reasons to know the size of the black population. The percentage of blacks indicates, first of all, the relative strength of blacks either as potential or actual political participants. The southern black populations that are generally free to register and vote in the 1980s are considerably smaller in every jurisdiction than the black populations that were effectively denied the franchise in the 1920s. In the contemporary period, assuming that the right to vote is a reality and that black voters are fairly united in their preferences, the size of the black population is a major determinant of potential black political leverage. The percentage of blacks also serves as an indirect indicator of the salience and intensity of white attitudes and behavior. "If the whites of the black belts give the South its dominant political tone," Key suggested, "the character of the politics of individual states will vary roughly with the Negro proportion of the population."[40] The larger the black population, the greater the likelihood for whites—threatened or feeling threatened by blacks—to be united in support of racial conservatism. Thus even in the midst of declining black populations, variations in the relative size of the black population within the South remain important for understanding the political behavior of white southerners.

One of the most telling demographic changes affecting twentieth-century southern politics is the diminishing weight of the black belt in statewide elections. In 1920 more than one-fourth (27 percent) of the region's total presidential vote originated in black belt counties (rural areas with black populations of 30 percent or more). Black belt whites accounted for 43 percent of the vote cast in the Deep South versus 21 percent of the Peripheral South vote. Six decades later, however, the potential influence of conservative whites from these areas had been substantially reduced. In the 1980 presidential compaign the rural black belts contributed only 10 percent of the total southern vote (23 percent in the Deep South, but merely 4 percent in the Peripheral South). Not only has the prominence of the black belt vote declined, but much of the vote emanating from the black belt comes from blacks. Black reentry into politics and massive population gains outside the black belt have made it virtually impossible for conservative black belt whites, the leadership echelon in classic southern politics, to control contemporary political agendas.

The New Southerners

The old southern politics flourished in a homogeneous electorate. Prior to midcentury most voters were whites, born and raised in the South of the late nineteenth or early twentieth centuries. Even after the adoption of the Nineteenth Amendment in 1920, most members of the active electorate were males who had experienced—or whose father or grandfather had experienced—the tumultuous, life-or-death struggles of the Civil War, Reconstruction, and disfranchisement. The majority had scant formal education; many were marginal farmers or otherwise employed in manual labor. Scarce indeed were "middle"-or "upper"-class voters. Stump-speaking abilities that entertained as well as argued, that employed grandiloquent boasting and pungent ridicule, that allowed audiences to vent their feelings were often required to command the attention and win the votes of these whites. Constituencies primarily composed of unlettered, rural, white, male Democrats nourished the region's reputation for spellbinding oratory, and often the speechmaking included racism of the most callous and blatant sort.

In no small measure the Solid South rested on the electoral dominance of its native white population. The revival of black participation has obviously altered the electorate's racial composition, but critical changes in the South's white population have contributed as well to the new southern politics. In the early 1960s Philip E. Converse directed attention to two demographic trends, interregional migration and generational replacement, that were changing the South's population and would, in time, change its electorate.[41] To the extent that white southern populations traditionally attached to the Democratic party have been diluted by the arrival of migrating nonsouthern whites and by younger whites native to the South who are more predisposed toward political independence or Republicanism, challenges to one-party politics should be anticipated.

Steady increases are evident (see table 1.2) in the proportion of "Yankees"—defined as whites born in the United States but outside the Census Bureau's sixteen-state South—in the white populations of the South.[42] Nonsouthern whites, who composed at midcentury only 8 percent of the region's white population, accounted for 20 percent of the southern white population in 1980. Yankees have especially penetrated the Peripheral South. Nonsouthern whites constituted 25 percent of the Peripheral South's white population in 1980, and that subregion has consistently contained 85 percent of the South's Yankee population. Immigrant whites made up only a tenth of the Deep South's whites in 1980, a fact that contributes significantly to the Deep South's continuing reputation for racial and political traditionalism.

With regard to the political impact of whites born outside the region, the states may be divided into three groups. Florida, whose tropical climate attracted retirees and military installations in abundance, was unique in the scope of its northernization. In 1980 it possessed two-fifths of all the Yankees living in the South and was the only southern state in which northern-born whites were a majority of the total white population. Less impressive rates of in-migration, with nonsouthern whites accounting for approximately one-fifth of the 1980 white population, were visible in the Peripheral South states of Virginia (substantial federal gov-

Table 1.2. Incremental northernization of white populations in the South: percentage of native whites residing in the South who were born outside the South, 1950–1980, by state, subregion, and region

Political unit	Percentage of native whites born outside South							
	1950		1960		1970		1980	
Florida[a]	30	(29)[b]	30	(39)	42	(39)	51	(41)
Virginia	11	(13)	14	(11)	18	(12)	21	(10)
Texas	9	(27)	10	(23)	14	(20)	20	(20)
Arkansas	9	(6)	10	(4)	12	(4)	18	(4)
Georgia	4	(4)	6	(5)	8	(5)	12	(6)
South Carolina	3	(2)	6	(2)	8	(3)	12	(3)
Tennessee	4	(6)	5	(4)	7	(4)	11	(5)
North Carolina	3	(5)	5	(5)	7	(5)	11	(5)
Louisiana	5	(4)	5	(3)	6	(3)	9	(3)
Mississippi	3	(2)	5	(2)	6	(2)	8	(2)
Alabama	3	(3)	5	(3)	6	(3)	8	(3)
Deep South	4	(15)	5	(15)	7	(15)	10	(15)
Peripheral South	10	(85)	14	(85)	18	(85)	25	(85)
South	8	(100)	11	(100)	14	(100)	20	(100)

Sources: Calculated from the following publications of the U.S. Bureau of the Census: *1950 Census of Population,* vol. IV, *Special Reports,* part 4, chap. A, State of Birth, tables 14 and 15; *1960 Census of Population,* State Reports, tables 39 and 98; *1970 Census of Population,* State Reports, table 50; and *1980 Census of Population,* State Reports, tables 75 and 85.

a. States are ranked (highest to lowest) according to the percentage of native whites in 1980 who were born outside the South.

b. Figures in parentheses report the percentage distribution within the South of all native whites born outside the South. For example, in 1950 Florida contained 29 percent of all the northern-born whites who resided in the South.

ernment presence, both military and civilian), Texas (defense installations), and Arkansas (retirement center). Except in these four states, however, extensive northernization failed to take place, at least through 1980. On the contrary, a majority of the southern states were characterized less by sizable advances in white in-migration than by the continuing homogeneity of their native white populations. When native whites born in the South compose between 88 and 92 percent of the total white population, as they did in 1980 in all five Deep South states, North Carolina, and Tennessee, such limited northernization cannot explain much of the political change that has occurred.

Where exactly have Yankees settled in the South? A map indicating

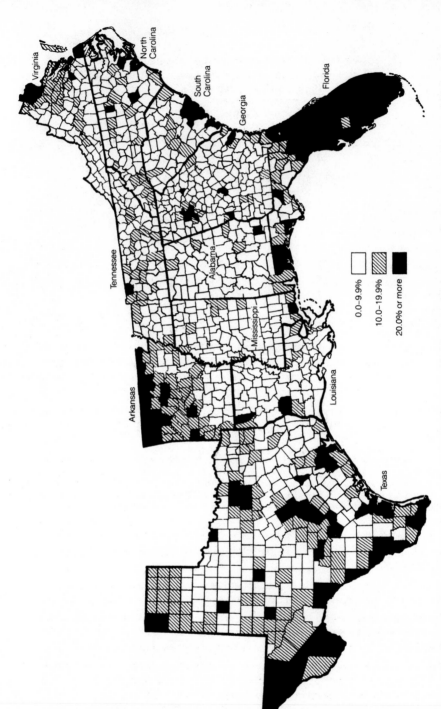

Figure 1.1. The geography of northernization: percentage of native whites in 1980 who were born outside the southern states. *Source:* Calculated from U.S. Bureau of the Census, *1980 Census of Population*, I, *Characteristics of the Population*, appropriate state reports, table 183.

Legend:
0.0–9.9%
10.0–19.9%
20.0% or more

the extent of northernization in 1980 reveals that the incidence of northern-born whites has varied radically among southern counties (figure 1.1). Aside from the wholesale northernization of peninsular Florida and smaller concentrations of white migrants in northern Arkansas, the few counties in which one-fifth or more of the native white population had been born outside the South appear as isolated enclaves.

We suspect that in most counties the high rates of northernization can be explained in terms of one or more of three basic forces: urbanization (with its attendant opportunities for employment), militarization, and retirement. By far the most important and dynamic factor with regard to political consequences has been the relocation of northern-born whites in the South's expanding metropolitan areas. In 1980 most of the counties containing the central cities of the South's principal Standard Metropolitan Statistical Areas (SMSAs) possessed Yankee populations of at least 10 percent. The relation between urbanization and northernization, critical for the creation of sustained southern Republicanism, was, nonetheless, much stronger in the Peripheral South (excepting North Carolina and Tennessee) than in the Deep South.

Another key source of white in-migration, though less important politically because of the brevity of military assignments, has been the ninety-one major military installations (sixty-one in the Peripheral South, thirty in the Deep South) operating in the South in the early 1980s.[43] A sizable majority of these defense bases were situated in the leading metropolitan centers and thus contributed to rapid urbanization. Virginia's Hampton Roads area, San Antonio, and Charleston illustrate defense-stimulated northernization in urban environments. Most of the solitary, nonmetropolitan counties with high rates of nothern-born whites contained military bases. A third factor driving white migration, less significant regionally because it is concentrated in South Florida and northern Arkansas, is the South's attractiveness as a retirement site. Retirees have numerous practical concerns that require political alertness, yet because of their age they are less likely to be agents of political change than, say, upwardly mobile executives in their thirties.

Attention should finally be drawn to the remarkable impenetrability of most southern counties to the entry of northern-born whites. Although there were 141 counties (12 percent) in 1980 where migrants represented at least 20 percent of the native white population, Yankees made up less than a tenth of the white population in 750 counties (65 percent). Persistently southernized counties—those left blank in figure 1.1—included 86 percent of all Deep South counties and 54 percent of all Peripheral South counties. Future censuses will probably reveal a deepening penetration of nonsouthern whites within areas already attractive to migrants and some dispersion to counties with smaller towns as more industries—chiefly branch plants—continue to spread throughout the region.

Generational changes in the South's native white population, the other demographic trend identified by Converse, have also weakened the ties that bound native southerners to the Democratic party. Paul Allen Beck has provided lucid analyses of successive generations of southern whites and, with Paul Lopatto, has distinguished three different political generations among white southerners: whites who came of voting age prior to 1946 (the Solid South generation); those who began to vote between 1946 and 1964 (the post–World War II generation); and those who became eligible to vote after 1964 (the post–Voting Rights generation).[44]

The Solid South generation of native whites contains the chief cultural bearers of southern Democracy. Although they supplied the vast majority of the region's voters in the early 1950s, aging has steadily reduced the clout of a group whose attitudes and behavior were virtually synonymous with the old southern politics. In the 1976-1980 elections the Solid South generation supplied only one-seventh of the region's voters, a ratio surpassed by both white migrants and blacks. By removing from the electorate those whites most likely to remain supportive of the old southern politics, the passing of this generation parallels the declining share of the regional vote contributed by black belt whites.

Now rising into political ascendancy among native white southerners are representatives of the post–World War II generation (middle-aged individuals who furnish most of the region's candidates and officeholders) and, to a lesser extent, members of the post–Voting Rights generation. More educated, more middle-class, more at ease in urban settings than their parents and grandparents, members of the post–World War II and post–Voting Rights generations are less inclined to identify themselves as Democrats than as independents or Republicans.

The growing diversity of the South's population and electorate is readily apparent in the election year surveys of the Survey Research Center–Center for Political Studies (SRC-CPS; see table 1.3). In the 1952-1956 elections native whites represented 69 percent of the southern population. Because white migrants were scarce and most blacks were excluded from politics, native white southerners almost completely monopolized the electorate (83 percent). Since the early 1950s major demographic and political shifts have reshaped the southern political universe. Whites raised outside the South (chiefly in the Northeast and Midwest) have increasingly perceived the South as a land of opportunity, either for work or retirement, and they have moved southward in such numbers that they constituted one-fifth of the population in 1976-1980. Not all migrants are cut from the same cloth, but as a group they are better educated,

Table 1.3. Changing demographic composition of the southern population and electorate, 1952–1956 to 1976–1980[a]

Group	Population				Electorate			
	52–56	60–64	68–72	76–80	52–56	60–64	68–72	76–80
Blacks	22	18	20	20	6	11	19	18
Migrant whites	9	16	16	21	11	17	17	25
Native whites	69	66	65	60	83	72	64	57
Post–Voting Rights generation	—	—	6	24	—	—	5	23
Postwar generation	12	19	27	19	11	20	25	20
Solid South generation	57	47	32	17	72	52	34	14

Source: SRC-CPS presidential election year surveys.
a. Data are presented as percentages and are averages of successive pairs of presidential election year surveys. Columns may not sum to 100 percent because of rounding.

more prosperous, more ethnically diverse, and much less Democratic than native southern whites. And because they usually vote at higher rates than native white southerners (56 percent versus 44 percent in 1980, for example), white migrants are more prominent in the electorate (25 percent in 1976-1980) than in the population. In addition, southern blacks have risen to almost a fifth of the region's voters. The entry of non-southern whites and the revival of black participation have substantially weakened the native whites' previously commanding position in the southern electorate. In the 1976-1980 elections whites born and raised in the South cast 57 percent of the vote, a decline of 31 percent from their share of the region's voters in 1952-1956 (83 percent). These critical changes in the composition of the active electorate have hastened the demise of one-party politics.

Whereas the electorate that underlay traditional southern politics was by and large composed of like-minded individuals in many important ways, the southern electorate of the 1980s includes groups that are markedly dissimilar in crucial aspects. The contemporary electorate contains *blacks* and whites, *Yankees* and natives, *women* and men; and it is made up principally of individuals whose formative political experiences are far removed in time from the traumas of the turn-of-the-century South. Reflection on key demographic trends suggests why many of the abiding concerns of the old southern politics—unquestioning loyalty to the Democratic party, heartfelt hatred of Republicans, the primacy of strict racial segregation—proved irrelevant or no longer compelling to many of the South's new people.

two

Industrialization and Urbanization

IN PART the old southern politics was the product of a rural and small-town region whose economy revolved almost totally around agriculture. The rise of the industrial and urban South, which profoundly changed the region's society and economy, has also helped to reshape the central institutions and practices of southern politics. This expansion of "industry and trade in a region hitherto more completely directed to agriculture"[1] has produced state power structures of greater complexity and has created a new socioeconomic class structure.

Industrialization has altered the composition of state power structures, those large organizations and institutions that are strategically positioned to invest ample resources and exert exceptional influence concerning the leading controversies of state and regional politics. In every southern state industrialization has multiplied and diversified the number of institutions—banks, insurance companies, utilities, construction firms, real estate interests, transportation companies, communications businesses, leading law firms—that make up state power structures, while simultaneously augmenting the collective resources at the disposal of state "establishments."

As viewed by the elites themselves, the power structures may seem pluralistic and competitive; examined from the perspective of those seeking to challenge the values and priorities of the dominant institutions, the power structures may appear to be monolithic and unitary. More and more, state and regional controversies stem from the "maintenance and enhancement needs of large formal organizations."[2] Even if the established organizations cannot always obtain their goals, they quite often succeed in defeating matters they oppose.

Key argued that "the growth of cities contains the seeds of political change for the South." Though whites residing in metropolitan areas were still strongly racist at midcentury, they tended to be less preoccupied with perpetuating all the aspects of traditional race relations than were whites in the black belt counties. Furthermore, the complexity of economic activity in urban environments, in contrast to the simplicity of the black belt's one-crop agricultural economies, seemed likely to enlarge both the urban working class and the urban middle and upper classes, thus generating socioeconomic cleavages within the metropolitan South that could foster challenges to one-party politics in the long run. Other things being equal, the more urban the state, the less "southern" its political life would be.[3]

The Industrial Transformation of the South

"Every southern state," generalized T. Harry Williams in his monumental work, *Huey Long,* "had a tradition of government by an elite. The membership of the elite has been characterized by various phrases—an upper-class or upper-income group, an alliance of planters and businessmen, a ruling hierarchy, oligarchy, or caste. Southerners sometimes summed it up by saying that they lived under a government of gentlemen. Like all concepts of its kind, the tradition had both exaggerations and omissions, but it had more reality than most traditions." An elite "of planters and merchants and professional politicians," Williams concluded, "dominated every Southern state in the years between the 1870's and the turn of the century. But after 1900 new elements sought and won admission to the inner circle."[4]

Although our theoretical interest in southern industrialization is guided, in part, by this hypothesis of expanding state power structures, we cannot, in a study of this breadth, describe such structures with any precision. An adequate treatment would require historical studies embracing a wide range of policymaking activities in individual states, and several such studies already exist.[5] We can, however, analyze the growing complexity of institutional claimants to power in the age of "agribusiness," industrialization, and urbanization.[6]

Immense changes have occurred in agricultural employment, historically the most distinctive feature of the southern economy. Whereas America "was born in the country and has moved to the city,"[7] the South stayed in the country and continued to farm decades after the non-South had ceased to be an agrarian region. Throughout the late nineteenth century staggering majorities of southerners farmed for a living, and as late as 1920 agriculture accounted for fully half of the South's jobs compared to less than a fifth of the non-South's labor force. With each passing decade, however, smaller and smaller proportions of southerners have been employed in agriculture, and by 1970 the South and the non-South had essentially identical rates of agricultural employment. Because of extensive modernization of farming methods, this decline in the use of human resources by no means implies that agriculture is unimportant to the southern economy. Both sizable individual holdings and huge, corporate, agribusiness operations are commonplace, raising the economic stakes of farming and inescapably involving this sector in state and national politics.

Although the South was still disproportionately agrarian in the 1920s, substantial shifts in the old way of life had already transpired, for only half of the work force was directly engaged in agriculture. To understand the consequences of industrialization, it is necessary to observe the way in which industrialization came to the South. Two factors deserve emphasis: the increasing importance of county-seat elites in local and state politics, and the peculiar blend of industry and traditional white values that constituted the "new South" movement.

"The political center of gravity of the South," asserted Shannon, "changed from the countryside to the county seat between 1870 and 1900." During this era "the county seat, the little urban center, took possession of the countryside and a gradual reorientation of values began." What eventually appeared was a "new governing class, a county seat governing class," which evolved from the planter governing class and included prosperous large farmers. Shannon's wonderful description of the new elite was the "banker-merchant-farmer-lawyer-doctor governing class," a shorthand term to designate the white elites, the more affluent and successful townspeople combined with the more influential and wealthy planters. It was a group "caught between the agrarian and industrial mores," and Shannon contended that the standard of values shared by this white group "explains more about southern politics than any analysis of structure can possibly do, though it is the decentralization of power into these semirural units which makes its existence possible." The "self-evident" values of the governing group included the necessity and desirability of white supremacy, elitist control of all vital local and state political institutions, and allegiance to the conservative wing of the Democratic party. Shannon also believed that the governing class's "fundamental ethic is pecuniary. The inevitable popular epitaph of the county seat lawyer, merchant, banker, or editor is: how much was he worth?"[8]

Though acknowledging that the local elites shared a keen interest in making money, other scholars have emphasized that maximizing wealth was not the most important value for most of the small-town elites. Key thought that "the only possible long-run outcome of increasing the productivity of the Negro would be to make rich whites richer and more whites rich,"[9] and he was baffled by the region's inattention to economic development. Employing a more explicitly comparative perspective, in which "traditionalistic," "individualistic," and "moralistic" political cultures are distinguished, Daniel J. Elazar captured the essence of their working principles in his concept of the traditionalistic political culture. According to Elazar, this philosophy "is rooted in an ambivalent attitude toward the marketplace coupled with a paternalistic and elitist conception of the commonwealth. It reflects an older, precommercial attitude that accepts a substantially hierarchial society as part of the ordered nature of things, authorizing and expecting those at the top of the social structure to take a special and dominant role in government."[10] Acting out of this world view, the governing elites accepted new governmental programs and promoted economic development only if these innovations could serve their own interests. The proper role of government in a traditionalistic political culture is generally quite limited. " 'Good government' . . . involves the maintenance and encouragement of traditional patterns and, if necessary, their adjustment to changing conditions with the least possible upset," Elazar concluded. "Where the traditionalistic political culture is dominant in the United States today, unless political leaders are pressed strongly from the outside they play conservative and custodial rather than initiatory roles."[11]

Traditionalistic perspectives strongly influenced the dominant regional pattern of industrialization by setting the South on the path of "conservative modernization."[12] Long ago Cash argued that the shift toward industrialization in the late nineteenth century blended Yankee conceptions of manufacturing (subjecting men, women, and children to the new discipline of the machine) with the southern traditions of the color line (usually reserving manufacturing jobs for whites only) and elite control of the work force (as on the plantation).[13] For many whites rural poverty was exchanged for a slightly more secure form of industrial poverty.

"New South" industrialization provided jobs for some of the poor-white independent farmers, sharecroppers, and tenants who could no longer survive on the farm, as well as high rates of profits for the owners. This type of industrialization proved compatible with racism and the persisting influence of the wealthier whites; indeed, many of the planters seem to have invested in and promoted the new business enterprises.[14] James Cobb contends:

> By the 1930s the South's strategies for industrial growth were so intertwined with other traditions like white supremacy, minimal government, and regional chauvinism that political and economic leaders resisted threats to

one as threats to all. For example, labor unions promised to impede development efforts, subject the region to increased Yankee influence and undermine white supremacy. Likewise, more spending for public welfare would scare away tax-conscious industrialists and elevate blacks at the expense of whites. In the long run, the commitment to progress and the determination to preserve the southern way of life were often complementary rather than contradictory impulses.[15]

Conservative modernizers and their allies among the small-town elites were strongly opposed to the provision of services for the have-nots and were skeptical about rapid economic development that might topple or challenge local and state power structures. " 'We were secure. We were the old families. We had what we wanted. We didn't bother anybody,' " a member of the old Louisiana order told Huey Long's biographer, T. Harry Williams. " 'All we wanted was to keep it.' "[16] Although adherents of the traditionalistic political culture could tolerate some expansion of state governments as part of enlightened self-interest ("business progressivism"),[17] far more central to the realities facing most southerners was Williams's assessment of the effects of traditionalistic leadership in Louisiana. In explaining the paucity of state services for the have-nots after several decades of "new South" industrialization, Williams concluded:

> One reason why educational and other services were poor or non-existent was that the state was poor, unable to finance a broad program of social benefits. But they were poor for the additional reason that the ruling hierarchy was little interested in using what resources the state had available to provide services and was even less interested in employing the power of the state to create new resources so that more services could be supported. The hierarchy was smug, satisfied with things as they were, devoted to the protection of privilege. Its leaders were gentlemen in frock coats, string ties, and wide hats, and they gave the state a kind of government like themselves—dignified, usually honest, though sometimes discreetly corrupt, and backward-looking. It might be described as "government by goatee."[18]

The traditionalistic conception of government and economic progress did not go unchallenged. Two very different schools of criticism emerged among white politicians. Both were variations on major themes of Elazar's individualistic political culture, and both possessed considerable popular appeal. The Populist critique derived from the region's tradition of agrarian radicalism and produced politicans who flailed the haves and appealed in various ways to the have-nots. The second critique emerged from a small but growing group of urban industrialists, financiers, entrepreneurs, journalists, and educators; they too saw poverty as the region's basic problem and advocated economic development as the solution.

Part of their purpose was to free entrepreneurs to pursue economic growth without undue regard for possible changes in the South's social organization, culture, and power structure.

The aspect of the individualistic political culture most relevant to Populism was "the conception of the democratic order as a marketplace. In its view, government is instituted for strictly utilitarian reasons, to handle those functions demanded by the people it is created to serve . . . In general, government action is to be restricted to those areas, primarily in the economic realm, which encourage private initiative and widespread access to the market place."[19] Populism emphasized the need for genuine democracy in public policy decisions (government by and for the people) and merged this with a pronounced antipathy toward concentrated wealth, toward monopolies and oligopolies (government against vested interests).[20] "The elite instinctively dislikes any politician," Shannon suggested, "who injects issues which arouse the farmers to independence or consciousness of self-interest opposed to its leaders."[21] Key stressed the recurrence of conflicts aligning the poorer white farmers and some industrial workers against the more prosperous white farmers, small-town elites, and major industrial interests in southern politics. These controversies appeared irregularly, but they were usually agitated by different opinions concerning the purposes and burdens of state government.[22]

Although the descendants of the nineteenth-century Populists favored economic progress, they doubted that economic development overseen by the industrial elites would fundamentally improve the lot of poor farmers and workers. To the contrary, such economic development might only magnify the financial resources available to a few groups and individuals. Neo-Populists assumed that in the short run the region would remain impoverished and that therefore the interest of the white have-nots lay in extracting more taxes from the few haves in order to pay for more services and benefits to have-nots and have-littles. It was less a politics of economic growth than of redistributing fixed resources. Neo-Populist politics reached its zenith in state politics during the administration of Huey Long in Louisiana, the first to execute a politics based on realistic class interests.[23] Long increased the taxes of major corporations (chiefly out-of-state oil companies), provided more government programs and services than ever before, and regarded corruption with excessive benignity; it is small wonder that urban industrialists and people of substance generally feared, despised, and tried to destroy Longism.

This species of the individualistic political culture has always emphasized cleavages between the wealthy few and the nonaffluent many and has continued to see outside capital as an arch-villain. Much of the appeal of neo-Populist politicians among marginal farmers and blue-collar workers has resulted from their unfettered expression of class resentments, sometimes at the expense of presenting practical steps to improve the economy. A veteran Mississippi editor complained that "our politicians spent their time attacking Wall Street and industry. How did that help the poor farmers in the fields?"[24] In recent decades, as the region has experienced more economic prosperity, the old Populist demand to redistribute resources has had less appeal. It is not irrelevant, though; the modern progressive movement evolved from agrarian radicalism, and the neo-Populist tradition continues to speak to and for the interests of millions of southerners who are unacquainted with any centers of power. The growth and diversity of corporate enterprise in the southern states has actually given the progressives increasingly visible targets, though the objects of neo-Populist anger may have much vaster financial resources to invest in state controversies affecting their interests.

The second challenge to the traditionalists, that of the entrepreneurial individualists, was quite different. Many of its leaders were also nauseated by the traditional South's waste of human resources and viewed poverty as an unnecessary disgrace. But instead of redistributing scarce resources to the lower orders, the entrepreneurial individualists sought to expand the collective wealth of the region, its citizens, and themselves through rapid economic development. Many entrepreneurial individualists were native southerners who were staunchly conservative in their racial and class beliefs, but they were much less constrained by the traditionalists' desire to preserve established power structures. To the contrary, many of these men—and the institutional interests they represented—wanted access to the state power structures, wanted to direct them away from dependence upon plantations, multi-unit agriculture, and single industries.

In the entrepreneurial version of individualism, pursuit of self-interest, primarily the making and keeping of wealth, is the cardinal value despite potentially disruptive consequences for the larger society. Such entrepreneurs promoted changes—particularly visible in the more advanced Peripheral South states—that brought about greater economic diversity, augmented state power structures, and established truly large cities. Their main conviction concerned the need to expand their states' public and private resources to create services and institutions that would foster the production of additional wealth in the future. Economic growth would reward the working class and emerging middle class with steady employment, but state governments would not be used to distribute resources downward in the social structure. The purpose of state action was not to subsidize or support have-nots or have-littles, but to subsidize the institutional and individual creators of wealth.

Key was well aware that a single-minded emphasis on making money was different from the region's accustomed hierarchy of values, and he singled out Texas as the prime example of an atypical southern politics, a "politics of economics." "The changes of nine decades," he argued, "have weakened the heritage of southern traditionalism, revolutionized the economy, and made Texas more western than southern." As a result of these changes, the agenda of Texas politics was transformed: "White Texans, unlike white Mississippians, have little cause to be obsessed about the Negro. The Lone Star State is concerned about money and how to make it, about oil and sulphur and gas, about cattle and dust storms and irrigation, about cotton and banking and Mexicans."[25] Entrepreneurial individualism could surely thrive in such an environment. According to Elazar, in the individualistic political culture, politics becomes "just another means by which individuals may improve themselves socially and economically. In this sense politics is a 'business' like any other that competes for talent and offers rewards to those who take it up as a career."[26] It is no accident that the South's most visible examples in public life of the entrepreneurial individualist tradition were two Texans, Lyndon Johnson and John Connally.[27]

From political and industrial entrepreneurs like Johnson and Connally came an insistence on providing better-quality jobs, instead of relying mainly on low-wage employment, and a greater willingness to promote urbanization, to develop the infrastructure that would support the increasingly middle-class populations in the cities and help spin off new, better paying industries. From them developed a concerted effort to extract from the federal government programs and contracts that would raise industrial employment, even as such employment was beginning to alter the composition of the population, weaken the Democratic party's monopoly on politics, and bring in some labor unions. From them too would finally emerge belated, reluctant assent to modifications of the caste system in the mid-1960s. The South's entrepreneurial individualists were willing to take bigger risks with traditional southern values, to dream and then construct urban landscapes far beyond the imagination of the traditionalists. Their influence has been much stronger in Texas, Florida, Virginia, and, to a much lesser extent, Georgia, than in the other southern states, where the traditionalistic culture was more entrenched and had fewer competitors, and where the shift toward more high-wage industrialization and the growth of cities are much more recent developments.

By the time Key completed *Southern Politics,* most of the southern work force had already abandoned farming as a full-time occupation. At midcentury he analyzed a region where low-wage, anti-union industrialization had been underway for decades. The philosophy of conservative modernization had produced by 1950 a pattern of industrial growth in which manufacturing (as measured by the percentage of the labor force employed in these pursuits) was concentrated in a wide strip of roughly contiguous counties that began in southcentral Virginia, stretched across the piedmont of the Carolinas, extended into northern Georgia (where it was joined by a narrow band of counties in East Tennessee), and ended in northeastern Alabama. This was the textile mill and (in Alabama and Tennessee) foundry South, located far from the rural and still agricultural black belts.[28] Other pockets of industry had appeared, such as shipbuilding and repair in the urbanized coastal areas of Virginia, petrochemicals in the southeastern urbanized section of Texas, and more low-wage concentrations in southern Arkansas and southwestern Alabama; but in most of the region's counties the percentage of the work force engaged in manufacturing fell well below the national norm.

In 1950 southern working-class whites usually resided in small towns or semirural environments, frequently close to their jobs. The work places were dirty, noisy, often dangerous; the work itself was commonly tedious and exhausting; and the wages were very low. Nonetheless, the coming of industry to the small-town South did enable many white workers to live in familiar surroundings, near family and friends, and close to institutions that held meaning for them.[29] It was a living, as the people used to say. To enjoy a better standard of living—to make real money—workers would have to migrate to cities, either within the South or (less likely) in the strange and distant North.

Southern power structures varied considerably at midcentury. Every state still had powerful agricultural interests, for the production of raw materials remained the foundation of most state economies. Also represented were a fairly common group of industries essential to a modern economy: banking, public utilities (electric power companies and telephone companies), insurance, and construction (highway and building contractors). These interests varied in size and significance, but even the most impoverished southern state supported these functions, which in turn became the basis for a voice in state politics. And added to these concerns would be industries that were unique to a state or cluster of states: textiles in the Carolinas, Virginia, Georgia, and Alabama; oil and gas extraction and refining in Texas and Louisiana; mining in Alabama, Tennessee, and Virginia; steel production in Alabama and Tennessee; and food processing and tourism in Florida.

In every state the power structures included more claimants in 1950 than they had in 1900; theoretically, a continuum can be distinguished ranging from the purely agricultural states with minimal additions of industry and finance (Mississippi is the leading example), to states having more differentiated economies but still being basically controlled by the traditionalists (Alabama and South Carolina), to states where traditionalism and individualism were clashing (Florida), to states where an individualistic culture seemed to be edging out the traditionalist forces (Texas). Close analysis of state politics on key issues, with careful attention to mass and elite coalitions, and special attention to the small corps of state legislators who were returned, governor after governor, and who constituted the permanent government in many states, would be necessary in order to reach firm conclusions regarding changes within state power structures. Here we can only suggest a range of possibilities.

The waning of the exclusively agricultural South has been accompanied by other changes in the labor force that have produced increasingly similar distributions of industrial employment in the South and non-South. In the census immediately preceding the Second World War the South was markedly higher than the non-South in agricultural employment but considerably lower in manufacturing. Over the following forty years, stimulated initially by the war and its attendant opportunities for defense-related construction and manufacturing and later by the interstate highway system, which connected cities and opened previously inaccessible smaller towns to industry, employment patterns in the South have steadily approached those of the non-South. By 1980, with the further decline of southern agriculture and nonsouthern manufacturing, the two regions exhibited enormous similarity in the proportion of their labor forces engaged in various industrial sectors.[30]

Why has the southern economy become more similar to the economy of the rest of the nation? Suggestive explanations emerge from David C. Perry and Alfred J. Watkins's *Rise of the Sunbelt Cities* and Kirkpatrick Sale's *Power Shift*.[31] Studying manufacturing patterns between 1940 and 1960, Watkins and Perry divided industries according to above-average and below-average growth in employment. Forty percent of all southerners who worked in manufacturing during this period were employed in low-growth, low-wage industries.[32] This finding corresponded to the widely held view of a southern labor force employed in industries whose pay lagged far below the national average for manufacturing; it represented the continuing legacy of the region's devotion to apparel goods, textiles, lumbering, and food processing. Frequently located in the rural and small-town South and commonly nonunionized, these industries did not challenge or threaten local elites.

Though we cannot be certain that such industries account for most manufacturing concerns in the rural South, the post-1950 dispersion of manufacturing across the rural portions of most southern states (excepting Texas, Florida, and much of Louisiana) in combination with the historical strength of the traditionalistic political culture in the high-black rural counties strongly suggests that there is still a demand for such establishments in the hinterlands. Between 1950 and 1980 there was a tremendous surge of manufacturing away from the geographically concentrated pattern of 1950. The more recent industrialization of the high-black rural areas is unlikely to produce more political organization among workers, although blacks, who are now included in the industrial work force, have shown considerably more interest in labor unions than blue-collar whites.

While patterns associated with the old South still endure in much of the region, the more striking finding was that 60 percent of the South's manufacturing workers in 1960 were employed in industries that were growing faster than the national average. Employment in these "fast-growing, high wage industries" was a key to the region's economic development. To be sure, workers in these concerns have not fully escaped the sting of the traditionalistic culture. "Because of its lower pay scales and less stringent labor laws," Watkins and Perry state, "the South has emerged as a lower wage site for traditionally high wage activities."[33] Even so, the rewards are considerably higher than the economic payoff from employment in a textile mill or a lumber yard. Some of these plants brought with them organized labor, a willingness to hire blacks, managerial personnel who might be inclined toward Republicanism, and often a preference to locate in urban environments—consequences serious enough to sink the projects among die-hard traditionalists, but of less concern to individualist entrepreneurs whose main priority was growth. The establishment of such industries, together with an accelerated demand for workers to service, feed, house, clothe, and entertain the greater populations, has led to the rapid growth of cities like Houston, Dallas, and Atlanta. And there will be much more growth in the future.

Sale argued in *Power Shift* that the growth of the Sunbelt was supported by six "pillars": agribusiness, defense, high technology, oil and natural gas, real estate and construction, and tourism and leisure.[34] Watkins and Perry agree with Sale's emphasis on these categories but supplement the discussion by contending that much of this economic development was facilitated by the South's exploitation of its strong position within the Democratic party to extract financing from the federal government. Federal programs and policies stimulated the growth of southern defense industries (both production plants and military bases) during World War II; helped finance the infrastructure (highways, airports, water and sewage systems) needed for economic expansion; and then pumped more money into the region in the form of subsidies for agricultural products, defense installations, contracts for the electronics and aerospace industries, subsidies for oil and natural gas producers, encouragement of real estate speculation and construction through tax laws; and finally, through social security, facilitated retirement to warmer climates. Since the total amount of federal money spent in the South has always exceeded the region's contribution to the U.S. Treasury, southern economic development partially financed at the expense of Yankees and Westerners has been especially satisfying to many southerners.[35]

Sale's six pillars capture the significant features of the paramount trend toward further diversification of the economy—and hence of state power structures—that has occurred since midcentury. Because appropriate data are not readily available for all categories, we shall not attempt to compare the southern states according to the relative importance of the various pillars. Nonetheless, Texas, Florida, Virginia, and perhaps Louisiana stand out as the states most differentiated from the ancient agricultural power structures. Pockets of individualistic political culture have certainly appeared elsewhere; yet the dispersion of (presumably) low-growth, low-wage industry across formerly agricultural areas of the remaining states suggests that much of the spirit of traditionalistic politics has been preserved. By adding the common institutions of finance and commerce to the particular constellations of pillars in each state, the broad outlines of state power structures emerge. It is from these affluent interests that the funds to finance statewide campaigns are mainly drawn, and many of the candidates are either prominent players in state power structures or have established appropriately intimate connections with key figures therein. The votes needed to nominate and elect lie elsewhere, however, as can be seen by examining the South's changing political demography.

The Rise of the Urban South

The rural South of the past has increasingly given way to a region almost as urban as the non-South.[36] In 1920 no more than a fourth of all southerners, compared with three-fifths of all nonsoutherners, resided in localities with populations as large as 2,500. Ruralism pervaded every southern state, with the urban population ranging upwards from 13 percent in Mississippi to 37 percent in Florida. Though urbanization was underway in the 1940s, even at midcentury only Florida, Texas, and Louisiana were more than half urban. Urbanization accelerated between 1950 and 1970 but slowed during the 1970s. As of the 1980 census the southern states were approaching nonsouthern rates of urbanization and could be clustered in three distinct groups. The regional leaders, the "megastates" of Florida (84 percent urban) and Texas (80 percent),[37] were the only states whose urban populations exceeded that of the non-

South (76 percent). More typical of the South were Louisiana, Virginia, Georgia, Tennessee, Alabama, South Carolina, and Arkansas, where at least half but fewer than three-fourths of the population was classified as urban. Rural citizens continued to outnumber urban residents in North Carolina (48 percent) and Mississippi (47 percent). Although the Peripheral South has consistently been more urban than the Deep South, the subregions have been much more similar in the size of their urban population than in their racial composition.

To understand the implications of demographic change, we have classified southern counties on the basis of the demographic theory of political change implicit in Key's *Southern Politics*. We have grouped the counties according to the size of their black populations and their urban-rural status. Employing terms previously developed to operationalize Key's views, we have divided the southern electorates into four demographic sectors: large metropolitan, medium urban, low-black rural, and high-black rural. Beginning with the demographic sector that should be least "southern" in its political behavior, we have defined counties that are part of an SMSA with a total population of at least 250,000 as large metropolitan counties. Medium urban counties consist of all counties included in an SMSA of less than 250,000 population and all other counties possessing a city of at least 25,000 population. Counties not qualifying as large metropolitan or medium urban are defined as rural, and rural counties are classified according to the size of their black population. Low-black rural counties are rural counties with black populations of less than 30 percent; high-black rural counties, the counties whose behavior should be most "southern," are rural counties with black populations of 30 percent or more. To prevent underestimating demographic traditionalism, the very few medium-urban counties with black population majorities (for example, Montgomery County, Alabama, and Charleston County, South Carolina, in 1920) have been grouped with high-black rural counties.[38]

In order to visualize the changing political anatomy of the South, maps have been prepared showing the demographic standing of all counties in 1920 and 1980. Consider first the county-level demographic setting for politics in the 1920s (fig. 2.1). High-black rural areas, which Key characterized as "a skeleton holding together the South,"[39] appear as a broad band of counties extending without interruption from East Texas to East Virginia. Two-thirds of the Deep South counties qualified in 1920 as high-black rural, and the geographical concentration of these traditional political units was especially prominent in South Carolina and Mississippi. Although there were more low-black rural than high-black rural counties in the Peripheral South, rural counties with sizable black pop-

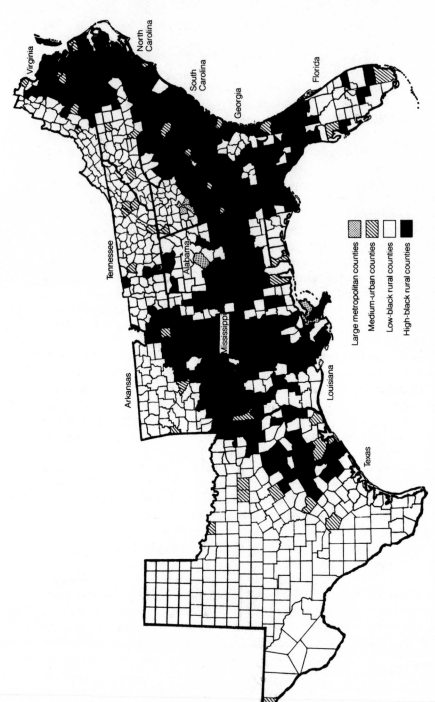

Figure 2.1. The rural South: regional political demography in 1920. Source: U.S. Bureau of the Census.

Large metropolitan counties

Medium-urban counties

Low-black rural counties

High-black rural counties

Virginia

North Carolina

South Carolina

Georgia

Florida

Tennessee

Alabama

Mississippi

Arkansas

Louisiana

Texas

ulations constituted significant minorities of all counties in every Peripheral South state except Tennessee and Texas.

If the geographical breadth of the high-black rural sector provided a firm demographic anchor for one-party politics, an equally significant feature of the South's political demography in 1920 was the virtual absence of big cities. New Orleans (population 414,000), Atlanta (326,000), and Birmingham (310,000) were the only large metropolitan areas in the entire South. These three Deep South cities possessed substantial black populations and were contiguous to high-black rural counties; accordingly, they were hardly free of black belt attitudes on race relations. The incredibly traditional character of the old South's political demography thus reinforced, rather than moderated, the region's heritage of one-party politics.

Glimmers of a less provincial political demography are evident in the 1950 census, at least for most Peripheral South states. Largely because of black out-migration from black belt areas, by midcentury there were fewer high-black rural counties in every state than there had been in 1920. The most important change in the setting of southern politics, however, was the growth of thirteen more large metropolitan areas. The South's new big cities emerged in Texas, Tennessee, Florida, and Virginia. Four of these urban centers first appeared as of the 1930 census (Houston, Dallas, San Antonio, and Memphis); five more (Miami, Tampa–St. Petersburg, Nashville, Norfolk and Richmond) were added in 1940; and another four (Fort Worth, Knoxville, Jacksonville, and the northern Virginia suburbs of Washington) qualified at midcentury. No additional large metropolitan areas emerged in the Deep South through 1950, leaving that subregion with few sources of potentially nontraditional leadership. Most politicians had been born in high-black environments, and many still resided there.

There have been substantial changes over time in the demographic setting of southern politics (compare figures 2.2 and 2.1). Rural counties with black populations exceeding 30 percent still accounted for nearly half (46 percent) of the Deep South's counties in 1980, but even there the high-black rural sector contracted noticeably between 1920 and 1980. In the Peripheral South, most obviously in Texas, Tennessee, and Florida, the backbone of southern traditionalism was brittle indeed.

The most telling metamorphosis in southern demography is the proliferation of major cities. A dozen new large metropolitan SMSAs were created between 1950 and 1960, with five in the Deep South (Mobile, Shreveport, Charleston, Columbia, and Greenville) and seven in the Peripheral South (Orlando, Fort Lauderdale–Hollywood, Charlotte, Chattanooga, Beaumont–Port Arthur, El Paso, and Corpus Christi). Only

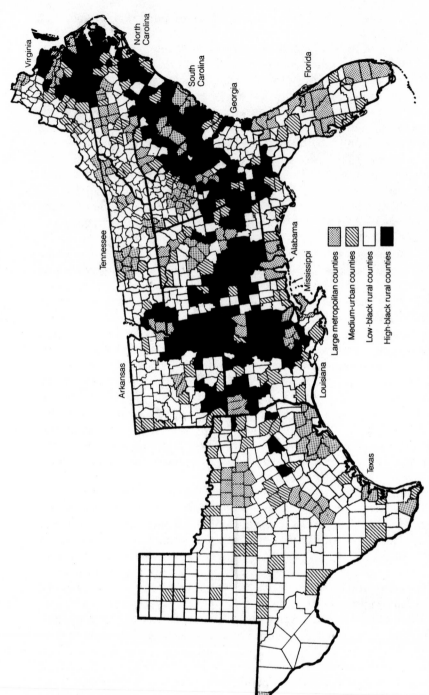

Figure 2.2. The urban South: regional political demography in 1980. Source: U.S. Bureau of the Census.

Large metropolitan counties
Medium-urban counties
Low-black rural counties
High-black rural counties

Virginia
North Carolina
South Carolina
Georgia
Florida
Alabama
Mississippi
Tennessee
Arkansas
Louisiana
Texas

seven more large metropolitan areas (Baton Rouge and Jackson in the Deep South, and Little Rock, West Palm Beach, Greensboro–Winston Salem–High Point, Austin, and Newport News–Hampton in the Peripheral South) were identified in 1970, but by 1980 there were eleven more big cities (Huntsville, Montgomery, Augusta, and Macon in the Deep South, and Lakeland–Winter Haven, Pensacola, Melbourne-Titusville-Cocoa, Daytona Beach, Raleigh-Durham, Johnson City–Kingsport-Bristol, and McAllen-Pharr-Edinburg in the Peripheral South). As of 1980 the South possessed forty-five large metropolitan complexes, two-thirds of which were in the Peripheral South.

Counties differ radically in population size, of course, and more political relevance can be injected into the analysis by using aggregate election returns. Changes in the relative weight of the four demographic sectors in electoral politics may be determined by plotting the distribution of the total southern vote among the sectors for the sixteen presidential elections from 1920 through 1980.[40] During the period covered by Key, ruralism undergirded the Democratic party's supremacy in presidential politics (figure 2.3). Four-fifths of the region's voters in 1920 lived in rural or small town settings, and the combined rural sectors accounted for nearly three-fifths of the 1948 presidential vote. Over time, however, the rural electorate has steadily declined. In 1980 rural and small-town counties produced less than one-third of the vote, a figure too high for politicians to ignore but paltry by historical standards.

Gradual expansion of the large metropolitan vote represents the most significant break with the past (see figure 2.3). In 1920 less than a single vote out of every twenty originated in large metropolitan areas, compelling evidence of urbanism's unimportance. Yet by 1948 the large metropolitan sector supplied more votes than either the medium urban or high-black rural counties, and in 1956 large metropolitan counties became the leading source of votes. In 1980 the large metropolitan counties provided 54 percent of the southern presidential vote, roughly the same as the majority (53 percent) cast by the low-black rural counties six decades before. When the large metropolitan sector is combined with the medium urban sector, it is evident that the South's center of political gravity has decisively moved from the rural and small-town voters to those who live in urban settings. Presumably political influence has shifted as well from individuals residing in the rural sectors to those occupying key positions in the larger cities.

The South is not of a single piece, however, and regional trend lines mask critical differences between the subregions and among the states. In the Deep South the distribution of the presidential vote among demographic sectors still reflects a traditional electoral milieu. The high-

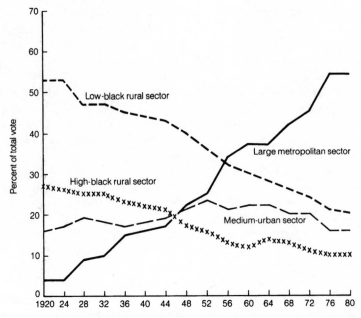

Figure 2.3. The changing political demography of the South: percent distribution of the total vote in presidential elections, 1920–1980, by demographic sector. Sources: Richard M. Scammon, ed., *America at the Polls* (Pittsburgh: University of Pittsburgh Press, 1965); and appropriate volumes of Richard M. Scammon, ed., *America Votes.*

black rural sector was the largest contributor to the presidential vote through 1952 and subsequently furnished the second highest share of the Deep South vote. Because few blacks voted before 1968 in the high-black rural counties of the Deep South, the political leverage of the black belt whites is manifest. After 1964 the large metropolitan sector became the greatest producer of votes, but only toward the end of the period did its vote surge far ahead of the high-black rural sector. Although the Deep South electorate in 1980 was much less "southern" than it had been in earlier decades, demographic traditionalism persists to an important degree in that subregion.

Peripheral South electorates have been composed of voters situated in substantially different demographic settings. One-party politics in the Peripheral South was grounded in ruralism, but the predominant county there possessed a low-black population. Between 1920 and 1980 the political environment in the Peripheral South was significantly reshaped, primarily through the replacement of the low-black rural sector by the large metropolitan sector as the key source of votes. With the expansion of previously established large metropolitan counties and the creation of new large metropolitan areas through the reclassification of counties after each census, the large metropolitan vote has increasingly dominated electoral politics. In 1980 this sector contributed almost three-fifths of the entire Peripheral South vote, far exceeding the size of the large metropolitan vote in the Deep South (44 percent). The proliferation of big cities in the Peripheral South has stimulated a politics less rooted in loyalty to the Democratic party, and the growth of fairly stable interparty competition has also been indirectly encouraged by the absence of a sizable high-black rural vote. High-black rural counties accounted for no more than 4 percent of the Peripheral South vote in 1980, a figure one-sixth the size of the high-black rural vote in the Deep South.

The same logic that emphasizes the advantages of subregional controls for regional findings implies that subregional generalizations should be examined for variations among states. On the basis of comparisons of the high-black rural and large metropolitan sectors, four broad categories of demographic settings may be established (see table 2.1).

Mississippi, the single state in 1980 in which the high-black rural vote far exceeded the big city vote, presents the most traditional demographic environment. In Mississippi the only large metropolitan area is Jackson, which is a dwarf compared with the major southern cities. The political community has expanded through the pressure of the civil rights movement, and racial cleavages remain salient in many rural and small town settings.

Most of the people in Arkansas and North Carolina do not live in large metropolitan areas, but these Peripheral South states lack the sizable high-black rural populations characteristic of Mississippi. Mississippi, Arkansas, and North Carolina all possess demographies more similar to the traditional way of life than other southern states, and the last two states have become attractive to retirees seeking small-town life as well as to people who simply prefer to live and work away from large cities. Little Rock, Charlotte, and Greensboro have grown enormously over the past decades, but they do not resemble the region's "megacities."

The other groups of states follow subregional outlines. With the exception of Mississippi, the Deep South states in 1980 combined fairly substantial high-black rural populations with large metropolitan populations amounting to about half of the total state electorates. In South Carolina, Louisiana, Georgia, and Alabama, the big city vote strongly outweighed the high-black rural vote—a striking reversal of the 1920s pattern for all of these states save Louisiana. Yet in none of these states could residents of a single city be said to dominate or control state politics.

Table 2.1. Southern demographic traditionalism in decline: percentage distribution of the total vote among demographic sectors in the 1920, 1952, and 1980 presidential elections, by state, subregion, and region

Political unit[a]	1920				1952				1980			
	LM[b]	MU[b]	LBR[b]	HBR[b]	LM	MU	LBR	HBR	LM	MU	LBR	HBR
Mississippi	0[c]	0	28	72	0	22	22	55	15	19	21	45
Arkansas	0	10	57	33	0	23	54	23	17	28	44	11
North Carolina	0	10	58	32	0	34	45	21	36	22	29	13
South Carolina	0	4	20	76	0	38	17	46	48	10	13	29
Louisiana	41	4	20	35	33	26	17	24	47	18	16	19
Georgia	11	10	34	46	21	20	30	29	50	13	20	17
Alabama	14	4	55	27	17	20	41	23	49	19	18	15
Virginia	0	28	50	22	34	16	36	14	57	15	20	8
Tennessee	0	22	69	9	37	10	51	3	63	5	30	2
Florida	0	32	33	35	47	27	17	9	74	14	11	1
Texas	0	25	59	15	32	21	43	4	62	18	20	0
Deep South	15	5	36	43	18	24	25	32	44	16	18	23
Peripheral South	0	20	58	22	27	22	40	10	59	16	21	4
South	4	16	53	27	25	23	36	16	54	16	20	10

Sources: Same as figure 2.3.

a. States are ranked from most traditional to least traditional according to the rationale explained in the text.

b. LM, large metropolitan sector; MU, medium urban sector; LBR, low-black rural sector; HBR, high-black rural sector.

c. Figures are rounded to the nearest whole percentage and may not sum to 100 percent.

South Carolina's large metropolitan vote, for example, was divided among Charleston, Columbia, and Greenville-Spartanburg, cities that by no means always see eye-to-eye on state politics. And though New Orleans, Atlanta, and Birmingham were the undisputed leaders of the big city vote in their respective states, other large metropolitan areas had priorities of their own in statewide campaigns.

The least traditional demographic settings occurred among the remaining four states of the Peripheral South. In Virginia, Tennessee, Florida, and Texas, much larger majorities of voters resided in large metropolitan counties, while the high-black rural vote (apart from Virginia's modest 8 percent) was negligible. The demographies of these Peripheral South states were not distinctively "southern," and single cities were even less likely to control state affairs than in the urbanized Deep South states. Virginia's metropolitan voters extended from the Washington suburbs to Richmond to Newport News, Norfolk, and Virginia Beach; and Tennessee's big city vote was divided among cities with conflicting partisan histories and current political orientations (Memphis, Nashville, Knoxville, and Chattanooga). Florida's metropolitan diversity was legendary. Three-fourths of its 1980 electorate inhabited ten large metropolitan complexes, which ranged from such cities as Miami, Tampa–St. Petersburg, Jacksonville, and Orlando to suburbanized portions of the eastern coast and of central Florida. Whereas Houston, Dallas, and San Antonio accounted for most of Texas's large metropolitan vote, Texas also contained a number of smaller but expanding big cities.

Over the past six decades the demographic setting in which politicians and political parties function has changed in fundamental ways. Despite important differences among the individual states and between the subregions, the demographic traditionalism historically associated with southern electoral politics has been sharply modified through the growth of scores of urban areas and by the decline of the high-black rural counties.

Political Implications of Metropolitan Growth

What have these secular changes meant for southern politics? Prior to midcentury, with most voters residing in rural and semirural counties, the most immediate sources of local political influence lay in the hundreds of county seats that dotted the South. In statewide campaigns the local elite's main function was to turn out a reliable county vote for the "right" candidates. Conservative elites supplied cues to the lower orders, many of whom were sufficiently naive and ignorant to justify Key's image of the "simple clodhopper" manipulated by conniving politicians.[41] Shannon explained the elite's operating procedures in these terms:

> Generally, the county seat and its politically conscious courthouse officers control politics by the process of influence percolating down to the substratum of small farmers and tenants. The humbler element seeks overtly the advice of their betters partly from inertia and partly hoping to gain from the subtle flattery of giving their landlords and merchant neighbors the feeling of being politically important . . . Where poll taxes or literacy tests exist they are helpful to the local elite in maintaining its position. The leaders control the election process and thereby keep political and economic power alike in their own hands.[42]

But if the votes necessary to win state campaigns came from the hinterlands and smaller towns, the big money flowed primarily from businessmen; "in a region predominantly agricultural," Key observed, "the funds for gubernatorial and senatorial campaigns come mainly from business and finance."[43] Key's research suggests that the key to electoral success during the 1920-1950 period frequently involved linkages between the money of various business and financial concerns and the activation of grassroots support by members of the county-seat crowds. These alliances generally produced governors and senators who were acutely sympathetic and attentive to the interests of both the small-town elites and leading industries. Perhaps even more important in controlling state activities were the veteran politicians who returned again and again to leadership positions in the legislatures. Careful inquiry over long periods of time would probably reveal power structures whose geographical roots were in the rural and small-town counties but whose political connections formed extensive networks of influence with major business and financial interests.[44]

The demographic trends of the last three decades have produced yet another decisive shift in the center of southern political gravity. Most voters, most political activists, and the region's predominant financial and business enterprises are now located in metropolitan areas and medium-sized cities. Because only three-tenths of the South's electorate still lives in rural and small-town counties, the political influence of the old county-seat crowds has declined sharply in importance. Grassroots politics, as a practical necessity, is now much more likely to be conducted in a large metropolitan or medium urban setting. Though the proposition would be difficult to demonstrate, our impression is that county-seat elites are much less capable of providing political cues that local voters will accept and act upon than in the past. Even in rural and small-town environments, mass education has vastly improved, potential voters are exposed to a much broader array of mass media, and the electorates—in the post–Voting Rights era—are more racially diverse. "You can't fool people the way you used to," was the blunt appraisal of one extraordinarily successful Deep South legislator (the epitome of a county-seat elite) when asked the main difference between the "old" and "new" southern politics.[45]

Rural electorates are still large enough to compel statewide politicians to give some attention to their problems and concerns, and candidates would be foolish indeed to allow themselves to be perceived as the advocates of exclusively urban interests. But the principal arena for the continued representation of the views of small-town white elites is the state legislature. Through extended reelection, long service on major committees, and careful supervision of administrative appointments, skillful members of the old county-seat crowds continue to exert formidable—sometimes decisive—influence on state politics. It is here, rather than in the governor's chair, that the real flavor of old-style, small-town southern politics persists in many states.

The rise of the metropolitan South has contributed to several prominent political trends, including the dilution but not elimination of the traditionalistic political culture, the increasing use of state and federal resources to accelerate the growth and improve the attractiveness of the urban South, the development of a wider range of political choice in gubernatorial and legislative elections, and the modernization of political campaigning.

Historically, as we have seen, southern cities were few in number and small in size. According to Peter A. Lupsha and William J. Siembieda, the region's cities typically developed "to provide market centers, points of transshipment, and transportation nodes for the distribution of goods and services to and from the hinterlands," rather than to bring together dense concentrations of industrial workers, as occurred in many northeastern and midwestern metropolises. The values of the dominant elites derived from the rural South, and "local government functions were narrowly defined and the business community was actively recruited to govern the polity." Representation in local governments and in state legislative delegations was determined by at-large elections, rather than by wards or by election from many single-member districts, and consequently the demand for services to the working and impoverished classes never took hold in southern cities. "Political organization in the Sunbelt cities has never been designed to accommodate mass demands or create services," Lupsha and Siembieda concluded. "It was designed to function as an adjunct to the business and economic community providing a mechanism for accommodating growth and development."[46]

All of this is consistent with Elazar's traditionalistic political culture, with a careful emphasis on controlled growth. Key reported at midcentury that workers in southern cities were generally unorganized and showed little interest in local politics;[47] several decades of traditionalistic political culture had eliminated blacks as voters and rendered the white working class politically impotent. But within southern cities there were individuals and institutions who perceived untapped possibilities in capital accumulation, in a more aggressive approach to industrialization, and in the growth of large—very large, by regional standards—metropolises. Against the background of controlled growth emerged the South's urban entrepreneurs in several key cities, individuals who sought to use both federal and state money, services, and programs to build the infrastructure that would make particular cities more attractive to outside industries and local entrepreneurs.[48] Big city banks, power companies, transportation firms, and communications media stood to gain from rapid economic development, from servicing constantly expanding markets. Their vision of uncontrolled growth appalled some, frightened others, but galvanized many. Entrepreneurial individualism promised to make some individuals very wealthy, some institutions very powerful, and to raise the income of countless others, even as it transformed the cityscape, dislodged many at the bottom of society, and increased the probability of environmental pollution. It was, in short, the southernization of the old American dream—to make and keep a lot of money.

The individualistic vision magnified the importance of controlling local governments and the cities' representatives to state legislatures and Congress because much of the money needed to construct the infrastructure would have to be extracted from higher levels of the federal system—and thus conveniently paid for, in part, by citizens with whom the benefits would not have to be shared. Little of this political history is known, but it would be fascinating to understand exactly how southern development was financed.[49] Urban individualists were eager to build institutions (employing many professionally trained workers) that would provide needed services for upwardly mobile individuals (state universities, for example) and for individuals requiring advanced medical treatment (hence the huge expansion of medical centers). They were less adept at anticipating and responding to transportation needs within metropolitan areas, as anyone who has driven in Houston, Dallas, or dozens of other southern cities can attest, and, like the traditionalists, they were strenuously opposed to subsidizing "unproductive" families or individuals ("throwing money down the drain").

As a result of the efforts of individuals and groups guided by individualistic orientations, many of the traditionalistic political cultures in southern cities have been challenged or even replaced by the individualistic culture. Elazar's depiction of the political cultures in southern cities about 1970 showed traditionalism still dominant in virtually all cities, but representing the exclusive culture in only a few metropolitan areas, such as Jackson, Charleston, and Memphis. In most cities traditionalism either existed along with or was synthesized with the individualistic culture; Dallas, Houston, and Atlanta were so classified. In isolated instances, as in northern Virginia and Fort Worth, individualism was considered the dominant culture.[50]

The blend of old and new political cultures suggests that southern cities will not be carbon copies of northern cities, either in their values or their public policies. Lupsha and Siembieda underscore this conclusion:

Wealth, increased urban population, sense of proximity, density, and complexity are now everyday aspects of life in metropolitan centers like Dallas, Miami, and Houston. At the same time, other conditions—the values of organization and participation by underclass groups, a belief that a high level of public services is an obligation of government—or any widely agreed upon notion of equity have yet to gain a major foothold in the Sunbelt cities. Furthermore, the sociocultural and political organizational structure of the Sunbelt will not enhance the rapid implementation of these conditions. The Sunbelt cities are on the rise, but they will continue—as far as public service delivery is concerned—to pay far less attention to the needs of their poor and people of color than to the needs of monied and propertied elites.[51]

Although southern cities have been and may continue to be different from nonsouthern cities, they are gradually becoming zones of heterogenity and political diversity in a region long known to be, apart from race, homogeneous. The large metropolitan and medium urban electorates are split among rapidly growing middle-class whites, large numbers of working-class whites (some of whom may belong to labor unions), an increasingly diverse group of blacks, and large groups of Hispanics (Cubans in Florida, Chicanos in Texas). In varying proportions local electorates include Democrats (progressives to conservatives), Republicans (moderates to extreme conservatives), and political independents of differing ideological persuasions. Though metropolitan elites are not without means of influencing electoral outcomes, the principal urban areas are not settings in which a handful of affluent, conservative white Democrats native to the South can "pass the word" and expect instant compliance from a restricted and "reliable" electorate. Metropolitan political diversity is sometimes disguised in statewide elections, where the voters' realistic choices may be limited and where the candidates who can raise the enormous sums necessary for television advertising often do very well. Diversity is readily observable, however, in the composition of metropolitan delegations to the state legislature when single-member districts are employed. To the extent that blacks, liberal Democrats, and Republicans are represented in state legislatures, they are most likely to come from districts located within large metropolitan areas.

Finally, the rise of urban electorates has accelerated the transition from old-style grassroots politics, which emphasized personal contact in meeting and greeting voters, to the more impersonal, remote, yet cost-effective techniques of video campaigning.[52] Modern campaigns require presentable candidates who can discuss issues, events, and personalities in a conversational style (as opposed to a fiery, stem-winding stump speech);

campaigners can speak with passion and conviction, but they must sustain the appearance of self-control. Part of the entertainment appeal of the old southern politics, with its public "speakings" before massive and expectant crowds, was the anticipation that speakers might get so carried away that they would say something especially shocking or memorable. Since winning electoral strategies in most southern states require respectable votes from both metropolitan and nonmetropolitan electorates, contemporary campaigning rewards candidates who are modern enough to appeal to the more sophisticated city voters but sufficiently humble and down-to-earth to attract small-town and rural support. In practice this has meant the emergence of a new generation of southern campaigners whose roots are frequently in the medium-sized cities but whose political ambitions have connected them to significant metropolitan interests.

The South today is more similar to the rest of the nation than ever before in its history. Judged by the standard indicators of industrialization and urbanization, regional distinctiveness is clearly waning. The region has moved in the general direction anticipated by Key, but it has not fully converged with the non-South, and in some respects continues to be quite different from the rest of the nation. Southern industrialization, though generating roughly comparable shares of workers in various industry groups, has differed from that of the non-South by dispersing into small-town and rural settings rather than concentrating in large cities. Southern urbanization, while remarkable in its scope and velocity, has been different as well from that of the non-South. No southern metropolitan area in 1980 contained half the inhabitants of New York, Los Angeles, or Chicago, although the South's largest metropolitan centers (Dallas–Fort Worth and Houston) were approximately the same size as San Francisco–Oakland or Boston.

As the twentieth century has proceeded, state power structures have been augmented by new producers of wealth emerging from industrialization. No longer constructed around a single crop or industry, southern power structures now encompass more institutional actors. The economic resources required for sustained and successful political activity remain highly concentrated, though the games of state, regional, and national politics involve more players than in the past. Large metropolitan areas and medium-sized cities, not the hinterlands, now produce the votes necessary to win statewide elections.

In recent decades the South has changed tremendously, and the cumulative impact of these vast transformations has been to undermine the complete supremacy of the traditionalistic political culture. The emergence of entrepreneurial industrialists promoting modernization, and the diffusion of a philosophy sanctioning unrestrained rather than controlled growth have produced a region energetically committed to rapid economic development. At the same time, the opposition of both traditionalists and urban entrepreneurs to public policies explicitly aiding the region's have-littles and have-nots constitutes a profound continuity in elite political orientations.

three

The Rise of
Middle-Class
Society

JUST AS observers of southern politics need to appreciate the vast demographic and economic changes that have occurred in recent decades, they need to understand as well the changing social structure of the South. Key argued in 1955:

> The enlargement of the urban middle classes and the increase in the ranks of non-agricultural workers are creating the foundations for a durable alteration in the politics of the South. The principle of politics underlying such an assertion is, of course, the assumption that political cleavages tend to parallel economic differences, a proposition that is only conditionally valid. In our relatively bland politics, without a historical habit of sustained conflict along rigid lines of social class, potential cleavages along economic lines attain fullest political reality only when opened cleanly by the cutting edge of sharp issues of economic policy. A long spell of general prosperity will mute political differences between those who have more and those with less. To suggest that deep economic differences will not recur sooner or later and have their political repercussions would be to envisage a reorganization of economic life of a sort not readily imaginable.[1]

Key proceeded to identify the region's victors for the foreseeable future. "It is probable, given the nature of resources and facilities of social classes for political action, that the new middle classes will be able to exert their full strength before the new working classes can be fully mobilized," he predicted. "Political leaders who seek to activate the emerging industrial working class, black and white, must overcome ingrained habits of non-participation in politics as well as the special handicaps to action inherent in most groups low on the ladder of status."[2]

One of the most penetrating social anthropological investigations of the traditional South, the work *Deep South,* by Allison Davis, Burleigh

B. Gardner, and Mary R. Gardner, offers a theoretical orientation based on caste and class divisions that can be adapted to gauge the extent and import of changes in the southern social order:

> The fundamental division in the social organization of Old City and Old County is that between the Negroes and the "white folks." This social cleavage is such that all privileges and opportunities, as well as duties and obligations, are unequally distributed between the two groups. The whites receive by far the larger portion of all economic and social rewards, while the Negroes have an undue share of the more onerous duties. Both Negroes and whites recognize the fact that the white group is superordinate in power and prestige, and they exemplify this awareness in both their behavior and thought . . . Each individual is born into the Negro or white group and must remain in it for life. He may neither earn nor wed his way out.[3]

Although the distinction between a superordinate white caste and a subordinate black caste was based on an analysis of a single Mississippi county in the late 1930s, few observers would question the appropriateness of the *Deep South* interpretation of race relations for the unreconstructed South in general. The authors of *Deep South* recognized a variety of secondary cleavages and concluded that "social class" (analyzed as upper, middle, and lower classes) was the "most fundamental of these divisions within each caste."[4]

Despite the intuitive appeal of the *Deep South* model of southern social structure prior to the civil rights movement, patterns of race and class relations for the region as a whole have not been systematically investigated over an extended period of time. Comparative analysis has been inhibited by the difficulty of estimating the relative size of the social classes identified in the caste and class model and by the need to take into account the South's transition from ruralism to urbanism. This omission needs to be corrected, not simply because of the intrinsic importance of social structure, but also because of the possible consequences for political life. Although it is not feasible to replicate the methods of participant observation used by the *Deep South* research team to determine social class, the occupational data reported in the decennial U.S. censuses can be aggregated to reveal the changing social structure of the South.

Borrowing and modifying concepts introduced by Leonard Reissman,[5] we shall distinguish the following four classes: an *agrarian middle class* of farm owners (an unknown proportion of whom would constitute the region's plantation elite); a *traditional lower class* performing laborious and exceedingly unremunerative tasks usually associated with agriculture; a *working class* increasingly situated in cities and towns; and a *new middle class,* over time the most likely source of innovative leadership for the South. The agrarian middle class is defined as the percentage of employed southerners who are farm owners. Farm tenants, farm laborers, and private household workers compose the traditional lower class. The working class is defined as the proportion of southerners employed in the following occupations: craftsmen and foremen, operatives, transportation, service, and laborers. Southerners with professional, technical, managerial, administrative, sales, and clerical positions constitute the new middle class.[6] These broad occupational categories are obviously blunt instruments, but we consider them reasonable classifications for analyzing social structure over time and think that the division of white and black southerners into four socioeconomic classes retains the spirit of the *Deep South* perspective.

The Changing Social Structure of the South

When the percentage distribution of the labor force among these four classes is charted from 1940 (the earliest census with comparable occupational classifications) through 1980 for all southerners with jobs, rather dramatic alterations appear in the region's social structure (figure 3.1). Even more impressive discontinuities would probably emerge if it were possible to stretch the comparisons farther back in time. Since 1940 the two occupational classes generally identified with the old South— the agrarian middle class and the traditional lower class—have steadily diminished in size. The new middle class and the working class dominate the occupational structure of the modern South.

Because the transformation of southern agriculture had begun in the nineteenth century, it is not surprising that the 1940 census depicts a South in transition from an agrarian to a mixed economy. Whites differed immensely from blacks in their occupations. In 1940 two-thirds of the white labor force were already part of the industrial working class or the new middle class. Few whites were economically secure during the Great Depression (many of those engaged in supposedly "middle-class" jobs were paid working-class wages or lower), but most whites were not directly and exclusively tied to the land for a living. By comparison, a sizable majority of southern blacks were trapped in the traditional lower class, and most blacks with working-class jobs could only be employed for tasks that whites did not want.

The Jim Crow system especially impeded the development of a substantial black middle class.[7] Only a limited number of middle-class positions (such as school teaching and nursing) were required to operate segregated institutions. Meager educational opportunities, poverty, and discrimination in hiring meant that middle-class employment was an

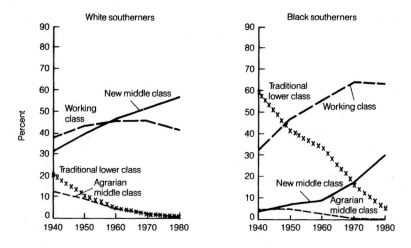

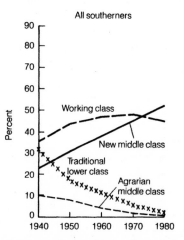

Figure 3.1. Reshaping of the southern social order: class composition of the labor force for white southerners, black southerners, and all southerners, 1940–1980. Sources: Calculated from publications of the U.S. Bureau of the Census, 1940, 1950, 1960, 1970, and 1980.

impossible dream for almost all black southerners. Although three-tenths of the whites possessed middle-class jobs in 1940, no more than four blacks in every hundred were able to obtain professional and technical, managerial and administrative, or even sales and clerical jobs. Whether middle class, working class, or lower class, the economic dependence of blacks upon whites was the general rule. The contrasting class positions of white and black southerners in 1940 documents for the region the historical subordination of blacks demonstrated for one county in *Deep South*.

Since 1940 millions of southerners have abandoned their accustomed occupations (or those of their parents) in search of improved standards of living, and the modern South's social structure bears little resemblance to that of the past. In 1980, for the first time in the region's history, a majority of southerners worked in new-middle-class jobs. Because most of the other employed southerners now hold working-class jobs, the unique features of the old southern social structure have dwindled to quite marginal proportions.

Yet despite significant changes over time in the relative size of the four occupational classes, it is equally obvious that white advantages have largely survived the transformation of the region's social order. In 1980 a majority of southern whites were employed in new-middle-class positions, compared with less than a third of southern blacks. Middle-class employment among black southerners increased sevenfold between 1940 and 1980, with the most impressive gains occurring during the 1960s (the decade of the civil-rights movement's most important successes) and the 1970s (the decade of affirmative action employment policies). The white new middle class has been a moving target, however, and the gap between the proportion of white and black southerners with new-middle-class occupations was almost as wide in 1980 (26 points) as it was in 1940 (27 points). It will be many, many years before racial parity in new-middle-class employment begins to be approached.

For black southerners who left or were displaced from jobs in the traditional lower class, the main source of reemployment was not the new middle class but the working class. By and large, black men who had once worked as farm laborers or tenants and black women who had formerly labored as domestic servants acquired working-class occupations, most commonly as unskilled laborers (for men) and service workers (for women). In 1980 the proportion of blacks with working-class jobs was roughly 1.5 times as high as the percentage of working-class whites.

A more precise understanding of race and class in the South can be obtained by controlling for sex. Between 1940 and 1980 there were two important changes in the racial and sexual composition of the southern labor force. White women, who accounted for only 14 percent of all employed southerners in 1940, entered the labor market in such numbers that they made up 34 percent of the 1980 work force. During the same period, due largely to out-migration, the proportion of southern jobs held by black men dropped from 20 to 9. Modest declines also occurred in the shares of jobs controlled by white males (56 percent in 1940 versus

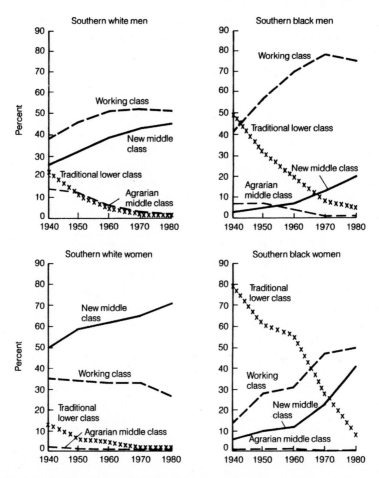

Figure 3.2. Southern labor force by race and gender, 1940–1980. Sources: Same as figure 3.1.

48 percent in 1980) and by black females (10 percent versus 9 percent). The southern labor force in 1980 was thus "whiter" than it had been in 1940, a function both of blacks leaving the region and white women finding work.

Employment opportunities within each race have been strongly conditioned by gender (see figure 3.2). The high rate of white southerners in the new middle class is due more to white women than to white men. As white females have increasingly joined the labor force, they have overwhelmingly acquired middle-class occupations. Likewise, the disproportionate concentration of blacks in the traditional lower class is far more characteristic of black women than black men. No contrast in southern race and class is more stark than the 1940 employment situations of black women (cooking and cleaning in middle- and upper-class white households or working in the fields) and white women (office work and teaching).

The trend lines establish several important points (figure 3.2). First, the class positions of black and white southerners of both sexes prior to World War II were generally consistent with the basic argument of *Deep South*. White command and control of a rigidly segregated social order was enormously facilitated by the microscopic size of the black new middle class. Second, with urbanization, economic development, the rise of the civil rights movement, and finally federal intervention into southern race relations, the sizes of the four classes have changed to such an extent that the South of 1980 was far, far less distinctive than it had previously been. By 1980, in every southern comparison, the proportion of jobs accounted for by a combination of the new middle class and the working class exceeded nine-tenths of all positions. Finally, despite unprecedented changes in class relations, black southerners of both sexes have remained far behind white southerners in acquiring the middle-class jobs that translate most readily into leadership roles.

Within the South the changing occupational order has progressed much further in metropolitan than in rural and small-town environments. To separate urbanized from nonurbanized areas is to demarcate the "dynamic" from the "static" South (see table 3.1).[8] By 1980 a majority of the southern labor force resided in urbanized areas, and a much larger proportion of the urbanized labor force was employed in the new middle class than in the working class. This was especially true for whites, while among black southerners the working class still outnumbered the new middle class.

In several crucial respects the occupational class structure of the rural and small-town South differed from that of the urbanized South. The nonurbanized South was dominated numerically by the working class, possessed a much smaller new middle class, had a larger proportion of farm owners, and contained a higher rate of black employment in the traditional lower class. In 1980 merely a fifth of black southerners residing outside the urbanized areas had secured new-middle-class jobs. Though most southerners even in the rural and small-town South had long since been employed outside the agricultural sector, it was in the region's hinterlands—and especially in those localities where blacks still constituted substantial proportions of the rural population—that the social order in the 1980s most resembled the old South, that many tra-

Table 3.1. The dynamic and the static South: comparison of the 1980 class composition of the southern labor force in urbanized and nonurbanized areas[a]

Population	Urbanized labor force					Nonurbanized labor force				
	NMC[b]	WC[b]	AMC[b]	TLC[b]	Urb[c]	NMC	WC	AMC	TLC	Nonurb[c]
All southerners	60	38	0	2	54	42	53	2	3	46
White southerners	66	33	0	1	53	45	50	3	2	47
Black southerners	37	58	0	5	60	20	70	1	9	40
White women	79	20	0	1	55	62	36	1	2	45
White men	55	44	0	1	51	34	59	4	3	49
Black women	50	43	0	7	61	29	61	0	10	39
Black men	25	73	0	2	58	13	78	2	8	42

Sources: Same as 1980 sources cited in figure 3.1.

a. Data are presented as percentages.

b. NMC, new middle class; WC, working class; AMC, agrarian middle class; TLC, traditional lower class.

c. Proportion of specified population residing in urbanized (or nonurbanized) areas.

ditional ways of interacting persisted, and that resistance was strongest to radical departures in employment practices.

Judged by labor force characteristics, the South's social structure is now scarcely distinguishable from the non-South. Astonishing changes in occupational structure between 1940 and 1980 have amounted to a "national incorporation of a region."[9] The two occupational classes that originally set the South apart from the rest of the nation—the agrarian middle class and the traditional lower class—have so steadily diminished in size that they amounted to no more than 3 percent of the entire southern labor force in 1980. Compared to the non-South, the South in 1980 had only a slightly larger working class (45 versus 42 percent) and a somewhat smaller new middle class (52 versus 56 percent). Whites in both regions had virtually identical labor force characteristics, and the principal difference between the regions was that the black middle class was smaller in the South than in the rest of the nation.

Political Predispositions of the New Middle Class

Momentous changes in the primary location of power and influence within the South are implicit in the preceding analysis. In 1940 the new middle class already outnumbered the agrarian middle class, but because many prominent members of the new middle class fully shared the beliefs, values, and interests of the large-scale landowners, the plantation elite could virtually control the political agenda in most southern states. By 1980 a quantum change had occurred, and the new middle class was twenty-three times greater than the agrarian middle class. Even conceding that black belt agricultural interests may continue to exert influence far beyond their numbers, the size, complexity, and resources of the new middle class means that it is positioned to exercise an increasingly decisive role in political affairs. Reissman argued in the mid-1960s that the "growth of a middle class to challenge the former aristocratic [agrarian] elite" is the only "valid way to explain the revolutionary changes now taking place, since there must be human agents behind that change."[10] Stated plainly, if the black belt elite was the dominant force in the old southern politics, the enormous expansion of the South's new middle class and the equally visible shrinking of the agrarian middle class strongly imply that elements within the new middle class have replaced the plantation elite as the paramount factor in the emerging southern politics.

Middle-class southerners occupy most of the region's political offices, dominate its key decisionmaking institutions in the private sector, and control most of its communications and mass media. From the South's new middle class have emerged the society's most conspicuous models of success and achievement.[11] Although the members of this middle class are obviously not all alike in occupation, education, or income, several important central tendencies clearly emerge concerning their political ideology, notions of governmental responsibility for the economic well-being of the citizenry, and likes and dislikes regarding salient political symbols. Knowledge of these themes is crucial in understanding the manifold advantages possessed by conservative and moderate-to-conservative politicians, in contrast to the multiple obstacles that confront flagrantly liberal campaigners in the South.

The best data for analyzing conservatism's popularity in the contemporary South come from the 1968 Comparative State Elections Project (CSEP).[12] The CSEP questions about political ideology allow us to analyze respondents either in terms of three broad groups (conservatives, middle-of-the-roaders, and liberals) or in terms of seven smaller groups (strong conservatives, not very strong conservatives, middle-of-the-roaders leaning toward conservatism, middle-of-the-roaders with no leanings, middle-of-the-roaders leaning toward liberalism, not very strong liberals, and strong liberals). The data reported here (see table 3.2) describe the three broad groups, though we shall occasionally refer to the more detailed categories in describing the shape of southern public opinion concerning political ideology. Because the vast majority of middle-class southerners are white, we shall concentrate on their views.

Most whites who categorized themselves as "middle class" thought of themselves as some sort of political conservative (table 3.2).[13] Almost half explicitly identified themselves as conservatives, and another fifth (not shown in the table) classified themselves as leaning toward conservatism. All told, nearly two-thirds of the South's white middle class expressed some affinity for the political right. Self-designated liberals, on the other hand, made up only one-sixth of this group. Even after adding white middle-of-the-roaders who leaned toward liberalism to the self-identified liberals, no more than a quarter of the white middle class expressed any sympathy for political liberalism.

The ideological tendencies of the southern white middle class persisted after 1968. Surveys of the American electorate conducted by the University of Michigan's Survey Research Center—Center for Political Studies (SRC-CPS) have asked respondents to place themselves on an ideological continuum. Though the wording of the SRC-CPS questions is not identical to the CSEP questions, individuals can still be classified as liberals,

Table 3.2. Class, race, and ideology in the South: ideological self-placement in 1968 and 1972–1984[a]

Category of southerner	1968 CSEP				1972–1984 SRC-CPS[b]			
	Con[c]	MR[c]	Lib[c]	C/L[c]	Con	MR	Lib	C/L
Entire middle class	46	38	15	3.1	48	31	21	2.3
Entire working class	37	49	15	2.5	42	36	23	1.8
Middle-class whites	47	38	14	3.4	50	32	18	2.7
Working-class whites	42	49	10	4.2	47	36	17	2.9
Blacks	25	44	32	0.8	21	31	48	0.4

Sources: 1968 CSEP; 1972–1984 presidential election year surveys of SRC-CPS.

a. Data, except for ratios, are presented as percentages.

b. The results are averages of the 1972–1984 presidential election year surveys.

c. Con, conservative; MR, middle-of-the-road; Lib, liberal; C/L, ratio of conservatives to liberals.

Coding: In the 1968 CSEP survey, respondents were asked, "When it comes to politics in general, do you usually think of yourself as a conservative, as a liberal, as middle-of-the-road, or don't you think of yourself along liberal or conservative lines?" The results in this table include respondents who think in ideological terms and those who placed themselves in a category after probing by the interviewer.

In the SRC-CPS surveys, respondents were asked to place themselves on an ideological continuum. The question was as follows: "We hear a lot of talk these days about liberals and conservatives. Here is a seven-point scale on which the political views that people might hold are arranged from extremely liberal to extremely conservative. Where would you place yourself on this scale, or haven't you thought much about this?" With the exception of those who had not given any thought to the question and who therefore were omitted, respondents were classified as extremely liberal, liberal, slightly liberal, moderate or middle-of-the-road, slightly conservative, conservative, or extremely conservative. In the table we have condensed these categories so that liberals are the sum of the first three categories and conservatives are the sum of the last three categories.

conservatives, or middle-of-the-roaders. Because the Michigan surveys contain much smaller samples of middle-class southerners, we have averaged the results of the 1972, 1976, 1980, and 1984 surveys. These averages give ideological distributions for middle-class whites—conservatives almost three times as numerous as liberals—that are essentially similar to the CSEP results (table 3.2). Survey research in this instance confirms conventional wisdom about middle-class white southerners; liberalism remains a minor theme compared with conservatism.

In addition to the conservatism of middle-class whites on the general dimension of ideology, we can demonstrate a more specific set of beliefs supporting economic conservatism through an SRC-CPS question that asks respondents to choose between individual responsibility and governmental responsibility for providing a job and a good standard of living. Both the traditionalistic and entrepreneurial individualistic cultures emphasize personal responsibility for financial success and minimize the responsibility of government to provide a good living standard for their citizens. The main sources of support for governmental responsibility derive from the Populist tradition and from the extremely limited moralistic tradition, neither of which has been especially prominent among the new middle class.

The SRC-CPS question is as follows: "Some people feel that the government in Washington should see to it that every person has a job and a good standard of living. Suppose that these people are at one end of this scale—at point number 1. Others think that the government should just let each person get ahead on his own. Suppose that these people are at the other end—at point number 7. And, of course, some other people have opinions in between. Where would you place yourself on this scale, or haven't you thought much about this?" Those who had not given much attention to the question were ignored. Although we shall occasionally refer to the individuals who believed in either complete governmental responsibility or complete individual responsibility, most of our discussion will be based on the results of collapsing the categories into those favoring governmental responsibility (points 1, 2, and 3), those who are neutral (point 4), and those who prefer individual responsibility (points 5, 6, and 7).

Again averaging results for the 1972-1984 SRC-CPS surveys, we found that whites who favored individual responsibility (56 percent) outweighed those who believed government had a duty to provide employment and a good standard of living (23 percent) by more than 2:1 (see table 3.3). Although many middle-class white southerners would recognize unusual circumstancces necessitating governmental intervention, truly extraordinary conditions—on the order of widespread, severe, and

Table 3.3. Class, race, and the conservative edge in placing responsibility for economic well-being, 1972–1984[a]

Type of southerner	Greater stress on individual responsibility	Midpoint	Greater stress on governmental responsibility	IR/GR[b]
Entire middle class	53	20	27	1.9
Entire working class	38	21	41	0.9
Middle-class whites	56	21	23	2.4
Working-class whites	49	23	29	1.7
Blacks	13	14	72	0.2

Sources: 1972, 1976, 1980, and 1984 SRC-CPS presidential year surveys.

a. Data, except for ratios, are presented as percentages and are averages of the four surveys.

b. IR/GR, ratio of respondents emphasizing individual responsibility to respondents stressing governmental responsibility.

Coding: Greater stress on individual responsibility = points 7, 6, and 5; midpoint = point 4; greater stress on governmental responsibility = points 1, 2, and 3.

prolonged economic hardship—would be required to disrupt their commitment to individual responsibility.[14]

The popularity of conservatism allows conservative politicians to deploy an impressive array of positive and negative symbols to win the hearts and minds of the southern white middle class. Liberal politicians, by comparison, have a much smaller group of positive symbols with which to work and a much larger set of negative symbols to defend against. This utter imbalance in symbolic politics can be illustrated with survey data. In a series of SRC-CPS surveys participants have been asked to give "thermometer ratings" to a variety of political symbols. A score of 50 represents neutrality or indifference; ratings lower than 50 indicate coolness or hostility; and ratings higher than 50 signify warmth or friendliness toward a given symbol. Using symbols we consider relevant to southern politics, we have computed the average percentages of middle-class white southerners who expressed warmth or coolness toward particular symbols during the 1972-1984 period.[15]

The political landscape revealed by our computations is exceedingly advantageous to conservatives (figure 3.3). At one extreme in the symbolic political universe of the southern white middle class are positive valence symbols, objects or groups so overwhelmingly liked and valued that only one "proper" response seems to have been possible.[16] These symbols— "police," "whites," "southerners," "military," "conservatives," and "Republicans"—represent the emotional and cognitive importance of authority, continuity, stability, armed might in defense of the homeland,

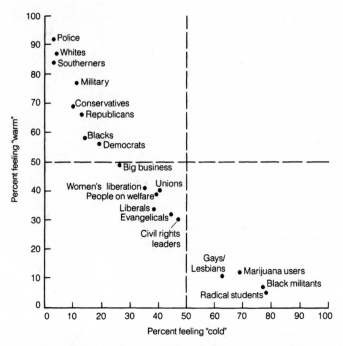

Figure 3.3. The political landscape of the southern white middle class: mean percentages of respondents who expressed "warm" and "cold" reactions to selected political symbols, 1972–1984. Feeling thermometer scores of less than 50 are considered to be unfavorable and are classified as "cold"; scores greater than 50 are considered to be favorable and are classified as "warm". Source: SRC-CPS presidential election year surveys, 1972–1984.

regional and racial pride, and the new political instrument of southern conservatism. Constituting a panoply of sacred or near-sacred objects, all of these symbols have been employed and will continue to be evoked, in subtle and not-so-subtle appeals, to support conservatism.

"Democrats" and "blacks" elicited favorable ratings from over half of the middle-class whites, but the majorities were smaller than for the premier symbols. The position of "Democrats" is especially intriguing. In decades past, before the civil rights movement and federal intervention took place under Democratic auspices, the Democratic party probably would have been one of the white middle class's sacred symbols, occupying territory similar to "whites" and "southerners." By the 1970s, however, "Democrats" received less approval than the historical partisan enemies of conservative whites—the "Republicans"—and drew about the same level of support as did "blacks." The symbol "Democrats," it is important to note, was not evaluated similarly to the symbol "liberal." In the South many middle-class whites still perceive the Democratic party as a necessary instrument for rule.

More balanced position symbols, stimuli that generated both considerable support and opposition, were "big business," "people on welfare," "unions," "liberals," and "women's liberation." "Big business" won more support than opposition, but its mixed reviews signify that large corporations were not universally respected and admired even among the white middle class. The other divided thermometer ratings illustrate why liberal politicians usually have difficulty appealing to the white middle class. If liberalism is associated with more people on welfare, unions, and an acceleration of women's liberation, many middle-class white southerners want no part of it. Considerably more coldness than warmth appeared for two potential disrupters of the status quo—"evangelicals" and "civil rights leaders." And much stronger expressions of opposition characterized responses to the symbols "gays/lesbians," "marijuana users," "radical students," and "black militants." Seen as negative valence symbols by most southern middle-class whites, these groups represented racial and cultural radicalism: strange people, strange ideas, very strange and threatening behavior.

Consideration of the white middle class's central tendencies—its affinity for conservatism in general, its emphasis on individual rather than governmental responsibility for finding a job and securing a good standard of living, and its warmth and coolness toward different political symbols—makes clearer the tasks of conservative and liberal compaigners, at least concerning their appeals to this crucial segment of the South's electorate. Conservative strategists, who basically run with the grain of popular sentiment, have a much easier job. Facing a population that wants to side with conservatism, that prefers to define governmental responsibility narrowly and keep taxes low, and that is predisposed to respond warmly to most symbols of conservatism, political consultants who have the requisite experience, imagination, and shrewdness can easily create visceral symbolic appeals that will engage most middle-class white southerners in the service of political conservatism. In many cases the critical problem for conservative strategists is less how to discredit liberal (or moderate) opponents than how to defeat fellow conservatives.

From the standpoint of liberal compaigners, the political landscape of the southern white middle class is bleak and forbidding. The symbolic terrain is filled with groups and causes for which proximity probably spells political disaster, and the positions frequently championed by liberals generally do not coincide with the values prevalent among middle-class whites. A liberalism directed toward the problems of the average citizen (as it seemed to be during the New Deal era), rather than a liberalism perceived as a holding company for an agglomeration of special interest groups, might win more acceptance among middle-class southerners. Aggressive presentation of the rationale for increased investment in quality public education is an issue that liberal candidates might use effectively with middle-class audiences, and informed attacks on large corporate interests, though alienating many middle-class whites, would be approved by a sizable share of this group. Probably the most realistic prognosis is that liberal campaigners will achieve no more than sporadic victories among the white middle class. Southern liberals have been unable to define issues that positively excite middle-class whites, and they must compete in an environment in which their ideological opponents maintain distinct superiority in finance as well as symbols. Middle-class conservatives can afford to put their money where their mouth is. Emphatic and enthusiastic support for conservative and moderate-to-conservative campaigners will continue to be the predominant political tendency of middle-class white southerners.

The Failure of Organized Labor in the South

Although the emergence of the new middle class in 1980 as the South's largest class is a signal development, a sizable minority of the southern labor force (45 percent) were employed in the working class. Moreover, the new middle class's predominance is primarily due to the exceptionally high rate of new-middle-class jobholding—amounting to seven-tenths of the work force—achieved by white women. Among the other three race-and-gender categories, blue-collar employment in 1980 exceeded new-middle-class employment. Most black men (75 percent) held working-class positions, as did half of all white men (51) and black women (50).

The sizes of the southern and nonsouthern working classes have become very similar, but Key's expectation that southern industrialization would significantly enhance the economic and political leverage of organized labor has yet to be realized. No more than a small fraction of southern workers have joined unions, and there is little prospect of dramatic change in the foreseeable future. Figures on union membership underscore organized labor's enduring weakness. Although the absolute number of southern unionists rose from 0.5 million in 1939 to 3.2 million in 1980, the percentage of union members among the region's nonagricultural work force has remained quite low.[17] In 1939 a mere tenth of southern workers belonged to unions. There were percentage gains in the 1940s and earlys 1950s (peaking at an estimated 17 percent in 1953), but union membership in the South (and the non-South) has been gradually diminishing.

In the North, labor unions historically flourished in metropolitan areas and constituted a significant presence even in nonmetropolitan settings. According to the 1968 CSEP survey, for example, 36 percent of the North's metropolitan households contained a union member, compared to 26 percent of nonmetropolitan households. The apparently more hospitable environment of large cities led some observers, Key included, to view southern urbanization as a hopeful sign for the rise of organized labor. Within the South, though, reported labor union membership was equally low in metropolitan (15 percent) and nonmetropolitan (13 percent) households. If this pattern continues, the growth of more and more cities will not mean a commensurate strengthening of the southern labor movement. Even in the late 1960s, unionism in the metropolitan South lagged far behind the proportion of union households in the smaller cities, towns, and rural sections of the North.

Beyond the South, organized labor's greatest appeal was among skilled and semiskilled workers. In 1968 three-fifths of all northern households headed by an unskilled worker also contained a union member, as did 55 percent of northern households headed by a skilled worker. The organizational ties of southern workers were utterly different. Only one-quarter of southern households headed by either a skilled or unskilled worker also contained a union member. The vast majority of the South's manual workers, blacks and whites, maintained no formal association with organized labor in the late 1960s, and this situation remained unaltered in the mid-1980s.

Unionization's halting pace has frustrated supporters of organized labor; yet the southern states are neither homogeneous nor unique in their patterns of union membership. Although their 1980 rates of union membership placed them at the low end of the distribution of American states, the southern rates ranged from 8 percent in South Carolina to 22 percent in Alabama. The most inhospitable environments for labor unions in the entire nation were the textile-saturated Carolinas and the most populous southern states, Texas and Florida.[18] In most southern states, nonetheless, at least 15 percent of the nonagricultural work force belonged to unions, and Tennessee joined Alabama in achieving rates that were comparatively robust within the region. The dearth of union membership in the South was not unique. Thirteen nonsouthern states, chiefly in the Great Plains, the Rocky Mountains, and the least industrialized and urbanized portions of New England, had lower rates of unionism than Alabama.

Many factors have contributed to the persistent enfeeblement of organized labor in the South. There has been a longstanding surplus of unskilled and untrained workers who can do little but accept low-wage employment, as well as an abundance of firms operating in highly competitive industries and dependent upon cheap labor for economic survival. In a pervasive ideological climate that perceives unions as impediments to capital formation and thus to economic development, specific businesses and industries have relentlessly fought attempts to organize their employees, and many politicians have eagerly used their influence to prevent unionization. The dispersal of much of the southern labor force among smaller cities, towns, and rural areas has inhibited union recruitment, and cleavages between white and black workers have often been exploited by management to divide the labor movement. Finally, though far from least important, southern unionization has been hampered by a tenacious strain of individualism that leads many workers to be inordinately skeptical of collective efforts to improve their economic standing.[19]

Despite particular areas of strength and the examples of two southern states (Louisiana and Arkansas) where organized labor is reputed to exert influence beyond its numbers, labor's continuing weakness means that the principal institution through which many workers in the North were motivated to participate in politics is largely missing for most southern workers.[20] The absence of an influential voice for organized labor has given the South's most powerful business interests more leverage than they would normally command in fixing agreeable levels of taxation and financing appropriately sympathetic candidates.

Ideological Tendencies within the Southern Working Class

Considerable evidence exists concerning the ideological self-placement of working-class southerners, their feelings toward a variety of political symbols, and their beliefs about governmental versus individual responsibility for providing full employment and a good standard of living. Familiarity with these attitudes is useful in understanding why most white and black workers have not continuously united around liberal—much less radical—goals and objectives and why conservative and moderate-to-conservative politicians have often won substantial majorities among the South's working-class whites.

According to the 1968 CSEP survey, a slim majority (53 percent) of southerners who thought of themselves as working class also expressed an affinity for political conservatism. This majority included middle-of-the-roaders who leaned toward conservatism as well as those explicitly describing themselves as strong or weak conservatives. By a comparably generous assessment, political liberalism was supported by fewer than a fourth of the region's working class. Moreover, the single largest category among working-class southerners (26 percent; not shown in table 3.2) was ideological neutrality, exemplified by middle-of-the-roaders without *any* tendency toward conservatism or liberalism. This is a category which George Rabinowitz has argued is disproportionately associated with indifference to or unconcern about the particular dimension being measured, and its practical consequence is greater disengagement from the stuff of politics.[21] The southern working class is composed, primarily, of individuals who do have ideological preferences—preferences much more sympathetic to conservatism than liberalism—and, secondarily, of individuals who do not follow or care about ideological politics.

These data hardly suggest a political system on the brink of widespread, sharply polarized ideological conflict between its middle and working classes. For that to happen millions of southern workers would have to be converted to opposite political viewpoints, and millions more would have to be converted *and* activated. Barring economic catastrophe, the probability of sustained ideological conflict between a liberal or radicalized southern working class and a conservative middle class is remote. What *is* likely is a political system in which most elections are won by conservatives, progressive conservatives, and conservative progressives— that is, by politicians who do not present themselves to the electorate as overt liberals.

Because blacks are a sizable fraction (one-fifth in 1968) of the southern working class, it is crucial to distinguish between the ideological preferences of white and black workers. Among white workers, 57 percent considered themselves conservative or leaning in that direction, 26 percent were neutral, and merely 17 percent described themselves as liberal or inclined that way. Working-class blacks, as might be expected, expressed very different ideological preferences: 43 percent were liberal or leaning toward liberalism, 26 percent were neutral, and 31 percent considered themselves conservative or tending toward conservatism. These data show a deep ideological split by race within the southern working class, a philosophical division hardly favorable or conducive to the establishment of a durable biracial coalition committed to a liberal agenda. For such a coalition to succeed, enormous mental earthquakes would have to occur in the self-understanding of most white and many black workers.[22]

The main ideological tendencies of southern workers have remained unchanged since the late 1960s. Consider, for example, the average percentage of working-class white southerners and black southerners who identified themselves as liberal, conservative, or moderate in the 1972, 1976, 1980, and 1984 SRC-CPS surveys (see table 3.2). Almost half of southern white workers, compared with a fifth of southern blacks, labeled themselves conservative, while almost a majority of blacks, but only one-sixth of the working-class whites, thought of themselves as some sort of liberal. The essential political orientation of the southern working class is fixed primarily by the predispositions of its much larger component—white workers—and hence the addition of blacks with acutely different views produces only minor changes in the ideological preferences of the region's entire working-class population.

Liberalism's vulnerability and conservatism's attractiveness also stand out in the white working class's evaluation of selected political symbols. Four items—"southerners," "whites," "police," and "military"—emerged as positive valence symbols (figure 3.4). In addition to the obvious appeal of symbols representing people like themselves, working-class whites were drawn to symbols of law and order at home and strength abroad. "Conservatives," "Democrats," and "Republicans" received less overwhelming majority approval but evoked little coolness. The symbol "Democrats" was appraised about as favorably as the term "conservatives," suggesting a possible overlap in support. Working-class whites, unlike middle-class whites, still evaluated "Democrats" more positively than "Republicans" in the 1972-1984 surveys. Only a few decades earlier "Democrats" would doubtless have been a sacred symbol for white southern workers, and "Republicans" would probably have attracted less warmth than coolness. "Blacks" produced mild majority approval, combined with hostility from a sixth of the white workers.

More evenly matched position symbols include "big business," "liberals," "people on welfare," "women's liberation movement," "unions," and "evangelicals." All of the symbols conventionally associated with American liberalism divided the southern white working class and yielded only small net gains or losses. Perhaps more important, conservative politicians can capitalize on the hostility some of these symbols generate among working-class whites in order to attract votes. The main symbol identified with conservatism that progressive campaigners might exploit among the white working class is "big business." Attacking the costs and services of large corporations—electric and gas utilities, or telephone companies—is no surefire formula for victory, for the thermometer data indicate substantial warmth among white workers toward big business, which employs thousands of working-class southerners. Yet these businesses become more visible targets as they loom larger in the region's economy, and dissatisfied consumers make up a constituency that could be mobilized on behalf of progressive candidates. Symbols that attracted more coolness than warmth among the South's white working class involved race ("civil rights leaders" and "black militants") and cultural

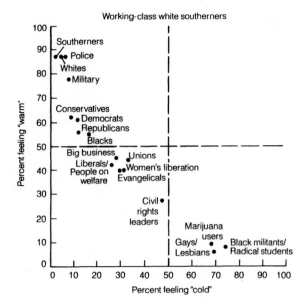

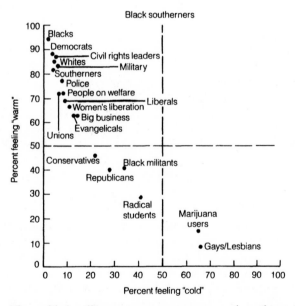

Figure 3.4. The unlikely alliance: mean percentages of working-class white southerners and black southerners who expressed "warm" and "cold" reactions to selected political symbols, 1972–1984. Source: SRC-CPS presidential election year surveys, 1972–1984.

radicalism ("marijuana users," "gays/lesbians," and "radical students"). These symbols illustrate forbidden terrain for politicians cultivating southern white workers.

Despite minor differences in detail, the political landscape of the white working class is remarkably similar to that of the white middle class (compare figures 3.3 and 3.4). Both white classes have similar positive and negative valence symbols and both evaluate position symbols in comparable ways. This fundamental congruence in whites' likes and dislikes across class lines provides enormous practical advantages to political conservatives in their search for elective office, whereas candidates running unmistakably as liberals have few positive valence symbols to project, few position symbols to manipulate, and many negative valence symbols to avoid or finesse.

If whites preferred liberal symbols far, far less than conservative symbols, the opposite situation prevailed among black southerners. Blacks differed from whites in producing a more elaborate set of positive valence symbols; at least two-thirds of black southerners, for example, expressed warmth toward eleven of nineteen symbols (figure 3.4) Though some positive valence symbols were shared by blacks and the white working class, these commonly respected items—"whites," "military," "southerners," and "police"—were uniformly conservative in their broad political implications.

More significant from the standpoint of creating and maintaining political alliances between black and white workers are the symbols that divide the races. Preponderant majorities of black southerners also treated "blacks," "Democrats," "civil rights leaders," "people on welfare," "liberals," "unions," and "women's liberation" as positive valence symbols, but these terms did not attract similarly large majorities of whites. In further contrast to white southerners, the symbols "Republicans" and "conservatives" did not evoke expressions of warmth from majorities of black southerners. The political landscape of black southerners was thus highly conducive to working-class politics, but their peers in the white working class by no means professed comparable feelings. Politicians who openly championed the entire range of symbols with greatest appeal to blacks would encounter immediate and widespread resistance among substantial portions of the white working class, as well as visceral opposition from huge majorities of the white middle class.

Thus far our analysis of ideological preferences and political symbols has led to pessimistic conclusions about sustained cooperation between blacks and working-class whites. Because it might be thought that a more appropriate test of these groups' common beliefs would focus on economic matters, we have examined the responses of working-class whites and blacks to the question of governmental or individual responsibility for employment and a good standard of living (see again table 3.3). At first glance it might indeed appear that prospects for a biracial coalition improve considerably as the issues narrow to governmental versus individual responsibility for economic well-being. When blacks and working-class whites are combined, a plurality of working-class southerners side with governmental rather than individual responsibility for employment and a good standard of living. These views are quite different from those of middle-class white southerners, where large majorities emphasize individual rather than governmental responsibility.

When the opinions of blacks and working-class whites are examined separately, however, no consensus appears on this question. An enormous majority of blacks (72 percent) placed greater stress on governmental responsibility, while almost half of the working-class whites (49 percent) emphasized individual responsibility as the primary value. Moreover, if we compare the percentages within each group favoring *purely* governmental or *purely* individual responsibility, the prospect of white working-class support for what most blacks prefer becomes virtually nil. Nearly a majority of blacks, 48 percent on the average, took the strongest possible position in support of total governmental and no individual responsibility for employment and a good standard of living. Although such complete reliance on the federal government among southern blacks may be understandable in light of the historical experiences of many blacks, their persistently high poverty rates, and their limited employment options today, the practical consequence is that what most blacks want from the federal government goes far beyond what most working-class whites support for themselves, much less for blacks. Only 14 percent of working-class white southerners adopted the stance of complete governmental responsibility. Most working-class whites preferred a mixture of individual and governmental responsibility (only one-fifth advocated total individual responsibility). Working-class whites did not face rigid group discrimination comparable to that met by blacks, and, as Robert Botsch's valuable study of North Carolina furniture workers indicates,[23] there are sufficient examples of individuals advancing from working-class origins to legitimize the norm of individual responsibility.

Prospects for political alliances between black and white workers are directly tied to the performance of the southern economy. In times of prosperity and widespread economic growth the desire for governmental responsibility for employment will be less salient than the belief in individual responsibility, while working-class opinion in recessionary periods will probably shift more in the direction of governmental intervention. Conditions of general economic hardship offer more opportunities and incentives for working-class whites and blacks to discover common interests, but even here goals and objectives will not perfectly coincide.

Our overview of the southern social order between 1940 and 1980 has shown that the South has become steadily less different in comparison with the rest of the nation. The near disappearance of both the agrarian middle class and the traditional lower class and the simultaneous expansion of the new middle class and the working class have culminated in a region whose social structure is no longer distinctive.

The South's transformed social order has *not* been associated with many statewide elections pitting sizable majorities of the middle class against broad majorities of the working class. As we have shown, an overwhelming majority of the white middle class and nearly half of the white working class believe in the primacy of individual, not governmental, responsibility for economic well-being. These beliefs unite whites who differ in socioeconomic status. Only a minority of the white working class leans toward governmental responsibility, which is desired by most blacks.

Finally, there is the matter of southern expectations about politics. "Southerners may have learned not to expect a great deal from the commonwealth," argues John Shelton Reed. "I believe that there is an individualistic ethic more common in the South than elsewhere, an ethic that says: in the last analysis, you (or at best you and your neighbors) are on your own. The greater world, many Southerners have learned, is indifferent if not actively hostile, disappointing if not actually dangerous, and it is a mistake to expect too much from it. It is easy to see how the distinct but intertwined histories of black and white Southerners could have led both to that same conclusion."[24] If working-class whites and blacks do have low expectations about governmental goods and services, the most likely consequence is not active participation and robust conflict over particular policies but indifference to and avoidance of the political process. Although middle-class southerners have low expectations, we think they do have strong preferences concerning the scope and substance of government. Southern states do not tax their middle classes heavily, do not engage in extensive redistributive programs designed to assist the working class, and tend to spend large amounts of money mainly on goods and services directly connected with the continued expansion of the middle classes. A politics constructed around the problems and aspirations of have-littles and have-nots can make little headway in such a climate.

II

The Transformation of Southern Race Relations

four
___

The
Old
Order

ONE CAN no more understand politics in the South without studying its system of race relations than one can comprehend politics in South Africa without analyzing apartheid.[1] As Key recognized with characteristic clarity, the old southern politics was mired in the defense of a totally segregated society: "The predominant consideration in the architecture of southern political institutions has been to assure locally a subordination of the Negro population and, externally, to block threatened interferences from the outside with these local arrangements." Key concluded *Southern Politics* by emphasizing the necessity of resolving the region's racial dilemma. "The race issue broadly defined," he argued, "must be considered as the number one problem on the southern agenda. Lacking a solution for it, all else fails."[2] Indeed, the emergence of a "new" southern politics became possible only when the traditional system of racial segregation collapsed. For these reasons it is of the utmost importance to show how—and to what extent—southern race relations have changed and to interpret the effects of renewed black participation on southern politics generally.

The system of race relations that emerged in the aftermath of emancipation was the closest functional approximation to the outlawed institution of slavery that white southerners could conceive, impose, and sustain. Gunnar Myrdal observed in 1944 that "Southerners still think of Negroes as their former slaves" and that "in the South, the master-model of economic discrimination—slavery—is still a living force as a memory and a tradition."[3] Southern racism involved an intricate code of interracial etiquette that symbolized white supremacy and black inferiority, the legalization of racial segregation in every important institution, the attempted (and largely successful) repression of educational and economic achievement among blacks, the routine denial of full human dignity to blacks, and the rationalization of legal and extralegal force to maintain the norms of the system. It is no wonder that millions of blacks voted with their feet and abandoned the South.

Two compelling motivations—fear of potential challenges to white supremacy and determination to perpetuate a way of life that provided many benefits and advantages to whites—undergirded the centrality and intensity of racism to white southerners. Herbert Blumer has argued convincingly that southern racism developed "through many generations of critical experience in which the self-identity and survival of the whites as a given kind of group were at stake." Slavery, secession and war, the Reconstruction era, and the eventual return of racist white Democrats to power contributed to the primacy of maintaining crucial distinctions between whites and blacks. As a consequence, Blumer contended, "the collective definition or social code elaborated from this experience came to be deeply embedded in the mores. The color line came to be felt by whites as natural, proper, and sacred, and as such to be zealously guarded against trespass by Negroes and preserved from disrespect by whites."[4] "The elementary determinant in Southern politics," Marion D. Irish concluded in 1942, "is an intense Negro phobia which has scarcely abated since Reconstruction."[5]

Fear was conveniently wedded to interest, since southern racial traditions allocated enormous advantages to whites at the expense of blacks.[6] Color lines in industrial jobs shielded many working-class whites from direct black competition, while creating a surplus of black labor that could be hired cheaply for work in traditional lower-class jobs (farming and housekeeping occupations). The almost total exclusion of blacks from voting eliminated the possibility of direct political pressure for more benefits to the black community and undercut any efforts to construct coalitions of have-nots against the much smaller group of haves. By defining whites as biologically and culturally superior to blacks, southern racism conveyed to whites an immense psychological gain. In the realm of sex, the color line placed a stringent taboo on sexual relations involving black men and white women.

Defense of racial interests became the fundamental "given" of southern politics. In order to maintain the southern way of life, popularly expressed as "white supremacy versus Negro domination," constant vigilance was required. As Key bluntly stated, "considerations of race relations" (the twin imperatives of subordinating blacks within the region and simultaneously preventing national intervention in regional racial practices) powerfully "moulded southern political institutions."[7]

Traditional Race Relations and the Illusion of Stability

In considering the traditional form of race relations it is helpful to draw on Blumer's concept of "the color line," defined as "a line which separates whites and Negroes, assigning to each a different position in the social order and attaching to each position a differential set of rights, privileges, and arenas of action . . . The color line stems from a collective sense held by whites that Negroes as a racial group do not qualify for equal status, and that because of their racial differences Negroes have no claim to being accepted socially." Blumer stressed the *multiplicity* of color lines in the United States. "As a metaphor, the color line is not appropriately represented by a single, sharply drawn line but appears rather as a series of ramparts, like the 'Maginot Line,' extending from outer breastworks to inner bastions," he explained. "Outer portions of it may . . . be given up only to hold steadfast to inner citadels."[8]

Black Americans have confronted massive discrimination in each of three broad categories. Controversies in the outer color line have concerned "the segregated position of Negroes *in the public arena*"; disputes in the intermediate color line have focused on "economic subordination and opportunity restriction"; and tensions in the innermost ring have involved white acceptance of blacks in intimate friendships and private associations.[9] In Blumer's analysis the "costs" to whites of changes in race relations and thus the intensity of white resistance to change are assumed to increase as attention shifts from the outer to the intermediate to the inner color line.

Embracing rights that "stem from the legal status of Negroes as citizens," the outer color line is exemplified by struggles over "free access to public accommodations and public institutions, the enjoyment of the franchise, the equal protection of laws, and equal rights as consumers."[10] Much of the early civil rights movement in the South was directed toward the desegregation of public accommodations and the exercise of voting rights. Indeed, for many whites, the demise of public segregation brought to an end legitimate "civil rights" issues. Blumer cautions against such a narrow interpretation of interracial controversies:

> It is a serious mistake, however, to regard the achievement by Negroes of civil rights, as presently defined, as equivalent to removing the color line. Whites are generally disposed, it is true, to view the matter in this way. They believe that if Negroes can vote, enter into politics, eat in any restaurant, go to any theater, ride on any public conveyance, have access to any hospital, attend any public function, enroll in any public school, apply for any job, and freely enter government employment, in short enjoy the os-

tensible rights of citizenship, the color line will have disappeared. However, the area of civil rights constitutes only a part, even though a highly significant part, of the larger region from which the Negro has been barred by the color line.[11]

The intermediate color line involves conflict between whites and blacks over employment opportunities, quality education, and residential integration. Progress in these areas is inherently more difficult, not only because of past massive racial discrimination which rendered many blacks less educated and less trained than whites, but also because each of the targets "is highly complicated by private and quasi-private property rights, managerial rights, and organizational rights."[12] The racial cleavages that have arisen over efforts to weaken the intermediate color line (metropolitan school desegregation, busing, affirmative action programs) are among the most controversial ever to appear in American politics.[13] Blumer was on the mark when he argued in 1965 that economic subordination and opportunity restriction constitute "a much more formidable part of the color line than is represented by the debarment of the Negro from the exercise of civil rights in the public arena."[14]

Finally, the "inner citadel of the color line," the most resistant part of all, concerns intimate friendships between whites and blacks. "Its presence can be noted most clearly among whites who are willing to accept Negroes as having equal social status," Blumer suggested, "yet who are not disposed to admit them into intimate and private circles, represented by social sets, cliques, private clubs, friendship sets, family circles, courtship, and marriage." Feelings and emotions generated by prospects of undesired intimacy may well fuel white hostility to changes in the other color lines.[15] But since the inner color line involves voluntary actions, beyond the formal control of government policy, we shall mainly consider the first two color lines.

From the perspective of many southerners, white and black, prior to World War II "the institution of racial segregation appeared to be an immutable feature of the American social order."[16] Perpetuation of southern racial customs involved the explicit socialization of white children concerning their roles as members of the superordinate group. Most southern white children learned early in life, through the cues of their parents, other adults, and peers, that they were different from and superior to blacks. A white youth who had absorbed the region's dominant values would fervently believe that racism was altogether "natural, proper, and sacred," a belief that would not ordinarily be reconsidered for the rest of his or her life.

Pondering the white South in 1941, Cash found much to admire:

"Proud, brave, honorable by its lights, courteous, personally generous, loyal, swift to act, often too swift, but signally effective, sometimes terrible, in its action—such was the South at its best. And such at its best it remains today, despite the great falling away in some of its virtues."[17] Unlike many apologists for the white South, Cash also emphasized recurrent defects in the temperament of the typical white southerner:

> Violence, intolerance, aversion and suspicion toward new ideas, an incapacity for analysis, an inclination to act from feeling rather than thought, an exaggerated individualism and a too narrow concept of social responsibility, attachment to fictions and false values, above all too great attachment to racial values and a tendency to justify cruelty and injustice in the name of these values, sentimentality and a lack of realism—these have been its characteristic vices in the past. And, despite changes for the better, they remain its characteristic vices today.[18]

This interpretation of the white South's racist obsessions and predisposition toward a violent defense of its racial practices—what Cash fittingly terms "the savage ideal"—made it impossible for most observers to expect significant reformation of southern racial traditions based on any moderation of white public opinion. It also encouraged the belief that changes in race relations imposed from outside the region or demanded from within by black southerners would be violently and massively resisted.

With the rewards of the Jim Crow system so completely biased against members of the lower caste, how were black southerners motivated to perform the duties appropriate to their subordinate status? The implicit long-run strategy of white leaders was to keep as many blacks as possible in positions of dependency upon whites and to limit the growth of the black middle class to the bare minimum needed to perform tasks for other blacks that whites did not wish to undertake.[19] Several complementary strategies were pursued to sustain black dependency: the education of the lower caste was generally limited to the values and skills useful for manual labor; through the pervasive symbolism of a segregated society, as well as white admonitions and directives, blacks were constantly reminded of their inferior status; prompt and pitiless application of the "savage ideal" insured that blacks who violated or defied racial mores were subjected to severe deprivations; and, finally, the system allowed an escape for the most discontented blacks—exit from the region.

All of these features of the traditional system of race relations are illustrated in the autobiography of Benjamin Elijah Mays, *Born to Rebel.* Rising from poverty to become president of Morehouse College in Atlanta and a leading supporter of the civil rights movement, Mays first encountered the "perilous world" of American race relations as a child in South Carolina's black belt. His earliest memory, which haunted him thereafter, was the experience of racist terrorism in 1898. "I remembered a crowd of white men who rode up on horseback with rifles on their shoulders," he wrote. "I was with my father when they rode up, and I remember starting to cry. They cursed my father, drew their guns and made him salute, made him take off his hat and bow down to them several times. Then they rode away."[20]

Adding to the precariousness of daily life were customs requiring blacks to be "humble, meek, and subservient" in the presence of whites and condoning their verbal and physical abuse if whites believed racial improprieties had occurred. "If a black boy wanted to live a halfway normal life and die a natural death," Mays recalled, "he had to learn early the art of how to get along with white folks." Even this cruel knowledge failed to guarantee security or survival. "How could a Negro avoid trouble when his 'place' was whatever any white man's whim dictated at any given time?" Mays observed how whites used intimidation to motivate blacks to conform to racist expectations. Race relations in Greenwood County, South Carolina, and, by implication, in hundreds of other southern localities "certainly 'put the rabbit' in many Negroes," Mays concluded. "They were poor, inadequately trained, and dependent upon the white man for work. Few dared stand up to a white man. When one did it, he got the worst of it."[21]

From this oppressive situation came a sense of alienation and fear, an intense estrangement from white affairs and institutions. "I never felt completely at home in my native county," Mays wrote. "The experiences I had in my most impressionable years . . . left me with a feeling of alienation from the county of my birth." It is not surprising that Mays was intensely afraid of white southerners, that he perpetually feared that "someday I might be lynched" by a "murderous mob" and became acutely "ill at ease" at the very sight of a "crowd of whites together."[22]

Young Benjamin Mays's experiences illustrate many of the obstacles that blacks would have to overcome in order to change their subordinate status. A central problem in challenging southern racial traditions was the facing and surmounting of fear arising from the thoroughly realistic anticipation of terrible physical reprisals, of the loss of employment or property, of yet another assault on one's dignity.[23] For many of the blacks who remained in the South, the principal psychological defense seems to have been public acquiescence and the disguising of their true feelings. Because black southerners lacked resources to challenge the system effectively, it became necessary to play the role of an accommodating victim in order not to arouse the oppressor. The psychic costs of such passivity and accommodation were often deadly. As Mays put it, the system "killed the spirit of all too many of my people."[24] Southern whites often interpreted black acquiescence to the prevailing power realities as spontaneous and voluntary support by the subordinate group. This collective white illusion blinded whites to the real feelings of blacks about southern race relations and encouraged the dangerous fantasy that blacks enthusiastically supported a social order that daily victimized them and their children.

Yet if fear, passivity, and superficial compliance had been black southerners' only responses to the caste system, little change in race relations would have occurred. The significance of Mays's account is that he identifies other reactions—anger, skepticism, and the need to achieve—that would ultimately sustain successful protest against the Jim Crow system. Many studies of the traditional South missed these feelings and consequently greatly underestimated the potential for a revolt by blacks against their assigned caste roles.[25] Mays first of all felt anger and rage. These emotions were directed primarily against the victimizers, with Mays concluding that "the southern white was my enemy—not only my enemy but the enemy of all Negroes." But he was also extremely angry that black southerners did not rebel openly against their treatment, even though he understood why rebellion seldom occurred. In addition, Mays refused to believe the racist propaganda of black inferiority. "Everything I had seen, and most of what I had heard," he recalled, "should have convinced me that the white man was superior and the Negro inferior. But I was not convinced; I was bothered; I was haunted night and day."[26] A final question disturbed him, one that would become a signal motivating factor in the civil rights movement—the search to be "somebody." "This was a 'white man's world;' " Mays wrote. "How could I be free in this world? How could I grow to my full stature as a man? . . . How could I exist, let alone live, without cringing and kowtowing to white men as I had seen my elders do? How could I walk the earth with dignity and pride?"[27]

All of Mays's questions developed naturally from the black experience in the South, and all were profoundly subversive of the racial status quo. The traditional system of race relations could not survive if members of the lower order rejected their prescribed roles and acted upon that rejection. Some black southerners, angry at the system that ensnared and entrapped them, repudiating the label of "inferior," and aspiring to personal freedom and dignity, nourished the motivations for revolt. For the most part, however, these feelings were hidden in the traditional South, and the illusion of a stable system of race relations persisted. Mays's initial solution to the problem of southern injustice, for example, was to leave

South Carolina in search of higher education in the North. But implicit in his early reactions to obtrusive racial discrimination were attitudes that would someday ignite the southern civil rights movement.

Acquiescence and Cautious Protest

Accommodation to the reality of white power was the predominant pattern of interracial leadership in southern black communities prior to the creation of a genuine civil rights movement. Protest emerged only sporadically (usually in the larger cities) and typically assumed the form of lawsuits attacking specific discriminatory practices, rather than direct action confrontations of black groups—large or small—with the Jim Crow system. This was surely the primary mode of black politics during the period examined in *Southern Politics* (roughly 1920–1950).

"Accommodating leadership" derived fundamentally from white control of all significant resources. As Myrdal observed, "The selection and the behavior of Negro leaders in the South is an outcome of this fact, that practically all the economic and political powers are concentrated in the white caste while the small amount of influence, status and wealth that there is in the Negro community is derivative and dependent." Although whites controlled race relations, they were not indifferent to the various "moods" of the black community. Whites had every incentive to motivate blacks to be "faithful and fairly efficient workers." Maintaining minimal levels of hygiene and a semblance of law and order in black districts was of concern "so that at least contagious diseases and crime will not react back upon the whites too much," and the "superior" group wanted blacks to be "willing, and not only forced, to observe the complicated system of racial etiquette." Whites particularly required assurance that local blacks were quarantined and immunized against dangerous ideas and organizations ("red agitators," "outside meddlers," and labor union organizers, among others).[28]

To fulfill these goals southern whites needed "liaison agents in the persons of Negro 'leaders.'" Governing in part through indirect rule, whites were eager to permit some blacks to "obtain as much prestige and influence in the Negro community as possible—so long as they cooperate with the whites faithfully." As Myrdal summarized the whites' perspective, "the whites should 'look after their Negroes.' Negroes should not protest but accommodate. They should not demand their rights but beg for help and assistance. Everything then works out for the good of both groups." Whites accordingly tried to install in leadership roles only those blacks reputed to be " 'cautious,' 'sane,' 'sober,' 'safe,' 'restrained,' and 'temperate.' "[29]

From the other side of the color line, blacks, as a practical necessity, required "leaders who can talk to, and get things from, the whites." Substantial rewards might be available for blacks who successfully performed this "leadership" role. To black leaders would flow not only material benefits and favors from prominent whites but also greater influence and status among blacks. Yet the "go-between" role exposed the leader to misperceptions, criticism, and possible rebuke from both sides. What whites could give, they could easily take away. Myrdal thought that black southerners generally understood the constraints that limited their leaders' effectiveness: "They know that a Negro leader who starts to act aggressively is not only losing his own power and often his livelihood but might endanger the welfare of the whole Negro community." Despite this awareness, black "leaders" were often accused of exploiting their privileged position for personal gains, selling out the interests of blacks as a group, and spying on behalf of the white leaders. Whatever the facts were concerning individual black leaders, their position was inherently precarious and insecure.[30]

Accommodation to white power was virtually the only option for blacks in the rural South. The situation was slightly different in the region's larger cities, where Myrdal discovered that "single individuals and small groups of followers around them . . . use the protection of the greater anonymity of the segregated urban Negro community to raise cautiously the banner of Negro protest." By far the most significant criticism developed under the aegis of the National Association for the Advancement of Colored People (NAACP), which had branches in most of the bigger cities. Many NAACP chapters had few members and were usually inactive, but the organization helped sponsor the main attacks on racial discrimination before 1950. Most white and some black southerners viewed the NAACP with hate and derision, and, as a consequence, many local branches were ineffective in winning immediate rewards.[31]

Within the South mass acquiescence and elite accommodation ruled out sustained black challenges to Jim Crow. Nor did much aid in resisting segregation appear likely from beyond the region. Although direct action protests were being pioneered by the Congress of Racial Equality (CORE) in the early 1940s in Chicago, that small organization decided not to attack southern segregation directly.[32] Without direct action techniques, the only way to alter the racial status quo was to initiate lawsuits against those aspects of southern race relations that seemed especially vulnerable to constitutional challenge. Thus the NAACP, with its small team of lawyers, became the central organization for improving the lot of black southerners in the era of accommodation and acquiescence.

Two principal challenges to the traditional caste system were initiated.

The first attack, directed against the outer color line, challenged the southern Democrats' practice of limiting participation in Democratic primaries to whites only; the second effort, aimed at the intermediate color line, consisted of attempts to equalize (and later abolish) racially segregated public schools. Both protest objectives aroused strenuous white opposition, and white authorities worked vigorously to limit and contain black gains. Consistent with Blumer's theory of the greater difficulty of achieving racial change in the intermediate than in the outer color line, blacks made more progress in securing voting rights than in desegregating public schools.

Abolishing the White Primary

The most common and convenient device for preventing black participation in the selection of public officials was the white primary, the constitutionality of which rested on the doctrine that the Democratic party in the southern states was a purely private, voluntary association that performed no official functions. As members of a private association, southern Democrats were free to establish whatever membership criteria they wished; in state after state, Democrats wanted only whites to vote in the party's nominating primaries to select candidates for the general election. But because Democratic nominees ordinarily faced no serious competition in general elections, the Democratic primaries actually functioned as the sole arena of meaningful choice in state politics. Barred from participating in the region's real elections, the few blacks who managed to become registered voters had only the Alice in Wonderland option of voting in general elections. The proposition that southern Democratic parties were simply private organizations with no implicit state functions was so preposterous that only small children believed it and only constitutional lawyers debated it. Certainly it was not seriously entertained by the South's politicians or journalists, who habitually described the outcome of Democratic primaries as "tantamount to election."

Against this background of institutional racism and constitutional formalisms, a handful of black litigants began a long, difficult, and expensive struggle to reconcile prevailing practices with the spirit of the Fifteenth Amendment to the Constitution.[33] The original claimants—professional, well-educated, middle-class individuals who lived in the metropolitan South and were eager to revive black political participation—were exactly the type of blacks whom the social order was designed to minimize. NAACP lawyers helped plan the legal strategy, argued the case in the federal courts, and financed the costly appeals. Finally, in 1944, the Supreme Court ruled in *Smith v. Allwright* that, since state action was involved, blacks had been unconstitutionally excluded from participation in the primaries of the Democratic party.[34] Few southern states accepted the abolition of the white primary gracefully, and a fresh round of lawsuits was necessary to enforce the decision. Key detected an important subregional division in southern solidarity. "The states around the rim of the Deep South did not react violently and concretely to reestablish the form of the white primary," he emphasized. "The reality in no small measure remained everywhere, but the area of maximum intensity of reaction was more circumscribed than it would have been 40 years ago."[35]

Smith v. Allwright provided the first major stimulus to black voter registration since the turn of the century. As Donald R. Matthews and James W. Prothro have pointed out, "Once the white primary had been killed, the number and proportion of Negroes registered to vote in the southern states increased with startling speed."[36] Between 1940 and 1947 the number of registered blacks increased by 444,000, and another 414,000 new registrants were added by 1952. In little more than a decade, estimated black registration climbed from only 151,000 in 1940 to 1,009,000 in 1952. But while the rate of increase was impressive, southern blacks achieved only marginal changes in the central pattern of disfranchisement. In 1952 some four-fifths of the black voting age population were still ineligible to vote.[37]

Black voting gains were minimal for many reasons, the chief of which was undoubtedly the enduring opposition of most white southerners to this change in the outer color line. In their reactions to black suffrage most white southerners in the 1940s seemed to begin not with the requirements of the Constitution but with their perceptions of the unworthiness of black southerners. As Key summarized the conventional wisdom of the white South, "The Negro is poorer than the white, more plagued by disease, less literate, less trained in manual and professional skills, less experienced in the management of group affairs. Whether all these characteristics flow from inherent incapacity or simply from environmental oppression, they are there and have to be faced in dealing with the question of the Negro and the suffrage."[38]

Conservative and "progressive" white southerners, though united by their perception of vast differences between whites and blacks, drew somewhat different conclusions about assimilating blacks into the political community. Conservatives interpreted the observed racial inequalities as the inevitable outcome of inherent black inferiority and argued against extending the franchise to any blacks at all. Permitting some blacks to vote, even educated and middle-class blacks, would simply encourage other blacks to register and, more important, would embolden blacks to request or demand reform in other parts of the caste system. In effect, conservatives contended that marginal changes in one aspect of the outer color line would inevitably lead to substantial changes in the other color lines, including the inner sanctum of social equality.[39] When expressing themselves uninhibitedly in the regional vernacular, southern racists could fashion powerful arguments to arouse antiblack emotions and direct them toward such concrete issues as poll tax reform and the administration of literacy tests. Mississippi politicians were the most prominent advocates of this defiantly inflexible stand, but counterparts could be identified in every state.

A much smaller group of white southerners, who admitted the differences between whites and blacks, refused to accept the "biological inferiority" argument and favored assimilating some blacks into the political system as voters. The solution of the liberal whites was to extend the franchise to those blacks presumably best qualified to vote. As Key urged, "permit, even encourage, Negro doctors, lawyers, ministers, businessmen, and upper-class Negroes to vote and such others as are known to be 'responsible' citizens." Under this gradual approach blacks would be offered an incentive for achievement; the policy's attractiveness to white progressives was that "gradualism postpones the full consequences of enfranchisement and offers a workable approach." Nonetheless, gradualism had severe disadvantages. Because gradualism "concedes the entire argument on the question of racial superiority and looks toward the eventual assimilation of the Negro into the political life of the community," it was a stance "taken publicly with hesitation by southern whites." Nor would gradual assimilation satisfy many black southerners, most of whom would find their voting rights still sacrificed to "practical necessities." Neither conservative nor liberal whites had a doctrine capable of either maintaining the traditional system intact or managing the rate of change so that white southerners would peacefully accept reforms. Key expressed the dilemma best in a line borrowed from Lincoln that erupts amid dispassionate analysis and conveys the spirit of the times: "Southern whites have a bear by the tail and don't know what to do about it."[40]

In the short run, though, politically active white southerners did know "what to do about it." The marginal gains in black voting occurred generally in the larger cities; in much of the Deep South, as well as most Peripheral South jurisdictions with sizable black populations, black exclusion from the political system continued much as though *Allwright* had never been decided. White officials employed a variety of devices, including literacy tests, "understanding" and "good character" tests, and poll taxes, to prevent black registration. In early 1949 four states (Alabama, Mississippi, South Carolina, and Virginia) mandated both literacy tests and poll taxes; three states (Georgia, Louisiana, and North Carolina) required literacy tests but not poll taxes; three states (Arkansas, Tennessee, and Texas) had poll taxes alone; and only Florida used neither a literacy test nor a poll tax.[41] Enormous discretion rested with local registration authorities in deciding whether a prospective voter was qualified under state law.

Literacy and understanding tests were the most significant deterrents to black registration. Seven states required literacy tests in the late 1940s, and Key scathingly denounced their corrupt administration. "The southern literacy test is a fraud and nothing more," Key concluded. "The simple fact seems to be that the constitutionally prescribed test of ability to read and write a section of the constitution is rarely administered to whites. It is applied chiefly to Negroes and not always to them. When Negroes are tested on their ability to read and write, only in exceptional instances is the test administered fairly." In this critical arena of white domination and control, Key wrote, "a solemn recapitulation of the formal literacy and understanding requirements verges on the ridiculous. In practice literacy and understanding have little to do with the acquisition of the right to vote. Whether a person can register to vote depends on what the man down at the courthouse says, and he usually has the final say. It is how the tests are administered that matters."[42] Despite widespread knowledge of discriminatory administration, the Supreme Court had refused to invalidate literacy and understanding tests; indeed, the arbitrary, unfair, and corrupt administration of such devices remained a problem in parts of the South until these devices were finally suspended under the Voting Rights Act of 1965.[43]

Key contended that the rationale and consequences of the poll tax had shifted over time: "Originally designed chiefly to discourage Negro participation, it became obsolete for that purpose, with the invention of the white primary." Following the subsequent demise of the white primary, the poll tax reemerged as a potentially serious obstacle to black registration. In 1949 five states (Mississippi, Arkansas, Alabama, Virginia, and Texas) required payment of some fee in order to vote in Democratic primaries, and two more states (South Carolina and Tennessee) used the poll tax for general elections but waived it for party primaries. Though Key discounted the impact of the poll tax on black voting in comparison with other considerations (both "extralegal restraints" and the white primary were much more determinative), he recognized that the poll tax could become an important deterrent in the future if other barriers to participation fell.[44]

The NAACP's legal attacks on the white primary led to significant and impressive advances in black voting rights. Nevertheless, southern white resistance to change in this portion of the outer color line remained pronounced, and voter registration authorities still possessed other means to handle the few blacks who attempted to register in the rural and small-town South. Additional litigation and new types of protest and organization would be required to penetrate thoroughly the outer color line, to enable blacks throughout the South to exercise freely a right supposedly guaranteed by the Fifteenth Amendment.

Challenging Public School Segregation

The second major focus of NAACP litigation concerned the refusal of southern school officials and politicians to provide equal educational opportunities. The NAACP's effort challenged the South's segregated public schools, one of the most entrenched institutions of the intermediate color line. In the 1940s, nearly half a century after the Supreme Court's decision in *Plessy v. Ferguson* (1896) had sanctioned "separate but equal" public facilities, every southern state offered blacks separate and distinctly unequal schools. Few southerners of either race graduated from high school in 1940, but whereas one-quarter of whites over the age of twenty-four had completed high school, a scant 5 percent of blacks possessed a high school education. Only 1 percent of blacks, compared with 5 percent of whites, had graduated from college.[45] Even comparisons of high school or college graduation rates are somewhat misleading, for the blacks who finished school had typically received an "education" considerably inferior to that provided for whites.

Black educational deficiencies flowed from the whites' racist assumptions concerning black intellectual capabilities, as well as from white interest in preventing the development of a truly educated group of blacks who might also become economically independent of whites. Many white politicians justified inequalities in school expenditures on the grounds that white and black education served fundamentally different purposes. Governor James K. Vardaman came to the crux of the matter in a 1909 address to the Mississippi legislature. "Money spent today for the maintenance of public schools for Negroes is robbery of the white man, and a waste upon the negro," the governor announced. "You take it from the toiling white men and women, you rob the white child of the advantages it would afford him, and you spend it upon the Negro in an effort to make of the negro what God Almighty never intended should be made, and which men cannot accomplish." The task of improving the intellectual skills of blacks was doomed to failure because "God Almighty created the negro for a menial—he is essentially a servant." Accordingly, Vardaman proposed that the future education of blacks should concentrate on "his hand and heart," imparting those vocational skills and moral obligations appropriate for a passive member of the lower caste in a biracial, agricultural society.[46] Since black teachers were not expected to develop their students' cognitive skills, black schools did not need to be as well equipped or staffed as white schools.

In varing degrees the mentality epitomized by Vardaman seems to have guided white leaders across the South in the first decades of this century.[47] Racist attitudes, combined with the total concentration of power among whites, produced a collection of wretched elementary and secondary schools. "The South is the section of the country least able to support even a single system," complained Horace Mann Bond in 1934. "As compared to the Nation at large, it may be said categorically that Southern states are not able to support systems for the two races comparing favorably with national norms of achievement. The result is that Negro children are discriminated against universally in states with a heavy Negro population, all available funds being devoted as far as possible to the needs of white school children."[48] In per capita educational expenditures, teacher salaries, value of buildings and equipment, length of the school term, and overall quality of the curriculum, black students compared poorly with their white peers.[49]

How could gross inequalities in educational resources be narrowed or eliminated? The direct approach involved challenging the constitutionality of segregated public education. But since *Plessy* was the controlling precedent and southern white acceptance of school integration was inconceivable, a straightforward assault on segregation seemed certain to fail. Instead, in the early 1930s the NAACP commenced an indirect maneuver. At the center of this effort was a document written by attorney Nathan R. Margold, a report setting forth a legal strategy for attacking inequalities in educational opportunity in the southern and border states. "At its heart, the Margold Report of 1931 was a conservative instrument," Richard Kluger has stated. "But it was conceived against the background of an exceedingly conservative Supreme Court. Abrupt reversals of precedent were hardly likely . . . By moderate Supreme Court decisions requiring the South to draw up fair laws and to administer them in a way to provide truly equal schools, the NAACP would improve Negro education and in the process put so much financial pressure on the white community that in time it would be forced to abandon the far more costly dual system and integrate the schools."[50]

Charles W. Houston, dean of the Howard University Law School and later special counsel to the NAACP, added other twists to the basic strategy. Litigation should commence over the absence of opportunities for graduate and professional education. "Here was an area," Kluger wrote, "where the educational facilities for blacks were neither separate nor equal but non-existent. The Supreme Court . . . would have trouble turning its back on so plain a discrimination and denial of equal protection." By first initiating suits in the border states, the NAACP hoped to win legal precedents that could later be used to desegregate higher learning and, eventually, elementary and secondary schools in the South.[51]

Whereas desegregation appeared achievable in graduate and professional education, in the 1930s the immediate abolition of dual public school systems was a remedy too improbable to help black school children. Consequently, the NAACP decided to seek the equalization of racially separate elementary and secondary schools rather than their integration. As Houston put it, the goal would be "absolute equality . . . If the white South insists upon its separate schools, it must not squeeze the Negro schools to pay for them."[52] From the 1930s until 1950, the NAACP pursued two different strategies to reform southern education: suits to desegregate—or at least equalize—graduate and professional education; and suits to equalize elementary and secondary education.

In higher education the NAACP strategy yielded important precedents. *Murray v. Maryland* (1936) resulted in the admission of a black student to the University of Maryland law school because the state provided no facilities for the legal training of blacks. Two years later, in *Gaines v. Canada,* the Supreme Court invalidated the common southern practice of financing higher education for blacks at some other state's facilities rather than providing in-state training for its black citizens. The University of Missouri was ordered to admit a black plaintiff to its all-white law school, since there were no comparable in-state institutions open to blacks.[53]

World War II brought a pause in litigation, but activity quickened in the late 1940s and culminated in two cases decided on the same day in 1950, *Sweatt v. Painter* and *McLaurin v. Oklahoma.* The Supreme Court's decision in *Sweatt* ended the legal debate about what *Plessy* meant for graduate and professional education, for the Court "identified the requirements of separate equality piece by piece and did the job in such a manner that it was made impossible for a state to afford to establish a law school for Negroes with equal facilities."[54] In the *McLaurin* case the Supreme Court "decreed that once a school admits a student it must not discriminate against him but must accord him the same rights and privileges accorded other students." Both cases represented significant victories for blacks against the traditional caste system. "By mid-century," Henry Allen Bullock noted, "the NAACP had successfully abolished segregation in public education at the graduate and professional levels. There was still some bickering on the part of the states that were to resist the desegregation process, but in the end, racial segregation in this area of American life was to disappear."[55]

The NAACP's success in higher education encouraged blacks to demand equalization of resources devoted to elementary and secondary education. In the late 1930s and early 1940s, black southerners "turned to the Federal courts as a major resort in their fight for better elementary and secondary schools for their children. Thereafter, protests against and appeals for the correction of inequalities between whites and Negro schools came increasingly to be followed by litigation."[56] Through legal action blacks managed to equalize the salaries of white and black teachers of similar educational achievement and teaching experience. Efforts to equalize salaries of teachers and administrators began in 1940 and were substantially achieved a decade later.[57]

Profound differences between white and black education had long existed not only in teacher salaries but in the value of school property, the breadth and depth of the curriculum, and the availability of transportation to and from school. Improvements commenced in the late 1940s, as blacks again resorted to lawsuits to compel local school authorities to raise black schools to local white standards. Because black schools had been so inadequately funded in the past, true equalization required the construction of thousands of modern buildings, the consolidation of numerous tiny schools into larger institutions, and the development of bus systems to transport black students from outlying areas to the consolidated schools. To assist localities several southern states passed large bond issues or increased taxes in the early 1950s to finance the belated equalization efforts.

The equalization movement produced concrete benefits for black students in segregated schools. In 1940, before the equalization drive started, black students in the Deep South usually received one-third or less of the amounts spent on white students for current expenditures and only about one-tenth of the monies expended for capital improvements in the white schools. Blacks residing in the Peripheral South were typically better financed, but there too systematic discrimination against black school children was the central pattern. By 1952, after more than a decade of litigation and threats of lawsuits, every southern state was providing more financial resources—both absolutely and relative to whites—than in the past.[58] "To meet this situation," Governor James F. Byrnes of South Carolina acknowledged in 1950, "we are forced to do what we should have been doing for the past fifty years."[59] Even in 1952, however, parity in current expenditures was nonexistent, and in most states capital expenditures were still disproportionately allocated to white schools.

Despite signs of "progress" in the educational statistics, "doghouse education" remained a daily reality for many black students.[60]

By 1950 it was clear that the NAACP could easily win equalization suits under the equal protection clause of the Fourteenth Amendment. Yet this was not the road the NAACP wished to travel, for the equalization strategy had been adopted as a concession to practical necessity; the ultimate goal had always been the repudiation of *Plessy v. Ferguson* through the unequivocal abolition of legalized racial segregation. Although the equalization strategy had succeeded in the area of higher education in the border states and some Peripheral South states, it was not working and had virtually no chance of succeeding in the infinitely more emotional field of elementary and secondary education. Most white southerners loathed and despised the idea of jointly educating white and black students. Precisely because of their antipathy toward racial integration in the public schools, many whites had reluctantly begun to support equalization of segregated black schools. Prominent white politicians at midcentury were actively promoting the equalization movement as the only practical alternative to desegregation. "Except for the professional agitators," claimed Governor Byrnes, "what the colored people want, and what they are entitled to, is equal facilities in their schools."[61] For whites born and raised in the traditionalistic political culture, the economic waste involved in financing two entirely separate school systems was categorically less important than maintaining white supremacy.

And so the NAACP lawyers began to rethink their strategy. Victories in the law school cases had reaffirmed *Plessy,* but the Supreme Court's willingness to pay closer attention to the requirements of equality raised the possibility that the Court might be persuaded to find separation itself—irrespective of equality—a violation of the Fourteenth Amendment. In the summer of 1950 Thurgood Marshall and other leading NAACP attorneys reached a momentous decision. At a conference on the organization's legal strategy, Marshall announced that the NAACP Legal Defense Fund would no longer bring equalization suits.[62] By seeking the overthrow of *Plessy,* a constitutional cornerstone of the "southern way of life," the NAACP shifted to a direct attack on the intermediate color line, a challenge to the Jim Crow system so fundamental that the ensuing political convulsions persisted for decades. Interested parties clearly understood the implications of the revised NAACP strategy. Within the white South the promise of equitable treatment under the "separate but equal" formula went hand in hand with a renewed emphasis on the permanence of segregated schools, and many white authorities began to threaten the destruction of public education entirely should *Plessy* be overturned and school desegregation ordered.[63]

Having discarded the equalization strategy, attorneys for the NAACP began to search for plaintiffs to challenge the constitutionality of segregated public schools. Two cases eventually emerged from the black belt South that became part of the Supreme Court's *Brown v. Board of Education* decision in 1954. *Briggs v. Elliott* originated in Clarendon County, South Carolina; and Virginia produced *Davis v. County School Board of Prince Edward County*. Richard Kluger has superbly portrayed the human drama underlying both lawsuits in his book *Simple Justice*.[64]

In the South Carolina case, white school officials summarily rejected black requests for adequate transportion. "We ain't got no money to buy a bus for your nigger children," the chairman of the local school board reportedly told a delegation of black parents. The humiliating dismissal stimulated black political organization and an eventual lawsuit. Despite vicious reprisals against the complainants, Clarendon County blacks were determined to make a stand. The suit was first heard in 1950 by Federal District Judge J. Waties Waring, a maverick Charleston aristocrat who had become an outspoken critic of racial discrimination.[65] Dissatisfied with the way NAACP lawyers had framed the issue, Judge Waring invited Marshall to make constitutionality of the state's school segregation laws the central issue. Challenges to the constitutionality of a state law were heard by a three-judge panel, rather than by a single judge, and in 1951 *Briggs v. Elliott* came before a court consisting of Waring, George Bell Timmerman, a staunch segregationist, and John Parker, a North Carolinian who had ruled in the NAACP's favor in the past. Lawyers for South Carolina conceded inequalities in funds for the black schools in Clarendon County and promised that public money would be provided to equalize the segregated schools. In opposition, the NAACP attorneys argued that equalization was no longer a sufficient remedy for the discrimination implicit in racially segregated schools.

As expected by the NAACP lawyers, two of the three judges refused to declare school segregation unconstitutional. Judge Parker reasoned that "it is a late day to say that such segregation is violative of fundamental constitutional rights," since these practices had been occurring for more than seventy years and had received Supreme Court approval in the past. But South Carolina was obliged to provide equality in its racially separate school facilities, and the local school board was ordered to do so. Judge Waring dissented strongly. "*Segregation is per se inequality*," he concluded, using language remarkably similar to Chief Justice Earl Warren's opinion three years later in the *Brown* decision.

Denouncing racial segregation, Waring recommended the immediate abolition of dual school systems. "All of the legal guideposts, expert testimony, common sense and reason point unerringly to the conclusion that the system of segregation in education adopted and practiced in the state of South Carolina must go and must go now"—advice that was not taken by the Warren Court in its 1955 enforcement decision.[66]

A few months later, in *Davis v. County School Board of Prince Edward County*, another three-judge panel ruled against the NAACP. A student strike at the black high school protesting inequities in equipment and curricula became the basis for a lawsuit challenging segregated education. After lengthy testimony and rough cross-examination by both sides, the federal judges (all native white southerners) identified "no hurt or harm to either race" in segregated schools and ordered the Prince Edward school board to continue its equalization program.[67] NAACP attorneys had anticipated the outcome, and another school segregation case from the South entered the federal appellate process. The stage was now set for the Supreme Court's reconsideration of the constitutionality of racially separate schools, even if the facilities provided to each race were substantially equal.

Following protracted deliberation, the Supreme Court ruled unanimously in *Brown v. Board of Education* (1954) that laws requiring or permitting racial segregation in public education violated the Fourteenth Amendment. Chief Justice Warren concluded that "in the field of public education the doctrine of 'separate but equal' has no place. Separate educational facilities are inherently unequal."[68] *Brown* stirred hope among southern blacks and outrage among southern whites, and in its aftermath civil rights controversies became the most prominent issues in southern politics for more than a decade.

In the initial school desegregation decision (*Brown I*), the Supreme Court deliberately avoided the problem of enforcement. The Court's implementation order, handed down a year later in *Brown II,* was a victory for the white South. In effect the Supreme Court delegated enforcement to the South's local school boards and federal district courts, institutions ordinarily controlled by native white southerners who vehemently disagreed with the *Brown* decision.[69] Mandating no specific date by which dual school systems had to be dismantled, the Court offered only the nebulous enforcement standard of "all deliberate speed" to guide the desegregation process. And before long the prevailing interpretation of the white South's obligations became Judge Parker's opinion (in the remanded *Briggs* case) that "nothing in the Constitution or in the [*Brown*] decision of the Supreme Court takes away from the people the freedom to choose the schools they attend. The Constitution, in other words, does not require integration. It merely forbids discrimination. It does not forbid such discrimination as occurs as the result of voluntary action." For all practical purposes, Parker interpreted *Brown* to mean that "if the schools which [a state] maintains are open to children of all races, no violation of the Constitution is involved even though the children of different races voluntarily attend different schools, as they attend different churches." Under the "Parker doctrine" no actual integration of schools was necessary for southern school districts to be in compliance with the *Brown* decision; it was a prime example of how southern federal district judges could eviscerate a potentially monumental decision.[70]

The *Brown* decision strongly aroused white southerners.[71] Eminent white politicians actively promoted a "massive resistance" movement against even the slightest compliance with school desegregation.[72] Militant segregationists defined the issue as segregation or integration, and, thus understood, the vast majority of white southerners preferred strict segregation of the races in public schools. Massive resistance was concentrated in the Deep South and Virginia, where legislatures passed new laws requiring state schools to be closed if blacks and whites were placed in the same facilities. But as small numbers of black students began to apply for admission to all-white schools, and as federal judges began to order school integration in states that required racially mixed schools to be closed, the costs to whites of unyielding resistance escalated sharply. The turning point for the massive resistance movement came during the 1958–59 school year, when the public schools of Norfolk, Virginia, were closed by state authorities to prevent desegregation. As the year passed without public schools, and as Norfolk citizens began to understand the implications of massive resistance more fully, a crucial redefinition of the situation occurred. The primary issue shifted from the desirability of segregation or desegregation to the desirability of desegregated schools versus no public schools at all. Public opinion surveys of Norfolk whites during this critical school year have documented this basic change in white perceptions of the price of maintaining racial separation.[73]

Even though the stupendous folly of massive resistance became more widely appreciated, the collapse of massive resistance did not signal the emergence of substantial school desegregation. Through the early 1960s the main exceptions to totally segregated schools were instances of token school desegregation, where small numbers of black students entered otherwise all-white schools. Most southern states adopted pupil placement plans that utilized multiple criteria for determining school assignments. As administered by reliable school authorities, the plans allowed all of the white students to be placed in "white" schools and virtually all of the blacks to be assigned to "black" schools. "Freedom of choice" plans had an appealing rhetoric, but their main function was to keep the races separated in public education.[74]

Considering the resources possessed by white southerners to defend racial segregation and the minimal pressure exerted by the federal judiciary to enforce the *Brown* decision, it is hardly surprising that (at best) only token school desegregation occurred during the next decade. In the 1964–65 school year 97.75 percent of the South's black schoolchildren still attended all-black schools.[75] This dismal outcome was entirely consistent with Key's skepticism about white compliance with unpopular federal court decisions. In discussing the constitutionality of "gradual enfranchisement," for example, he assumed that "the rulings of the Supreme Court on this question will mean in practice not much more than the dominant white groups of the region are willing to have them mean."[76] After the *Brown* decision, representatives of the traditional southern political culture rose in defiance and deflected the blacks' attack against segregated public education, a cardinal institution of the intermediate color line.

Supreme Court decisions outlawing the white primary in 1944 and school segregation in 1954 were the most notable successes of the NAACP's effort to reform southern race relations through the federal judicial system. In neither instance did the formal establishment of constitutional principles translate immediately and directly into effective participation by most black citizens in those activities and institutions from which they had been previously excluded. In both episodes, the central tendency of white southerners was anger and opposition to the Supreme Court's rulings. But the two cases showed critical differences in the intensity and scope of white defiance, differences consistent with Blumer's theory that changes in the intermediate color line were judged by whites as much more "costly" than changes in the outer color line. Greater change occurred in voting rights than in school integration. A decade after *Smith v. Allwright,* between one-fifth and one-fourth of eligible black southerners were registered to vote, while a decade after *Brown v. Board of Education* only one out of every fifty black students attended a desegregated school.

Following the NAACP's victory in *Brown I* and its defeat in *Brown II,* black southerners who sought to desegregate elementary and secondary schools occupied exposed positions. The outer color line was still securely intact against most black southerners in the mid-1950s. Most blacks did not vote and all blacks suffered the stigma, injustice, and inconvenience of rigid segregation in places of public accommodation. Most blacks were impoverished or only slightly above poverty, and few were economically independent of whites. Given their vulnerabilities, many blacks who might have wished to send their children to desegregated schools were undoubtedly deterred because of their realistic assessment of white hostility. The small number of black families who actually tried to desegregate schools often suffered tremendous harassment and abuse.[77] Their situation was similar to that of clusters of attacking troops who have unexpectedly broken through an enemy's outer line of defense, but who find themselves exposed at the rear and on the flanks and facing a more formidable enemy fortress ahead; without significant reinforcements from the outside, success is unlikely. The well-publicized episodes of disruptive southern school desegregation in the late 1950s and early 1960s, as in Little Rock and New Orleans, illustrate the gauntlet that blacks had to run to claim the promise of *Brown I* and also explain why so few black parents were willing to let their children try.

Although the NAACP's legal strategies had established important principles, they could not secure immediate and effective implementation of voting rights and school desegregation. To break the deadlock in southern race relations, to mount a more fundamental challenge to Jim Crow, blacks needed a strategy of protest with more mass appeal, tactics that could arouse and effectively channel the discontent of many southern blacks with the color lines, and a return to targets that whites could more easily surrender.

five

Penetrating
the Outer
Color Line

FOR PROGRESS to resume in civil rights, it would be necessary for blacks to concentrate on unfinished business in the outer color line. In theory, the outer color line was the most promising area in which to confront southern racism; in practice, of course, efforts to end Jim Crow in public accommodations and voting rights met tremendous hostility and resistance. Save in the rarest situations, little or nothing was given away or conceded. The main targets of protest activity were segregated public accommodations, such as hotels, motels, lunch counters, restaurants, theaters, and other privately owned businesses ostensibly open to the public, and, in some parts of the region, discriminatory administration of voting rights. Through strenuous efforts to organize black communities against segregation, and through such techniques of direct action protest as mass marches, demonstrations, sit-ins, Freedom Rides, and boycotts, black southerners and their allies directly challenged many racist practices in the outer color line. Eventually the civil rights cause became a movement, and gradually the movement developed a successful and effective strategy of protest against targets in the outer color line.

The new strategy involved drawing national attention to flagrantly racist practices in the South through media exposure of nonviolent and nonprovocative demonstrators suffering terrible physical and verbal assaults by white southerners. When southern brutality in its most explicit forms began to be televised, the arena of political conflict expanded from scattered southern localities to the entire nation. As a consequence, national politicians and interest groups were educated—and finally activated—to intervene on behalf of the South's unprotected racial minority.[1] Years of harsh, often dangerous struggle were required but ultimately two significant laws were passed by Congress and signed by President

Lyndon B. Johnson—the Civil Rights Act of 1964 and the Voting Rights Act of 1965. These acts were the enduring national accomplishments of the civil rights movement. They symbolized the defeat of conservative white southerners over the issue of preventing federal intervention in race relations, and they destroyed the most conspicuous elements of the outer color line in most of the South.

Revolt from Below: Rise of the Civil Rights Movement

The crucial transitional episode in the history of civil rights protest, a year-long protest against Jim Crow practices on the buses of Montgomery, Alabama, occurred shortly after the first *Brown* decision but several years prior to the first sit-ins. The Montgomery protest, which consisted of negotiations between white and black leaders, the refusal of blacks to ride segregated city buses, and a constitutional test of ordinances requiring segregated seating on buses, combined old and new ways of challenging racism in the outer color line. It began in December 1955, when Mrs. Rosa Parks, a respected local NAACP activist, was arrested for violating a city ordinance requiring segregation on public buses. Outraged by her arrest, blacks formed an organization, the Montgomery Improvement Association (MIA), and selected a twenty-six-year-old Baptist minister, Martin Luther King, Jr., as its president. The MIA organized an immediate boycott of the bus system and attempted to discuss their grievances with white officials.[2]

Initially, the organization asked *not* for integrated public transportation, but for fairer treatment of blacks within a public facility that would remain segregated—a position similar to the NAACP's objectives in "equalization" lawsuits. According to King, the original resolution of protest asked blacks not to ride the buses "until (1) courteous treatment by the bus operators was guaranteed; (2) passengers were seated on a first-come, first-served basis—Negroes seating from the back of the bus toward the front while whites seated from the front toward the back; (3) Negro bus operators were employed on predominantly Negro routes." These modest goals were flatly rejected.[3]

Whites were especially angered because blacks reinforced their demands with a boycott of the bus company. After the protest started, participants were harassed by Montgomery police and subjected to abundant verbal abuse and intimidation. Blacks watched as the Ku Klux Klan and the White Citizens Council advocated white solidarity against any concessions to the boycotters and experienced the terror of the "savage ideal" as the homes of several protest leaders were bombed. Despite repression, the MIA's campaign of organized, massive noncooperation was sustained. Mass meetings energized, motivated, and directed the protesters toward purposeful action, and, at great personal hardship and inconvenience, most of Montgomery's blacks refused to ride the city buses for over a year.[4]

MIA goals and strategy changed after King's house was dynamited on January 30, 1956.[5] As King explained, Montgomery's black leaders "discovered that our optimism was misplaced. The intransigence of the city commission, the crudeness of the 'get tough' policy, and the viciousness of the recent bombings convinced us all that an attack must be made upon bus segregation itself. Accordingly a suit was filed in the United States Federal District Court, asking for an end of bus segregation on the grounds that it was contrary to the Fourteenth Amendment."[6] Shifting its objective from moderating segregation's harshness to abolishing segregation itself, the MIA won its victory neither through persuasion nor economic pressure, but by utilizing a constitutional principle established less than two years earlier in *Brown I*. Alabama's state and local laws requiring segregation in public transportation were struck down by a three-judge federal court on June 4, 1956, and the Supreme Court upheld the decision on November 13, 1956. Slightly less than a year after the boycott had begun, racially desegregated buses appeared in the Cradle of the Confederacy.

The Montgomery bus boycott catapulted Martin Luther King, Jr., into political prominence. The son of a Baptist minister and a native of Atlanta, Georgia, King was highly educated and already commanded rhetorical skills that would make him one of twentieth-century America's finest public speakers. There is no better succinct characterization of King's appeal to many southern blacks and nonsouthern whites than August Meier's label of the "Conservative Militant." "In this combination of militancy with conservatism and caution, of righteousness with respectability," Meier writes, "lies the secret of King's enormous success."[7] These traits were already visible, if not so widely recognized, in Montgomery. Recalling his first speech to the protesters, King wanted it to be "militant enough to keep my people aroused to positive action and yet moderate enough to keep this fervor within controllable and Christian bounds."[8] Though King had not yet learned how to win with the strategy of nonviolent resistance, he guided the movement in a peaceful direction that eventually culminated in major national legislation. From King's activities in Montgomery emerged a new civil rights organization, the Southern Christian Leadership Conference (SCLC), that became his instrument for civil rights work.[9] SCLC was primarily a group of urban southern black ministers who shared King's beliefs.

King's approach to attacking segregation became known as "nonviolent resistance." The civil rights movement ought to avoid violence, King argued, because it "would be both impractical and immoral." To create a society in which blacks and whites saw each other as equals, and treated each other with mutual respect, the minority group could not use means that would injure or harm their opponents. According to King, nonviolence "does not seek to defeat or humiliate the opponent, but to win his friendship and understanding." He also put this another way: "The end is redemption and reconciliation. The aftermath of nonviolence is the creation of the beloved community, while the aftermath of violence is tragic bitterness." But not only was violence immoral; its use would be counterproductive. In the South, where whites decisively outnumbered blacks, and where some white southerners were all too eager to engage in a shoot-out, black violence would be more than answered in kind. Consequently, the struggle against segregation had to be conducted within the limits of peaceful dissent. Yet King also emphasized the importance of resisting rather than acquiescing in second-class citizenship.[10]

King quickly understood that "the Christian doctrine of love operating through the Gandhian method of nonviolence was one of the most potent weapons available to the Negro in his struggle for freedom." MIA's frequent rallies in black churches were used to motivate and sustain the protesters, to overcome their fears of white retaliation. For many blacks the very act of defiance, supported by the mass meetings, released buried energy. The "true meaning of the Montgomery story," in King's view, lay in the emergence of "a new Negro in the South, with a new sense of dignity and destiny." In turn, "this growing self-respect has inspired the Negro with a new determination to struggle and sacrifice until first-class citizenship becomes a reality."[11]

The philosophy of nonviolent resistance successfully motivated many blacks to participate in the bus boycott, but its dramatization of injustice failed to change the attitudes of white officialdom. For some time to come, King continued to support a strategy that had not worked. According to David J. Garrow, "What King believed in and advocated in the late 1950s and the very first years of the 1960s was nonviolent *persuasion*. This was resistance that employed moral suasion upon one's opponents, and it was basically not coercive."[12] In retrospect King's emphasis on reconciliation and reasoned persuasion proved ineffective in changing racism in the outer color line; gains in the early 1960s were due far more to strategies that sought to coerce local whites into changing their treatment of blacks.

What happened in the heart of the Alabama black belt in the aftermath of the *Brown* decision symbolized a potential for widespread revolt by black southerners against their assigned roles in a caste society. Though Myrdal had identified powerful strains in southern race relations that he thought likely to erupt in the immediate future, not one sentence in Key's *Southern Politics* anticipates a sustained protest like the Montgomery bus boycott.[13] Key's model of change in race relations assumed the gradual absorption of a relatively few better-educated blacks into the political system as voters. Assuming these controlled conditions of entry, Key developed a scenario of an emerging class politics replacing racist politics as a coalition of working-class whites and the more highly educated blacks formed the nucleus of a progressive movement in the South. But as Numan V. Bartley and Hugh D. Graham have previously emphasized, the revival of the school desegregation issue in the 1950s meant that the old preoccupation with maintaining white supremacy again became the central issue of southern politics.[14] In the late 1950s conservative white southerners organized themselves to preserve all aspects of the color lines. King became preoccupied with fund raising and speech making on behalf of his organization, and from 1957 to 1960 SCLC achieved no prominent victories in applying principles of nonviolent resistance to targets of the outer color line.

Desegregation of Public Accommodations

Prior to the 1960s black southerners were routinely denied service or served in segregated and distinctly unequal facilities when they sought to obtain food and lodging from establishments owned and operated by whites. In instances where service was denied, the law rested with the management, which could ask police to remove the "undesirable" customer. This blatant discrimination had always irritated many blacks, not simply because it humiliated and insulted them, but also because it was a practical nightmare. Yet there was no obvious solution to this predicament. The Supreme Court had refused to prohibit racial discrimination as long as establishments were privately owned, and businesses had the antitrespass law at their disposal. As a result, the NAACP strategy of bringing lawsuits held no promise of success.[15] Some form of direct action was required to publicize the situation and to change the laws that permitted discrimination in privately owned places of public accommodation.

The impetus for change came from black college students in the winter and spring of 1960. Four students from North Carolina Agricultural and Technical College were denied food service at the lunch counter of a Greensboro department store. Their initial rejection motivated other students from the same college to join the demonstration, and by the end of the first week of protest, black students had organized lunch counter sit-ins in eight more North Carolina cities. Sit-ins spread quickly across the urbanized South, and by mid-April they encompassed all southern states and involved an estimated 50,000 demonstrators.[16]

Participation demanded courage and patience, for demonstrators frequently encountered verbal and physical abuse from hostile whites. The very act of collective protest enabled southern black students to change both their own self-image and the image that others held of them. Black demonstrators were "suddenly proud to be called 'black,' " and each protesting student achieved "a new awareness of himself."[17]

Sit-in demonstrations were a major innovation in civil rights protest. "In an almost visceral way," argues William H. Chafe, "the sit-ins expressed the dissatisfaction and anger of the black community toward white indifference." The protest "was expressed in a manner that whites could not possibly ignore—the silence of people sitting with dignity at a lunch counter demanding their rights. Thus, from a white point of view, the message was different, because for the first time, whites could not avoid hearing it."[18] The larger message was simply to bring the South into conformity with the less discriminatory treatment of blacks in nonsouthern eating places. Protesters thus "concentrated on eliminating overt southern racism by portraying it as anachronistic and irrational, contrary to the American creed, and damaging to the interests of the nation."[19]

Notable gains were achieved through the lunch counter sit-ins. Less than a year after the first protest, "more than one hundred cities had engaged in at least some desegregation of public facilities in response to student-led demonstrations."[20] The targets had expanded to include motels, hotels, theaters, clothing stores, amusement parks, and other types of privately owned businesses that were technically open to the public but were operated in such a manner as to exclude blacks or treat them differently from whites. Desegregation was more likely in larger cities than in smaller towns, in the Peripheral South than in the Deep South, and in businesses owned outside the region.[21] Most southern businesses, however, still either refused to serve blacks or deliberately provided inferior service. The sit-ins had attracted some national media coverage and the conflict had been expanded beyond the region; yet comprehensive national legislation to remove the grounds for the protest was not even close to enactment. Dissimilar treatment of blacks, both within different types of public accommodations in a given city, and from city to city across the region, was bound to create more tension and pressure "from below" for a permanent reformation of race relations. If southern whites could no longer avoid "hearing" the message of black discontent, many of them had not really "got the message."

The main organizational legacy of the sit-ins was the Student Nonviolent Coordinating Committee (SNCC), which was to become the most militant and radical of the major civil rights groups in the 1960s. SNCC grew out of an April 1960 meeting in Raleigh, North Carolina, that involved more than 100 student activists who had been participating in sit-ins, and it operated independently of all other civil rights organizations. Exactly what the organization would do was not clear, since most student activists believed that "local autonomy was the basis of sustained militancy."[22]

In the spring of 1961, the Congress of Racial Equality (CORE), a northern-based civil rights group, "rejuvenated the southern protest movement" through its "Freedom Rides."[23] According to Pat Watters and Reese Cleghorn, this tactic soon elicited the "first large infusion of young Northerners, whites among them, into the Southern movement" and converted a "largely spontaneous uprising by young Negro Southerners" into "a national movement."[24]

As originally planned, a small number of dedicated protesters, trained in the philosophy and tactics of nonviolent resistance, would ride buses through the South to test the desegregation of public waiting room facilities. A 1960 Supreme Court decision, *Virginia v. Boynton,* had declared such segregation unconstitutional, but the ruling was widely ignored. CORE wanted to demonstrate that these constitutional rights of blacks were not being enforced and to arouse public opinion and (more important) national authorities to intervene. In this exercise in nonviolent resistance, "the Freedom Ride would penetrate the Deep South, it would focus on terminal facilities, and the riders would pledge, if arrested, to remain in jail rather than to accept bail or pay fines."[25] Anticipating white violence and seeking as much publicity as possible, CORE distributed advance copies of the route to federal officials and the news media.

The first arrest occurred in Charlotte, North Carolina; the first beatings took place a few miles farther south in Rock Hill, South Carolina. Ferocious mob violence awaited the Freedom Riders in Alabama, where a crowd of whites assaulted the bus as it pulled into the Anniston depot. Later that day the same bus was bombed and set on fire after it left Anniston, and many of the protesters were attacked as they desperately tried to escape from the burning bus. More mob violence erupted in Birmingham, and no driver was immediately willing to take the remaining riders to Montgomery. The Freedom Ride did not resume until ten days later. When the bus entered the Montgomery terminal, however, police were absent. Again the welcoming party was a large crowd of angry whites, who "savagely assaulted" the emerging Freedom Riders. Faced with the recurrent failure of state and local law enforcement officials to preserve order and protect the demonstrators, the Kennedy administration was forced to dispatch 600 federal marshals to restore order. An even more dangerous situation developed the next night when a "howling, rock-throwing mob" of Alabama whites surrounded a black church where King was speaking in support of the Freedom Riders; federal marshals had to be supplemented by Alabama national guard troops to disperse the white rioters.[26]

Uncontrollable white violence was central to the initial national appeal of the Freedom Riders. As Watters has argued, the Freedom Rides "provided the kind of all-out violence from whites that made the movement big news."[27] The protesters' immediate goal was not so much desegregating local bus terminals as eliciting the type of unrestrained white resistance that would attract national attention and interest. CORE's approach required enormous courage and often entailed horrible personal suffering, both on the streets and later in the jails of the Deep South, but the ultimate result was that "the freedom rides achieved a prominence in the national consciousness that the sit-ins (which were gentler in tone, more purposeful, and almost entirely an indigenous southern movement) never did."[28] Television was the primary instrument for communicating the reality of the southern caste system to the nation at large. "The techniques of physical control used by the closed society were revealed by the searching eye of the camera and projected into the homes of most Americans every night," Allison Davis concluded. "They nauseated even those who did not accept the goals of the civil rights movement."[29]

Outrage over the treatment of the original Freedom Riders was so strong that SCLC and SNCC joined with CORE to form a Freedom Ride Co-ordinating Committee. Its main objectives were to "fill the jails of Montgomery and Jackson [Mississippi] in order to keep a sharp image of the issue before the public," as well as to force Attorney General Robert F. Kennedy to protect the constitutional rights of interstate travelers. The attorney general responded to the Freedom Rides in late May by requesting that the Interstate Commerce Commission issue regulations enforcing the *Boynton* decision (these regulations were issued in September), and by asking the civil rights groups for a "cooling-off period."[30] Fearful of additional violence, reluctant to exacerbate cleavages between the national administration and various state and local officials, worried about the erosion of support for the Democratic party in the Deep South, and concerned over the international consequences of the protests, federal officials conceded the justice of the Freedom Riders' demands but saw no constructive purpose in continuing the protest.[31]

Most of the civil rights activists, especially members of CORE and SNCC, viewed the matter very differently. By any standard, the Freedom

Rides were their most successful tactic for dramatizing segregation in the outer color line. The rides initially produced widespread and favorable media attention outside the South, attracted many volunteers who wished to take part in the protests, and stimulated financial contributions to the civil rights organizations. Moreover, the type of discrimination targeted by the Freedom Riders was only part of a much broader agenda, and they had no intention of abandoning their newly discovered tactic. SNCC and CORE leaders rejected Kennedy's plea. "We had been cooling off for 100 years," explained James Farmer, the head of CORE. "If we got any cooler, we'd be in a deep freeze."[32]

Meanwhile, the Freedom Rides continued as large numbers of fresh volunteers answered the call to "fill the jails." Jackson now became the central target, and more than 300 Freedom Riders were arrested in the summer of 1961. This new wave of protesters altered the cultural style of the civil rights movement. "Here come upon the South," observed Watters and Cleghorn, "was the menace of the unshaven, the invasion of the unkempt." Here also came many Yankees, both white and black, which further enraged native white southerners. "If the mannerly students, carrying their textbooks to jail with them, drew stern and self-righteous imprecations for daring to provoke racist violence," they concluded, "the bearded, 'outside agitator' Freedom Riders sent segregationists of all degrees, including many editorialists who should have known better, into fits and frenzies. Where would it all end?"[33]

Mississippi authorities hoped it would end in their penal system. Freedom Riders were quickly arrested and placed in various Mississippi jails, an experience that further radicalized many demonstrators. Watters and Cleghorn summarize what happened: "Many of them, once released from Mississippi's Parchman state penitentiary and other places of incarceration, stayed on, as had some sit-inners before them, in the ranks of the 'professional' freedom fighters, mainly as workers for SNCC and CORE."[34]

CORE's strategy—in Farmer's words, "to create crises and apply pressure"[35]—via the Freedom Rides was successful, and segregation in interstate transportation facilities largely disappeared from the South after the Interstate Commerce Commission issued an order in the early fall of 1961.[36] In victory the Freedom Riders "suddenly became aware of their collective ability to provoke a crisis that would attract international publicity and compel federal intervention."[37] As full-time activists, some members of SNCC and CORE initiated direct action struggles against segregation in the rural and small-town areas of the Deep South's black belt, challenging Jim Crow in the counties that had been the backbone of southern racism.

The far more difficult task remained of desegregating privately owned places of public accommodation. For the most part, however, the main civil rights groups shifted their energies to voter registration in 1962, and not until King led demonstrations in Birmingham in the spring of 1963 did public accommodations again become a truly national controversy. The gains of the early 1960s had not come through demonstrations initiated by SCLC. Indeed, within the movement there was widespread skepticism concerning King's philosophy and strategy of nonviolent persuasion. "The themes of reconciliation and the beloved community preached by Martin Luther King, Jr., had little relevance to many who had suffered in the jails of Mississippi," Harvard Sitkoff notes. "They believed that power alone counted, that only power could induce change."[38] And in SCLC's own campaigns, King's emphasis on nonviolent persuasion had not yet worked. According to Garrow, the original strategy of persuading white southerners to abandon segregation

> was given its first real trial in the Albany [Georgia] campaign of 1961 and 1962. Albany was not a success for King and the SCLC. Much of the reason for the movement's failure there was the conduct of the Albany police chief, Laurie Pritchett, who peacefully arrested all of the SCLC's numerous groups of marchers. The Albany campaign indicated that a strategy of nonviolent persuasion would not necessarily move the SCLC's opponents toward reforms and a lessening of racial injustice, and Pritchett's quiet conduct aroused neither the interest of the news media nor the anger of the movement's potential allies.[39]

From this defeat, Garrow argues, SCLC's leaders concluded that "a strategy of nonviolent persuasion which focused on changing the hearts and minds of one's opponents was unrealistic and ineffective."[40] In its place came an emphasis on nonviolent coercion:

> Only in the wake of Albany did King begin to realize that *coercive* nonviolence would be necessary if progress was to be achieved. While progress could not be achieved through efforts to convince the movement's white opponents that they were mistaken, progress could be achieved if the movement, and its external allies, could *force* southern localities to implement progressive changes. Federal legislation, King increasingly realized, was one route by which effective change could be brought about. The path to such legislation, in turn, lay through the national news media and the audiences to which they could convey the movement's pleas for assistance and reforms.[41]

But because "the news media's interest in a campaign quickly waned when no violent or unusually dramatic confrontations were occurring,"[42] the revised strategy required demonstrations to be staged in communities where police brutality could be expected.

After careful deliberation King and the other SCLC leaders selected

Birmingham, a city with a history of racial violence extraordinary even by Deep South standards, as the site of the next major confrontation. King's presence assured mass media coverage, but Birmingham's attractiveness to SCLC lay in the anticipated response of its police force. The chief law enforcement official of this totally segregated city, Eugene T. ("Bull") Connor, had long employed harsh methods in repressing blacks. Watters later reconstructed the probable calculations of SCLC leaders: "The supposition has to be that, at least in part, SCLC, in a shrewd, normal-American, cynical stratagem, knew a good enemy when they saw him—one who could be counted on in stupidity and natural viciousness to play into their hands, for full exploitation in the press as archfiend and villain." By dramatizing unjust encounters between "saintly Negroes" and "depraved and savage whites," SCLC hoped to create the same type of crisis that the Freedom Riders had produced two years earlier in Alabama.[43] Racial conditions in Birmingham were the immediate targets, but influencing national public opinion and pressuring relevant federal authorities were the ultimate objectives.

For more than two months the largest city in Alabama was the scene of continuous protest activities, including a boycott of downtown stores, marches, sit-ins, mass arrests, flagrant police brutality, and various kinds of public disorder. In due course the demonstrations stimulated the expected responses from Connor's police. Before the protests ended, Birmingham had yielded pictures seen around the world of firehoses blasting women and children and police dogs attacking demonstrators. These scenes revolted many observers—reportedly including President John F. Kennedy, whose emotional commitment to civil rights intensified in the spring and summer of 1963.[44] "Like the Greensboro sit-ins," wrote August Meier and Elliott Rudwick, "the Birmingham demonstrations both epitomized the change in mood and became a major stimulus for direct-action campaigns across the country." Even more important, "the Negro protest movement became suffused with a new militance. 'Freedom Now!' became the slogan."[45]

Although the Birmingham protests renewed the civil rights movement and initiated a political chain reaction that ultimately produced the Civil Rights Act of 1964, events in Birmingham did not immediately elicit either federal intervention or new federal legislation, primarily because the protest "lacked a clear, single goal that could be easily conveyed both *to* and *by* the news media," and secondarily because "on several occasions black citizens not formally involved in the movement had themselves employed weapons or violence against white officials."[46] Both points merit discussion, for what happened in this Deep South city in 1963 was symptomatic of changes in black protest behavior across the South.

Bayard Rustin stressed the multiplicity of grievances confronting southern blacks; in Birmingham, he argued, "the single-issue demands of the movement's classical stage gave way to the 'package deal.' No longer were Negroes satisfied with integrating lunch counters. They now sought advances in employment, housing, school integration, police protection, and so forth." In Birmingham, for example, King listed six demands as the goals of the demonstrations. These demands began to overlap between the outer and the intermediate color lines, between what came to be understood as issues of "equality of opportunity" and "equality of results."[47] The second group of issues was much more controversial among nonsouthern whites than the first. If the Birmingham protests reflected a broad range of black grievances, they increased the difficulty of conveying to the media and, in turn, to its distant audiences the depth and magnitude of the conflict.

National reactions to Birmingham were also shaped by the conduct and behavior of some blacks. More than once in Birmingham the discipline of nonviolent resistance broke down as anger and rage erupted. Instead of always behaving as "saintly Negroes," some Birmingham blacks began to curse, taunt, and bait the police, to throw rocks, carry weapons, and, after two bombings (in one night) of the property of prominent blacks, to take to the streets in furious and destructive protest. These actions blurred and undermined the intended portrait of good versus evil that SCLC was trying to present to the nation, threatened public order, and produced among distant media audiences some sympathy for the local police, who were occasionally being provoked by onlookers.[48]

By now, many blacks were so angry, enraged, and frustrated with the Jim Crow system that massive social disorder could be expected to increase. Neither black leaders nor white politicians could totally ignore the larger implications of the demonstrations. After Birmingham, black protests escalated across the South, producing almost 800 demonstrations in more than 200 cities and towns.[49] As city after city began to experience organized protest, white community leaders had to reassess the price of continuing segregation in public accommodations. Some white politicians, more often in the Peripheral South than in the Deep South, began to revise their position.[50]

Yet though demonstrations occurred in many communities in 1963, their outcomes again made clear why national legislation was necessary to resolve these problems of the outer color line. Reform appears to have been blocked in more than three-quarters of the communities in which protests occurred, and in numerous other communities, where there were no demonstrations, public accommodations generally remained rigidly segregated.[51] Although more fissures had occurred in the pattern of segregation, the results of the events of 1963 were similar to those of the challenges of 1960: uneven change among and within southern cities and towns, and in many places, no change at all.

The public accommodations controversy was largely resolved by the Civil Rights Act of 1964, signed into law on July 2 by President Johnson. Title II of the act banned racial discrimination in privately owned businesses that were open to the general public. According to Harrell R. Rodgers, Jr., and Charles S. Bullock III, "a businessman could not refuse service to blacks if (1) he served people traveling from state to state, or (2) a substantial portion of the products used in his business had moved in interstate commerce."[52] The Civil Rights Act thus created a new right for consumers that took precedence over the management's right to select customers on the basis of such arbitrary and unreasonable classifications as race. Throughout most of the South, especially in metropolitan areas and in stores that were part of national chains, there was immediate compliance with the law. If segregation still prevailed in many privately owned businesses, particularly in black belt environments, the law of the land was now unequivocally on the side of the blacks.

Many events of the preceding year contributed to the act's passage. The upsurge in civil rights militancy in the spring and summer of 1963 demonstrated the urgency of black demands for reform and dramatically increased white awareness of civil rights problems. Since 1935 the Gallup organization has periodically asked a representative sample of Americans to identify "the most important problem facing the nation."[53] Until the mid-1950s civil rights problems were only rarely perceived by the American public as matters of highest priority; after the mid-1950s attention was episodic and usually represented a short-lived reaction to crises over southern school desegregation. The spring of 1963, however, "marked an historical turning point in the nation's perception of the civil rights issue and in the administration's approach to it."[54] With the Birmingham demonstrations stimulating other civil rights protests and activating non-southern groups that were only indirectly concerned with southern racial traditions, the share of Gallup respondents selecting civil rights as the nation's most important problem increased phenomenally, rising from 4 percent in early spring to 52 percent by early summer. During the next two years civil rights problems remained near the center of national attention; no less than one-third and sometimes more than one-half of the Gallup respondents considered these controversies the nation's most urgent concern.[55]

Popular support for national civil rights legislation was symbolized by the August 1963 March on Washington, which attracted some 200,000 peaceful demonstrators. As millions of Americans watched on television, the rally reached its climax with King's magnificent vision of a South in which whites and blacks were harmoniously united in mutual respect and dignity. King's speech fused militance and brotherhood, change and reconciliation. "To the extent that any single public utterance could," Sitkoff concludes, "this speech made the black revolt acceptable to white America."[56] Public opinion surveys found that nonsouthern whites favored federal action on two of the most publicized issues of the day— the rights of southern blacks to be served in places of public accommodation and to register and vote without discrimination.[57] The white South was now becoming isolated in national public opinion.

Against this background President Kennedy began to pursue civil rights much more vigorously than in the past.[58] The administration's original civil rights proposals were strengthened in the summer of 1963, but they still faced formidable congressional opposition. President Kennedy's assassination shifted the presidency to a native white southerner who had long thought of himself more as a Texan than as a southerner. Though Lyndon Johnson had maintained firm ties with many of the conservative southern senators, he had never allowed himself to be seen as a completely unreconstructed southerner.[59] Johnson disarmed many potential critics when he wholeheartedly accepted leadership of the slain president's civil rights program and helped guide the new legislation through Congress in 1964.

Title II of the Civil Rights Act had implications for the South's economic development, for the Jim Crow system impeded the growth of natural markets. Continuing social unrest and turmoil over desegregation often hurt local economies. In addition, for the national corporations that were playing an increasingly larger role in southern communities, a desegregated South presented the prospect of much larger markets than the old segregated South. Blacks with money to spend and white businesses desiring to increase sales would both benefit from the desegregation of public accommodations. As Rustin properly emphasized, "In a highly industrialized twentieth-century civilization, we hit Jim Crow precisely where it was most anachronistic, dispensable, and vulnerable—in hotels, lunch counters, terminals, libraries, swimming pools, and the like. For in these forms, Jim Crow does impede the flow of commerce in the broadest sense; it is a nuisance in a society on the move (and on the make)."[60] Rodgers and Bullock observed that many southern businessmen led the way in urging compliance with the Civil Rights Act.[61]

Waning opposition to this alteration of the outer color line is evident in survey data. SRC-CPS surveys show that the percentage of white southerners who opposed federal responsibility for desegregating public accommodations dropped by 36 percent betwen 1964 and 1972, the last year in which this question was asked. Around the time the Civil Rights Act was passed, 80 percent of southern whites opposed federal intervention on this issue; eight years later, only 51 percent remained in opposition. We suspect that opposition to the principle of desegregated public accommodations would be much, much lower in the South of the 1980s.

With the dismantling of segregated public accommodations, the South was compelled to take a long stride toward practices commonly accepted in the rest of the nation. It was a significant shift away from one of the most obvious markers of regional distinctiveness in traditional race relations.

Securing the Right to Vote

The Civil Rights Act of 1964 effectively reformed segregationist traditions in public accommodations, but altering another crucial feature of the outer color line—the voting rights of black southerners—required a separate national law, the Voting Rights Act of 1965. To understand why whites in some parts of the South continued to offer tenacious resistance to political democracy, it is necessary to examine trends in black participation during the 1950s and early 1960s.

Although approximately 1,000,000 black southerners were registered to vote by 1952, the massive resistance campaign against school desegregation stiffened white opposition to further black registration. Only 454,000 new black registrants were added to southern electorates in the next decade, about half the increase that had occurred from 1944 to 1952. In 1960 an estimated 29 percent of the South's eligible blacks were registered, still leaving the vast majority of black southerners politically immobilized. Registration rates among voting age blacks varied widely among the states, ranging from 5 percent in Mississippi to an estimated (and no doubt exaggerated) 59 percent in Tennessee. Only Georgia and Louisiana approximated the regional norm. Much lower rates of black registration occurred in Mississippi, Alabama, South Carolina, and Virginia; considerably higher registration figures appeared in Tennessee, Florida, North Carolina, Arkansas, and Texas.[62]

Even more arresting differences in black participation prior to the modern civil rights movement characterized the region's counties. County estimates of black and white voter registration for 1958 and 1960 became available through the United States Commission on Civil Rights. These data are invaluable but imperfect, and in using them we necessarily enter a shadowland of accuracy mingled with more or less informed guesswork.[63] We have chosen to use 1960 data (supplemented by 1958 results for Georgia and South Carolina, for which no 1960 estimates were available), primarily because calculations of black registration rates were made on the basis of 1960 voting age populations. Since we are concerned to establish broad regional patterns, we have put each county which had at least 2 percent blacks and at least 100 blacks of voting age into one of three categories of mobilization: (1) counties in which no more than a small minority of blacks (0-24 percent) were registered; (2) counties where sizable minorities of blacks (25-49 percent) were enrolled; and (3) counties in which majorities of blacks (50 percent or higher) were registered. These broad classifications—exclusion, undermobilization, and mobilization—allow us to observe the distribution of three different patterns of black mobilization across the South prior to the rise of the civil rights movement.

Unlike other aspects of the outer color line, the color line on voting was not universally rigid. In 1960 the South was decidedly "unsolid" (figure 5.1). Fifteen years after the white primary had been abolished, black participation remained negligible in many counties. In other areas, however, substantial minorities of eligible blacks were registered, and more than half of the potential black electorate was registered in a small group of counties. The South's bedrock centers of nonparticipation began in northern Virginia, became more pervasive in Southside Virginia and northeastern North Carolina, blanketed South Carolina, and ran along Georgia's eastern border. Then began a huge stretch of monolithic exclusion that included southwestern Georgia, southern Alabama, the entire state of Mississippi, and nearly all of northern Louisiana before petering out in the eastern third of Texas. Along with a few additional localities in Florida, Tennessee, and Arkansas, these counties represented areas where electoral politics was still almost exclusively reserved for whites.

On the other hand, *majorities* of blacks were registered to vote in most of southern Louisiana, western North Carolina, West Texas, most of Tennessee, and scattered counties in northwestern Arkansas, East Texas, and Florida. In the remaining groups of counties, composing much of penisular Florida, central and northern Virginia, northwestern Georgia, northern Alabama, southern Arkansas, and pockets of East Texas, *sizable minorities* of the potential black electorate were registered. Taken as a whole, exclusion and undermobilization were the two most common patterns in 1960; two decades earlier, exclusion had been the sole pattern.

The geography of exclusion in 1960 was generally consistent with Key's theoretical emphasis on the influence of racial composition, as well as Matthews and Prothro's analysis of 1958 voter registration data, which concluded that the percentage of blacks in counties was the single most important correlate ($r = -.46$) of black registration rates in the South. In addition, Matthews and Prothro confirmed for the first time with

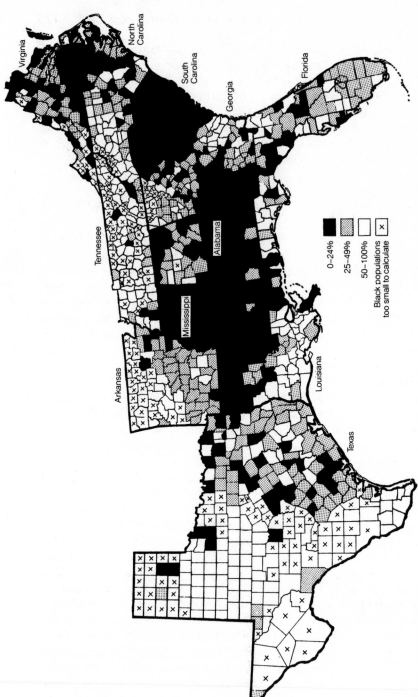

Figure 5.1. Black voter registration prior to the Voting Rights Act of 1965: percentage of eligible blacks registered in 1960. Results for Georgia and South Carolina are based on 1958 data. Sources: *Report of the U.S. Commission on Civil Rights, 1959* (Washington, D.C.: Government Printing Office, 1959); and *1961 U.S. Commission on Civil Rights Report* (Washington, D.C.: Government Printing Office, 1961).

survey data Key's stress on the extraordinarily racist attitudes of black belt whites. "The more Negroes in the population of a county," they observed, "the fewer the whites who give even abstract endorsement of the right of Negroes to vote." Yet even as they affirmed that black concentration was the single most important factor influencing partici-pation by the minority group, Matthews and Prothro carefully empha-sized that this factor alone could not account for most of the variance—indeed, it left 79 percent of the variance "unexplained"—in black reg-istration rates across the region's counties.[64]

Key's suggestions about the potentially liberalizing impact of urbani-zation and industrialization were severely challenged by the 1958 voter registration data. Matthews and Prothro found no strong correlation between black registration rates and either urbanization (.07) or indus-trialization (.08). "Urbanization and industrialization are vastly overrated as facilitators of Negro voter registration," they concluded. "Urbaniza-tion and industrialization may provide necessary conditions for high levels of Negro political participation, but by themselves they are not sufficient to ensure such levels."[65] The 1960 voter registration estimates confirm the persisting weakness of black mobilization in southern met-ropolitan areas, where registration was generally limited to sizable mi-norities of black adults.[66]

To interpret this rather surprising finding—that urbanization made no difference to black political mobilization, at least during the late 1950s—it is necessary to examine more closely black politics in city and rural environments. Urban areas did absorb the largest influx of new black voters after *Smith v. Allwright,* but the early urban political mobilization stopped far short of encompassing majorities of potential black voters. In 1960 white racism remained a formidable barrier against exercise of the franchise by many urban blacks. Through their complete control of the registration process, white officials could make black voter registra-tion easy or difficult, practical or impractical. "The chances are that in the long run the most effective force for the promotion of Negro partic-ipation in politics is the actions of white men who think that they need and can win Negro votes," Key had observed. "When whites split among themselves and seek Negro support, the way may be opened for the Negro to vote."[67] Preferences of urban white politicians appear to have ranged all the way from diligent efforts to restrict black registration to the lowest feasible numbers to enthusiastic encouragement of participation by ma-jorities of eligible blacks, with the most common preference being an acceptance of voting by more or less sizable minorities of eligible blacks.

Opposition to voting by urban blacks was strongest in the Deep South. In most Deep South cities blacks made up 30 percent or more of the total population, a threshold established by Matthews and Prothro as critical in deterring substantial black registration.[68] Fewer than one-quarter of eligible blacks were on the registration rolls in 1960 in the counties that included the cities of Birmingham, Charleston, Columbia, Greenville, Jackson, Mobile, and Montgomery; and only in Baton Rouge, Atlanta, and New Orleans, where limited black involvement had sometimes been encouraged by local white politicians, were slightly more than a fourth of eligible blacks registered. All of the Peripheral South counties that contained large cities (Memphis and Richmond excepted) had black populations of less than 30 percent, and that subregion's central tendency was the political mobilization of more than one-quarter but less than one-half of the possible black electorate. Counties containing such cities as Dallas, Houston, Miami, Little Rock, Charlotte, Greensboro, Norfolk, and Richmond showed incomplete, partial registration of blacks; but in five of the Peripheral South's metropolitan counties, estimated black registration exceeded 50 percent. In the two Florida counties that included Tampa and Jacksonville, local Democratic politicians had sought out black voters to improve their electoral margins.[69] White politicians had also encouraged massive black participation in the three Tennessee counties containing Memphis, Nashville, and Knoxville. Indeed, Memphis represented the anomaly and sole exception to the rule of "high black concentration, low black registration." Black participation had originated in the factional electoral interests of Boss Ed Crump's political machine and did not pose a threat to racial segregation.[70]

Variation in the racial composition of southern cities and in the electoral needs of white Democratic politicians, important as they are, do not provide a convincing explanation of the failure of most urban black southerners to participate in politics in the late 1950s and early 1960s. Prior to the direct action demonstrations of the civil rights movement, minority politics in the urban South was generally characterized by small and fairly cohesive leadership groups, rather limited goals (mainly amelioration of segregated institutions, but also growing protest against segregation itself), and weak mass bases. "Urban Negro political organization in the past usually was limited to what a few principal Negro political leaders saw fit to establish and utilize," explained Watters and Cleghorn. "Even in Atlanta, with a large Negro middle class, the political leadership was small and fairly tight in discipline. In New Orleans, a very few Negro leaders guided the Negro community politically. This was the pattern in most Southern cities."[71]

Thus small political organizations, commonly led by middle-class blacks, faced black populations primarily composed of individuals who were not middle class, not well educated, and not economically secure. "Negro political organizations have not yet drawn in all potential voters nor have they stabilized their participation," Harry Holloway concluded of Texas's urban blacks. "Probably part of the difficulty lies not just in the low education and income typical of this group but also in the influx of rural voters not used to voting regularly and the departure of some of the most energetic and enterprising individuals from the city. The cities gain population from the country and lose population to other cities in the North."[72] The observations of a black Greensboro school teacher who had lived in rural, eastern North Carolina during part of her life are pertinent: " 'Blacks were out of it and didn't even think about it in the east,' she said. 'They were out of it and they knew they were out of it in Greensboro. There's a difference.' "[73] The comparatively low levels of registration in large cities could be attributed in part to the changing composition of the black population in these cities, as migration from the rural areas brought into southern cities some people who still "didn't even think about it."

For those urban residents who already "knew they were out of it," active political involvement—an uphill struggle at best—was not the only alternative. White candidates rarely campaigned in ways that stimulated black participation, and often choice was limited to different varieties of segregationists. Watters and Cleghorn correctly emphasized that "politics seemed irrelevant to Negroes in many locales partly because it *was* irrelevant. When it came to their own interests, Negroes had no real choices."[74] Holloway concluded from an intensive study of urban blacks that "the Texas city Negroes vote as a bloc, on the whole, in those races where there is a difference between the candidates on issues of importance to the group."[75] But with black candidates seldom on the ballot, and with few white candidates making open, positive appeals for black votes, the political agenda was typically dominated by racially conservative whites. The result was a tremendous reserve of untapped political resources among blacks in southern big cities. Yet although their rates of participation remained low, urban blacks had begun to demonstrate a degree of independence from white politicians by voting for their racial interests even against the opposition of influential white politicians. In Texas, for example, the urban blacks who did vote constituted a "surprisingly effective, cohesive, and stable bloc oriented toward the liberal Democratic candidate, especially if he is strongly pro-civil rights."[76]

Beyond the cities, blacks had also begun to vote in modest numbers—more accurately, perhaps, blacks had begun to be voted—in some parts of the low-black rural and small-town South. Key had been well aware that black participation, especially in rural areas, would be heavily constrained by the caste system. "A basic principle of the social system is that the black man does what the white man says," he stated. "This ingrained habit undoubtedly gives the Negro vote (not so much as it is, but as it might be on a larger scale) a high degree of organizability, which would probably be more marked in rural than in urban communities."[77] White opposition to political democracy was so pervasive and unyielding in the black belt sections that white politicians usually had no room to maneuver. But in counties where whites outnumbered blacks by over-whelming margins, white attitudes about black participation were some-what more permissive, though the white politicians who pursued black votes had to be cautious and discreet. Limited mobilization of rural and small-town blacks was permissible since it primarily served the electoral interests of groups of local white politicians and their backers, rather than expressing—much less satisfying—multiple black grievances.

"Manipulation" and "control" of black electorates by white politicians are the key concepts for understanding the relatively moderate rates of registration among rural blacks. Evidence for this interpretation rests on two especially fine examples of field research, Holloway's study of East Texas blacks, and Alfred B. Clubok, John M. DeGrove, and Charles D. Farris's comparative analysis of black politics in six small Florida com-munities.[78] Both studies demonstrated that black voting was encouraged by groups of local whites in order to win or retain control of local political offices. Electoral needs of local white factions helped to generate black participation in some rural counties but not in others. White politicians had no interest in mobilizing blacks who could not be controlled, and hence economic and psychological dependency on whites was essential for the system to work properly. Holloway concluded that the East Texas "rural Negro is still in good part bound by the caste system of racial relationships and casts his vote accordingly." In general, the black East Texan "has little trouble registering and exercising the right to vote but, with some exceptions, does not cast a free, self-willed ballot."[79]

In Florida researchers found a wider variety of black responses—in-cluding groups of blacks who were not controlled by white politicians—but again stressed that "the white politicians' encouragement of Negro registration was based either on actual or anticipated competition for public office. Organization and manipulation of a Negro vote was con-ceived of as a means of either obtaining or retaining control of public policy-making positions." And from the perspective of local whites who thought about such matters, this style of manipulated politics had an additional desirable consequence: it minimized the chances of outside intervention in local race relations by the federal government or civil rights organizations. In the words of a Floridian who was county judge in a small, medium-black rural county, "Hell, the Federals are interested only when you try to keep the colored from voting, and we're voting them to the hilt."[80]

The thesis of controlled black voting in rural areas suggests the process by which the caste system was "modernized" or "democratized" to continue furthering the interests of dominant whites. This much is certain: without the approval or acquiescence of local white politicians, who controlled entry into the political system, little black registration could have occurred prior to the civil rights movement. Arbitrary administration of literacy tests, poll taxes, availability of formal and informal cues to discourage potential black registrants—all these made it easy for white authorities to manage black participation in the rural and small-town South. Manipulative politics fed on black economic dependency. In lowland Arkansas, East Texas, southeastern Georgia, and parts of Florida and Virginia, white politicians and landlords pioneered techniques of control that would later be implemented in the heart of the black belt, once blacks had entered the system after the Voting Rights Act of 1965.

It would be inaccurate to portray this pattern of manipulation as one in which rural blacks received nothing in return for their votes. Both the Texas and Florida studies emphasized that the key payoff to blacks was more or less "friendly" law enforcement that minimized hostility and violence toward blacks—no small gain, considering the histories of police brutality, harassment, and intimidation in many southern communities. In all other aspects of life, however, "controlled" black political participation was consistent with the racial status quo. Indeed, Holloway found that rural blacks in Texas often voted for racially conservative candidates in state politics, whereas big city black voters supported candidates who were closest to their own positions.[81]

When we probe beneath the superficial similarities in the registration rates of urban and rural blacks in the late 1950s, we find in the rural areas—as Key would have predicted—the potential for much stiffer opposition to increased black voter registration. Except for those cities with sizable black populations and especially violent traditions of racial repression, the metropolitan South seemed ripe for increased minority voting, provided that blacks could become better organized. In the rural South, black participation was still unacceptable to most whites who lived in counties with high black concentrations, and adamant resistance to political democracy was the realistic expectation. Outside high-black rural areas, whether blacks had voted in the past depended largely upon the needs of local white politicians, and the controlled participation they sometimes fostered or allowed did not challenge racial segregation. White attitudes in the low-black rural counties would be less permissive toward black voting rights if segregation itself seemed to be at stake.[82]

In the aftermath of the Freedom Rides, the civil rights movement shifted priorities to expanding black voter registration. Anxious to enlarge the number of registered black Democrats in the South before the 1964 presidential election, as well as to get the Freedom Riders off the evening newscasts and front pages, Kennedy Administration officials and leaders of private foundations met with representatives of the major civil rights organizations in 1961 and 1962 to urge a change in movement priorities and to offer financial support for voter registration drives. Civil rights activists, aware of the dangers involved in registering blacks in much of the black belt South, left the meetings believing that they had been promised police protection by the administration, whose spokesmen subsequently denied making any such promise.[83] This dispute between the administration and civil rights leaders directly involved the safety of the volunteers and those blacks who were the targets of registration activities, and it grew into a cancer of insurmountable bitterness for many civil rights workers in the next few years.

The outcome of negotiations among foundation officials, government representatives, and movement leaders was the Voter Education Project (VEP), under the direction of Wiley Branton, a black Arkansas lawyer who was thoroughly familiar with the problems and prospects of black voter registration.[84] When the civil rights movement turned to voter registration as its main objective in the spring of 1962, hard choices had to be made concerning the best use of its scarce resources. With limited funds and few full-time activists, VEP clearly could not enter every southern county in which blacks were completely disfranchised, manipulated, or simply unorganized. Resources were channeled either to the "hardcore" areas, where white resistance was expected to be strongest, or to the "easy" situations, those cities where grassroots organizations might be able to recruit many blacks into the electorate without encountering much white opposition. "SNCC's work was almost entirely in areas of bad resistance," reported Watters and Cleghorn. "CORE was in bad territory mostly, but in some easier areas, too, as was SCLC, whose voter work was less. The NAACP was across all the South, good, bad, and inbetween."[85] The region's toughest sections generally were those in which less than one-quarter (and sometimes less than one-tenth) of adult blacks were registered in 1960 (see figure 5.1). During the first VEP (1962-1964), the hard-core areas received most of the resources but produced scant results; the easier areas got little of the money but secured the vast majority of new registrants.[86] An unavoidable consequence of the VEP's strategy was that many parts of the small-town and rural South having modest black populations were bypassed by the leading civil rights organizations, and in the mid-1980s such places could still be characterized by traditional patterns of black political participation.

In the hard-core areas civil rights workers confronted three principal obstacles: near-monolithic opposition from local whites who possessed ample informal and formal methods of intimidating and neutralizing registration activities; the continuing unwillingness of federal officials to protect civil rights workers in the exercise of their constitutional rights; and the reluctance of many black residents, especially prominent blacks, to become involved in registration work and thereby risk physical and economic retaliation from the dominant whites.[87] To enter many communities in Mississippi, Alabama, southwestern Georgia, or northern Louisiana as a known civil rights worker was to risk beatings, bombings, and shootings, to invite relentless harassment, and to enter a psychological state of permanent insecurity. Violent death had long been the ultimate punishment for violations of racial taboos, and civil rights workers were purposefully repudiating southern traditions in order to provide new role models for local blacks. As the civil rights movement consciously tried to replace passivity and accommodation with assertion and confrontation, participants and observers repeatedly stressed that fear was one of the primary obstacles to be overcome.[88]

It was all the harder to cope with one's personal fears and to persuade others to overcome their fears when southern law enforcement was completely hostile—sometimes, as in the notorious case of Neshoba County, Mississippi, murderously hostile—to efforts to change the system, and when federal officials could not be counted on to provide protection. The civil rights struggle in the Deep South is replete with pleas to the Department of Justice to secure law enforcement that would enable volunteers to carry out their constitutional rights of freedom of speech and assembly and of redress of grievances. As the months passed and the expected federal intervention did not come, many civil rights activists felt that they had been betrayed by the Kennedy administration.[89]

Because of this charged atmosphere of intimidation and retaliation, as well as the history and social structure of the black belt, the civil rights movement was not welcomed openly by all local blacks. Public association with the movement put blacks at risk of various reprisals, and middle-class blacks had the most to lose. As Watters and Cleghorn observed, "An arresting fact about the difference between white and Negro community leadership is this: businessmen have constituted the largest occupational group in the white leadership, and ministers have been the largest among Negroes. The explanation is obvious: ministers usually were, at least potentially, the most independent figures in the Negro community, barring only the undertakers . . . Virtually all other occupations brought middle-class Negroes into crippling situations."[90] For many middle-class blacks, whose incomes were controlled by whites, civil rights activism represented too steep a price to pay for objectives that might not succeed in the immediate future. Accordingly, middle-class blacks in the rural and small-town South frequently shunned the movement, though this did not happen in all instances. Many civil rights workers responded by viewing the leadership of the traditional black middle class as a major obstacle to the creation of a strong, cohesive, and united protest movement.[91]

Civil rights workers also encountered reluctance to participate that was generally labeled black "apathy." Apathy, which involved an apparent lack of knowledge about and interest in political affairs, left many blacks wary of involvment and skeptical about positive consequences from participation. It was an understandable (and intended) result of the historical treatment of blacks, but it proved to be extremely difficult for civil rights workers to combat.[92]

The problems that outside volunteers encountered in motivating and mobilizing many local blacks to participate in voter registration precluded immediate success in hard-core resistance areas. Where whites were determined to blunt registration efforts, virtually no gains occurred during the first VEP drive.[93] Even after the Civil Rights Act of 1964 was passed, conservative whites were still winning the battle against black voter registration in the closed societies of the black belt South.

Strenuous white resistance to minority voting rights was not confined to the rural black belt; voter registration drives in the Deep South's largest cities failed to mobilize majorities of the black voting age population.[94] Even dedicated efforts by local grassroots organizations were unable to overcome the opposition of white registration officials or to break through the reluctance, indifference, or antipathy of many blacks. Percentages of registered blacks did rise slowly during the first VEP, but in 1964 no Deep South city had even two-fifths of its eligible blacks on the voter rolls. In the counties that included Birmingham, Montgomery, Mobile, and Jackson, at least three-fourths of the potential black electorate were unregistered.

Different conditions prevailed, however, in the large cities of the Peripheral South as effective local black organizations, foundation money, and a more "permissive" environment combined to produce substantial increases in black voter registration. In 1964 majorities or near majorities of blacks were registered to vote in most of the Peripheral South's metropolitan centers, where extensive black mobilization could not conceivably result in black control of the primary decisionmaking institutions.

Prior to the Voting Rights Act, mobilization of urban blacks varied sharply by subregion. Majorities or near majorities of blacks were enfranchised in most Peripheral South cities, while most blacks in Deep South cities remained unregistered.

After the first VEP, there were even wider differences among states in the scope of black participation. According to the best estimates, in 1964 some 43 percent of eligible black southerners were registered voters, compared with less than 30 percent in 1962.[95] In that presidential election year, majorities of blacks were registered in Tennessee, Florida, and Texas; almost half of eligible blacks were enrolled in Arkansas; and around 45 percent were registered in North Carolina, Virginia, and Georgia. Slightly less than two-fifths of South Carolina's blacks were registered, less than one-third of Louisiana's blacks, less than one-fourth of black Alabamians, and, in Mississippi, only one black in sixteen had qualified to vote. The voting rights issue was dividing the Confederate states and was gradually isolating Mississippi and Alabama as centers of die-hard resistance to the Fifteenth Amendment.

The Civil Rights Act of 1964 outlawed some of the devices used by local registration officials to exclude blacks from registration. But it "did not result in the enfranchisement of any appreciable number of people. This was true primarily because the acts depended upon litigation for enforcement. Litigation, often involving countless appeals and retrials, to some extent merely played into the hands of recalcitrant officials and gave them further opportunity to evade their obligations under the law."[96] Essentially the same discriminatory practices continued in many southern counties; the many political compromises reached in passing the 1964 act had yielded a voting rights title that was demonstrably inadequate in view of the magnitude of the problems it was designed to correct.

It is not surprising, then, that civil rights groups immediately began to press for a new voting rights law, a law strong enough to bypass local registrars. The political strategy that led to the Voting Rights Act of 1965 has been superbly told in Garrow's *Protest at Selma*.[97] In the spring of 1965, King's SCLC and other civil rights organizations converged on Selma, Alabama, to dramatize continuing discrimination in voter registration practices. By now, Garrow argues, SCLC's philosophy of nonviolence was "based not upon a moral commitment to nonviolence or upon a desire to reform the hearts and minds of the likes of Jim Clark [the sheriff of Dallas County, where Selma was located], but upon the pragmatic knowledge that nonviolence, coupled with violent opponents, would best serve the movement in its effort to gain active support from the American populace." Plainly, "King accurately believed that nothing could be more effective in activating support among the national audience for the movement and its goal of equal suffrage than scenes of peaceful demonstrators, seeking their birthright as American citizens, being violently attacked by southern whites."[98]

On March 7, 1965 (Bloody Sunday), there occurred a gruesome physical clash between horse-riding, club-wielding Alabama lawmen and defenseless, nonviolent civil rights demonstrators. Television coverage showed white southerners forcibly repressing blacks who were protesting in support of a widely shared national value—the right to vote. Selma instantaneously activated public opinion in the rest of the nation in favor of the demonstrators, evoked immediate action from Congress to remove the causes for such a protest, and brought President Johnson directly into the voting rights controversy. Johnson spoke forcefully and eloquently to the Congress and the entire nation, urging immediate passage of new legislation that would finally put an end to blatant black disfranchisement.

SCLC's strategy of nonviolent "provocation" succeeded. Under Johnson's leadership Congress quickly passed voting rights legislation that departed significantly from the ineffective enforcement procedures of previous laws. The Voting Rights Act of 1965 completely abolished "tests or devices" as a means of qualifying voters; this meant that southern registrars could no longer arbitrarily exclude blacks through the use of "literacy tests, educational requirements, [or] good character tests." Further, the act set forth criteria by which certain states and counties came under the supervision of federal officials in the administration of their registration procedures as well as in the case of changes in their registration and election laws. In the 1965 law, jurisdictions "which used a literacy test or device for voting, and in which less than half of the voting age residents were registered or voted" in the 1964 presidential election were covered by the Voting Rights Act. These areas were eligible for federal intervention in the form of federal registrars and were required to "pre-clear" registration and election law changes with federal officials.[99] By the above criteria, the Voting Rights Act of 1965 did not apply to all of the eleven southern states. Covered were the entire states of Alabama, Georgia, Louisiana, Mississippi, South Carolina, and Virginia, as well as numerous counties in eastern and piedmont North Carolina. But completely exempt were those southern states with comparatively small black populations—Arkansas, Florida, Tennessee, and Texas.

The rigidity, extremism, and brutality of some Deep South whites had finally provoked the very federal intervention that conservative whites had long feared and struggled to prevent; the Mississippi of Ross Barnett and the Alabama of George Wallace had finally exasperated, embarrassed, and disgusted Americans outside the South and, to a much lesser degree, minorities of white southerners. In 1965 the Deep South's intransigence was rejected by nearly one-third of the entire southern congressional delegation, which had stood in almost total solidarity against the Civil Rights Act of 1964.[100] Initiatives of the civil rights movement, combined with the bloody resistance of Deep South law officers, had exposed all too memorably those negative qualities of some southerners that Cash had identified. Thus revealed, the South of old-fashioned, raw white supremacy found itself effectively isolated among nonsoutherners and repudiated by the President and Congress.

In the face of monolithic white opposition to the *Brown* decision, progress in achieving civil rights had required a return to controversies of the outer color line. The revolt from below protesting segregated public accommodations and discrimination in voting rights finally compelled levels of federal intervention unprecedented in this century. The Civil Rights Act of 1964 and the Voting Rights Act of 1965 established new legal principles that put racially conservative white southerners on the defensive; broadly construed, federal intervention so transformed regional behavior in portions of the outer color line that unreconstructed whites were placed in the reactionary stance of trying to reestablish older patterns of behavior.

six
—

The Limited Leverage
of a Franchised Minority

ONCE southern blacks won the right to vote, the difficulties of achieving political influence and wielding political power became the main controversies of the outer color line. Matthews and Prothro's *Negroes and the New Southern Politics,* the best book on regional politics in the 1960s, was plainly pessimistic about the impact of black voting. "A number of resources can be translated into political power—votes, money, prestige, information, skill, organization, and so on," they observed in 1966. "Southern Negroes have but one political resource in abundance—votes. Southern whites, most of whom still oppose the Negro's political objectives, tend to have the lion's share of *all* political resources, including votes." Accordingly, they warned that "the concrete benefits [to blacks] to be derived from the franchise—under the conditions that prevail in the South—have often been exaggerated."[1] There was every reason to expect that the consequences of expanded black participation, either in terms of securing public policies of direct and tangible benefit to blacks or of electing blacks to public offices, would be far, far less than revolutionary.[2]

The search for power and influence grew all the more difficult as disparities in jobs, income, and schooling became the central substantive problems facing black southerners. Widespread white resistance, North and South, to many changes in the intermediate color line was a formidable barrier. Another obstacle was a radical change for the worse in white perceptions of blacks, beginning with the 1965 Watts riot and accelerating with the "black power" slogan that emerged in 1966. Assessing the dilemmas of modern racial politics, James Q. Wilson identified numerous strains and inconsistencies between "what some Negroes are asking of politics" and "what politics seems capable of providing."[3] Black militancy, intense white opposition, and the issues of the intermediate color line immersed American race relations in a quagmire of insuperable problems and unfeasible solutions.

The Disintegration of the Civil Rights Movement

After 1965 the essential change in the political status of black southerners was that a *disfranchised* minority became a *franchised* minority. What remained unaltered was the minority status of blacks within most political constituencies. "Even the vote itself has limitations as a political resource for southern Negroes," explained Matthews and Prothro in analyzing the "new" southern politics. "They are in a minority almost everywhere in the South."[4] In 1960 blacks accounted for 12 to 42 percent of the population in southern states; twenty years later, in every state except Texas, blacks constituted still smaller proportions (12 to 35 percent) of total populations. Whites continued to hold majorities in nearly all of the region's counties and cities. Population movements since 1960 have created a few southern cities with black majorities but have reduced the number of rural black-majority counties. In 1980 there were black majorities in Atlanta, Birmingham, New Orleans, and Richmond; and blacks made up 40 percent or more of the population in Columbia, Durham, Jackson, Macon, Memphis, Montgomery, Portsmouth, Savannah, Shreveport, and Winston-Salem. In most large southern cities, however, whites decisively outnumbered blacks. Only eighty-six rural counties, four-fifths of them located in the Deep South, retained a majority of blacks.

Minority status has generally limited what blacks can achieve from politics because majorities of each race have commonly possessed very different political objectives and priorities. After federal intervention in 1964 and 1965, sharp differences between the races persisted over controversies in the intermediate color line. Across the South there was extensive white opposition to integration in housing, schools, and jobs and to the Johnson administration's antipoverty program. Only on the question of whether jobs should be integrated did whites in any of the demographic sectors (low-black metropolitan and medium-urban areas) express more support for racial liberalism than for racial conservatism. The predominance of racial conservatives over liberals was consistently greatest in the rural and small-town counties with black populations of 30 percent or more. And although the low-black, large metropolitan counties were the least conservative portions of the South, white conservatives generally outnumbered white liberals in such settings. Given white public opinion, changes concerning the intermediate color line would not be spontaneously initiated by southern white officeholders.

Southern white opposition to changes involving the outer color line had not previously been an insurmountable barrier to national legislation because of the superior political weight and influence of nonsouthern whites. As the specific racial issues at stake changed, the attitudes of nonsouthern whites became less reliable. Desegregating public accommodations and winning the right to vote were primarily regional problems, but changes in the racial patterns of schools, work places, and housing were national in scope. Over the entire nation, the gaps in living conditions between most blacks and most whites were so extensive, the problems so massive, that immediate fundamental changes in the social and economic position of most blacks seemed highly unlikely.[5] Such proposed solutions as metropolitan school desegregation, affirmative action programs in employment, and open housing, as well as large increases in taxes to pay for enhanced services and programs for urban blacks, directly affected whites in many parts of the nation. Substantial numbers of whites outside the South began to see reform of the intermediate color line as unrealistic, undesirable, or too expensive. To civil rights activists who hoped to organize another biracial coalition among northern and western whites to end racial discrimination in the intermediate color line, it was devastating that a majority of the nonsouthern whites with opinions on the subject (55 percent in 1968) opposed federal efforts to integrate schools and jobs.[6] Issues of the intermediate color line were inherently matters of complex justice rather than simple justice; there were few white allies, North or South, who saw the problems and solutions in exactly the same light as did many of the black activists.

White support and sympathy for the cause of civil rights also dropped precipitously in 1965 and 1966 because of startling—yet not truly surprising—revisions in the public image of black Americans. The image of southern blacks as dignified, unprovocative individuals who sought elementary human rights without resort to violence was critically important in generating understanding and approval among nonsouthern whites. When this forceful but controlled style of protest was combined with the eloquent rhetoric of a leader like King, who could communicate the goals of the civil rights movement in terms of values that whites also shared, the movement was able to take the high moral ground. This perception did not last, however. It was shattered in August 1965, when "the most destructive race riot in more than two decades began in Watts, Los Angeles's largest black ghetto. That explosion of bitterness over unmet demands for black dignity and a stop to racial oppression sparked a succession of 'long hot summers' and proclaimed an end to the era of nonviolence." Just as television had previously communicated vivid images of "saintly Negroes" and "savage whites," so now it portrayed angry, frustrated blacks in acts of arson, vandalism, and looting, often fighting police and national guard forces. "By the end of 1968, police reported some fifty thousand arrests and over eight thousand casualties in the nearly three hundred race riots and disturbances since 1965," Sitkoff observed. "An estimated half million blacks had participated in the burning and looting."[7] Most white Americans were thoroughly repelled by what they witnessed.

The changing civil rights agenda, widespread white opposition to significant reforms concerning the intermediate color line, and the new black militancy had profound consequences for the major civil rights organizations. Movement activists found it extremely difficult to devise feasible solutions for the formidable problems of the intermediate color line. "After the Selma campaign," concluded Sitkoff, "the leading organizations of the movement. . . . floundered in their search for new programs. But none developed a viable strategy for solving the complex problems of inadequate housing, dead-end jobs, no jobs, and inferior schooling."[8] As the movement's most prominent spokesman, King was under special strain. Having found a way to attack the outer color line, King and SCLC remained committed to the use of a highly visible leader to attract media coverage of protest campaigns, to nonviolent resistance, and to the creation of biracial national coalitions to pressure the federal government to pass new laws. Application of the old strategy to the new issues, however, left King and his organization exposed and vulnerable. Though nonsouthern white support was essential to implement the strategy, SCLC's advocacy of more controversial civil rights policies invited white defections. Dependence upon good-faith efforts by federal officials to implement existing laws evoked criticism from black civil rights workers, who often found little change in many rural areas and small towns; and King's insistence on nonviolence was increasingly out of step with the growing mood of militance among blacks in the North and South.

Much more militant expressions of protest, similar to the mood of revolt in northern and western ghettos set off by the Watts riot, began to be voiced by a growing number of younger blacks in SNCC and CORE.[9] Acutely aware that the interests of members of the northern biracial coalition were *not* synonymous with the needs of impoverished southern blacks, the militants were disgusted with the compromises needed to maintain biracial coalitions.[10] Disillusionment with whites had previously intensified in 1964 as a result of much greater national concern over the lives of assassinated whites than blacks in Mississippi, and had further accelerated when the Democratic party refused to seat the entire delegation of Mississippi Freedom Democrats and to reject the whole delegation of regular Mississippi Democrats at the party's 1964 presidential nominating convention. Over the next two years many black activists in SNCC and CORE (though certainly not all) came to view white civil rights volunteers as impediments to recruiting and developing indigenous black leadership. In both SNCC and CORE the replacement of top leadership in 1966 (John Lewis gave way to Stokely Carmichael in SNCC, James Farmer to Floyd McKissick in CORE) symbolized a radical change in the organizations' goals and a strong de-emphasis of the utility of biracial coalitions.[11]

Less than a year after the Watts riot, the slogan of "black power" erupted from the black belt South. Differences among the leading civil rights organizations over goals, strategy, and tactics came to a head in the summer of 1966. James Meredith, who had desegregated the University of Mississippi in 1962, attempted to demonstrate that black Mississippians could now register and vote without fear by walking from Memphis to Jackson. For his audacity he was shot and wounded by a white Mississippian before he had gone ten miles. Civil rights leaders rushed to Memphis to continue the walk, but they were deeply divided over its purpose. "The nightly rallies in Mississippi communities became contests in which the three leaders [of SNCC, SCLC, and CORE] competed for the support of black residents," Carson observed. "Carmichael and McKissick stressed the need for greater militancy and condemned the federal government for lack of strong action on behalf of southern blacks. King was on the defensive but made effective pleas for the continued use of nonviolent tactics." King was recognized as the "dominant participant" at the march's beginning, but his "more moderate rhetoric" could neither express nor arouse the "anger, discontent, and disillusionment" of many blacks in the audience.[12]

A member of the SNCC advance party, however, was using an expression that electrified the crowds. "[Willie] Ricks provided Carmichael with a new weapon in his ideological struggle with King when he demonstrated the enormous appeal of the slogan 'Black Power'—a shortened version of 'black power for black people,' a phrase used by SNCC workers in Alabama."[13] Carmichael began to use the slogan in Greenwood, Mississippi. As Carson recounts the episode, Carmichael "announced that blacks had been demanding freedom for six years and had gotten nothing. 'What we gonna start saying now is "black power." ' He shouted the slogan repeatedly; each time the audience shouted back, 'black power!' Willie Ricks leaped to the platform and asked, 'What do you want?' Again and again the audience shouted in unison the slogan that had suddenly gal-vanized their emotions."[14]

"Black power" stirred black audiences, first in the rural South and then across the country, by breaking taboos and releasing deeply felt but long repressed emotions. Adopting the white majority's pejorative label but reversing its emotional attachments was a striking way to remove the sting of felt inferiority;[15] and converting the connotations of "black" from derision to respect engendered positive feelings of self-worth, pride, and value for many blacks. Black power succinctly expressed what blacks in America had long wanted but never attained collectively—some degree of power or control over their own lives.

The black power slogan additionally appealed to many angry blacks because it expressed tremendous hostility toward whites. "SNCC work-ers' satisfaction with the black power slogan," Carson concluded, "was based largely on the extent to which it aroused blacks and disturbed whites." Many blacks sought to explain the meaning of black power, but most of the media attention centered on SNCC's new leader. "Car-michael consistently denied that he was anti-white or that his speeches incited anti-white violence," Carson stressed, "yet these connotations were an unmistakable part of the appeal of the black power rhetoric for many discontented blacks."[16] The racist content of the black power move-ment was especially emphasized by Samuel DuBois Cook, whose im-portant critique, "The Tragic Myth of Black Power," was published in 1966: "It is anti-white. It is separatist and isolationist. Make no mistake about it: Vigorous denials under pressure notwithstanding, the unique dimension of the Black Power myth is racism."[17]

Whites almost universally interpreted the black power slogan as pro-vocative, frightening, antiwhite rhetoric. Among black belt whites the term reactivated their ancient fears of black domination; among whites not immediately faced with potential black majorities, the media's fre-quent depiction of militant blacks intensified white resistance to any further changes in race relations. Short of a symbol or slogan that would explicitly advocate death for members of the majority group, it is hard to imagine a term more corrosive of white support for civil rights goals. "If the Negro had a cosmic enemy who had seized control of the de-partment of strategy and tactics of the civil rights movement," wrote Cook, "he could not invent a more disastrous political methodology."[18] Whites' rejection of the symbolism of black power is vividly apparent in their responses to "black militant" in the SRC-CPS election year studies. Of more than twenty symbols evaluated on a "feeling thermometer" from "cold" (less than 50) to "indifferent" (50) to "warm" (higher than

50), "black militant" elicited the least warmth and the most coldness of all the symbols used in 1976, 1980, and 1984. On the average, only 7 percent of white southerners felt warm toward "black militants," while 76 percent were cold.

The turn to black power by a racial minority inescapably dependent upon white allies reinvigorated the enemies of the civil rights movement and alienated some whites who might otherwise have supported the movement's goals. Many whites in the North and West, of course, would have opposed further racial changes regardless of the protesters' behavior. But other whites who remained sympathetic to the objective of improving the social and economic status of blacks turned away in anger or sadness from the behavior and rhetoric of black militants, whom they viewed as menacing to themselves and counterproductive for the cause of black civil rights.

Not all blacks were comfortable with or supported a political movement organized around the explicit goal of power. After observing that the black power movement could succeed—if at all—in only a small number of counties, Cook argued that the "Black Power philosophy . . . can have no strategy or program where Negroes are in a distinct minority." He contended that "because of political retaliation, it would do havoc with the movement for racial justice and paralyze the civil rights movement. It would gain an inch but lose miles and miles."[19] White financial support for SNCC and CORE, the major organizations identified with black power, all but vanished within months of the dissemination of the black power slogan. SNCC and CORE shifted their activities away from the rural South and eventually left the region.[20] The southern civil rights movement had begun to disintegrate.

Yet if the black power movement failed to transform the social and economic conditions of black Americans in the late 1960s, so too did the biracial civil rights movement. King's own organization turned to efforts to organize the poor, and, in time, King forcefully denounced the Vietnam War. Nonetheless, there were no more successful demonstrations like that at Selma. "The media repeatedly described King's criticism of the war as destructive to his people and his cause, and Lyndon Johnson did all he could covertly to destroy the minister's influence," Sitkoff has commented. "Deserted by the liberals for going too far in his remonstrance, derided by the more vitriolic radicals for not going far enough, King lost power and status. The intensification of black violence and white backlash in 1967 underlined his ineffectuality. King sank into despondency."[21]

In 1968 King again became involved in the controversies of the intermediate color line, chiefly the economic issues affecting poor people.

While organizing the Poor People's March on Washington, King accepted an invitation to participate in a sanitation workers' strike in Memphis, Tennessee, where he was assassinated on April fourth. His tragic death at the age of thirty-nine deprived the civil rights movement of its most honored spokesman, a man who symbolized the "beloved community" and whose dream of racial integration in the South and in the entire nation had pushed and prodded white leaders to adjust the old racial order. Though frequently treated as a prophet unhonored in his own land, his contributions to peaceful racial change and to the amelioration of southern racism were monumental.

King was a personal symbol for millions of American blacks and whites. While millions of Americans mourned his death, many blacks "went into the streets to express their anger. In a unique display of nationwide racial unity, blacks in numerous cities burned and looted white property and battled the police and military forces sent to suppress them. Over forty blacks were killed and more than twenty thousand arrested throughout the nation."[22] King's assassination ended an era. "His death meant the abandonment of the middle ground that had been rapidly disintegrating since the passage of the voting-rights act in 1965," Sitkoff writes. "No other black leader would succeed in convincing large numbers of both races to share his dreams; no other would galvanize the movement to heroic exertions. In countless ways, individual blacks would continue to battle for a better existence, but the grand passion of the organized struggle was moribund."[23]

Black militancy and white reaction dominated the aftermath of the Voting Rights Act. Just as black southerners were beginning to participate in electoral politics in significant numbers, prospects appeared remote for successful biracial coalitions built upon issues of central concern to blacks. In no southern state were there enough white allies to support a winning liberal politics, much less a radical politics. If advocates of black power cogently identified many of the weaknesses of coalition politics for the minority and sensitized many blacks to the probable limitations of electoral politics, the critiques of the black power movement compellingly demonstrated the practical futility of separatism for a minority in political systems where the majority controlled virtually all the political resources. The heart of the problem was that neither approach offered realistic prospects for immediately improving the adverse social and economic conditions affecting many blacks.

Apart from a small number of rural counties and villages where blacks constitute overwhelming majorities of the electorate, and an even smaller number of large cities where blacks constitute near majorities or actual majorities of the voters, the search for political power—real control over the formal institutions of government—has proved illusory. In the modern South the most that blacks can realistically expect is some share in decisionmaking, some degree of influence concerning important outcomes, some representation within state and local political systems that remain firmly under the control of whites.

Political Mobilization of Black Southerners

Although a slight majority of blacks in the Peripheral South had become registered voters before federal intervention, implementation of the Voting Rights Act of 1965, together with the organized efforts of local blacks to get on the rolls, were the main instruments through which majorities of blacks in the Deep South finally came to be registered voters. According to county registration data for the Deep South states (estimates that may well exaggerate black registration rates), by 1968 massive black exclusion from electoral politics (0 to 24 percent registered) persisted in only fourteen counties.[24] Sizable *minorities* of blacks were registered in the piedmont and sections of lowlands South Carolina, much of Alabama outside its black belt, clusters of counties in the eastern and delta portions of Mississippi, and a few parishes in northern Louisiana. Even more radically transformed from past conditions were the counties in which estimated *majorities* of blacks had become registered voters. These settings encompassed about three-fourths of Mississippi's counties, most of the Alabama black belt, southeastern and northwestern Georgia, and parts of the South Carolina low country.

Black political mobilization was hardly uniform across the entire region. A complete understanding of the differences between areas would require detailed knowledge of the counties' socioeconomic structures, the degree to which local white politicians impeded or facilitated black registration, and the extent to which local black groups mounted registration drives after passage of federal voting rights legislation. But certainly, part of the explanation for different rates of black mobilization lay in the enforcement strategy of the federal government.[25]

Congress had been reluctant to allow federal officials to supersede local authorities in registering potential black voters. Voter registration had long been the domain of state and local officials, and only after three previous laws (the Civil Rights Acts of 1957, 1960, and 1964) had failed to stop racial discrimination in voting rights was Congress persuaded to authorize (but not require) the attorney general to send federal registrars into areas where he had reason to believe that discrimination would occur. According to Scher and Button, "Lyndon Johnson, the most enthusiastic supporter of the bill, insisted that target areas be identified and federal examiners be sent to them within days of his signing the original legislation. By his rhetoric and decisive actions he gave clear signals to the South that the federal government was prepared to guarantee blacks the right to vote."[26] Consequently, the Justice Department needed to demonstrate results—actual increases in the numbers of registered blacks— and for this purpose it was necessary to direct some federal registrars into the heart of the black belt. At the same time, most of the politicians and officeholders in the states affected by the Voting Rights Act were white Democrats. The less prominent the federal intervention, the less political damage among whites to the Johnson administration.

Accordingly, Garrow argues that the Justice Department's objective was to "achieve as much voluntary compliance with the act's commands by local registrars as possible in an effort to minimize the number of examiners sent South."[27] The Johnson administration's strategy for securing voluntary adherence was to dispatch federal registrars only where no initial compliance by county registration officials could be expected, while relying upon and working with local voting authorities in all other counties to which the act applied. For almost 90 percent of the affected counties, therefore, the federal government chose to make use of some of the very officials whose previous misconduct had brought about the need for corrective legislation.[28] Direct federal intervention would be confined to counties in which whites continued to hew to the spirit, if not the actual techniques, of the pre–Voting Rights Act South. For all but the most obtuse and obstreperous white registration officials, federal intervention was exceedingly improbable. What was likely under these circumstances was radical variation from one county to another in rates of black political mobilization.

Federal intervention usually had a greater impact on registration than did local black organization, according to data collected by the Voter Education Project. (A second registration effort ran from 1966 to 1970 and sponsored organizations in more than 500 communities.) The highest degree of black registration occurred, of course, when an active grassroots organization was combined with federal intervention, and the least improvement in black mobilization resulted when local blacks were unorganized and local whites continued to act as registrars. In the mixed cases, though, higher registration rates occurred in counties with federal registrars and no organized black registration drive than in counties with organized registration activities but no federal registrars.[29]

What was the extent of federal intervention? Between 1965 and 1980, federal registrars entered no more than 60 of the 533 southern counties covered by the Voting Rights Act of 1965.[30] Forceful and vigorous implementation of the act was primarily limited to portions of three Deep

South states—Mississippi, Alabama, and Louisiana. South Carolina's earlier attitude of blatant resistance had begun to soften prior to the act, and Georgia was largely undisturbed by the Justice Department. Neither Virginia nor the North Carolina counties covered by the law received any federal examiners.[31] Virtually all instances (97 percent) of federal intervention to register blacks, as Mack Jones has pointed out, occurred within the first two years of the act. For all practical purposes, the registration assistance portion of the law came to an end in 1967.[32] The Nixon and Ford administrations sent registrars into only two counties in eight years, and the Carter and Reagan administrations dispatched no federal officials to supersede local registrars. On the basis of the Justice Department's enforcement strategy, it is hard to disagree with Jones's conclusion that "it would be a serious error to assume uncritically that the promise of the VRA has been realized or that it is destined to be."[33]

Although enforcement of the voting rights legislation fell considerably short of the expectations of many civil rights activists, and although the extent of black political mobilization has varied widely, it would be nonsense to conclude that the Voting Rights Act was worth little to blacks. The federal presence was felt in many locales where racist whites had monopolized the political arena for generations, and beyond the areas directly affected, many registrars either had to reform their practices in the direction of simple fairness or risk federal intervention.[34] The Voting Rights Act was the grand turning point in modern times for the reentry of blacks into southern politics. By 1966 2.6 million blacks were registered, about 52 percent of the black voting age population. According to data issued by the Voter Education Project, black registration subsequent to the Voting Rights Act has never dropped below 50 percent.[35]

The political mobilization of black southerners for selected years between 1940 and 1984 is summarized in table 6.1. Under the white primary system (about 1940), blacks were so uniformly excluded that subregional differences were of no consequence. Abolition of the white primary in 1944 brought a growing minority of blacks to the polls, and the Peripheral South began to emerge as a slightly less hostile environment for black registration than the Deep South. By 1964 a slim majority of blacks in the Peripheral South were registered voters, while less than a third of eligible blacks were enfranchised in the heartland of the old Confederacy. By the 1968 presidential election majorities of blacks were registered in every southern state. In recent years the convenient subregional distinction has lost its usefulness in isolating different levels of black political mobilization. In fact, estimates for 1984 show black registration highest in Alabama (69 percent) and Mississippi (68 percent), formerly the states with the fiercest resistance to black voting rights. In the 1980s roughly

Table 6.1.   The political mobilization of southern blacks, 1940–1984[a]

Year	South	Peripheral South	Deep South	Difference between Peripheral South and Deep South
1940	3	5	1	+4
1947	12	17	8	+9
1956	25	29	21	+8
1964	43	52	30	+22
1966	52	58	46	+12
1968	62	67	57	+10
1976	63	62	64	-2
1984	59	58	59	-1

Sources: For all data prior to 1976, various tables in David J. Garrow, *Protest at Selma* (New Haven: Yale University Press, 1978); for 1976 and 1984, appropriate volumes of the *U.S. Statistical Abstract.*

a. Each entry is the percentage of eligible blacks who were estimated to be registered to vote.

three-fifths of adult blacks were registered to vote. After long and costly struggles, blacks had become permanent participants in the new southern politics.

Though southern blacks remain incompletely mobilized, the traditional structure of black voter registration within southern states has been substantially altered. Before the Voting Rights Act took effect, black registration rates were usually highest in areas where blacks composed small percentages of the total population. County registration data by race are not available for all southern states. But 1976 figures acquired from the four states in which these data are officially collected (Louisiana, South Carolina, Florida, and North Carolina) indicate the reversal of the pattern established by Matthews and Prothro. In the counties with substantial black populations, the registration rates of eligible blacks were roughly equal to or greater than black registration rates in counties with small black populations.[36]

Changes in levels of black registration were also evident in the region's major cities.[37] Two years after the Voting Rights Act was implemented, subregional differences in black registration rates had largely disappeared; blacks were about as apt to be registered in Deep South as in Peripheral South big cities. Of even more practical importance, majorities of the black voting age population were registered in virtually all of the large metropolitian counties for which 1967 estimates are available. Three of the Deep South cities with the worst reputations for equitable treatment of potential black voters—Birmingham, Jackson, and Montgomery—received federal registrars, and the most spectacular improvement occurred in Jackson, where the proportion of registered black voters jumped from 16 percent in 1964 to 67 percent three years later.

Electoral politics in the urban South since the Voting Rights Act has received inadequate attention, and the paucity of readily available data makes generalization hazardous. Richard Murray and Arnold Vedlitz, who have analyzed registration and voting patterns in five of the region's biggest cities (Houston, Dallas, Memphis, New Orleans, and Atlanta) over the period 1960-1977, report steady increases in black registration rates.[38] Average black registration in these cities was only 40 percent of eligible blacks in 1960. By 1964 59 percent of blacks were enrolled, and by 1974 67 percent of blacks were registered voters, a registration rate only one percentage point below that of whites. In view of the lower socioeconomic status of black southerners, it is unlikely that the more or less spontaneous actions of unorganized individuals have been responsible for black registration rates that are fairly comparable to those of whites. Murray and Vedlitz suggest that "blacks are better organized in these communities than are whites, and this superior organization stimulates higher levels of registration and voting among blacks than we would expect given the relative socioeconomic deprivation of the group."[39] Should their findings hold for the South's largest cities generally, then it would seem that the combination of black grassroots organization and federal intervention have demolished the tremendous historical difference between the races in voter registration.

The New Biracial Electorate

Massive registration and voting by blacks is one of the most visible signs of the new southern politics. Yet it is impossible to judge the significance of greater black participation without simultaneously considering the behavior of the white majority.[40] It is certainly important that during the last quarter-century blacks increased from 11 percent of the southern electorate to 17 percent (see table 6.2), an improvement that has helped to eliminate much old-fashioned racism.[41] At the same time, it is crucial to keep in mind that whites still form an overwhelming majority—83 percent in 1984—of the region's registered voters.

Far more whites than blacks entered the southern electorate as new voters during the two decades from 1960 to 1980.[42] Although southern electorates expanded remarkably between 1960 and 1970, there were no states in which increased participation could be attributed primarily to new black registrants. During the 1960s, the period of the strongest

Table 6.2. The changing size of the black vote: percentage of blacks among registered voters in 1960 and 1984, by state, subregion, and region

	Percentage of blacks among registered voters	
Political unit^a	1960	1984
South Carolina	11	28
Mississippi	4	26
Louisiana	14	25
Alabama	7	22
Georgia	15	22
North Carolina	10	19
Virginia	10	17
Tennessee	12	14
Arkansas	12	14
Florida	9	11
Texas	10	11
Deep South	11	24
Peripheral South	10	15
South	11	17

Sources: U.S. Bureau of the Census, *Statistical Abstract of the United States: 1982–83* (Washington, D.C.: Government Printing Office, 1982), p. 488; *Statistical Abstract of the United States: 1985* (Washington, D.C.: Government Printing Office, 1984), p. 253.

a. States are ranked (highest to lowest) according to the estimated percentage of blacks among registered voters in 1984.

advance in black voter registration, three new whites were enrolled in the Deep South for every two new blacks. In the Peripheral South, where the much larger white populations and white population growth made it more difficult for blacks to achieve sizable proportions of new registrations, there were approximately four new white voters for each new black registrant. Disproportionate white strength was even more apparent in the following decade. With the decline of the civil rights movement and the growing white in-migration, whites accounted for 90 percent of the South's new registrants between 1970 and 1980.

It is difficult to say how much of this huge increase in white registration can be attributed to racism. We suspect that a good deal of racist countermobilization did occur in the Deep South states and in the black belt portions of the Peripheral South.[43] *Most* of the gains in white registration, however, were probably due to other factors. Rising educational levels, the shift toward a more middle-class society, and greater politicization of working-class white women surely motivated millions of white southerners to participate.[44] Moreover, the revival of party competition in presidential, senatorial, and gubernatorial elections gave southern whites additional incentives to join the electorate. Whatever their motivations, the practical consequence is that blacks are a smaller proportion of the electorate than they would have been had not larger numbers of whites concurrently decided to register.

Because blacks now regularly constitute respectable minorities of the total vote in southern general elections, it is interesting to consider the electoral strategies that either write off (concede?) the votes of black southerners or depend fundamentally upon a substantial and unified black vote.[45] The underlying racial structure in most closely contested general elections may be understood by examining the relationships between the size of the black vote, the cohesiveness of the black vote, and the cohesiveness of the white vote. The *size* of the black vote means the percentage of all voters who are black in a particular election, and the *cohesiveness* of the black (or white) vote refers to the percentage of the total black (or white) vote won by a specified party. We begin with estimates of the size and cohesiveness of the black vote and then calculate the cohesiveness of the white vote, rather than vice versa, because blacks have voted with substantially more cohesion than have whites.

The cohesiveness of the white vote needed by a given party to win a majority of the votes cast in a two-candidate election (defined for our purposes as 50.1 percent of the total vote) is a function of the size and cohesiveness of the black vote. Thus

$$wx = 50.1 - b_{p1}$$

where b is the size of the black vote (percentage of blacks among all voters); p_1 is the cohesiveness of the black vote for party 1 (percentage of total black vote won by party 1); 50.1 is the percentage of the total vote cast required for a majority; w is the size of the white vote ($100 - b$); and x is the cohesiveness of the white vote required by party 1 to win 50.1 percent of the total vote, given the size and cohesiveness of the black vote (percentage of all white votes needed by party 1 for victory).

To illustrate the equation, assume that blacks are expected to contribute 20 percent of the total vote in an election and that party 1 expects to win 90 percent of that total black vote. Then, solving for x, we get

$$80x = 50.1 - 20(.90)$$
$$80x = 50.1 - 18.0$$
$$80x = 32.1$$
$$x = 40.1$$

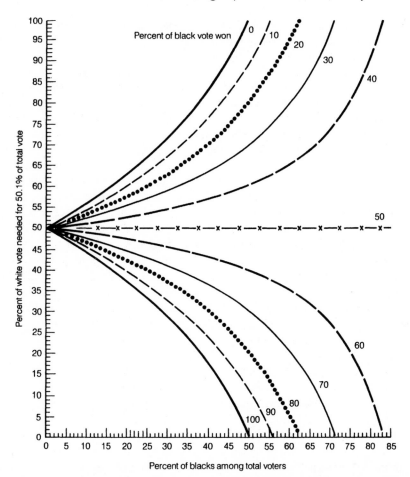

Figure 6.1. Forming a majority coalition: relationships between the size of the black vote, the cohesiveness of the black vote, and the cohesiveness of the white vote required by a given candidate to win 50.1% of the total vote.

Hence for the hypothesized size and cohesiveness of the black vote, party 1 must attract at least 40.1 percent of the total white vote in order to win 50.1 percent of the total vote cast in the election.

The percentage of the white vote that must be won to obtain a majority of the total vote, given particular assumptions concerning the size and cohesiveness of the black vote, can be readily specified (figure 6.1). The figure displays relationships between the size of the black vote (varying from zero to 85 percent along the horizontal axis), selected degrees of black cohesiveness (depicted by the curves representing the percentage of the black vote won), and the percentage of the white vote (ranging from zero to 100 percent along the vertical axis) required to produce an electoral majority for each combination of black size and cohesiveness.

The following hypothetical example will illustrate the use of the figure. Assume that blacks will cast 15 percent of the vote in a forthcoming election and that candidate Smith will receive no more than 10 percent of the entire black vote. Under these conditions, what minimum percentage of the total white vote must Smith win in order to secure a majority of the total vote? The answer to that strategic question may be found by locating the intersection of the two "givens"—the point on the chart where the estimated size of the black vote (15 percent on the horizontal axis) meets the curve indicating black cohesiveness of 10 percent—and reading across to the vertical axis. As the reader may quickly determine, the answer is 57 percent of the white vote. By experimenting with best-case and worst-case assumptions, a range for the needed white vote can be established and used as a benchmark to evaluate poll results, plan campaign strategy, and compare rival candidacies. The chart reveals the racial structure of majority coalitions for a multitude of conceivable electoral settings and can be used to analyze precincts, cities, counties, and congressional districts as well as the region, subregions, and states.

The information contained in table 6.2 and figure 6.1 suggests that the mobilization of blacks has partially altered political outcomes in the region. In most statewide elections, the white majority makes up 75 to 90 percent of all voters. The black minority is sizable enough to be taken seriously but insufficiently large to become the most important or most crucial target of campaign strategy. Several important consequences emerge from the strategic situation confronting blacks in the South: the cessation of explicit, old-fashioned racism in virtually all statewide campaigns; the long odds against biracial coalitions based on liberal agendas; the emergence of distinctive electoral coalitions and styles of campaigning on the part of Democrats and Republicans; and the rise of the Peripheral South as a superior site for Republican victories in state contests.

"Negroes, when they vote, can cause a startling change in the style, if not the substance, of southern politics," Wilson stated in the mid-1960s. "Segregationists will have to choose between abandoning race-baiting as a political tactic or getting out of politics."[46] This prediction has surely come to pass. Among southern politicians of almost all ideological persuasions the central tendency is to depict themselves as representatives of "all the people." Old-style racism has not been completely eliminated, but the few remaining politicians who are still able to win elections by using flagrantly racist appeals as part of their repertoire are campaigning the hard way.[47] They certainly do not serve as role models for the rising generation of southern politicians.

And yet the political mobilization of southern blacks has not produced the triumph of liberalism. Wilson was essentially correct when he contended that, "while there is little doubt that Negro voters will continue to exert a liberalizing influence on American politics, the possibility of a stable, organized liberal—to say nothing of radical—coalition is, I believe, slight."[48] In the years since the Voting Rights Act, few serious southern politicians have sought statewide office by campaigning forthrightly on those issues that are of central concern to most blacks. There is little mystery about the absence of full-fledged liberals, for the most likely outcome of this style of campaigning would be the rapid mobilization of a huge white majority in opposition. A successful biracial coalition based on liberal or radical issues presupposes a white electorate with very different experiences, concerns, values, and expectations from those documented in this book.

Because most black votes go to Democrats, the advent of black voting has contributed to slightly different campaign styles on the part of Democratic and Republican candidates for public office. For Democrats the essential task is to combine virtually all of the black vote with enough of the white vote to produce a majority in the total electorate. The need for black votes inescapably pulls Democratic candidates toward some progressive themes, but in most instances it has been possible for Democratic candidates in general elections to win votes from blacks without running exclusively "liberal" campaigns. Democratic candidates no longer need to win a majority among white voters, but they always need a sizable minority of the white vote. Successful Democrats have usually acquired that substantial white minority by emphasizing some mixture of progressive and conservative themes. Republican candidates, on the contrary, typically require landslide white majorities since they cannot depend upon any sizable contribution from blacks. The common Republican response has been to identify oneself strongly as a conservative, with the range of winning styles varying between "practical" conservatives and "extreme" or "ideological" conservatives.

Finally, the new biracial electorate has important implications for subregional differences in partisan politics. A basic determinant of Republican or Democratic majority coalitions is the proportion of blacks among actual voters. With blacks constituting almost one-fourth of the Deep South electorate compared with roughly one-seventh of the Peripheral South electorate, solid black support for Democratic candidates means that smaller white majorities are required in the Deep South for

Democratic victories. If Deep South Democrats are supported by 90-95 percent of blacks (as is frequently the case), only 35-40 percent of the white vote is needed to generate a Democratic majority. In the Peripheral South, similarly cohesive black support must be united with some 40-45 percent of the white vote in order for Democrats to prevail.

The inability of Republican candidates to secure more than token black support has frequently impeded their success in the Deep South. By contrast, the smaller proportion of black voters in the Peripheral South has made that subregion more conducive to Republicanism. Peripheral South Republicans need smaller majorities of the white vote (roughly 57-59 percent) than do Deep South Republicans (approximately 63-65 percent) in order to prevail. And since the Peripheral South also has a larger white middle class and a stronger heritage of grassroots Republicanism, its Republican nominees are less dependent upon short-term factors (gifted campaigners, Democratic blunders, advantageous issues) to create ad hoc Republican majorities.

Persistence of White Power after 1965

Almost all of the South's elected public officials were whites when the Voting Rights Act was passed, and two decades later the vast majority of the region's officeholders remain members of the majority racial group. Nevertheless, the South now offers numerous examples of successful black politicians, such as Lt. Gov. Douglas Wilder of Virginia and Atlanta Mayor Andrew Young. "The gains in black registration and voting have resulted in a substantial increase in black Southerners elected to office," conclude Scher and Button. "Thus far, this is perhaps the most striking outcome of increased black political participation in the South."[49] There has indeed been a sizable increase in the absolute number of black elected officials, from 72 in 1965 to 2,601 in 1982.[50] According to Jones, "the symbolic importance of BEOs [Black Elected Officials] can hardly be overemphasized, particularly in the rural South. The presence of Blacks in positions of responsibility in communities where only a decade ago Blacks were treated with utter contempt and disrespect may have far reaching implications."[51]

Nevertheless, Jones also emphasizes that "the [Voting Rights Act] has been met with studied opposition by southern whites;"[52] and there is good reason to believe that the advent of black officeholding is associated with less change than immediately meets the eye. Chandler Davidson argues that "the history of racial minorities in America, and in [the South and Southwest] in particular, is a troubling reminder of the skill, the resourcefulness, the fierce tenacity, and, above all, the patience of privileged groups in fighting to uphold the social and political structures that guarantee their dominance."[53] Not all white officeholders were opposed to the civil rights movement (some were progressive, others even indifferent); yet it would be naive to assume that many whites purposely tried to encourage or establish constituencies from which blacks could win offices in state and local government. In the words of a veteran civil rights attorney, the most realistic assumption is that whites who desired to minimize the impact of blacks on electoral politics revised their objectives from "preventing blacks from voting to preventing blacks from winning or deciding elections."[54]

After all, southern whites had been in a similar situation almost a century earlier, when the federal government established new election laws permitting black males to vote. Kousser concludes that "Reconstruction and post-Reconstruction southern Democrats used at least sixteen different techniques to hamper black political power without actually denying the franchise to sufficient numbers of voters to invite a strengthening of federal intervention." Specific practices and techniques included gerrymandering, at-large elections, white primaries, registration requirements, poll taxes, secret ballots, multiple-box laws, petty crimes provisions, annexation, and de-annexation. These devices had proven highly efficient in limiting "officeholding by blacks or black-influenced white officeholders."[55]

Similar techniques of minority vote dilution appear to have been used in the Second Reconstruction.[56] The work *Minority Vote Dilution* contains numerous examples of such practices throughout the region. Steven F. Lawson, too, observes that "while most southern jurisdictions complied with the letter of the 1965 law, many attempted to avoid its spirit by grafting sophisticated forms of bias onto existing electoral institutions." And Scher and Button argue that "the willingness of local officials in some areas to try to dilute the black vote through annexation, at-large elections, and redistricting (even gerrymandering) has become a problem."[57]

When blacks entered southern political systems as voters and potential elected officials, very few jurisdictions existed in which they could realistically challenge whites for control of key governing bodies. Even in these areas dilutive techniques may have assisted white elites in remaining in power despite being outnumbered by blacks. In many other settings blacks might realistically seek a minority presence in such decisionmaking forums as state legislatures, county and city councils, and school boards. "Many of the nineteenth century dilutive devices had no impact or only a marginal impact on blacks' ability to vote per se," Kousser concludes, "but they very often made the difference between winning and losing—

that is to say, between having some political influence and little or none."[58] This distinction strikes us as aptly specifying the probable effects of contemporary dilution on black representation in areas where blacks are a sizable minority of the population.

Usually constituting an electoral minority, always facing the possibility of a cohesive white vote if whites perceive their vital economic, social, or racial interests to be at stake, and at times confronting election laws and procedures that may have the effect of diluting their voting strength, blacks have been—and will remain—highly constrained in their possible impact upon southern politics.

No black candidate has ever been elected governor of a southern state. Only a few black politicians have attempted gubernatorial campaigns, and none has come close to winning a Democratic primary, much less a general election. To date, Wilder's election to the lieutenant governor's office in Virginia is the sole example of a black politician winning a state executive office in the South, a feat that surprised many observers. As a campaigner, Wilder visited numerous localities, stressed his experience in state government, and generally followed the example of successful white Democrats in blending progressive and conservative themes. His success has expanded the boundaries of what is now possible for black candidates in the South, though whites will still possess strong advantages in nearly all statewide contests in the foreseeable future.

In statewide elections black potential influence usually ranges from sharing in the victory of a *white* candidate to no influence at all. The actual exercise of political influence by the minority group is by no means assured, for it depends upon the goals, turnout, and cohesion of both blacks and whites.[59] Successful influence requires blacks to be united behind a chosen white campaigner and whites to be sufficiently divided in their candidate preferences. Even if a biracial coalition backs a successful office seeker, blacks can do little more than share the advantages of victory with their white allies. The issue agenda and policy priorities of winning white politicians are unlikely to coincide with those advocated by many blacks, and for this reason black politicians frequently complain that they are taken for granted by the whites whom they helped elect. In more than a few statewide races, of course, coalitions of blacks and a minority of whites are too small to win. When landslide majorities of whites opt for the more conservative candidate, blacks are cut off from any practical influence on the officeholder.

State legislatures are the most feasible point of entry into southern state governments for black elected officials. If blacks were represented in proportion to their share of the voting age population, all southern legislatures would have substantial minority blocs. Black representation has grown in recent years, and in 1982 (before the elections) there were 127 black state legislators in the South.[60] But since blacks were 20 percent of the 1980 southern population, yet only 7 percent of the region's legislators, they remained poorly represented in the legislative process. Underrepresentation was especially acute in state senates, where blacks accounted for less than 4 percent of the members, and was only slightly less severe in the lower houses (8 percent).

Among southern lower houses two distinct tendencies were apparent in 1982. In seven states (the Deep South states, Texas, and Tennessee), all of which used single-member districts in metropolitan counties, blacks accounted for 8 to 12 percent of the lower chamber. In the remaining four Peripheral South states, all of which then used multiple-member at-large districts in metropolitan areas, blacks made up no more than 2 to 4 percent of the lower houses. With respect to southern state senates, only Tennessee and Alabama had sizable black delegations; elsewhere, blacks composed 5 percent or less of the upper chambers and were completely unrepresented in Florida, South Carolina, and Texas.

Thomas R. Dye had predicted in 1971 that "for the foreseeable future, it is very likely that all, or nearly all, of the nation's black state legislators will come from majority black constituencies."[61] To move beyond token representation, blacks have had to challenge legislative reapportionment plans as unconstitutional dilutions of the black vote and have had to ask federal judges to create single-member constituencies, some of which would have black majorities. Such a legal attack increased the number of black state representatives in Texas, and blacks have successfully pursued the legal route in Alabama, Louisiana, Mississippi, North Carolina, South Carolina, and Virginia.[62] Most of the early gains were concentrated in metropolitan areas, but blacks have begun to make inroads among rural districts in Mississippi, South Carolina, and North Carolina.

Despite these advances, blacks remain severely underrepresented in southern state legislatures. In some states, no matter how district lines are drawn, because many blacks reside in rural and small-town counties where whites are in the majority, black representation will remain well below the minority's share of the voting age population.[63] Nearly twenty years after the Voting Rights Act, scarce numbers remain the central political problem of black legislators. The quest for enhanced black access to the legislative process inevitably places the federal judiciary in the political thicket of determining what constitutes equitable legislative districts. If this problem is resolved in favor of strengthening black representation, state legislative politics in the future could move to more

substantive conflicts between whites and blacks, a search by black legislators for white allies could begin in earnest, and a politics that more
accurately reflects the region's racial diversity could appear.

State senator and state representative are among the most important
elective positions won by blacks, but few of the South's black elected
officials are state legislators. Most of the 2,601 black officials in 1982
held seats on municipal governing bodies, school boards, and county
commissions, where they were unlikely to have sufficient political strength
to control or decisively influence policymaking. "In general, BEO's are
found either as isolated figures constituting a small minority (most often
a minority of one) on the governing boards of populous cities or counties,
or as a majority on the governing body of a few of the more than five
hundred preponderantly black and impoverished counties and villages
across the region," Jones concludes. "Even in cities and counties which
have preponderantly black populations, Blacks have not converted their
numbers into commensurate representation."[64]

Jones's generalizations are supported by our analysis of black officeholding across the South in 1982. Although the total number of black
elected officials seems impressive, 2,601 officials spread over the region's
1,147 counties and parishes amounts to an average of only 2.3 black
officials per county. When 223 counties are removed—those in which
blacks constituted less than 3 percent of the 1980 population—the average rises slightly to 2.8 officials per county. Using the *National Roster
of Black Elected Officials* (volume XII, 1982), we have counted the
number of black elected officials for every county and parish. For most
jurisdictions there were far greater continuities with the tradition of white
officeholding than there were revolutionary departures.

Putting aside jurisdictions in which blacks made up less than 3 percent
of the population, in the early 1980s there were no black elected officials
in nearly half (47 percent) of the region's counties, and only one to four
officials in another third of the counties. Blacks accounted for five or
more public officials in merely one-fifth of the southern counties. Substantial officeholding by blacks (defined here as ten or more elected officials) occurred in only 8 percent of the South's counties, but these 77
counties contained nearly half (48 percent) of all black elected officials
in the entire region. The paucity of black officeholding is shown geographically in figure 6.2. Except for Louisiana and South Carolina, where
parishes or counties with at least five black officials were fairly common,
grassroots politics in each of the southern states continued to be dominated by whites.

Black belt rural counties and large metropolitan counties accounted
for two-thirds of the localities with ten or more black elected officials in

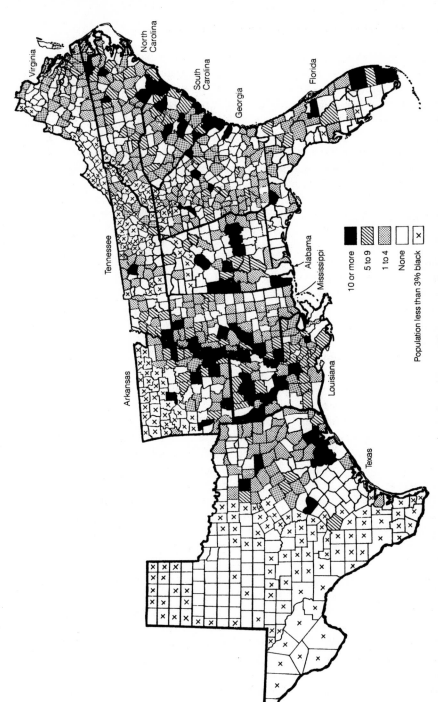

Figure 6.2. The paucity of black power: number of black elected officials in the South in 1982. Source: Compiled from Joint Center for Political Studies, *National Roster of Black Elected Officials*, vol. XII (Washington, D.C.: JCPS, 1982).

1982. The Carolina lowlands, the Alabama black belt, and the delta counties of Mississippi, Arkansas, and Louisiana have provided some settings in which blacks have successfully pursued political office. Yet great diversity in political achievement exists among the majority black rural counties. The historic pattern of total exclusion is waning (it appeared in only 10 percent of the majority black counties), but in another 34 percent of these counties, blacks constituted no more than a handful of local officials. Blacks held ten or more elected positions in slightly less than a third of the majority black rural counties. Only in a minute number of rural counties (such as Greene and Lowndes in Alabama, Hancock in Georgia), where blacks outnumber whites more than two to one, has it been possible for blacks to win majorities on county governing boards.

Blacks have won appreciable numbers of offices in some major cities. Substantial officeholding (at least ten offices) was concentrated in cities where blacks made up 40 percent or more of the population and, where blacks were less than 40 percent of the population, in the larger cities. Blacks did best, of course, in the few cities in which they held actual population majorities. Each of the South's four majority black cities had a black mayor in the early 1980s—Young in Atlanta, Richard Arrington in Birmingham, Ernest Morial in New Orleans, and Roy West in Richmond. Black officeholders thrived especially in the counties containing Atlanta and Birmingham. There were forty-four black elected officials in Fulton County, Georgia, and forty-five in Jefferson County, Alabama. Orleans Parish had nineteen black officials, compared with nine in Richmond, Virginia. Blacks also held numerous elected offices in seven of the nine counties with central cities in the 40-49 percent black range, and it is probably from this group of cities—Savannah, Memphis, Jackson, Durham, Macon, Portsmouth, Shreveport, Winston-Salem, and Columbia—that blacks will achieve their greatest future successes in southern city politics. The stakes of local control are very high, involving the possible transfer of formal political power from one race to the other. Though complete racial polarization is not inevitable, a close examination of similar transitions in other cities would probably show numerous examples of tense, conflictual politics, frequently interracial in character, over a wide range of issues.[65]

In most urban settings the practical thrust of black politics is not directed toward the realization of political control. The goals of black politicians are usually more equitable minority representation in decisionmaking bodies (wards and single-member districts rather than at-large elections), as well as a fair share of city services and programs. In metropolitan areas where whites are unquestionably in the majority, black politicians have been elected to office more frequently in the larger than in the smaller cities. A few southern cities with heavy white majorities (Raleigh, Charlotte, Little Rock, and Roanoke) have occasionally elected black mayors. For black politicians to succeed in such environments, it is obviously necessary for them to attract substantial white support.

Much media attention is properly devoted to the novel and atypical event, such as the election of a black mayor. Interesting and important as this phenomenon is, at least equal attention should be given to the continuity of the South's urban politics. Whites decisively outnumber blacks in most cities, and most elected politicians in these settings will be white. As in the rural South, the central tendency of metropolitan politics is steady white control of key offices.

Visible and irreversible changes have occurred in the South's outer color line since the mid-1960s. Majorities of blacks are now registered to vote, and this elementary right of citizenship is no longer controversial among most white southerners. Although the number of black elected officials continues to grow, the prominence of some black officeholders will not alter the more typical outcome of white governance. The adjustments that white southerners have been compelled to make concerning the outer color line have not seriously threatened—and will not seriously threaten in the future—white control of all state and most local political institutions. As in the past, the relevant political question is not whether whites or blacks will occupy most of the vital decisionmaking arenas in state government, but *which* whites will rule.

seven

Confronting
the Intermediate
Color Line

WITH PUBLIC accommodations desegregated and voting rights secured, the civil rights movement shifted its attention to the more enduring and intractable problems of economic subordination and opportunity restriction, the formidable barriers of the intermediate color line. Blacks and whites were often forced to address the dilemmas of opening schools, jobs, and housing to members of a racial minority against whom systematic discrimination had been practiced for more than three centuries. Desegregation of public education, the institution most immediately related to the promotion of upward social mobility, perhaps held the greatest promise of future gains; but in few southern settings was school desegregation achieved without unrest, frustration, and turmoil. Breaking the color line in public and private employment was similarly controversial, especially when conducted under the mandate of preferential treatment programs, because it often placed whites and blacks in direct competition for a scarce number of desirable jobs. And in the background of both school and work-place desegregation lay the problem of massive black poverty. With only limited political leverage, however, southern blacks have had mixed and uneven success in altering the intermediate color line. Much of the politics of race in the modern South revolves around the efforts of blacks to secure substantive gains in schooling, jobs, and income.

Public School Desegregation

Few conflicts have more convulsed southern political systems and more insistently engaged the attention and emotions of youths and adults alike than the federal government's efforts to desegregate public schools. The struggle to reform this part of the intermediate color line—so critical to the realization of equality of opportunity—has passed through three phases or stages, each marked by the imposition of increasingly rigorous standards of compliance with the national government's goal of biracial schools.[1]

From 1955 through 1964, a period of massive white resistance and avoidance, southern school desegregation was guided by the Supreme Court's vague enforcement standard of "all deliberate speed" and by an eviscerating lower court ruling in which *Brown* was interpreted to require not the actual integration of public schools but merely the abolition of legally required segregation.[2] Implementation of the *Brown* decision rested with federal district judges, most of whom were native southerners who vehemently disagreed with the decision they were charged to enforce.[3] Responsibility for abolishing legal segregation resided in local school boards, which were composed almost entirely of white segregationists. In view of the strategic placement of regional elites strenuously opposed to racial change, prospects for significant desegregation were not bright.

All southern states resisted school desegregation, and in the late 1950s, particularly after the 1957 Little Rock school desegregation crisis in which federal troops were dispatched to uphold a federal court order, opposition to racial change became a central theme in southern politics. Some states with comparatively few blacks adopted local option plans, and a few school districts with fractional black populations (mainly in West Texas and Tennessee) did desegregate. Desegregation took place as well in selected metropolitan areas, usually involving token numbers of blacks attending otherwise all-white schools. The most publicized responses to the *Brown* decision, however, occurred in the Deep South and Virginia, where new state laws were passed that required public schools to be closed if blacks and whites were intermingled.

When it eventually became apparent (as in Norfolk, Virginia, where schools were shut for an entire year) that the costs of total defiance were incredibly high, many whites came to view token school desegregation as preferable to no public schools. Creative administration of public placement plans, which used criteria other than race to place all white students in "white" schools and practically all black students in "black" schools, limited desegregation to tiny numbers of black students. Efforts by local school boards to subvert the spirit of the original *Brown* decision were consistent with the early appellate interpretation, never explicitly rejected by the Supreme Court, that compliance did not necessarily require actual desegregation. Rarely prodded by federal district judges, most local school officials continued to operate school systems that were completely distinct by race a decade after *Brown II* had been issued.

Almost 98 percent of the region's black students still attended all-black schools in 1964-65. If integrationists achieved scattered symbolic victories in the first phase of school desegregation, successful opposition was the characteristic southern response.

In the second phase, extending roughly from 1965 to 1968, school desegregation was spurred by administrative intervention. Limited compliance began when Congress finally passed legislation authorizing the Department of Health, Education, and Welfare (HEW) to penalize school districts that refused to desegregate and reward districts that did comply.[4] Title VI of the Civil Rights Act of 1964 required the withholding of federal funds from racially segregated state and local programs. Passage of the Elementary and Secondary Education Act of 1965 greatly encouraged racial change in public education, for the new federal grants were contingent upon a demonstration of some desegregation. HEW, acting under congressional authority, began to devise guidelines for school desegregation that southern school districts had to meet in order to qualify for federal aid to education. Postponing implementation in the highly resistant districts with black majorities until after the 1968 presidential election, HEW concentrated its enforcement activities on the theoretically "easier" districts with white majorities. In 1965-66 some 6 percent of the South's black students attended public schools with whites, a figure that climbed to 16 percent in the next school year.

The Solid South pattern of no appreciable desegregation in 1956-57 gave way in 1966-67 to a situation in which the proportion of blacks attending school with some whites was inversely related to the size of the black population. There were six times as many blacks in desegregated schools in the Peripheral South (24 percent) as there were in the Deep South (4 percent). Though the increased desegregation was hardly impressive compared with the proportion of blacks remaining in segregated schools, it represented the start of widespread compliance with the *Brown* decision. When the threat of federal pressure was balanced by the prospect of federal dollars, a "quiet social revolution [occurred] in the schools of the South."[5]

In 1968-69 an era commenced of more rigorous judicial intervention, sometimes reinforced by more coercive administrative sanctions. In this third stage of school desegregation the Supreme Court finally repudiated "all deliberate speed," tightened its standards for compliance, and ordered the immediate desegregation of the region's laggard school districts.[6] After first opposing the ruling, the Nixon administration initiated behind-the-scenes efforts to foster compliance by local school officials. During this stage of enforcement schools in every southern state were substantially desegregated.[7] By 1976-77, nearly four out of every five black students in the South were attending public schools in which whites constituted at least 10 percent—and usually a much higher proportion—of the student body. When measured against its history of totally segregated schools, the South's uneasy transition to biracial elementary and secondary schools was a most impressive social change. It is widely appreciated that by 1970 the South exceeded the North and the West in the percentage of black students attending desegregated schools. In the mid-1980s this area of the color line is more exclusionary outside the South than within it.[8]

Despite these strides toward desegregated schools, remnants of the separatist order endure. In 1976-77 slightly more than one-fifth of the South's black students still attended virtually or entirely all-black schools.[9] In order to show where schools have been desegregated and where segregated schools still exist, we have compared the scope of school desegregation for the current generation of young black southerners across different demographic settings.

Our data have been extracted from the massive HEW document, *Directory of Elementary and Secondary School Districts,* which reports the racial composition of every school district in the nation for the 1976-77 school year.[10] Because we needed to match school boundaries with counties or parishes, we aggregated data from the local districts in those many instances where countywide school districts did not exist. School desegregation was measured by calculating for each county or parish the percentage of black students who were enrolled in schools where whites formed at least one-tenth of the total student population. This criterion was chosen because we wanted to separate areas where blacks were still truly isolated from places in which there was a minimal degree of interracial contact. It should be emphasized that the requirement of a white student population of 10 percent represents a minimum threshold for whites; in most cases, the proportion of whites in each school is much higher.[11]

Setting aside counties with black populations of 1 percent or less, we found that almost all black students were attending desegregated schools in 846 (84 percent) of the region's remaining 1,009 counties. In 69 counties (7 percent) fewer than all blacks but at least substantial majorities were in desegregated schools, and in another 46 counties (5 percent) no more than sizable minorities of blacks remained isolated from whites. Only in 48 counties (5 percent) were majorities of black students still attending essentially all-black schools. To compare school desegregation rates across and within the region, each county has been put into one of five demographic categories—black belt rural (over 50 percent black population), medium-black rural (30-49 percent black), low-black rural

(0-29 percent black), medium urban, and large metropolitan—and school enrollment data have been aggregated over each demographic sector.

In rural counties with small and intermediate black populations and in counties with medium-sized cities, the historical isolation of black students has practically disappeared (see table 7.1). Forty-three percent of the South's black students, but only 14 percent of all racially isolated black students, lived in these areas. Here, of course, is a crucial demographic difference between the South and the rest of the nation. In the West and North, far fewer blacks reside in rural, white majority environments or in urban areas with less than 250,000 population.

Substantial racial isolation has persisted, however, at the opposite ends of the southern demographic spectrum, in the largest cities and in rural counties where blacks outnumber whites. The perpetuation of racially distinct schools in major cities is the most important common link in educational patterns between the South and the non-South. Racial isolation in the modern South is overwhelmingly a big city phenomenon; 69 percent of the region's racially separate blacks—but only 47 percent of the South's black students—attended classes in large metropolitan areas. Two types of cities were especially associated with low rates of school desegregation: Peripheral South metropolitan counties with comparatively low percentages of blacks but total populations in excess of one million; and Deep South big cities containing relatively large proportions of blacks and total populations exceeding 500,000. In the first category were the three counties which encompass the region's largest

Table 7.1. Demographic scope of southern school desegregation: percentage of black students attending desegregated public schools in the region and subregions, 1976–77, by demographic sector

Demographic sector	Deep South		Peripheral South		South	
Large metropolitan	56	(36)[a]	74	(57)	67	(47)
Medium-urban	83	(16)	95	(16)	89	(16)
Low-black rural	98	(10)	99	(13)	98	(12)
Medium-black rural	91	(21)	95	(9)	93	(15)
Black belt	55	(17)	90	(5)	63	(10)
Total	72	(100)	83	(100)	78	(100)

Source: Department of Health, Education, and Welfare, Office for Civil Rights, *Directory of Elementary and Secondary School Districts, and Schools in Selected School Districts: School Year 1976–77* (Washington, D.C.: HEW, n.d.), vols. I–II.

a. Figures in parentheses report the percentage of all black students found within a given demographic sector.

metropolitan centers (Houston, Dallas, and Miami)—Harris (68 percent of blacks attended schools with few or no whites), Dallas (59 percent), and Dade (42 percent). The second group included New Orleans, Atlanta, and Birmingham, the three leading population centers of the Deep South—Orleans (79 percent), Fulton (75 percent), and Jefferson (61 percent)—plus Memphis's Shelby County (45 percent).

Why have a small number of the South's principal cities lagged far behind the rest of the region in desegregating public schools? Gary Orfield's instructive *Must We Bus?* suggests several pertinent factors.[12] The 1974 Supreme Court decision in *Milliken v. Bradley,*[13] which restricts desegregation plans to single school districts, is a formidable obstacle to desegregation in a number of southern metropolitan counties (most notably in Texas) which contain multiple school districts. Although "much of the South can be desegregated under the one-district principle,"[14] countywide school districts do not exist in four of the five highly populated (over 500,000) counties in which more than half of all black students were isolated from whites in 1976-77. In Harris, Dallas, Jefferson, and Fulton counties most blacks (68 to 92 percent) attended schools in the central city district, whereas white public school students (69 to 78 percent) typically attended public schools that were outside the central city district.

Moreover, even within individual school districts, the discretion which the Supreme Court's *Swann* decision granted to federal district judges in shaping remedies for racial segregation has resulted in considerable variation in the breadth of desegregation court orders from one central city district to another.[15] Federal judges, confronted by widespread white opposition at both mass and elite levels to extensive busing to achieve racial balance, faced in some instances with disagreement among black political leaders over the goal of desegregation,[16] and aware of the practical complexities of desegregating central city districts involving scores of schools and high traffic densities, have usually declined to order extensive desegregation of the largest school districts.

Rural counties with black population majorities provide the other demographic setting in which a substantial minority of black school children (37 percent) have remained isolated from their white counterparts. The greater isolation of blacks in the Deep South's majority black counties (see table 7.1) is a function both of that subregion's more intense white opposition to racial change and its greater concentration of heavily black counties. White politicians had long predicted a huge white exodus from the public schools if desegregation ever occurred, and extensive white abandonment of public schools has been a major consequence of efforts to desegregate the black belt South. Mark Lowry's important study of

Mississippi whites' initial response to school desegregation identified large declines in the number of whites attending public schools (especially in counties with large black populations) and concluded that the new phase of desegregation in that state had brought about biracial public schools and white private schools, a pattern that seems typical of rural counties with black population majorities.[17]

With each new phase of southern school desegregation, initial increments in desegregation were followed by a plateau, until more stringent administrative guidelines or Supreme Court decisions forced a transition to a higher stage of compliance. The third phase of school desegregation appears to have leveled out with about one-fifth of the region's black students excluded from appreciable contact with whites. In the absence of revised administrative guidelines or court orders compelling greater desegregation, racial isolation among southern blacks is unlikely to decline. To the contrary, if whites either continue or accelerate their departure from the region's central city school systems, as many have done in the North and West, the racial isolation of metropolitan black students in the South may well increase.

Public school desegregation has been extraordinarily controversial, of course, and public opinion surveys portray an undiminished concern among whites and blacks over the results of school desegregation. Nearly three-quarters of white southerners opposed the principle of federal supervision of public school desegregation in 1964, and twelve years later (the last time SRC-CPS asked the question), three-quarters of them again objected to federal intervention. This is clearly one matter of national governmental policy that irritates most white southerners; without federal coercion, much less actual school desegregation would have occurred. Whites especially object to the use of busing to accomplish school integration. In 1974, when the Gallup poll asked whites and blacks in the North and South whether they favored or opposed "busing school children to achieve better racial balance in the schools," preponderant majorities of blacks and whites were in direct conflict: 75 percent of blacks supported busing while 72 percent of whites opposed it.[18]

Even though southern whites remain opposed to the principle of federal intervention in the racial composition of local schools and to the specific remedy of busing, changes have occurred in the extent to which white parents are willing to accept school desegregation. White acquiescence or opposition is mainly a function of the school's expected racial composition. For example, a 1973 Gallup poll found 84 percent of southern white parents willing to send their children to schools with "a few" blacks, 64 percent willing to allow their children to attend schools with "half blacks," but merely 31 percent willing to enroll their children in schools with black majorities. These figures are only marginally lower than corresponding percentages for nonsouthern white parents.[19]

Southern school desegregation usually involves racial mixes in which blacks are distinct minorities, and this is very probably a key to the breadth of school desegregation. Many white parents may resent federal intervention and strongly dislike putting their children on a school bus, but as long as white students are in the majority, they may remain loyal to public schools. Outside the South, with blacks typically concentrated in central city schools, the actual situation for many nonsouthern white parents may be classrooms in which whites are in the minority; this factor alone would be sufficient reason for many white parents to withdraw their children from public education and to strongly oppose desegregation in metropolitan areas. It is no accident that the lowest rates of public school desegregation in the South occur in black belt rural schools and big city schools where whites are frequently outnumbered.

School desegregation brought millions of white and black children into sustained contact for the first time. No one familiar with school desegregation could pretend that the transition to biracial education has been easy or that racial animosities and conflicts have been fully resolved. If the social distance between most whites and blacks in southern schools still seems wide, it is surely less than in the past, when Matthews and Prothro used the powerful metaphor of "living together as strangers" to describe white and black adults.[20] The sharp break with past practice is the abiding reality for most black children. In the words of Charles S. Bullock III, "The creation of unitary schools with biracial facilities and the participation of a biracial student body in a full range of academic and extracurricular activities is an impressive example of the ability of federal policy to achieve sweeping changes against long odds."[21] Though we have chosen to emphasize the areas where school segregation has endured, it is clear that the central tendency in southern public education is not racial isolation but desegregation.

Race and Family Income

The constraints of the traditional economic and social order doomed most blacks and many whites to exceedingly meager living conditions. "The economic revolution of the past thirty years," observed Robert J. Steamer in the early 1960s, "has transformed the region from one of poverty and deprivation to one of material adequacy for most, abundance for many, and downright luxury for some."[22] This generalization is much more apt for whites than for blacks (see table 7.2). Almost half of the South's white families had incomes of at least $20,000 in 1979, and one-sixth reported incomes of $35,000 or higher. Among southern blacks the economic situation was much less favorable. The obstacles of the intermediate color line remained intact for many, though an expanding economy and federal pressure to ensure improved educational and job opportunities enabled a growing minority of black families to escape the worst burdens of economic subordination and opportunity restriction. These findings, which confirm both the continuation of ancient disadvantages and the realization of new possibilities, are consistent with William Julius Wilson's emphasis upon the simultaneous rise of a black middle class and the continuing economic deprivation of poorly educated blacks.[23]

In general, the 1979 income data (table 7.2) confirm a *partial* penetration of the intermediate color line. Historically, the caste system so radically limited black economic opportunities that few black families could achieve earnings approaching those of the average white family. In 1979 this pattern was still evident, with 49 percent of the white families (those earning at least $20,000) reporting incomes larger than 77 percent of the black families. But to a much greater extent than before, an appreciable minority of black families—the 23 percent who made $20,000 or more—had larger incomes than 51 percent of the whites. This set of black families, when combined with the 32 percent in the $10,000-19,999 range who made incomes similar to whites, means that black earnings overlapped white earnings to an unprecedented degree.

As the South has moved "out of the quagmire and into the economic

Table 7.2. Magnitude of southern income disparities: percentage of black and white families with specified incomes in 1979, by region and subregion

Family income	Deep South			Peripheral South			South		
	Bl[a] (%)	Wh[a] (%)	B/W[a]	Bl (%)	Wh (%)	B/W	Bl (%)	Wh (%)	B/W
Less than $10,000	48	20	2.4	43	19	2.3	45	19	2.4
$10,000–19,999	31	32	1.0	32	32	1.0	32	32	1.0
$20,000–34,999	17	34	0.5	20	33	0.6	19	33	0.6
$35,000 or more	4	14	0.3	5	16	0.3	4	16	0.3

Source: Calculated from U.S. Bureau of the Census, *1980 Census of the Population,* I, *Characteristics of the Population* (Washington, D.C.: Government Printing Office, 1983), state volumes, tables 81 and 91. Data on white families exclude Spanish-speaking whites.

a. Bl, black families; Wh, white families; B/W, ratio of black families to white families.

mainstream," substantial improvement in southern family incomes has occurred relative to the standards of white families in the entire nation.[24] Gains have been especially impressive among whites. Except for those white families living in Arkansas, Mississippi, and Tennessee, southern white families commanded income levels in 1979 that were approximately 90 percent or better of the levels earned by white families in the entire United States. White incomes in most southern states were similar to those in the more rural and small-town nonsouthern states.[25] Black families in every southern state likewise improved their position in the 1960s and 1970s, though in 1979 they still lagged far behind white families generally as well as behind white families in all southern states. What continue to differentiate many southern states from the rest of the nation are not so much the smaller white incomes as the substantially smaller black incomes. Despite improvement in the relative position of both white and black families in the South, a pronounced color line in incomes has been perpetuated.

The Persistence of Southern Poverty

Thomas Naylor and James Clotfelter have emphasized that "although in terms of overall economic development, the gap between the South and the rest of the nation has certainly been reduced in the past thirty years, the South is still the nation's poorest region."[26] No discussion of the intermediate color line would be adequate without a comparative assessment of poverty, long and correctly perceived as a "southern" problem.[27] In exploring this subject we shall focus on the poverty rates reported in the 1970 census, the census nearest in time to the rediscovery of hunger in the United States in the late 1960s.[28]

As late as 1969 the South as a whole still experienced inordinate rates of poverty, rates that were approximately double those of the non-South (see table 7.3). In that year, when 8 percent of all families outside the South fell below the official poverty level, double-digit poverty rates prevailed in every southern state. With one southern family in six lacking income sufficient to purchase minimal amounts of food, clothing, and shelter, the findings of the 1970 census point to the persistence of poverty as a southern phenomenon.

A more complex (but not unexpected) pattern emerges, however, when racial comparisons are introduced. Higher proportions of southern than nonsouthern whites were impoverished, but the difference between white families was only 4 percentage points (11 percent for white southerners versus 7 percent for white nonsoutherners). Aside from Arkansas, Mississippi, Tennessee, and Alabama, where white poverty was at least twice

Table 7.3. Poverty and race in the South: percentage of families with reported income in 1969 below the poverty level, by state, subregion, region, and nation

Political unit	All families	Black families	White families	Ratio of black to white
Mississippi[a]	29	59	16	3.7
Arkansas	23	53	18	3.0
Louisiana	22	47	13	3.8
Alabama	21	47	14	3.4
South Carolina	19	45	10	4.3
Georgia	17	40	11	3.8
North Carolina	16	39	11	3.5
Tennessee	18	38	15	2.5
Florida	13	36	9	4.0
Texas	12	33	9	3.9
Virginia	12	30	9	3.3
Deep South	21	47	12	3.8
Peripheral South	14	36	11	3.4
South	16	41	11	3.7
United States	10	30	8	3.7
Non-South	8	21	7	3.0

Sources: Calculated from U.S. Bureau of the Census, *1970 Census of Population,* I, *Characteristics of the Population* (Washington, D.C.: Government Printing Office, 1973), U.S. summary, table 95, and appropriate state volumes, table 58.

a. States are ranked (highest to lowest) according to the percentage of impoverished black families. Data on white families exclude Spanish-speaking whites.

as extensive as it was in the non-South, fairly modest rates of poverty existed among white southerners. Although the absence of destitution does not imply affluence, in comparative terms the cardinal political fact about southern white poverty in 1969 was its narrow impact, affecting roughly one white family in nine.

If the South's economic development enabled most white families to escape poverty, radically different realities confronted a huge proportion of black southerners. Fully two-fifths of the region's black families, including nearly half of the Deep South families and more than a third of the Peripheral South families, were impoverished in 1969. Poverty among black southerners was twice as common as it was among nonsouthern blacks, almost four times as great as the percentage of impoverished white southerners, and nearly six times as extensive as the poverty rate among nonsouthern whites. In Mississippi and Arkansas, the states with the most appalling poverty rates, more than half of the black families reported income below the line of poverty; and the other southern states exhibited high levels of black poverty, ranging from 30 percent in Virginia to 47 percent in Louisiana and Alabama.

The magnitude of the poverty gap between black and white southerners can be depicted with greater specificity and immediacy through paired maps. County-level data on the racial incidence of poverty were published for the first time in the 1970 census. In comparing the geography of white and black poverty in 1969, it is important to keep in mind that most Americans would regard poverty rates affecting one family in four as scandalous and unacceptable.

Extreme white poverty was primarily (though not exclusively) mountain poverty (see figure 7.1). In the mountain and upland counties of East and Middle Tennessee, northern Arkansas, western North Carolina, and southwestern Virginia, white poverty was extensive. Yet apart from the mountain South and smaller concentrations of white poverty in northeastern Louisiana and the hill counties of eastern Mississippi, where, presumably, little economic development had occurred, there were very few localities in which one-fourth of the white families were impoverished. White poverty rates of 25 percent or greater were limited to 11 percent of the southern counties, led by Tennessee, Arkansas, Mississippi, and Louisiana.

When the geography of black poverty is mapped according to the same stringent benchmark established for whites (see figure 7.2), the net effects of southern living for many blacks are revealed with exceptional force and clarity. It would be difficult to imagine a more fundamental interracial contrast than the monumental differences portrayed in the two maps. High rates of poverty existed among black families in practically every county in which the Census Bureau was able to estimate black poverty. Extensive black poverty prevailed in 96 percent of the South's counties, compared with 99 percent in the Deep South and 90 percent in the Peripheral South, with metropolitan Virginia providing the chief exception.

Striking as the geographical comparison of white and black poverty may be, the paired maps do not fully convey the severity of black poverty in the late 1960s. Our criterion of 25 percent poverty simply underestimates the pervasiveness of black poverty. If we isolate counties in which the rate of black poverty reached or exceeded *one-half* of all families, the historical black belt—extending from East Texas to eastern North Carolina—emerges as the South's black poverty belt, the primary locus

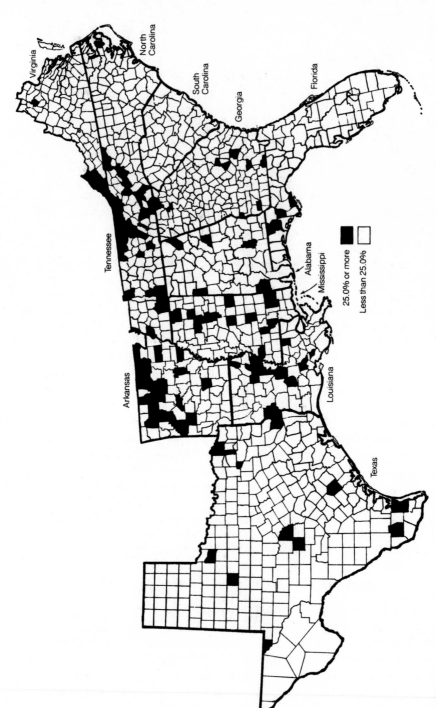

Figure 7.1. The geography of white poverty: southern counties in 1969 in which at least 25 percent of white families reported income below the poverty level. Spanish-speaking white families have been excluded. Sources: Same as table 7.3.

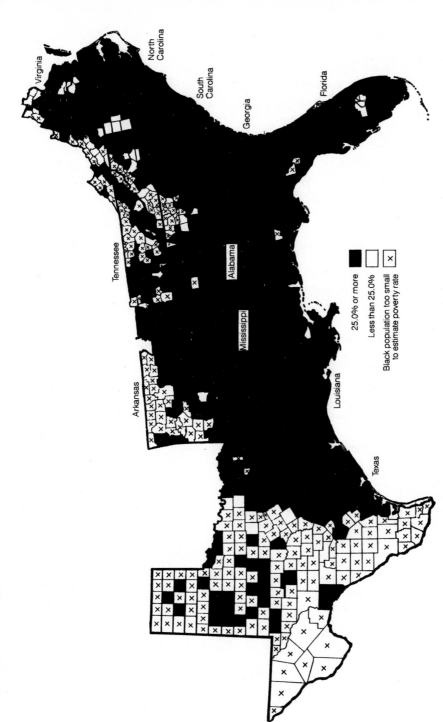

Figure 7.2. The geography of black poverty: southern counties in 1969 in which at least 25 percent of black families reported income below the poverty level. Sources: Same as table 7.3.

of exceptionally high rates of black poverty. As late as 1969 a majority of all black families were impoverished in some 359 of the 907 counties—40 percent—which possessed black populations large enough for the poverty rate to be estimated. Such counties constituted half or more of the relevant counties in Mississippi, Louisiana, Arkansas, and Alabama; only in Virginia were they rare.

In contrast to the rates of poverty that existed in the late 1960s, county-level data for 1979 show lower rates of poverty among both races in the South. The incidence of poverty among black families fell from 41 percent in 1969 to 30 percent ten years later, whereas the rate of poverty diminished from 11 to 7 percent among white families.[29] Most black families in the South were no longer impoverished, though the incidence of poverty among blacks was four times as high as the comparable figure for southern white families. The lowest black poverty rates appeared in counties of the urban corridor, Shenandoah Valley, and southcentral portions of Virginia, throughout the piedmont counties of the Carolinas and northern Georgia (where the color line in the textile industry had been broken), in portions of Tennessee, and in the Dallas and Houston metropolitan areas. Yet despite these pockets of economic progress, rampant poverty remained an abiding reality for substantial minorities of blacks across most of the South. Measured by counties having black family poverty rates of 25 percent or greater in 1969 *and* 1979, large fractions of black families remained impoverished in the typical southern county.

Because white and black southerners are so dissimilar in their incidence of poverty, it would be amazing if these economic differences were not reflected in political behavior. In view of the awesome poverty gap between the races it is realistic to assume that the economic priorities of most blacks will frequently diverge from those of most whites. Such issues as the relative importance of controlling inflation as opposed to reducing unemployment, support for increased welfare spending versus support for budgetary reductions, and reliance on individual or governmental responsibility for jobs and a good standard of living are apt to produce divisions, sometimes very sharp divisions, between most blacks and most whites.[30] Even when political campaigns do not explicitly focus on racial matters, the economic cleavages reflected in differential rates of poverty will frequently culminate in general election coalitions in which majorities of whites and blacks oppose each other.

In terms of political feasibility, the road out of poverty does not seem to lie through preferential treatment programs. In his important study of working-class southerners, Robert Botsch concluded that "the most troublesome issues with which the architects of a populist alliance must deal are those that raise the question of reverse discrimination. Many white working-class southerners who are otherwise fairly moderate and tolerant on racial issues are greatly disturbed by what they perceive to be an effort by the national government to change the rules of the game so that the darkness of one's skin is more rewarded than is hard work."[31]

Botsch's findings coincide with the depth of white opposition to preferential treatment revealed by Gallup surveys. On several occasions Gallup has posed the following question: "Some people say that to make up for past discrimination, women and members of minority groups should be given preferential treatment in getting jobs and places in college. Others say that ability, as determined by test scores, should be the main consideration. Which position comes closest to how you feel on this matter?" Typically, over four-fifths of the Gallup samples have said that ability should be the determinant of jobs or entry into college. "Rarely is public opinion, particularly on such a controversial issue, as united as it is over this question," Gallup reports. "Attitudes are fairly uniform from region to region and among all age groups . . . All groups back objective data such as test scores as the main qualifications in jobs and education."[32] Overwhelming majorities of whites and substantial majorities of blacks, according to the Gallup poll, oppose preferential treatment. If preferential treatment is to be the way out of massive poverty for many blacks, the political costs among the white majority will be extremely high. The more feasible political course lies through the accumulated educational achievements of individual blacks.

Education, Race, and New-Middle-Class Employment

Systematic comparisons of white and black occupations have shown that the southern social order has been substantially transformed over recent decades (see chapter 3). Nonetheless, in the midst of striking occupational changes, black southerners have lagged far behind white southerners in obtaining new-middle-class employment. Since jobs in the new middle class ordinarily require at least minimal skills in reading, writing, and mathematics, and since blacks were historically subjected to severe discrimination in educational opportunities and have only recently gained access to mainstream educational institutions, our examination of contemporary color lines properly concludes by investigating the relationship between formal education and new-middle-class employment.

Without question black entry into the new middle class has been severely impeded by low levels of education. In 1980 almost a quarter of the South's employed black males and a seventh of all employed black females had completed no more than eight years of elementary education, while only 8 percent of black men and 11 percent of black women had finished four or more years of college. Among whites with jobs only one-tenth of the men and one-twentieth of the women had eight years or less of formal education, compared with 21 percent of the males and 16 percent of the females who were college graduates or better (see the figures in parentheses in table 7.4). Because the black population was highly skewed toward the least educated end of the spectrum (a telling commentary on the rank injustice of the traditional economic and social order), far greater proportions of blacks than whites were effectively disqualified from middle-class employment.

Inadequate education, despite its significance, does not fully account for the racial imbalance in new-middle-class employment. As the table demonstrates, at each level of education except the most advanced, much larger proportions of white than black southerners acquired new-middle-class positions. The differential impact of formal education can be illustrated by comparing the educational level at which majorities of each race-and-sex group entered the new middle class. A high school diploma enabled most white women to obtain white-collar (mainly clerical) work; one to three years of college were needed before majorities of white men and black women joined the new middle class; and black men did not regularly gain middle-class jobs without college degrees. White southerners, in short, effectively penetrated the new middle class one educational level below black southerners of the same gender.

If the table discloses effects of racial discrimination that many older blacks cannot change, glimmerings of a fairer future are also discernible in the inverse relation between white advantage and black education and, more significantly, in the disappearance of an appreciable white advantage among college graduates. Like their white counterparts, blacks with four or more years of college were overwhelmingly employed in the new middle class. Since younger and better-educated blacks are much better situated to capitalize upon employment opportunities than older, less educated blacks, the table probably understates the competitiveness of the younger generation of black southerners. Hope for a more equitable future lies in the expansion of the college-educated black population.

Color Lines in the Modern South

Evaluated against the standard of promoting and rewarding individual achievement irrespective of race, the modern South is neither so bad as it once was nor so good as it may become. Only in the early 1960s did southern blacks, victimized and handicapped by two centuries of slavery and another century of legal segregation, succeed in shaking the foun-

Table 7.4. Education and the southern new middle class: percentage of employed southerners with new-middle-class occupations in 1980, by race, sex, and education

Years of education completed	Male southerners			Female southerners		
	Blacks	Whites	Black/white	Blacks	Whites	Black/white
Up to 8 years of elementary education	7[a] (23)[b]	15 (10)	0.5[c] (2.3)[d]	9 (15)	27 (6)	0.3 (2.4)
1–3 years of high school	10 (24)	21 (17)	0.5 (1.4)	19 (23)	48 (17)	0.4 (1.3)
4 years of high school	16 (32)	33 (33)	0.5 (1.0)	39 (35)	72 (41)	0.5 (0.9)
1–3 years of college	37 (13)	57 (18)	0.6 (0.7)	71 (16)	85 (20)	0.8 (0.8)
4 or more years of college	76 (8)	87 (21)	0.9 (0.4)	93 (11)	95 (16)	1.0 (0.7)
Total	20 (100)	45 (100)	0.4 (1.0)	42 (100)	71 (100)	0.6 (1.0)

Sources: Calculated from the U.S. Bureau of the Census, 1980 Census of the Population, I, Characteristics of the Population (Washington, D.C.: Government Printing Office, 1983), state volumes, table 223.
a. Percentage of a given group with new-middle-class jobs.
b. Percentage distribution of educational levels within each race-and-gender group.
c. Ratio of percentage of blacks with new-middle-class jobs to percentage of whites with new-middle-class jobs.
d. Ratio of percentage of blacks with a given level of education to percentage of whites with the same level of education.

dations of white racism. Race relations in the contemporary South reflect neither strict segregation nor thorough integration; rather, they embody a complex blend of old and new practices, old and new attitudes. Our analysis has shown remarkable areas of progress as well as a lengthy agenda of still controversial and unresolved interracial differences concerning the intermediate color line.

Some black southerners have penetrated the intermediate color line. In the mid-1980s many blacks occupy jobs once reserved for whites alone; most black students attend desegregated schools; and some blacks live in desegregated neighborhoods. About one-quarter of all black families in the South had 1979 incomes exceeding the median family income for white southerners. Despite these easily noticed signs of progress, *most* blacks remain far behind or separated from *most* whites in occupation, income, schooling, and housing. Vast differences in the living conditions and socioeconomic status of blacks as a group and whites as a group provide abundant material for bitter and protracted interracial conflicts.

Many blacks interpret the differences as evidence of continuing racial discrimination, while many whites see them as "natural" outcomes of the gaps between whites and blacks in education and training. Of all these changes, black access to public education on an equal basis with whites is probably the most far-reaching in its cumulative effects, effects which will not be fully apparent for many years. Whatever its shortcomings may be, public education clearly remains the key institutional facilitator of upward mobility for gifted children who are born into families with modest or impoverished incomes. More blacks are in desegregated schools than ever before in the region's history, and the increase in highly educated blacks will make blacks more competitive with whites for leadership positions.

Finally, the races remain separated, for the most part, in terms of the innermost color line—the circle of friendship and intimacy. Although some blacks and some whites share and enjoy equal-status friendships, the reality for most is socialization within their own race. In 1976, after more than a decade of desegregation, merely one in twenty white southerners said they felt 'close to' blacks, and only one in five blacks acknowledged feeling 'close to' whites.[33] It is not necessary for members of different racial or ethnic groups to "like" one another in order to have mutual respect, but estrangement at the core of the color line encourages mutual misunderstandings and misperceptions and may add hostile emotions to the substantive conflicts of the outer and intermediate color lines. In light of the South's long and tumultuous struggle over virtually every aspect of race relations, it may not be possible for majorities of whites and blacks to feel truly comfortable with each other. Though they are not drawn in the same way or with the same rigidity as in the past, color lines remain part of life in the South, as well as in the rest of the nation. Efforts to understand the politics of the South—past, present, and future—will always require careful examination of patterns of conflict and consensus between whites and blacks.

III

The Southern Electorate

eight

The Changing Electorate

"THE SIZE and composition of the South's voting population determine the matrix within which the struggle for political power is carried on," Key asserted; and, indeed, the character of any supposedly democratic regime can only be understood by analyzing patterns of mass participation.[1] Most adults did not vote in the old southern politics. Around the turn of the century conservative southern Democrats had vanquished their opposition and reduced the electorate to manageable proportions, mainly by eliminating blacks as voters and by constructing many barriers to participation by lower-class whites. During the 1920s, after women became eligible to vote, scarcely more than a fifth of adult southerners voted in either general elections or Democratic primaries.

Nor had circumstances appreciably changed by midcentury, when Key placed the South's lack of participation in an international perspective. "Among the great democracies of the world," he observed, "the southern states remain the chief considerable area in which an extremely small proportion of citizens vote." Southern nonvoting was so pronounced that Key thought the adjective "democratic" was not warranted. "The marking of the ballot, an act by which a citizen can participate in the choice of his rulers, epitomizes and symbolizes the entire democratic process," he wrote. "The simple fact is that a government founded on democratic doctrines becomes some other sort of regime when large proportions of its citizens refrain from voting."[2] Walter Dean Burnham's description of the American political system after 1896 as a "broadly based oligarchy," a government of the few,[3] applies with particular force to the old southern polity.

Since midcentury several significant factors—the revival of vigorous interparty competition for the presidency and some important state offices, notable reforms in suffrage requirements (abolition of poll taxes and tests of literacy and "understanding"), the rise of a much more middle-class and educated citizenry, and the reentry of black voters—have altered both the size and composition of the region's active electorate. The most significant change has occurred in *presidential elections,* in which approximately half of the voting age population now participates. Although this rate of participation is hardly awesome, it represents a doubling of the turnout characteristic of the old southern politics. In general elections for governor, however, the legacy of nonparticipation still lingers. Scarcely more than a third of the region's adults exercised their right to vote in the gubernatorial contests of the late 1970s and early 1980s. With a few exceptions here and there, southern *state governments* continue to rest upon the active consent of the few and the acquiescence or indifference of the many.

The present composition of the southern electorate is very different from that of the past. Most voters in the mid-1980s are totally unaware, or retain only the dimmest memories, of the events, circumstances, and experiences that created and sustained Democratic hegemony. With the revival of black voting, the electorate is now racially diverse. A considerable proportion of white voters were born and raised outside the region, and the southern electorate is no longer largely a male preserve. Though many of the region's voters are engaged in working-class occupations, the electorate is much more middle-class than before. Most voters have finished high school, and a growing minority have attended college. More voters now live in large and medium-sized cities than in rural and small-town areas. By any yardstick, the modern electorate is far more diverse than the comparatively homogeneous voters who sustained and nourished the classic one-party system. Trends in the size and composition of the active electorate suggest much about the likely winners and losers in contemporary southern politics.

The Increasingly Active Electorate

Southern turnout rates from 1920 through the early 1980s for the two most important offices, the presidency and the governorships, are displayed in figure 8.1. (Gubernatorial results have been calculated in four-year waves for the Democratic primaries, Republican primaries, and general elections). Until about 1950 turnout was persistently meager in southern elections. The South's tiny electorate was different in kind from the rest of the nation during the first half of the twentieth century, for nonsouthern presidential elections usually attracted more than three-fifths

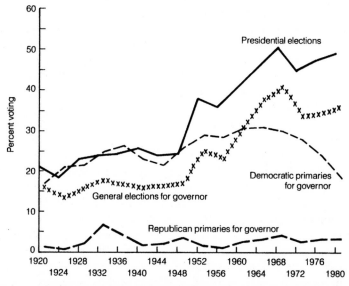

Figure 8.1. Changing patterns of participation in southern elections: percent of voting age population estimated to have voted in presidential elections, general elections for governor, contested Democratic primaries for governor, and contested Republican primaries for governor, 1920–1983. Sources: Richard M. Scammon, ed., *America at the Polls* (Pittsburgh: University of Pittsburgh Press, 1965); *Congressional Quarterly's Guide to U.S. Elections* (Washington, D.C.: Congressional Quarterly, 1975); and appropriate volumes of Richard M. Scammon, ed., *America Votes.*

of the eligible voters, and nonsouthern governorships typically involved majorities of the potential electorate.[4] Key's sobering appraisal of the old southern politics was correct: "It is practically impossible under the one-party system to formulate issues and to maintain political organization that will activate the electorate to the extent that a two-party system does."[5]

In recent decades major changes have occurred in the region's participation rates. Turnout has vastly increased in presidential elections; the general election for governor has displaced the Democratic nominating primary as the main arena for popular participation in state politics; and, with the gradual spread of two-party competition, general election turnout has begun to move upward for the governorship. Within the region a two-tier pattern of popular participation is evolving, with the presidency far ahead of the governorships (and other state offices) in stimulating voter interest.

The most impressive change is the tremendous increase in the percentage of eligible southerners who vote for president. Participation first surged when Republicans, taking advantage of a growing unease among many southern whites toward the national Democratic party, and also of the rise of a more urbanized middle-class society, began to compete seriously for the presidency in 1952. "Eisenhower campaigned more widely in the South than any previous Republican candidate," observed George B. Tindall. "Never again would presidential candidates of either party take the South for granted."[6] Turnout swelled again in 1964 (when Barry Goldwater and Lyndon Johnson offered something of value to vastly different groups of southerners), and reached its modern zenith in the turbulent contest of 1968. In that year Richard Nixon appealed to traditional Republicans and the white urban middle class in the Peripheral South; Hubert Humphrey mobilized blacks and the few remaining loyalist white Democrats; and George Wallace aroused whites in the Deep South and black belt areas of the Peripheral South. The result was a turnout that, for the first time in this century, exceeded half of the eligible voters. Turnout rates declined slightly in the early 1970s as the electorate expanded to include those aged eighteen to twenty, the Wallace movement collapsed, and conflict waned over renewed black voting; but in recent presidential elections participation has hovered around 50 percent.

Competition for the South's electoral college votes has thus vastly stimulated voter participation. Increased southern participation, coupled with turnout declines outside the South, have almost eliminated the stark regional differences in turnout previously characteristic of presidential elections. Turnout in the South still lags behind that of the non-South, but the difference is only a few percentage points.[7] The South is rejoining the nation.

In the old southern politics, one of the most important indications of the Democratic party's dominance in gubernatorial elections was the tendency for Democratic primary turnout to exceed general election participation. "The Democratic primary in the South is in reality the election," Key concluded. "The Democratic 'nominees' not only usually win the general election but in an overwhelming majority of instances, if one includes local officials in the calculations, are unopposed."[8] As is shown in figure 8.1, the Democratic primary remained the central focus of political participation through the late 1950s. By the early 1960s, however, slightly more southerners were attracted to general elections than to Democratic primaries, and in all subsequent electoral waves the general election has consistently been the main arena for voting in gubernatorial politics. As an institution, the Democratic primary is declining in importance.[9] Though it is still used in most southern states to nominate candidates, such nominations are no longer equivalent to election. Waning popular interest in the primary is yet another sign of the breakdown of classic one-party politics.

General elections for governor are now far more likely to be genuine contests than empty rituals. Nonetheless, close two-party competition is much less frequent in these races than in presidential elections. Participation in the most important state elections has never involved as much as half of the southern voting age population, and it has usually been much lower. Participation peaked during the 1968-1971 wave of general elections, when 43 percent of the region's adults—almost three times the rate of their predecessors five decades earlier—took part in gubernatorial contests. Since 1972, however, turnout has diminished to slightly better than one-third of the potential electorate.

Southern turnout rates remain low in part because most elections for governor do not coincide with presidential campaigns, a separation now common in nonsouthern states also. Alabama, Georgia, Mississippi, South Carolina, and Virginia had severed state and national elections before 1952, and subsequently all other southern states except North Carolina have followed their example. Although this separation may produce a state politics less "influenced" or "contaminated" by whatever national political trends are momentarily ascendant, it also removes a powerful stimulus for citizen involvement.[10]

Since 1952 the turnout in southern gubernatorial elections that coincide with presidential elections has run about 10 percentage points above the rates typical for off-year gubernatorial contests. In the 1970s the dwindling number of gubernatorial elections scheduled in presidential years attracted between 45 and 48 percent of these states' eligible voters, while off-year gubernatorial campaigns drew only slightly more than one-third of the voting age population. Splitting state and national elections places an additional burden on the Republican party, since it deprives that party of the surge of white voters who might be attracted by a conservative Republican nominee or repelled by the presidential candidacy of a northern liberal Democrat. Saving southern Democracy from Republican governors requires a considerable sacrifice in democratic participation.

During most of this century differences in gubernatorial turnout between southerners and nonsoutherners were often dramatic: most nonsouthern citizens voted in elections for governor; most southerners did not. Gradual increases in southern participation and deteriorating rates of nonsouthern participation have narrowed the regional turnout gap. Though southern turnout rates are still lower than those of the non-South, the differences have become matters of degree. In the non-South as well as the South nonparticipation is now the central tendency.

Composition of the Old Southern Electorate

Sometimes dramatic, sometimes only modest, shifts in rates of southern participation have occurred during the past six decades. More fundamental changes have appeared in the composition of the region's active electorate. To explain the significance of the new southern electorate, it is necessary to discuss the electorate that underlay traditional one-party politics. For reasons that are abundantly clear, the traditional electorate has often been analyzed in terms of race and socioeconomic class. We have no quarrel with these emphases, but we think one other factor— gender—is extremely important in clarifying which groups participated and which abstained from voting in the one-party South.

With the adoption of the Nineteenth Amendment in 1920, the electorate expanded to include females. This constitutional change in the definition of women's political roles was not assimilated with equal speed by all groups of southern women. Black women, of course, were unaffected. Among whites, middle- and upper-class women were far better situated to participate in political affairs than were working-class women. If they had the inclination, leisured women certainly had the time to make politics a prominent "volunteer" activity. Tradition required the male head of the household to establish the family's politics, to which lesser members were expected to conform. Deviations from the cultural norm no doubt occurred in the privacy of the voting booth, but deference to male authority and say-so on political matters had a long history and was not easily overturned. Always outnumbered by the unlettered masses, the more sagacious middle-class males welcomed another secure vote for their interests.

In working-class homes the woman's role was much more restricted. Burdened with all the child care, cooking, and cleaning, many working-class women were completely absorbed by the practical demands of daily life. Politics was usually left to the men, and the women had little time for it even if they were keenly interested. All of the factors that would induce political sterilization—limited formal education, isolation from ideas, otherworldly religion, religious acceptance of fatalism, absence of activist role models—together with so little cash income that few working-class families could afford to pay two poll taxes, must have acted with tremendous negative force on southern working-class women living in small-town and rural areas.

We think that interest in politics in the traditional South (about 1920-1950) can be ranked according to the following factors: race, gender, and family class position. Because race was the main principle of division, whites would generally be more interested in politics than blacks. Among whites, we believe that gender was more important than family social class in affecting levels of political interest. Because women's suffrage was a recent achievement, voting was a novel experience for southern females. By comparison, despite barriers against voting by working-class men, many of them had managed to vote for years. As a result, we expect that family social class made less difference to political participation than did the simple distinction between males and females. If this perspective is correct, traditional southern politics needs to be interpreted in terms of race, gender, and class, rather than simply race and class.

Among blacks, however, there is reason to anticipate that class differences were more important than gender in conditioning political involvement. Few blacks of either sex voted in the traditional South. Participation was somewhat more common among the minute number of blacks with middle-class status but most working-class blacks were politically inert.

At this point we confront a practical dilemma. Lacking sample surveys of the inhabitants of the old South, how can we reach back into the past to examine interest in politics? Historians have made creative use of oral interviews with individuals who attempt to recollect events and persons long past; skillful use of such data has provided new interpretations of the past.[11] Because particular stress is placed on independent validation of an individual's memories, usually the scope of investigation is quite specific—a particular event in a community, or details in the life of a given individual. Microscopic information is gained at the expense of breadth. We want to apply the basic idea of oral history—the use of individual recollections about a past situation—to the goal of generalizing about levels of interest in politics among different groups of southerners. Precise knowledge will be sacrificed to breadth, for there is no way to confirm the accuracy of any individual's perceptions. We have hypothesized, on theoretical grounds, a rank ordering of southerners according to levels of interest in politics, and our empirical task is to determine how well the available data fit the hypothesized ranking.

Our data are drawn from the 1968 Comparative State Elections Project, in which respondents were asked to recall several matters of information about their parents, including their parents' social class. In addition, they were asked a broad question about their parents' interest in politics: "Was your father (or mother) very interested, somewhat interested, or not interested at all?" Answers to this question may be used to recreate the rank ordering of political interest in the first half of the twentieth century that offspring ascribed to their parents.

Several cautionary words are appropriate at this point. On the level of each individual, these data are probably very "soft." Perception of one's own interest in something is highly subjective; perception of some-one else's interest remains subjective and is open to many forms of error. We simply do not know—nor is there any way to find out—whether an individual's recollection is correct. This is not a major problem, though, because we are not really interested in the individual respondents; we are interested in *groups* of individuals, and in whether the answers for groups correspond to the anticipated rank ordering. The predicted pattern has never been shown for the region during this period of time, much less compared with the non-South. Although the results cannot be defin-itive, they can be suggestive; in fact, we think the results are "within shouting distance of the realities," to use Key's apt phrase for approxi-mations of truth.

These recollections of parental interest in politics, displayed in figure 8.2, reveal clear and consistent differences in interest among various groups of southerners. As their offspring recalled the past, keen interest in politics prior to midcentury was limited largely to substantial portions of only two groups: white males of the middle class *and* working class. Overwhelming majorities of the other five groups were not remembered as having been highly interested in politics. While white women were more frequently recalled as being "very interested" in politics than were blacks, the females of the dominant racial group were much more similar to the legally disfranchised black population than to white males in terms

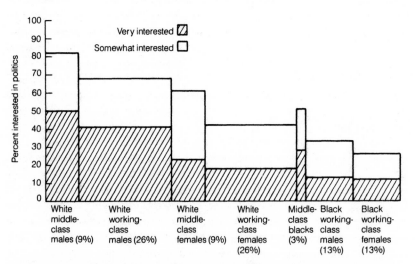

Figure 8.2. Levels of political interest among different types of southerners as recalled by their offspring in 1968. Source: CSEP.

of high political interest. The "oligarchy" of white males stands out vividly in the recall data.

The shape of political interest in the traditional South is slightly altered when individuals remembered as "somewhat interested" are added to the base of the "very interested" southerners. The two groups of white males hold their own but are now joined by middle-class white women. White women of higher status were much more likely than working-class white women to be classified as "somewhat interested" in politics. Possessing at least some political interest, middle-class white females appear to have been a group that could be episodically mobilized for political action. Four-fifths of the middle-class white males, two-thirds of working-class white males, and three-fifths of middle-class white females were remembered as possessing either some or a lot of interest in politics. Measured by the same standard, few members of three other groups seemed to be much concerned about politics: only two-fifths of working-class white women, one-third of black working-class males, and one-fourth of working-class black females were recalled as manifesting any interest in politics.

According to the memories of their offspring, political interest among southerners in the first half of this century was powerfully associated with the tradition and practice of white supremacy, the legacy and persistence of sexism, and family position in the social structure. The strongest division followed the color line. Fifty-nine percent of the white parents were remembered as having been interested in politics, almost double the 31 percent of black parents who were similarly recollected. Having anesthetized most blacks through suffrage laws, inferior educational opportunities, economic dependency, and periodic doses of intimidation, white southerners could correctly observe that most blacks seemed indifferent, apathetic, or unconcerned about voting; the victims were blamed for attitudes that were realistic adaptations to their opportunities for participation. These findings are consistent with the modal black response to life in the South prior to the civil rights movement: pervasive acquiescence to the system of white racism.

The only exception to the color line occurred among blacks of middle-class status. Middle-class blacks were the most likely to have been registered voters; to the extent that white politicians encouraged or permitted any voting by members of the minority group, it was usually by a handful of relatively high-status blacks who could act as conduits between white leaders and the larger black community. This partial exception to black exclusion by no means threatened whites. Less than 10 percent of the 1968 sample reported being raised in a middle-class family, and middle-class blacks only accounted for 2.5 percent of the respondents in the southern sample. Except for this tiny group of middle-class blacks, the recall data are consistent with an entrenched and pervasive system of white supremacy that left most whites with some political interests and most blacks with none.

As expected, among whites differences between males and females were much more important than class differences in ranking levels of political interest. Whether groups are ranked according to high interest or the combination of high and moderate interest, the results remain the same: middle-class white males at the top, followed by working-class white males, middle-class white females, and, at the bottom, working-class white females.

It is not surprising that the strongest levels of recollected political interest should be attributed to white males of the middle and upper classes. From this group came the "banker-merchant-farmer-lawyer-doctor governing class" that dominated most small-town and rural areas, as well as the rising urban middle classes based on business, commerce, and industry. Owning and controlling most of the South's wealth and property, they had the greatest reason for wishing to control state and local governments. Female suffrage appears to have strengthened the region's middle classes. Although middle-class white women were far outnumbered by their working-class counterparts, they are attributed by their children with much more interest in politics and were probably much easier to motivate to vote than were working-class white women. The impression that emerges from the recall data is of a stratum of middle-class white men highly attentive to politics and of a stratum of middle-class white women potentially interested in politics.

By contrast, the white working class was split by gender differences in political interest, a division that must have hampered the development of working-class cohesion in the traditional South. The traditional role of the southern woman as uninterested and uninvolved in political affairs continued to reduce the potential influence of the southern working class.

Among black southerners the relative importance of gender and family social class was reversed. Discrimination against southern blacks was so widespread that only minor differences separated men and women. Insufficient sample size prevents a comparison of women and men among middle-class blacks, but the black middle class as a group was clearly recollected as being more politically alert than either males or females of the working class. Most of the accommodating and—eventually—some of the protesting leadership was drawn from middle-class blacks.

The implications of these findings for the development of successful working-class politics are clear. Of the four groups of working-class southerners, only white males were recalled as having more than half of their members interested in politics. Black disfranchisement had already removed almost 30 percent of the region's adult population from the political universe, and women's suffrage brought in a large bloc of (usually) nonparticipant females. Although the white working classes—both male and female—could be aroused to political action, this seems to have occurred infrequently. Patient, determined, and occasionally successful efforts to raise and follow through on issues of great concern to white have-littles and have-nots would have been required in order to stimulate continuous participation by most of the region's lower-status whites. But this was not at all the type of politics that most members of the upper and middle classes favored, nor the type of politics on which most ambitious politicians sought to base their careers. Victories in statewide races went mainly to the champions of the dominant strata of whites.

The recall data also permit comparisons between reported political interest in the South and in the rest of the nation. In actual voting, southern turnout rates were far lower than those of non-South in the first half of this century. Are these behavioral differences paralleled by shortfalls among southerners in reputed political interest? As a matter of fact, levels of political interest attributed to parents did not differ between the regions for three of the four white groups. Neither middle-class southern whites (male and female) nor working-class southern white males appear to have been less concerned about politics than their non-southern peers. Only among white females of the working class did the interests of white southerners dip more than 5 percentage points below the level for the non-South.

If these data are reasonably correct, southern white males of the working class possessed levels of political interest comparable to those of white male workers outside the South. Despite suffrage laws that made voting difficult, despite the absence of candidates who appealed forthrightly to the economic interests of working-class whites, and despite the minimal education of most of these whites, an interest in and concern for politics apparently persisted. This does not mean that working-class whites in both regions actually participated at the same rates. Even assuming similar levels of interest, in the North the organizational networks linking workers to politics, such as party organizations in working-class neighborhoods and union halls where political activity was the norm, were much stronger. Although working-class white males with an intense interest in politics could be expected to vote regularly, those with weaker intrinsic interest probably needed assistance from political organizations, assistance that was far more readily available in the non-South than in the South. We suspect that the South's white male workers were more interested in politics than is usually assumed and that ineffective political organization was the main reason for their lower participation rates.

Among the three remaining groups of working-class southerners, however, the recall evidence does support the proposition that the southern working class was disproportionately anesthetized. Southern white women of the working class were credited with less interest in politics than working-class white females in nonsouthern states. Regional differences in political organizations appealing to working-class women compounded the regional differences in interest and probably contributed to the very low rates of turnout for white working class women in the South. Key's characterization of southern working-class indifference to politics was much more apt for females than for males. Finally, there were considerable differences in reputed interest between southern and nonsouthern blacks. Not only were blacks outside the South remembered as having much more interest in politics than southern blacks, but the comparatively few nonsouthern blacks were able to vote in elections that mattered. In the long run, the expanded opportunities for political activity available to northern blacks would be a major factor in pushing nonsouthern politicians to reopen the question of Jim Crow in the South.

Composition of the New Southern Electorate

Race, gender, and social class—in that order of importance—structured reputed interest in politics during the one-party era. In our treatment of voting in the modern South, we shall retain the spirit of our previous analysis but change two of the variables. To measure voting behavior, we shall rely upon individual accounts of participation (self-reports in the 1950s, validated turnout in 1980). To indicate social class, we shall use degree of formal education (those who have attended college versus the remainder whose education stopped before college), rather than perceived social class among individuals. Although these last two variables are not identical, they are essentially similar, and education provides a clearer picture of the variation in turnout.

According to presidential election year surveys, in recent decades access to higher education has become the main factor distinguishing southern voters from nonvoters, and the racial and sexual characteristics of southern adults have become much less significant. Since the early 1950s the SRC-CPS has polled representative samples of the national population, routinely asking respondents whether they had voted in the current presidential election. Although these data have serious drawbacks (self-reports of voting generally produce inflated turnout rates), they can be used to compare rankings among various groups of respondents (see table 8.1).[12]

At midcentury the imprint of the old order was still visible, for the color line remained the most important cleavage separating voters from nonvoters. Some three-fifths of white southerners, compared to one-seventh of black southerners, claimed they had voted for president in the 1950s. According to the more detailed rank ordering of subgroups presented in table 8.2, the single exception to low black participation involved the tiny group of southern blacks who had gone to college. Another continuity with the past lay in the clear differences between male and female turnout, differences that were especially large among the bulk of

Table 8.1. Reported turnout in the 1952–1956 and 1980 presidential elections of southerners and nonsoutherners, by race, gender, education, and political generation[a]

	1952–1956		1980	
Category	South	Non-South	South	Non-South
All	51	80	47	57
Whites	62	81	48	59
Blacks	13	61	42	44
Males	63	84	45	60
Females	41	76	48	55
College	84	91	62	66
High school or less	44	78	38	52
Solid South	—	—	50	67
Post–World War II	—	—	56	63
Post–Voting Rights Act	—	—	36	44
Whites only				
Males	76	85	46	63
Females	51	78	49	55
College	85	91	62	68
High school or less	56	79	38	53
Solid South	—	—	50	68
Post–World War II	—	—	58	65
Post–Voting Rights Act	—	—	37	46

Source: SRC-CPS presidential election year surveys. Figures for 1952–1956 are averages.
a. Data are presented as percentages.

Table 8.2.   Southern and nonsouthern participation rates in presidential elections of the 1950s, by race, access to college, and gender

Group[a]	Percentage voting		Net difference
	South	Non-South	
White men with college education	87	92	−5
White women with college education	82	90	−8
White men without college education	72	83	−11
Blacks with college education	57	93	−36
White women without college education	44	76	−32
Black men without college education	18	70	−52
Black women without college education	6	54	−48

Source: SRC-CPS presidential election year surveys. Figures are averages of the 1952 and 1956 surveys.

a. Groups are ranked (highest to lowest) according to the proportion of participating southerners.

the population that had not been to college. Based on their own reports, most white women and practically all black women whose educations had terminated before college did not vote in presidential elections.

Although race and gender continued to affect voter turnout, there was one crucial departure from the earlier ordering of subgroups according to recollected interest in politics. Only a slight gap in participation separated white southern men and women who had been exposed to higher education, and college-educated white women reported voting at a higher rate than white men who had not attended college. This finding, of course, is not new. In their analysis of a 1961 survey of southerners, Matthews and Prothro emphasized the impact of college education in eliminating the gender gap in voting, and Carol A. Cassel's subsequent examination of SRC-CPS data from the 1950s found similar results.[13] Access to higher education had already begun to emerge as a dynamic factor that might someday prove more important than sex and race in distinguishing rates of voter turnout. In the early 1950s southern electoral politics was conditioned by race, educational achievement, and gender—a ranking of characteristics slightly different from that of the past.

Noticeable differences in presidential voting still prevailed between the South and the non-South. What distinguished the South from the rest of the nation was not only massive black disfranchisement but also excessively low participation rates among less educated white women.[14] It was essentially the same pattern of regional uniqueness that had appeared in the recall data.

Since the 1950s several major changes, particularly increased voting by blacks and women and the broad shift toward a more middle-class society, have reshaped and reorganized southern electorates. Enhanced black political participation is the most visible innovation. Though it is impossible to be certain about the precise rates of black (and white) turnout in presidential elections, black participation surged in the 1960s, apparently peaked in 1968, and subsequently leveled off during the 1970s.[15] Surveys of presidential elections have consistently found black turnout trailing white turnout, but the differences have usually been less than 10 percentage points.

Other trends include increased voting by southern women, especially those without a college education, and a simultaneous decline in reported voting by southern white males, particularly those with a high school education or less.[16] Southern women were better educated and more apt to be employed than in previous generations. As they left the home, they more frequently voted. By the 1970s wide gaps in participation rates no longer separated men from women. The expansion of state university systems increased the number of southerners who came into contact with higher education. Central campuses of state systems attracted new students by the thousands, but even more important was the proliferation of branch campuses into many small towns and rapidly growing metropolitan areas. Assisted also by the migration of whites who had received a college education elsewhere in the nation, the percentage of southerners who had attended college doubled from 17 percent in the 1950s to 35 percent in 1980. Highly educated white southerners had always participated at high rates, and the contemporary South contains far more of these individuals than before.[17]

By 1980 the southern electorate was substantially more diverse in its racial, sexual, and educational composition than at any point in this century. In marked contrast to the past, race and gender were no longer associated with pronounced differences in voter participation. Although blacks voted 6 percentage points lower than whites and males were 3 points lower than females (see table 8.1), neither difference was substantial in comparison with past voting patterns. Instead, educational achievement was the principal dividing line between participants and nonparticipants: 62 percent of southerners who had attended college voted in 1980, compared with only 38 percent of those without any college training. Because of the large turnout differential, college-educated southerners furnished 47 percent of the region's voters in 1980, well above their share of the population. Among whites the college-educated even constituted a slight majority (51 percent) of all voters. The southern electorate was disproportionately middle class, a tilt that has already assisted Republican presidential candidates and should benefit future GOP gubernatorial and senatorial nominees.

The 1980 results are especially intriguing, for they are based on an unusually accurate measurement of turnout in presidential contests. Respondents' reports of having voted were actually verified with official voting records. By eliminating interviewees who falsely claimed to have voted, the survey's findings for the nation and the regions are very close to estimates obtained from aggregate voting statistics. Patterns observed in 1980 may or may not be typical of future elections, for candidates with different appeals could presumably activate more of the noncollegiate sector of the electorate. Nonetheless, the 1980 results do provide a benchmark for comparisons of past and future elections.

When voter participation rates for 1980 are calculated for the same subgroups previously examined in the 1950s (see table 8.3), a very different ordering appears. College attendance displaced race as the most significant attribute isolating voters from nonvoters. Within each of the two educational categories, moreover, there were no consistently large differences according to race or gender. Whether male or female, white or black, most southerners who went to college voted in 1980, while most southerners whose education ceased before college—regardless of race or sex—failed to participate. Educated white women, two-thirds of whom voted in 1980, led the South in voter turnout. At the bottom of the region, symbolically rubbing shoulders with relatively uneducated black men, were white men of similar educational status.

Though neither race nor gender was systematically related to 1980

Table 8.3. The primacy of educational achievement: participation in 1980 presidential election varied according to access to college

Group[a]	Percentage voting		Net difference
	South	Non-South	
White women with college education	66	64	2
Blacks with college education	64	43	21
White men with college education	58	71	− 13
White women without college education	41	51	− 10
Black women without college education	39	45	− 6
Black men without college education	35	44	− 9
White men without college education	35	57	− 22

Source: 1980 SRC-CPS presidential election year survey.

a. Groups are ranked (highest to lowest) according to the proportion of participating southerners.

Table 8.4. Education, political generation, and participation in the 1980 presidential election

Group[a]	Percentage voting		Net difference
	South	Non-South	
Pre–Voting Rights generations with college education	67	77	−10
Post–Voting Rights generation with college education	56	52	4
Pre–Voting Rights generations without college education	47	59	−12
Post–Voting Rights generation without college education	20	37	−17

Source: 1980 SRC-CPS presidential election year survey.

a. Groups are ranked (highest to lowest) according to the proportion of participating southerners.

turnout, the political generations identified by Beck and Lopatto (see chapter 1) show differences in voting.[18] A pronounced division separated the post–Voting Rights generation (aged 18-33 in 1980), few of whom voted, from the two older generations, most of whom were voters (see table 8.1). When individuals of different educational achievement are cross-tabulated by their membership in either pre–or post–Voting Rights generations, a clear and consistent ranking of southerners according to participation is discernible (see table 8.4). Voting was most likely among older, college-educated southerners, and exposure to college was comparatively more important than age in distinguishing the second and third highest voting groups. Massive political abstention prevailed among young southerners with little education; four of every five southerners in this category—regardless of race or gender—did not vote in 1980. This analysis reconfirms the importance of access to college education in influencing which groups vote in the modern South. The participation gap should narrow as the younger cohort ages. If it fails to moderate, the South's electorate will become even more skewed toward middle-class values than it is at present.

Finally, the 1980 data indicate that regional differences in voter participation have lessened but not totally disappeared. Only 47 percent of southerners voted in the Reagan-Carter-Anderson contest, compared with 57 percent of nonsoutherners. Southern distinctiveness formerly rested upon nonvoting blacks and low rates of participation among white females with little formal education. By 1980, however, the turnout rates of black southerners were generally similar to those of nonsouthern blacks. Apart from a substantially higher turnout among college-educated blacks in the South, regional differences in participation were concentrated among white southerners. Southern white females with no exposure to college voted at a rate 10 percentage points below their nonsouthern counterparts, but their behavior was no longer grossly exceptional. The largest regional imbalance involved less educated southern white males; only 35 percent of them voted in 1980, compared with 57 percent of similarly educated white men outside the South. Southern white men without a college education, the group whose relative importance in the southern electorate has deteriorated the most in recent decades, thus produced the principal interregional difference.

Political Implications of Changes in the Electorate

Over the past six decades the composition of the active electorate in the South has substantially changed, and with these changes have come differences in the style—the public face—of electoral politics. Vivid, picturesque, boisterous, and often sensationally racist, the paramount style of the old southern politics reflected the imperative of aspiring Democratic politicians to attract attention and demonstrate "leadership" qualities in a crowded primary field where the party label counted for nothing. Uneducated white males, residents of small towns and rural areas who had come of age politically during the late nineteenth or early twentieth century, were the principal consumers of this spectacle. One of the most important secular trends in reshaping the style of southern politics is the declining proportion of uneducated white males in the active electorate. It is difficult to know precisely what share of the contemporary electorate consists of this group, but even a generous estimate would put it no higher than one-fourth. Though a large enough segment to remain significant in close elections, poorly educated white males no longer constitute the bulk of the voters.

Generational replacement, the Voting Rights Act and black political mobilization, the shift of women from the home into the work place, and the steady rise of an urban middle class have profoundly transformed the simple and fairly homogeneous electorate of yesteryear into today's diversified entity. Just as the reentry of blacks raised the costs of race-baiting and removed much overt racism, so increased voting by women has generally ruled out candidates who conduct themselves in patently sexist ways. Astute campaigners acknowledge the electorate's diversity by avoiding negative characterizations of various subgroups of southerners. Television has reinforced these changes in campaign style. Though this medium can be used to disseminate old-fashioned "whispering campaigns" based on gossip, rumor, and innuendo, it eliminates most ranters and ravers, who appear to be simple arm-waving and rostrum-pounding fools and are unwelcome guests in most homes. A few southern politicians continue to use language with zest and originality, but the rhetoric of many modern campaigners is tepid stuff indeed.

Meager rates of participation in state elections remain a significant feature of the enduring South, and no one has provided a better analysis of the consequences of nonparticipation than Key. "The influence of levels of citizen-interest on the nature of the politics of an area is by no means a spectacular phenomenon," he argued. "Low levels of popular participation rather constitute a conditioning influence that over the years makes itself felt in unobtrusive ways." This "conditioning influence" has shaped and guided the working assumptions of most politicians. "The blunt truth," Key asserted, "is that politicians and officials are under no compulsion to pay much heed to classes and groups of citizens that do not vote." Key identified blacks, poorer rural whites, and industrial labor as the chief nonparticipants in the classic southern politics, to which we would add white women of lower socioeconomic status. Politicians typically devoted much more attention to the rural and small-town elites, and especially to the leading planters and farmers; in Key's words, "it would be fairly accurate to conclude that public policy discriminates in favor of the most prosperous, rural landowners."[19] The substance of state politics in the South was consistent with the values and objectives of the traditionalistic political culture: repression of blacks, limited taxation, virtually no large-scale state spending.

Since midcentury the proportions of eligible southerners who actually vote for their governors has increased only marginally. Although a few southern states plausibly resemble thriving democracies, most remain broadly based oligarchies, even if contemporary nonvoting is usually voluntary. The huge expansion of the middle class has created a setting in which most candidates for public office emphasize values and symbols that appeal to majorities in society's most successful strata, as well as to those members of the working class who believe in and aspire to the culturally dominant standards of reasonableness and legitimacy.

Southern state governments obviously provide more services than in the past; but as a rule they tax fairly lightly, regulate mainly where the public interest is so compelling that governmental intervention cannot be avoided, and spend comparatively little except where there are unmistakable direct benefits for the middle and upper-middle classes. In general, southern governments give scant attention and few tangible benefits to those in the bottom half of the social structure. Public policies are by and large consistent with the dominant philosophy of entrepreneurial individualism, which is more progressive in its use of public funds to stimulate economic growth than was the earlier traditionalistic philosophy. The main winners in the new southern politics have been the growing middle classes, particularly in the urban areas. Successful candidates for state office commonly blend elements from the individualistic political culture with traditionalistic themes. In the process they can often create cross-sectional support, uniting middle-class southerners and those who aspire to such status, urban residents and rural and small-town voters, and, on occasion, whites and blacks. In the small electorates of state politics, Democratic politicians have thus far prevailed more often than Republicans.

Although turnout in southern state elections has remained comparatively low, participation in presidential contests has greatly increased. In an environment where roughly half the potential electorate still does not bother to vote, the tone of the presidential electorate is set by the values and beliefs of the white middle class. As the national Democratic party has moved to the left and the national Republican party has moved toward the right, Republican presidential candidates have been ideally positioned to merge traditionalistic and individualistic themes in their appeal to members of the white majority. Dynamic enough to appeal to the urbanized middle class, traditional enough to win the votes of whites who have felt abandoned by the national Democratic party, Republican presidential nominees have been the main beneficiaries of the enlarged southern electorate.

nine

Contemporary
Racial
Attitudes

SOUTHERN politics is still powerfully conditioned by the historical experience of native southerners. From the "collective experience of the Southern people" developed a conscious regional identity among most members of the dominant racial group.[1] "Southern identification—a sense of the South as an entity over and above the states and localities that make it up and some sense of patriotism toward it—was shaped by the sectional conflict of the early 19th century," John Shelton Reed has argued. This state of mind intensified profoundly as a result of the Civil War. "The war itself, with its legacy of defeat, occupation, and subordination, gave the former Confederates another common basis for identification, a distinctiveness based on history rather than current circumstances," he points out. "They had not only their own flag, anthem, and holidays, but a heritage of economic—and allegedly, cultural and moral—inferiority to set them apart from other Americans."[2]

Among most residents the symbol "Southerner" is a powerful uniting force. Tremendous majorities of southern whites have responded favorably to this symbol in SRC-CPS surveys. As the South became more like the rest of the nation, only a modest decline (from slightly less than 90 percent in 1964 to 85 percent in 1980) occurred in the percentage of whites giving "warm" ratings. Although 13 percent of southern whites were indifferent to "Southerner" in 1980, much of this neutrality was predictably concentrated among migrants. Native white southerners, the most important and influential bearers of the cultural symbol, remained overwhelmingly positive in their responses to "Southerner."[3]

The persistence of highly favorable reactions to this symbol of regional identification is crucial in understanding the environment in which southern politics proceeds. "This ill-defined mass of Americans," Reed observes, "has resisted and continues to resist the assimilating effects of powerful 20th-century political, economic, and social forces, and maintains, in the face of those forces, a sense of its own distinctiveness." In Reed's view, "Southerners retain a strong sense of themselves as different from other Americans," even though "in some important respects they differ less than before."[4] In examining the often conflicting political attitudes of white and black southerners, it is important to keep in mind the durability of southern identity—this proud consciousness of being a southerner.

Patterns of public opinion concerning race relations (the subject of this chapter), the relative strength of conservatism and liberalism, and the degree of satisfaction with life in states and communities (the topics of the next chapter) are crucial for understanding central tendencies in contemporary southern politics.[5] In some instances we shall describe an unchanging South, a region characterized by the persistence of values generally associated with a traditionalistic political culture. In other cases we shall discuss patterns of belief more closely identified with an individualistic political culture, an emerging South preoccupied with individual freedom, especially the freedom to make and keep money. The political culture of the modern South blends traditionalistic and individualistic themes, and the broader meaning of the old and the new in public opinion data is captured in Thomas Pettigrew's observation that "the South is becoming more American and less Confederate."[6] Though undeniably the region is less isolated and parochial, less "southern" than in the past, key elements of the traditional way of life persist, as anyone who has ventured beyond a regional shopping mall, an affluent metropolitan suburb, or a large state university campus can easily attest. Accordingly, even though they are far more conventionally "American" than before, southerners' beliefs and attitudes are not identical with those of nonsoutherners, and there is no reason to suppose that the region will soon be completely absorbed into a homogeneous national political culture.[7]

The Preferred Form of Race Relations

An integral part of the traditionalistic political culture was the assumption of white supremacy and black inferiority. At times, as in the 1928 formulation of U. B. Phillips, white supremacy—the conviction that the South "shall be and remain a white man's country"—has been interpreted as "the cardinal test of a Southerner."[8] White southerners were commonly presented as monolithically supportive of white supremacy and unalterably opposed to desegregation in any form. Other observers of the region, however, had suggested the possibility of attitudinal changes on even such a basic cultural belief as segregation. Tindall argued in 1960 that Phillips had exaggerated the importance of white supremacy and that a significant erosion of the white supremacy doctrine had long been under way. "A gradual diminution in the force of the Southern Credo has now been apparent for several decades," wrote Tindall. "Though persisting in most of its aspects, the new peculiar institution itself began to show signs of strain under pressure in the thirties, in the forties it began to crack, and now, in the fifties, its chief symbol and support, Jim Crow, has come under virtual sentence of death by the federal courts."[9] A year earlier, Pettigrew had suggested that much of the region's enthusiasm for white supremacy derived not so much from deeply rooted personality needs of white southerners as from strong pressures for social conformity. Contending that many white southerners were even "latent liberals" on the racial issue, Pettigrew argued that the success of the desegregation process "rests on the effectiveness with which the racial integration now going on in the South can restructure the mores to which many latent liberal Southerners conform."[10]

Tindall's perspective suggests that some southerners would already be dissenting from white supremacy orthodoxy by the early 1960s, whereas Pettigrew's interpretation leads to an expectation of diminishing white preferences for racial segregation over time since some patterns of interracial behavior have demonstrably changed. Yet even if many white southerners would probably not desire a return to Jim Crow conditions, it is also unlikely that many would prefer the opposite form of race relations—integration or desegregation. Because most white adults were thoroughly socialized to white supremacist beliefs, embracing integration would appear to be too radical a shift for most white southerners to accept. As we have shown in previous chapters, interracial practices in the South have only been partially transformed. If most whites were to seek to bring their beliefs into conformity with their practices, support for some type of race relations occupying an intermediate position between total segregation and complete integration would be the most likely possibility. Even such a limited change would amount to a significant revision of the values underlying southern political customs and institutions.

To analyze the shifting beliefs and preferences of white southerners concerning race relations, we shall first examine a question that goes to the heart of the traditional southern culture: "Do you prefer strict segregation, integration, or something in-between?" This question elicits beliefs about the desired structure of race relations in general, rather than tapping attitudes toward specific areas of interracial behavior. First devised and asked of a representative sample of southerners in 1961 by Matthews and Prothro, it was subsequently replicated (with "desegregation" replacing integration as one of the options) in the 1964-1976 SRC-CPS presidential election year surveys.[11]

Had white southerners been asked this question in 1940, near unanimity would have been expressed for strict segregation.[12] At that time even organizations strongly opposed to the Jim Crow system commonly sought only equal treatment or equal facilities for blacks within a segregated social order. If our assumption of almost total white support for segregation in the early 1940s is combined with Tindall's observation of fissures in the system during the 1940s and 1950s, we have a reasonable basis for interpreting trends in segregationist sentiment prior to the 1961 survey. Although Matthews and Prothro found most white southerners (65 percent) still committed to the traditional form of race relations, fully one-third were not—a magnitude of regional "disloyalty" to the "central theme" that would have been inconceivable before World War II. A marked decline in strict segregationist beliefs must have occurred between the early 1940s and the early 1960s. But the decline was *not* associated with the growth of substantial integrationist sentiment, for only 7 percent of white southerners identified with that goal. Most whites who failed to support strict segregation wanted "something in-between" strict segregation and integration.[13]

Most of the early white mavericks resided in the Peripheral South, which provided 77 percent of the survey's white respondents but 98 percent of the integrationists and 90 percent of those in the middle. Three-fifths of Peripheral South whites were still strict segregationists, but a third adopted the intermediate position and 8 percent favored integration. No such diversity existed among Deep South whites. A massive 86 percent preferred strict segregation; merely 14 percent took the something-in-between option, and only one of 154 respondents (0.6 percent) expressed a preference for integration. Across the region segregationists were far more dominant in rural and small-town areas (72 percent) than in the medium-sized cities (56 percent) and large cities (52 percent).

As the effects of the civil rights movement and federal intervention were felt, abrupt changes occurred in the expressed preferences of white southerners (see figure 9.1). In each successive election year survey after 1961 smaller percentages of whites have favored strict segregation, while the proportion of respondents choosing desegregation has increased (before leveling off between 1972 and 1976). The greatest relative decline in strict segregationist sentiment occurred between 1964 and 1968. Battered by the actual changes in race relations that took place during the Johnson administration, adherents of the traditionalistic culture no longer constituted a majority of white southerners by 1968, and certainly not a majority of the most educated whites. Percentages of segregationists and desegregationists were equal by 1972, and four years later, in a region where segregation had once been synonymous with a distinctive way of life, the percentage of desegregationists slightly exceeded that of strict segregationists. Since 1968 the central tendency of white southerners has been to opt for something in-between the theoretical extremes. Though the overarching belief in a totally segregated society is disappearing, the past lingers on in the absence of extensive white support for the goal of desegregation.

Many considerations underlie the shifting preferences shown in figure 9.1, but we think waning support for strict segregation results primarily from two conclusions that white southerners seem to have drawn about the process of desegregation. First, many whites appear to have decided that the price of maintaining complete segregation—the cost of preserving the undiluted traditionalistic culture—was prohibitive. To insist on total segregation in the face of escalating black protest and increasing federal intervention meant that other valued goods—public schools, economic development, an orderly and peaceful society—might be denied white southerners.[14] Second, many white southerners came to perceive desegregation of public accommodations and expansion of the franchise as marginal adjustments in interracial relations, as reforms that were compatible with sustained white control. In every southern state, and in most city and county governments, whites continued to maintain the key positions of power and influence.

Thus far whites socialized within the region have not been distinguished from those whose formative years were spent in the North and West. To make the case that a central cultural belief of southern whites has been modified, it is necessary to show that the traditional bearers of the culture—whites native to the region—have discernibly shifted their views and that the changes visible among all whites are not just a consequence of increased Yankee immigration. The racial preferences of native whites and immigrant whites are charted separately in figure 9.1. As expected, whites raised outside the South have been much less committed to racial segregation than have native whites. Yankee immigration has measurably affected the distribution of white racial beliefs; without the influx of nonsouthern whites, strict segregationists would still have outnumbered desegregationists in 1976.

Most white southerners are natives, however, and northern newcomers could not possibly account for all of the observed changes in segregationist beliefs. A marked decline in support for strict segregation among whites who were raised in the South is evident in figure 9.1. By 1968,

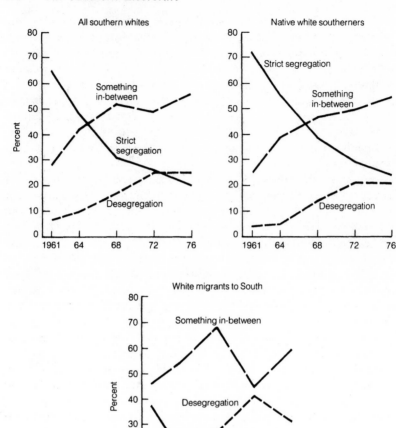

Figure 9.1. Diminished white support for strict segregation: preferred form of race relations among all southern whites, native white southerners, and white migrants to the South, 1961–1976. Sources: 1961 data from the survey conducted by Donald R. Matthews and James W. Prothro; all other data from SRC-CPS presidential election year surveys.

even among whites native to the region, strict segregation had been re-placed by something in-between as the preferred form of race relations. Yet overwhelming majorities of native southern whites, it should be emphasized, have continued to reject "desegregation." Only 21 percent chose this option in both 1972 and 1976, compared to larger minorities who still favored strict segregation.

We have also analyzed differences in these beliefs among white south-erners according to education, perceived social class, size of place, and age. Of these four variables, the strongest and most consistent relation-ships link preferences in race relations to differences in level of formal education, a finding similar to Matthews and Prothro's results.[15] The trends reported in figure 9.2 should not be interpreted as attributing *leadership* on this issue to the most educated white southerners. On the contrary, it was far more a matter either of responding to new conditions presented by protesting blacks and federal authorities or of forestalling anticipated protest activity. White resistance, acquiescence, and adap-tation to a redefined situation, rather than bold white initiatives to re-shape the society, are the main themes.[16]

The basic pattern of attitude modification appears to have been initial resistance by white southerners of all educational levels, followed by reluctant acquiescence sifting slowly downward from the most educated to the least educated whites. More than half of all southern whites with some exposure to college had abandoned strict segregationist preferences as early as 1961, and by the mid-1970s the segregationist perspective was so unusual among whites who had attended college that it was only admitted by one in ten. Although whites with a college education were considerably more supportive of desegregation than whites who had not gone to college, the leading tendency (1972 excepted) among these whites has been something in-between segregation and desegregation. Strict seg-regation, favored in 1964 by nearly half of the whites who had finished high school, was preferred by less than a fourth of this group by 1968 and by smaller percentages in subsequent surveys. Segregationist senti-ment was most pervasive and resistant to change among southern whites whose formal education had ended before completing high school. Eighty percent of whites without a high school degree identified themselves as strict segregationists in 1961, and not until 1972 did fewer than half of them opt for segregation. As late as 1976 almost one-third of the least educated whites preferred the traditional form of race relations while only one-seventh supported desegregation.

It is instructive to examine the stance of white segregationists, of "in-betweeners," and of desegregationists vis-à-vis specific civil rights pro-posals. The degree of support for the anti-civil-rights position by each

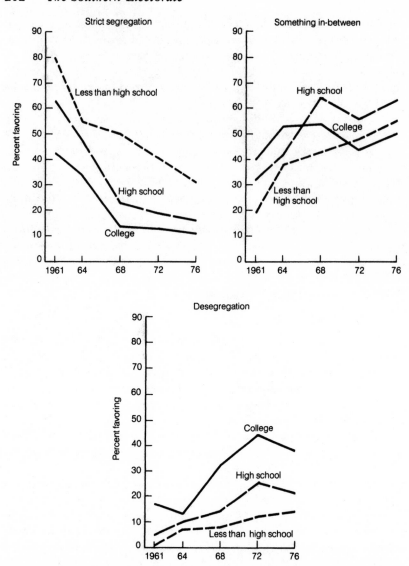

Figure 9.2. Education and white racial attitudes: white southerners' preferred form of race relations, 1961–1976, by level of education. Sources: Same as figure 9.1.

of these groups on selected racial issues that were included in the 1964-1976 SRC-CPS election year surveys is reported in table 9.1. The table's summary of white racial attitudes helps explain what is and what is not discussed in contemporary regional politics.

Few strict segregationists found anything to favor in any specific civil rights proposal. Unreconciled to the changes that had occurred, they remained opposed to additional revisions of the color lines. Though proponents of strict segregationist views are seldom seen any longer in campaigns for major state offices, strict segregationists persist as a minority of the mass public and in some states are probably as numerous as black voters.

In contrast, most white desegregationists supported additional changes in race relations. Almost all of the racial progressives thought blacks had the right to buy a house in a "white" neighborhood, and large majorities of them favored federal enforcement of equal access to public accommodations. Nonetheless, desegregationists departed from liberal ortho-

Table 9.1. Persistence of southern racial conservatism: percentage of white southerners supporting conservative position on specific racial issues, by their preferred form of race relations, 1964–1976ᵃ

Racial issues	Whites' preferred form of race relations		
	Strict segregation	Something in-between	Desegregation
Outer color line			
Federal responsibility to desegregate public accommodations			
1964	94	75	29
1968	96	57	15
1972	80	51	24
Intermediate color line			
Federal responsibility to desegregate schools			
1964	95	69	26
1968	94	76	33
1972	91	82	47
1976	96	78	56
Federal responsibility to prevent job discrimination			
1964	78	75	34
1968	80	73	35
1972	68	66	40

Table 9.1.   (continued)

| | Whites' preferred form of race relations | | |
Racial issues	Strict segregation	Something in-between	Desegregation
Right of blacks to buy home in white neighborhood			
1964	82	55	5
1968	93	36	2
1972	76	36	8
1976	64	14	6
Prefer entirely white neighborhood			
1976	95	67	41

Source: SRC-CPS presidential election year surveys, 1964–1976.

a. Each entry reports the percentage of white southerners who supported the conservative alternative on a given question. In calculating the conservative position among white southerners, we have set aside those respondents who said they had not given any thought to the issue, as well as the small number of individuals whose opinions were qualified or ambiguous. The specific questions (with the "conservative" response in parenthesis) are as follows:

"Should the government support the right of black people to go to any hotel or restaurant they can afford, or should it stay out of this matter?" (stay out)

"Do you think the government in Washington should see to it that white and black children go to the same schools or stay out of this area as it is not its (the government's) business?" (stay out)

"Should the government in Washington see to it that black people get fair treatment in jobs or leave these matters to the states and local communities?" (leave to states and local communities)

"Which of these statements would you agree with: white people have a right to keep black people out of their neighborhoods if they want to; or black people have a right to live wherever they can afford to, just like anybody else?" (whites have a right to keep blacks out)

"Would you personally prefer to live in a neighborhood that is all white, mostly white, about half white and half black, or mostly black?" (all-white neighborhood)

doxy on two public school issues. They strongly opposed busing (not shown) as a means of desegregating schools (their views on this issue were similar to those of the strict segregationists), and many of them became increasingly skeptical about the federal government's responsibility for school desegregation as this change in race relations was actually implemented. For whatever reasons—chiefly, we suspect, perceived negative consequences for white children from busing and from the desegregation experience—federal intervention to desegregate schools has not elicited attitudinal acquiescence among most southern whites. Racial conservatives and in-betweeners were initially hostile and have remained opposed, and more and more desegregationists have begun to agree with the conservatives. Public opinion data on this aspect of the intermediate color line bear out Blumer's prediction of much greater white resistance there than to issues of the outer color line.

Far more numerous than segregationists or desegregationists are the whites whose preferred form of race relations is something in-between. To label them "moderate" would be a misnomer because their concrete preferences lean decisively in a conservative, antichange direction. Overwhelming majorities of this group opposed busing, rejected federal responsibility for school desegregation and equal employment practices, and preferred an all-white neighborhood. On two other questions not reported in the table, strong majorities of the in-betweeners believed that minorities should help themselves rather than relying on the federal government and thought that blacks already possessed too much political influence. In these areas far more members of the intermediate group sided with the strict segregationists than with the desegregationists. Only on two issues did the white in-betweeners display signs of increasing liberalism. By 1976 only 14 percent still belived that whites had the right to refuse to sell a house to a black. They may still prefer an exclusively white neighborhood, but they now recognize that whites no longer have the "right" to exclude minorities. In addition, intermediates increasingly accepted federal responsibility for the desegregation of public accommodations. Though we cannot be sure of their present attitudes (the public accommodations question has not been asked since 1972), it is probable that most in-betweeners no longer contest federal responsibility for prohibiting racial discrimination involving the outer color line. Current civil rights controversies, however, are much more likely to focus on the intermediate color line, and on many of these issues—questions concerning affirmative action, quotas, busing, open housing preferences, and additional school desegregation—most of the in-between whites are hardly progressive. Strict segregationists and in-betweeners in the modern South compose an extensive white majority dead set against further government-sponsored assaults on the intermediate color line.

Political Consequences of Revised Racial Attitudes

What have been the principal political consequences of changed white attitudes concerning the preferred form of race relations? Three developments—the partial resolution of extremely divergent interracial preferences, the alteration of elite political behavior to reflect nonsegregationist but not necessarily integrationist beliefs, and the softening of attitudinal differences between southern and nonsouthern whites—are particularly important.

Within the South, black protest and federal intervention revised white attitudes and stimulated a partial transformation of the "crisis of southern politics." In their 1961 survey Matthews and Prothro discovered that large majorities of whites and blacks not only desired completely different patterns of race relations but were also unaware of the opposite race's true preferences. "Only a significant change in white racial attitudes, awareness, and expectations," they warned, could "ensure the avoidance of a racial holocaust and the preservation of political democracy in the South."[17] Between 1961 and 1976 the magnitude of cleavage separating the races had moderated, with most of the change concentrated among white southerners. No longer does an atmosphere of impending crisis pervade the region. It must be underscored, however, that most blacks and most whites still hold conflicting views on their preferred form of race relations. Four-fifths of black southerners endorsed desegregation in 1976, while only one-fifth of the native whites shared this preference.

Massive white opposition to liberal positions on specific civil rights controversies underlines the limited transformation of southern racial attitudes. Throughout southern history most whites have *always* objected to what most southern blacks have wanted in race relations, and this generalization still largely holds (see table 9.2). Contemporary white public opinion is scarcely permissive regarding the federal presence in ending job discrimination, combating racially separate housing patterns, and supervising the racial composition of public schools. That some changes in actual behavior have occurred over the objections of southern whites indicates that the region's white majority no longer maintains an informal veto over the national government's racial policies, but it does *not* signify that most whites prefer or support these federal policies. Save for the right of blacks to purchase homes in "white" neighborhoods, *southern whites and blacks disagree on virtually all of the issues of the intermediate color line.*

The new racial status quo is clearly different from that of the past, but it is a status quo that was essentially imposed upon white southerners. Nearly all influential white subgroups oppose the positions on current racial issues that are preferred by majorities of southern blacks. Whether white southerners are examined by age, formal education, or social class, it is difficult to identify a substantial corps of racially "progressive" whites. Moreover, nine-tenths of black southerners in 1976 thought that blacks exerted too little influence in politics, compared with slightly more than half of white southerners who believed that blacks had too much political influence. Although individual instances of racial amity certainly occur and interracial coalitions may be possible here and there, the central themes of survey research on southern race relations are the persistence

Table 9.2. Racial attitudes on issues of the intermediate color line: percentage of respondents supporting the conservative position on particular questions, by race and region, 1964–1976ª

Issues of the intermediate color line	White southerners	Black southerners	All southerners	White nonsoutherners	All nonsoutherners
Federal responsibility to desegregate schools					
1964	77	13	65	46	44
1968	74	8	61	55	52
1972	75	13	62	55	52
1976	76	11	61	66	63
Federal responsibility to prevent job discrimination					
1964	73	3	58	53	49
1968	69	8	57	55	52
1972	60	8	47	49	46
Right of blacks to buy home in white neighborhood					
1964	64	2	51	29	27
1968	50	2	41	21	20
1972	38	0	29	14	13
1976	20	2	16	8	7
Prefer entirely white (black) neighborhood					
1976	67	21	58	44	41

Source: Same as table 9.1.

a. Each entry reports the percentage of respondents who supported the conservative alternative on a given question. For question wording, see table 9.1.

of conflict on racial issues and the continued political impotence and frustration of black southerners.

In view of their conflicting attitudes on the ideal form of race relations, it is not surprising that white and black perceptions of the scope and pace of racial change have often differed (see figure 9.3). Since 1968 majorities of whites have thought "a lot" of change has occurred in race relations, whereas blacks have increasingly come to think that only "some" change has taken place. Measured against what most whites prefer—strict segregation or something in-between—the desegregation of public accommodations and black political participation may well qualify as "a lot" of change; set against the objective of most blacks—desegregation—the struggle against racial discrimination has been only partially won. Black and white perceptions may well be moving again on a collision course. In the past, one restraining influence has been the feeling among black southerners that the pace of racial change has been "about right,"

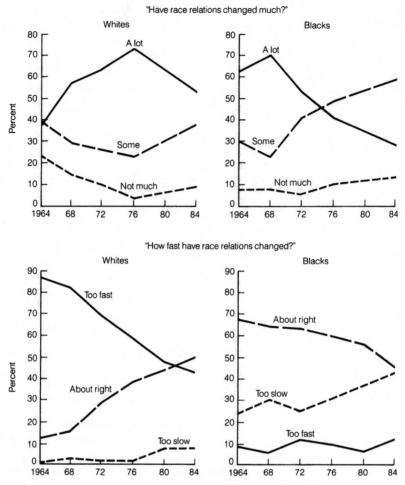

Figure 9.3. Contrary perceptions of racial change in the South: white and black views on the scope and speed of racial change, 1964–1984. (First question was not asked in 1980.) Sources: SRC-CPS presidential election year surveys.

rather than "too slow" or "too fast." Although black respondents in 1984 were about as likely to give an "about right" answer as a "too slow" reply, trend lines on this question indicate growing impatience among southern blacks with the speed of change in race relations, a mood of frustration that seems certain to persist. As for southern whites, after the organized civil rights movement collapsed in the late sixties, increasing percentages began to interpret the rate of racial change as "about right" rather than "too fast." In 1984 whites who believed race relations were changing "too fast" were outnumbered by those who believed the pace of change was "about right." Two decades earlier almost nine-tenths of the white southerners had thought race relations were being reformed too swiftly. On fundamental questions of race relations, whites and blacks in the South still "see" the past and the present very differently.

The destruction of the Jim Crow system undermined the strict segregationists' political effectiveness. A politician advocating segregation as a moral guide for the modern South would speak for a declining segment of whites and would risk electoral repudiation by many whites who no longer pledge allegiance to the old order of race relations. Shifts in mass beliefs away from strict segregation are highly correlated with the rise of nonsegregationist southern politicians. Trends in mass beliefs and elite campaign behavior have been mutually reinforcing. Politicians who campaigned on issues other than preserving white supremacy in its accustomed form helped redefine priorities for white voters, and the movement away from strict segregation among white voters helped liberate campaigners from the necessity of emphasizing racist perspectives.

Yet care should be taken not to exaggerate the extent to which white candidates altered their racial beliefs after federal intervention. In *Southern Governors and Civil Rights,* Earl Black emphasized that "changes in campaign stances" were "significant but less than revolutionary." "If the principle of racial segregation was rarely championed by the early 1970s, and if most white candidates have accepted the necessity of soliciting black support," he argued, "the rise of the nonsegregationist campaigners has usually not meant that southern politicians have become discernibly pro-black in their campaign rhetoric."[18] The main reason why most southern politicians still do not campaign as unequivocal integrationists lies in white public opinion. As we have seen, the isolation of the South's extreme racial conservatives has *not* meant that "latent liberals" have become the new regional majority among whites. Far from it.

Possessing an intuitive understanding of these cleavages, most white politicians have responded by not moving against the dominant tide of white public opinion, by not endorsing obviously unpopular positions. Although some white campaigners have attempted to educate their audiences to the benefits of more inclusive economic, social, and political citizenship for all groups of southerners, progressive leadership on racial topics in southern state politics has been infrequent and generally unsuccessful. The safer strategy has been to ignore, de-emphasize, or obfuscate interracial differences and to treat sensitive questions in the most bland and uncontroversial language. It is no small matter than most of these politically delicate racial issues concern the national government (especially its courts and bureacracies) and not the institutions of state and local governments. Southern state governments have undertaken few serious and thorough initiatives to alter race relations; and in the rare instances where governors have urged faster rates of racial change, state legislatures and bureaucracies have typically been unsympathetic and unresponsive. To emphasize the desirability of additional alterations of the color lines is to invite defeat among the large majority of whites who do not wish to see their traditions undergo further reform.

Finally, regional trends in the preferred form of race relations need to be placed in national perspective. At the level of general preferences, whites in the South and non-South have become increasingly alike. Although the South still contains a larger percentage of strict segregationists (20 versus 8 percent in 1976), and the rest of the nation still has more self-professed desegregationists (38 versus 25 percent in the same year), in both regions white majorities (56 percent in the South, 54 percent in the non-South) pick something in-between as their preferred form of race relations. The scope and tenacity of racist beliefs historically differentiated the South from the non-South, and federal intervention narrowed the effective range of white racism in the South. On this central question, the waning of sectional differences has proceeded far more through the "nationalization" of white southerners' attitudes than through any "southernization" of the racial preferences of nonsouthern whites.

But the matter of race relations in general is only part of the story. Far more consequential for practical politics are white attitudes on specific racial controversies, and on some issues related to the intermediate color line the survey evidence shows nonsouthern whites becoming more conventionally "southern" in their views. There is practically no difference, for example, between nonsouthern and southern whites in their strong opposition to the use of busing to achieve school desegregation, and there has been a striking change in nonsouthern white attitudes concerning the principle of federal responsibility for school desegregation. Only 46 percent of nonsouthern whites opposed federal involvement in this issue in 1964, but by 1976, after the federal government had become involved in school desegregation suits in many northern cities, two-thirds of them opposed the federal presence (see table 9.2). Majorities of whites across the nation also repudiated federal involvement in job discrimination issues, and the use of quotas to ensure minority hiring has been almost universally opposed.[19] In these crucial areas of the intermediate color line, whites in the two regions are far more similar than dissimilar in their preferences. If whites are especially opposed to governmental intervention in such conflicts, they are much less resistant to (or concerned about) racial changes that result from the actions of individual members of minority groups. The only section of the intermediate color line where white attitudes have become more liberal is that which concerns the right of blacks to purchase homes in "white" neighborhoods, and the main difference in white preferences is that a sizable majority of white southerners still prefer to live in an all-white neighborhood, while slightly fewer than half of the nonsouthern whites have the same preference.

Though southern and northern whites are now more similar in their racial attitudes than ever before, the regions are still not identical. On issue after issue white southerners are regularly more racially conservative than their counterparts outside the South, and the white majorities whose vision of ideal race relations does not include the goal of a thoroughly desegregated society are still larger in the South than in the non-South (76 percent versus 62 percent in 1976).

Despite all the disadvantages and obstacles still confronting blacks, immeasurably more freedom, dignity, and respect are accorded members of the minority group in the modern South than in earlier years. One of the consequences of reformed race relations has been the creation of more positive attitudes among blacks about southern identity. SRC-CPS presidential election year surveys from 1964 through 1980 have included "Southerner" as one of the groups that respondents were asked to evaluate on a "feeling thermometer." Southern blacks who awarded "warm" ratings to the symbol "Southerner" increased from only 50 percent in 1964 to 84 percent in 1980. The principal explanation for this change must lie in the civil rights movement, the resulting federal legislation, and the general acquiescence of most southern whites to reform of the outer color line. Southern blacks apparently responded by thinking somewhat better of their white fellow southerners and by beginning to think of themselves also as southerners.[20]

Yet a telling reminder of the color line's intensity still persists. Historically, the term "southerners" connoted whites who were native to or resident in the region and represented part of Blumer's "innermost" citadel of the color lines, the area of equal status among all members of the "superior" race. Has this color line been breached? It appears that white southerners have changed their feelings far less than black southerners. Not until 1980 did as many as three-fifths of white southerners express warmth toward blacks as a group, and merely 9 percent volunteered feeling "close" to blacks. On the basis of the available evidence, Merle Black and John Shelton Reed have concluded: "We suspect that 'Southerner' still means 'white Southerner' for most of the region's majority racial group, although many Southern whites would—on second thought—probably allow that Southern blacks are indeed Southerners, too."[21] If the day ever arrives when most white southerners think of blacks as fellow southerners on *first* thought, that will be a monumental change. It will signify reformation of the most impregnable line of all, through genuine acceptance of blacks as the equals of whites.

ten
———

The Conservative
Advantage in
Public Opinion

CONSERVATISM occupies an exalted ideological position in the South. Although the region has sometimes been portrayed as ripe for the construction of successful biracial coalitions of have-littles and have-nots, the growth of the urban middle class and the popularity of middle-class beliefs among southern white workers have worked against explicit class politics and in favor of conservative politics generally. When southerners are queried about their ideological preferences, their beliefs concerning individual versus governmental responsibility for securing jobs and a good standard of living, and their satisfaction with life in their states and localities, the collective thrust of their responses reveals a region in which conservatism flourishes and liberalism withers.

Conservatism and Individualism

Individual responsibility is a major theme in southern Protestant culture (and in American culture generally), one that few natives could have escaped in childhood. "Ask God for help in your work," goes a Protestant prayer, "but do not ask Him to do it for you."[1] The traditionalistic and the entrepreneurial individualistic political cultures emphasize conservatism and the desirability of rewarding individual effort and achievement; both cultures are comfortable with pronounced inequalities in family income, regarding them as the natural consequences of differences in ability, effort, skill, and opportunity as well as conducive to the successful motivation of leadership and achievement.

At the same time, virtually all southerners—as well as all Americans—also believe that "government ought to help the common man," and, by implication, that "government ought not to hurt the common man."

Recognizing that vast social forces and particular events may be far beyond an individual's control and that Americans begin life with very unequal chances for success, beliefs about the importance of the "common man" can support broad notions of governmental responsibility for economic well-being as well as notions of fairness and equity in taxation and expenditure policies. In the South an emphasis on liberalism and governmental responsibility derives mainly from the moralistic culture among blacks and the Populist version of the individualistic culture among a minority of whites; each of these traditions stresses short-term assistance for low-income groups in the form of redistributing income or power from groups at the top to groups at the bottom of society. The entrepreneurial version of the individualistic culture, though hostile to short-term redistribution from haves to have-littles and have-nots, recognizes government's positive obligation to "solve" the problem of inadequate income by promoting rapid economic growth.

The beliefs of white southerners concerning the national government's propensity to help or hurt the region's common whites have changed during this century. Southerners historically expected little or nothing from the national government, expectations that were generally matched by the government's performance. The Great Depression pushed many whites and blacks who had meager economic resources into unimagined poverty. As Cash described the South of 1932, "Everybody was either ruined beyond his wildest previous fears or stood in peril of such ruin." Southern whites became progovernment from sheer necessity; their options were limited and their short-term self-interest clear. Whites wanted national authorities that could understand, sympathize, and do something about the devastated economy. The New Deal meant direct financial aid for many whites without a concomitant burden of heavy taxation since most of the recipients were too poor to pay much in taxes. By not supporting civil rights issues or programs that would provide substantial, obtrusive aid to blacks, the Roosevelt administration avoided entangling the national government in the one issue that would assuredly have infuriated white southerners. Under such favorable conditions of exchange, which provided material benefits for southern whites without much taxation and without threatening the racial status quo, "no section of the country greeted Franklin Roosevelt and the New Deal with more intense and unfeigned enthusiasm than did the South."[2]

There was an underlying strain, nonetheless, in the region's acceptance of the New Deal. "It was obvious enough," Cash wrote, "that the basic Rooseveltian ideas, with their emphasis on the social values as against the individual, and on the necessity of revising all values in light of the conditions created by the machine and the disappearance of the frontier, ran directly contrary to the basic Southern attitudes." But these ideological conflicts were generally either ignored or set aside, for "Roosevelt was hope and confidence after long despair."[3] What needs to be emphasized is the constricted character, the narrow bounds, of New Deal "liberalism" in the South. The turn to the national government on economic matters was a situational response of a desperate, impoverished people who had nowhere else to go. Southern whites had not abandoned their belief in the work ethic but had simply recognized its irrelevance after the entire economy had collapsed. In many other aspects of their lives—religious beliefs and practices, race relations, opposition to basic civil liberties—most white southerners remained fundamentally conservative.

By the 1960s economic circumstances were vastly improved over the depression years, and many whites viewed the federal government as hurting rather than helping people like themselves through its taxes and expenditures. Economic development shifted most whites out of poverty and into stable working-class or middle-class jobs, but relatively few white families commanded truly comfortable incomes. Most of the new working-class and middle-class white families lived in a gray zone of personal finance where expanding needs and wants collided with limited cash. As David Halberstam explained, white southerners increasingly began to feel the bite of higher federal tax brackets. " 'They're having to pay for the first time in their lives for what they've always been getting in the past,' " a person who handled tax returns for southern workers told Halberstam. Some families worked hard, lived within their means, tried to save for retirement, and expected others to do the same—to provide by themselves for their own family's needs. Others remained, or fell, deeply in debt, a situation pregnant with political implications, for "out of this comes an enormous amount of frustration, to be making that much money, to be paying that much tax, and still be in debt."[4]

To make matters worse, many white southerners perceived themselves as being forced to contribute, against their convictions and desires, to programs for which blacks were highly visible beneficiaries. Many black southerners, we have stressed, remain in chronic poverty or have incomes only slightly above poverty levels, and their economic realities fuel demands for more and more benefits and services from the federal government. These demands, in turn, are viewed negatively—to understate the situation—by many white southerners, who see some of their taxes going to support individuals who cannot or will not provide for themselves and their dependents. " 'They've made about $7,000 a year in the factory and picked up another $2,000 through the soil bank,' " Halberstam was told in 1970. " 'You go through their returns and they owe $1,500 in taxes. And they're pissed off. Mightily. You can see them thinking, "Where does the tax money go? Welfare. And who gets the welfare? The niggers. And who did I just see on my color TV raising hell and carrying on and burning some damn thing? The niggers." And so they're angry as hell.' "⁵ That such programs as welfare or food stamps accounted for only a small percentage of federal spending, especially in comparison with defense expenditures, was either unknown or considered irrelevant. In 1968 more white southerners wanted the federal government to stop spending money on poverty than to continue doing so, with the strongest opposition centered in large cities and rural areas with large black populations. The federal government was becoming an enemy to the average white person in the South.

Tremendous disparities in what black and white southerners want from the federal government have persisted since the Great Society brought together what the New Deal had kept apart. In 1982 SRC-CPS asked a national sample to evaluate spending levels in different federal programs. In each of six areas where whites favored spending less money and blacks favored spending more, blacks were prominent as potential beneficiaries, even though they might not form the majority of recipients. Federal expenditures for food stamps and welfare produced the sharpest interracial cleavages, but aid to blacks, unemployment, aid to large cities, and student loans also split the races. Only a handful of areas—military spending, protecting the environment, and combating drugs—elicited similar preferences from both blacks and whites. In the remaining policy areas, the net balance within each racial group was similar, but large differences still separated the races.

The data do suggest a small core of important federal programs—social security, health care, education, the environment, and drugs and crime—for which there is biracial support to maintain or even enhance the national government's role. Whites have not totally abandoned their reliance on the federal government in fostering a "good standard of living," but they have become much more skeptical about federal programs that give them few direct benefits.

One of the most notable consequences of the federal government's changing role in the South has been the destruction of feelings of trust toward and respect for public authorities that white southerners had previously displayed.⁶ From 1952 through 1976 the SRC-CPS asked respondents, "Do you think that public officials care about people like yourselves?" Most white southerners answered affirmatively in the 1950s. Only a minority, disproportionately concentrated in the southern working class, dissented from the prevailing view. During the eight years of Democratic rule in the 1960s, however, the proportion of distrustful working-class whites increased from 44 percent in 1960 to 66 percent in 1968. Subsequent surveys usually found three-fifths or more of this group doubting that public officials cared about people like themselves. Of the many factors that have contributed to the greater sensitivity and alienation on the part of working-class whites than of middle-class whites, several stand out: as a group, the members of the white working class were less insulated from many of the changes in race relations, they had far less "surplus" in their personal finances to absorb increases in taxation, and they were more likely to be drafted and to participate in the Vietnam War. George Wallace was the southern politician who most powerfully communicated the anger and frustration of the southern white "little man" in the 1960s, and Wallace's strident contempt for "briefcase totin' bureaucrats" is mirrored in the whites' repudiation of public officials.

By the early 1970s alienation had spread to the region's white middle class. The pace of public school desegregation actually accelerated during the Nixon administration, disappointing those middle-class whites who believed Nixon would halt federal intervention; and inflation began to push many middle-class people into higher tax brackets, even as their real purchasing power deteriorated. In 1976 a majority of middle-class whites thought that public officials were not concerned about them. In this tumultuous period of social and economic change, most southern whites shifted to a stance of alienation and distrust of government officials that had previously characterized black southerners alone. For very different reasons, millions of white and black southerners in the 1970s felt that public officials in America were indifferent to their vital interests.

Bearing in mind the continuing differences between the personal finances of blacks and whites, the enormous divergencies between the two races' taxing and spending priorities, and the widespread doubt across races that public officials cared about people like themselves, let us next examine southern ideological preferences. Asking individuals to label themselves "conservative," "middle-of-the-road," or "liberal" may elicit ambiguous responses (since we do not know precisely what people mean when they use these terms), but the information gained is useful as a rough indicator of the distribution of ideological preferences within a given political system.

Conservatism's disproportionate appeal to southerners is evident in both the 1968 CSEP data and the 1972-1984 SRC-CPS surveys (see table 10.1). In both comparisons the conservatism of white southerners stands in stark contrast to the robust liberalism of black southerners. In most states the propensities of whites (especially native whites) continue to set the basic ideological tone of political life, a tone that is far more likely to emphasize conservative than liberal themes. Accordingly, for southern white politicians who give primary concern and attention to the central

Table 10.1. The conservative South: ideological self-placement of southerners in 1968 and 1972–1984[a]

	1968 CSEP				1972–1984 SRC-CPS[b]			
Category of southerner	Con[c] (%)	MR[c] (%)	Lib[c] (%)	C/L[c]	Con (%)	MR (%)	Lib (%)	C/L
All southerners	41	44	15	2.7	45	33	22	2.1
Whites	44	44	12	3.7	49	34	17	2.8
Blacks	25	44	32	0.8	21	31	48	0.4

Sources: 1968 CSEP; 1972–1984 presidential election year surveys of SRC-CPS.
a. Data, except for ratios, are presented as percentages.
b. Results are averages of the 1972–1984 presidential election year surveys.
c. Con, conservative; MR, middle-of-the-road; Lib, liberal; C/L, ratio of conservatives to liberals.
Coding: For coding procedures, see table 3.2.

tendencies of white public opinion, some version of political conservatism is virtually irresistible. To campaign statewide as a full-fledged liberal is—under ordinary circumstances—simply to invite defeat. Even if the vastly different ideological preferences of blacks are included in the analysis, conservatives still hold a commanding superiority over liberals in mass predispositions. Black reentry into southern electoral politics has diluted but not destroyed the advantaged position of white conservatives. Conservatives can still evoke multiple issues, symbols, and appeals to elicit favorable emotional and intellectual responses from most white southerners, while at the same time placing liberal opponents (when they exist at all) on the defensive.

Conservative views also appear in response to questions probing whether the individual or the government should be responsible for securing a good job and a good standard of living (see table 10.2). For the region as a whole those favoring individual responsibility were slightly more numerous than those who looked to government. Racial differences are so salient, however, that white and black preferences must be examined separately in order to understand the politics of this issue. In table 10.2, respondents are grouped according to whether they supported individual responsibility or governmental responsibility for economic well-being. An even starker view of the differences that separate whites and blacks emerges when we consider only those respondents who took the most extreme positions possible (not shown in table 10.2). Almost half (48 percent) of black southerners advocated *total* governmental responsibility in providing a job and a good standard of living, a position that seemed proper or reasonable to merely 11 percent of white southerners. And

Table 10.2. Southern opinions on individuals versus governmental responsibility for obtaining a job and a good standard of living, 1972–1984[a]

Type of southerner	Greater stress on individual responsibility	Midpoint	Greater stress on governmental responsibility	IR/GR[b]
All southerners	44	20	36	1.2
Whites	51	22	27	1.9
Blacks	13	14	72	0.2

Sources: 1972, 1976, 1980, and 1984 SRC-CPS presidential election year surveys.

a. Opinion data are presented as percentages, which are averages of the four surveys used as sources.

b. IR/GR, ratio of respondents emphasizing individual responsibility to respondents stressing governmental responsibility.

Coding: For coding procedures, see table 3.3.

whereas only 4 percent of blacks put the entire burden of personal economic well-being on the private individual, 20 percent of white southerners assumed such a stance.

White southerners who incline toward individual responsibility clearly outnumber whites who profess a greater reliance on government to promote employment and a good income, thus confirming conventional wisdom. At the same time, though, the self-placement results show that most whites do not take an extremely right-wing position on this issue. Over time there has been a steady decline in the percentage of whites favoring a stance that, in effect, denies *any* governmental responsibility for the economic well-being of individuals: 36 percent desired "complete individual responsibility" in 1972, but only 9 percent did so in 1984. The public opinion data depict a white South leaning much more toward conservatism than liberalism, yet not dominated at the grassroots level by whites who would make individuals solely responsible for their own economic success or failure.

The Satisfied South: "Best" Communities in "Best" States

Historically, the advantages and disadvantages of southern living have been evaluated very differently by southern and nonsouthern whites. Whites who were born, raised, and still resided in the region generally absorbed an affection for things southern that encompassed places, people, institutions, and mores. Many acquired an abiding sense of regional patriotism, and some expressed as well a prickly defensiveness against any criticism of the homeland. American whites not immersed at a susceptible age in mainstream southern orthodoxy have usually viewed the region with indifference, bemusement, or ridicule, often perceiving southerners as impoverished, lazy, ignorant, racist, benighted, and morally and culturally inferior to themselves. These may be standard images of a vanquished people by their one-time conquerors, but long after the demise of the Civil War generations, negative impressions of the South were prevalent among nonsoutherners.

In many respects the national aversion to the South was understandable. As Reed has observed, in the South of the 1930s "per capita income was roughly at the level used today to distinguish developed from underdeveloped countries, and the usual implications for social welfare, public health, and education followed."[7] For a nonsoutherner, migration to the South frequently entailed a lot of explaining to a reluctant family. It meant participation in a social system that emphasized white supremacy and black repression far more bluntly than was customary in the North, the likelihood of earning much less income for comparable work elsewhere in the nation, the prospect of settling in a small town or rural area with a dearth of "sophisticated" entertainment and amusement, the near certainty of inferior public education, and, perhaps worst of all, intellectual and emotional suffocation in a parochial culture that emphasized the superiority of lineage and race and the unending perfidy of Yankees— and in the old days practically every nonsoutherner was regarded as a Yankee. Southern living was not an enchanting or enticing prospect for the uninitiated, and under these conditions few northern whites and virtually no northern blacks yearned for permanent acquaintance with the southern way of life.

Decades ago, in the early 1930s, the common national perception of the South as backward and reactionary was supported by a pioneering comparative study of the quality of life in the American states. Using census data to rank the states according to the relative degree of wealth, education, health, and public order, Charles Angoff and H. L. Mencken concluded that Connecticut and Massachusetts were the "best" American states and that Mississippi was the "worst" state. The other southern states clustered near Mississippi at the bottom of the rankings.[8] These results no doubt reinforced Mencken's sneering, unsympathetic appraisal of southerners which had earlier compelled him to dismiss the entire region as a cultural and human wasteland, "The Sahara of the Bozart."[9]

Since that time, however, the economic bases of the southern states have improved substantially. A few of the region's states have surpassed the national median income, and most of the rest seem to be on a slow track to eventual convergence. Although taxable wealth has increased, southern states tax at rates below the national average and tend to rely heavily on regressive taxes. Per capita spending on education, health, and social welfare has grown, but most southern states still rank toward the bottom of the fifty states in their provision of important state services.[10] Another comparative study in the Angoff-Mencken tradition, a 1973 report of the Midwest Research Institute entitled *The Quality of Life in the United States,* again found southern states lagging nonsouthern states in most of the comparisons, including such categories as individual equality, living conditions, agriculture, technology, economic status, education, health, welfare, and state and local government. The majority of the southern states' services and institutions in most of these fields were classified "substandard," and in the study's "quality of life" index the southern states were in their familiar position as the worst American states.[11]

Studies in the Angoff-Mencken tradition employ "measures of economic well-being and governmental services" as indirect indicators of the quality of life among the American states. Conclusions obviously turn on which indicators are used, and Reed argues that "there are reasons to doubt the perennial conclusion that the quality of life in the South is relatively poor. We find striking differences in the South's favor, for example, in suicide rates, in rates of mental illness, in rates of alcoholism and heart disease and other stress-related health problems. Each of these differences is open to several interpretations, of course, but taken together they suggest we shouldn't jump to conclusions about the quality of Southerners' lives."[12]

Another method of evaluating states and localities is through public opinion polling. The subjective appraisals obtained in such polls may only skim the surface of what a person thinks or feels about his or her state or community, but they do provide direct measures of perceived satisfaction or dissatisfaction. These studies give a very different picture of the quality of life in the South and non-South—a portrait of a South that is evaluated much more highly than the non-South. Reed, who has analyzed Gallup poll results on such questions from 1939 to the present, reports that "when Americans are asked where they would most like to live if they could live anywhere they wanted, a constant finding is that Southerners like it where they are better than any other Americans, except possibly Californians."[13]

In the 1968 CSEP poll the following statement was read to representative samples in thirteen states and six regions: "All things considered, (name of state) is the best state in the United States to live in." Respondents were asked if they agreed, disagreed, or were not sure about the statement. According to the evaluations of current residents in the various regions, the South and the West Coast contained the best American states, and the worst states were in the Northeast.[14] To quote Reed's pungent summary, "The Northeastern states were civilized and discontent, the Southern states were happily backward, and the Midwest was, as usual, mediocre all the way around."[15]

The CSEP study also asked interviewees to evaluate their communities of current residence. Respondents were asked if they agreed, disagreed, or were not sure about the following statement: "All things considered, this community is the best one in (name of state) to live in." Because a person is a citizen of the nation and a state but really lives in a particular community, a more reliable indicator of the perceived quality of life in particular states can be created by combining the responses to the "best state" and "best community" questions. Accordingly, we shall examine the proportions of "doubly satisfied" individuals across the American states in the late 1960s, those people who thought they were living in the best state *and* the best community.

Enormous variation emerges between the South and the non-South, and among the southern and nonsouthern states, in the evaluations of state and community by representative samples of the population. Three-fifths of southerners—a landslide majority—were apparently enjoying life in their subjective version of the best state and best community, compared with only 43 percent of nonsoutherners. Wider differences appeared among the thirteen states, ranging from an amazing 70 percent of North Carolinians to only 29 percent of New York's residents. Among the other southern states, Alabamians were almost as satisfied with life in that state as Tar Heels were with North Carolina; residents of Texas and Louisiana placed their states well above the national figure; and only Florida looked more like the nation itself than a true southern state. Grouped at the bottom, in addition to New York, were Massachusetts and Illinois, where about one-third or less of the inhabitants awarded high marks to both state and community.

What accounts for the much higher degree of satisfaction with life reported by southerners? The most promising theoretical explanation derives from Reed's suggestion that "people are more comfortable in culturally homogeneous communities."[16] Yet important as culture is, why should homogeneity be restricted to a single aspect of life? A more general proposition would be that individuals are more comfortable when they interact with people like themselves. In states with diverse populations—social, economic, and cultural—the average individual is likely to interact frequently with people unlike himself or herself and to experience the environment as more uncomfortable than would an individual in a state with a homogeneous population, where he or she would be dealing mostly with similar individuals. If the "best state" and "best community" questions are essentially tapping feelings of security or comfort, then a measure of population diversity among the American states may tell us much about the disproportionate popularity of southern states.

Fortunately, John L. Sullivan has created just such an index for the fifty states.[17] Using six variables (education, income, occupation, housing ownership, foreign or native stock, and religion), Sullivan measured the social, economic, and religious diversity of the American states in the 1960s. Each state score can be interpreted as the percentage of measured characteristics on which two randomly selected residents of a state would differ. The higher the score, the more diverse the state's population and, presumably, the less likely individuals would be to agree that they were living in the best state and best community. For theoretical reasons, Sullivan excluded race from his diversity index. The American states varied considerably in their diversity scores, ranging from Mississippi's comparatively homogeneous population (.330) to the much more heterogeneous population of New York (.556).

It is instructive to examine the scattergram displaying the association between support for state and locality and the Sullivan Diversity Index (see figure 10.1). The correlation (-.94) is extraordinarily high, and the fit is so good that no glaringly "deviant" cases appear, though there is some fluctuation in the middle range of the scores. The Sullivan Diversity Index accounts for almost 90 percent of the variance in the scores. It is precisely among the most socially, economically, and religiously homogeneous of the southern states—North Carolina and Alabama—that the greatest levels of approval for state and community appeared in the entire nation. If the same relationship prevailed among the southern states not sampled in CSEP, then Mississippi, Arkansas, South Carolina, Tennessee, and Georgia would cluster around North Carolina and Alabama, and Virginia would approximate the regional norm. All of the more heterogeneous southern states—Louisiana, Florida, and Texas—were included in CSEP, and considerably smaller percentages of their populations were doubly satisfied.[18] At the opposite end of the diversity index, the northeastern states—repositories of wave after wave of different types of people—were far and away the settings where individuals were least likely to feel that their states and communities were the best.

These findings are consistent with the relative ethnic homogeneity of the white population in the South. Until recently, with only minor notable exceptions, southern whites were primarily descended from Protestants of the British Isles. Historically the slave economy discouraged settlers from other ethnic groups since slaves were the chief competitors of free laborers. The ethnic homogeneity of the dominant racial group, the region's lag in economic development, and the South's institutional weak-

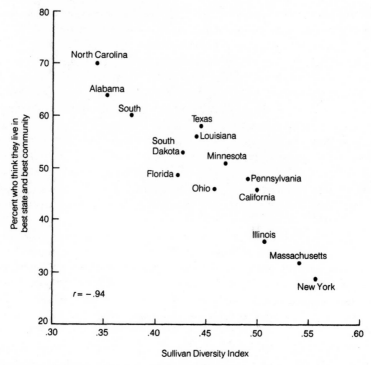

Figure 10.1. Perceived quality of life and diversity of state populations, 1968. Sources: CSEP for survey results; state diversity scores from John L. Sullivan, "Political Correlates of Social, Economic, and Religious Diversity in the American States," *Journal of Politics*, 35 (February 1973), 73, 82.

nesses culminated in comparatively undiversified populations in the most rural of the southern states. Segregation reduced racial interactions to white terms; and although it produced many deeply discontented blacks, in the twentieth century out-migration provided an escape valve for the blacks who were most dissatisfied. For the most part, then, both blacks and whites interacted with members of their own races—people essentially like themselves.

Even if the homogeneity of the southern population is the basic explanation of high rates of satisfaction, it is not a wholly adequate interpretation. What do its residents especially like about the South? Two factors that are associated with the Sullivan Diversity Index, mean winter temperature and the 1971 robbery rate, have been previously stressed by Reed in his analysis of the popularity of southern living. Beyond the conclusion that "people like safe, warm places," Reed emphasizes that each indicator "is standing in, so to speak, for a host of other characteristics. The average winter temperature has all sorts of implications for people's way of life (or 'life-style,' if you prefer). And the robbery rate tells us something about personal relations and social stability. I suggest that this is the sort of thing people have in mind when they say that North Carolina is the best state—or that Massachusetts isn't." A 1971 survey of North Carolinians asked them to name the best things about the South. "More than two-thirds of our respondents," Reed reports, "mentioned natural conditions: the benign climate, the clean air, the forests and wildlife, the easy pleasures of a life lived largely outdoors." Reed's second indicator of southern livability, robberies per 100,000 population, is even more fascinating. Though the South has usually been described as an especially violent region, such a sweeping generalization may be unwarranted. "It has been almost traditional to put the homicide rate into quality of life indexes—and the South doesn't do too well on that score," Reed argues. "But the thing about homicide, especially in the South, is that it's not 'in the streets.' It's often in the home and usually among friends, and even in the South it's pretty unusual. What is more common, and what people are scared of, is being robbed, mugged, raped, or burgled by a *stranger*. And North Carolina's robbery rate is only one-tenth of New York's." Reed thinks the meaning of low robbery rates extends beyond the absence of crime:

> The most important implications of the robbery rate are indirect. Suspicion and distrust, the absence of easy and cordial interaction with strangers— this kind of thing is important to people, too. When we asked what the best thing about the South was, half of our respondents said the *people* were, that Southerners are friendly, polite, take things easy, and are easy to get along with. . . We all rely on face-to-face interaction for the greater part of the satisfaction we get from life. But the North Carolinians in our poll seemed to feel (and I agree with them) that the texture of day-to-day life is pleasanter in the South, particularly in fleeting, secondary interactions (like those with salesclerks and secretaries and cabdrivers and policemen).[19]

The accessibility of nature, low rates of crimes against the person by strangers, and the more agreeable texture of life—all of these result in powerful bonds to places and people among a population that is fairly homogeneous. Life in the South has, indeed, many positive aspects.

There is also a darker side, an apparent satisfaction with life that is rooted in disproportionate percentages of people "who don't know any better," individuals whose realistic options have been bound by "limited experience and narrow horizons."[20] A continuing legacy of the region's underinvestment in public education is a much higher proportion of poorly educated people than in the rest of the nation. Persons whose formal education ended short of a high school diploma constituted a majority of the southerners sampled in 1968, and in the most backward states they made up huge majorities (65 percent in Alabama and 61 percent in North Carolina). Belief that one resided in the best state and best community was much higher among southerners without a high school education (69 percent) than among those who had attended college (43 percent).

Why should people at the bottom of society express such strong attachments to state and locality? Again Reed provides a persuasive answer: "What is a poor and ignorant Tarheel telling us when he says that North Carolina is the best state? Why, he's telling us that it's better to be poor and ignorant in North Carolina than in any other state. Sure, he would rather be rich, but he probably doubts that he can really improve his economic condition by leaving. If he thought that, he would probably leave." Finally, Reed observes that "Southerners know what Mencken was trying to tell them. Very few of our respondents mentioned politics or economics when we asked them what they liked about the South, and nearly a third mentioned them when we asked them what they liked least about their region. All in all, I read these data to say that state and local politics don't make much of an impression on most folks just living day-to-day, except as an entertaining sideshow (perhaps especially entertaining in the South)."[21] Attachment to place does not rule out dissatisfaction with other aspects of southern life (relatively low wages and salaries, for example) that some southerners might feel strongly about, and which under conditions of acute economic distress (high unemployment, high inflation, or both) might serve as a basis for collective political action; but life in the region does seem to provide many poorly educated southerners with things to value and cherish.

The popularity of southern states and communities, at least in the late 1960s, stemmed from a dominant population of native-born and relatively uneducated whites, homogeneous in social, economic, and cultural traits, and living, for the most part, in safe, civil, and temperate environments. Despite some discontent, most of the southern residents questioned in 1968 endorsed this way of life as meeting their standards of "the best."

Strong majorities of both white (59 percent) and black (65 percent) southerners agreed with the "best state" and "best community" labels. The high level of positive black responses may be surprising, but it is consistent with the composition of the black sample and with the changes in race relations that occurred in the early and middle 1960s. A higher percentage of blacks than whites had not finished high school, many had never traveled outside the South, and most were still living in the same state in which they had been raised—all of which suggests bonds of familiarity, affection, and attachment to life in their native state. Furthermore, southern blacks, in contrast to blacks residing in nonsouthern big cities, had recently witnessed many major improvements in their lives as a result of the civil rights movement. Outside the South, whites and blacks differed substantially in their assessments of life in state and community. Whereas 44 percent of nonsouthern whites were doubly satisfied, a mere 26 percent of nonsouthern blacks thought they lived in the best community and the best state. Indeed, 18 percent of nonsouthern blacks believed they resided in the worst state and community, three times the rate of doubly dissatisfied black southerners.

We can usefully extend the analysis by comparing racial differences among three types of residents: natives of states, intraregional migrants, and interregional migrants. The distinction between intraregional and interregional migrants to southern states is especially useful, for "with the exception of Florida, most of the population movement to particular southern states was composed of individuals born elsewhere in the South."[22] Among blacks and whites currently residing in the South, about two-thirds of those native to the state agreed they were living in the best state and best community, about half of those who had been raised in another southern state had a similar opinion, and less than two-fifths of the whites who had migrated from a nonsouthern state agreed that southern living was ideal. So few blacks raised in the North had migrated to the South as of the late 1960s that their absence from the sample indicates the feelings of northern blacks about Dixie. Southerners who had been raised in another southern state apparently adjusted more readily to their new home than did Yankees and midwesterners. If the subsequent flow of migration to the South has tipped more toward interregional transfers, much more criticism and displeasure with southern life and institutions can be anticipated. Such discontent might appear more readily if nonsoutherners clustered in particular locales rather than settling randomly across the region.

Beyond the South, the region where one had been raised had little systematic impact on expressed satisfaction. Almost half of the nonsouthern black sample consisted of individuals who had left the South for the "promised land," and only one-quarter of them thought they had found it. Low levels of satisfaction with life in nonsouthern big cities, coupled with improvements in southern race relations, suggest why a small stream of black "return migration" to the South has commenced.

Finally, it is instructive to consider the relationship between formal education and support for the best state and community in the South and non-South. Outside the South formal education was inversely associated with support for best state and community (see figure 10.2), with only a third of the nonsouthern states' most highly educated native whites expressing double satisfaction with their quality of life. A somewhat different pattern prevailed among native white southerners. Seven-tenths of the native whites with less than a high school education indicated support for their states and communities; nearly two-thirds of those who had finished high school gave similar responses; and only among native white southerners who had attended college did approval fall to a mere majority. Whereas most native white nonsoutherners with graduate or professional training harbored some reservations, some doubts, about the quality of life in state and locality, the southern professionals (lawyers, doctors, executives, accountants, educators, and the like) acted less as critics than as regional promoters, that is, "educated boosters." Almost three-fifths (58 percent) of the homegrown professionals—from whom most of the South's politicians, business executives, and opinion leaders are drawn—thought they were already living in the best state and community.

Here is an indicator, in our view, of an exceedingly significant difference between southern and nonsouthern politics. If political leaders are overwhelmingly selected from the more educated natives, then southern politics will be much more predisposed toward consensus, boosterism, and the absence of controversy than nonsouthern politics. It is not that the South lacks well-educated, native critics of the status quo—every

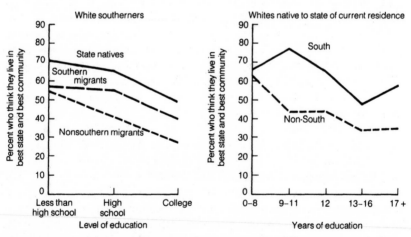

Figure 10.2. Satisfaction with state and community for different groups of whites, by education, 1968. Source: CSEP.

southern state has some dissenters from prevailing orthodoxies—but rather that the region possesses relatively fewer of them than does the rest of the nation. There are, of course, critics in abundance among highly educated migrants, particularly recent Yankee arrivals. But in most southern states these malcontents can be easily—easily—ignored or dismissed as unreasonably hostile to "the way we do things here." It is hard enough to be a native-born critic and win respect from other native southerners; it is almost impossible for those raised elsewhere to gain acceptance as "loyal critics."

Whether the South needs loyal critics or can "get by" with uncritical loyalists is a matter of opinion. We side with Key, who complained about the absence of a progressive leadership drawn from the ranks of the better-educated. "The upper bracket that goes unchallenged develops privileges and repressions destructive of mass morale and often restrictive of the potentialities of the productive system," he argued. "And ruling groups have so inveterate a habit of being wrong that the health of a democratic order demands that they be challenged and constantly compelled to prove their case."[23] If most citizens in a political system believe their present way of life is satisfactory, and all other things are held constant, such a system ought to generate fewer political controversies than a system in which the magnitude of perceived dissatisfaction is much higher.

Responses to the "best state" and "best community" questions in 1968 provide two reasons why southern politics has often appeared "issueless." The findings suggest a relatively quiescent, acquiescent, and content mass base (where many individuals, despite low incomes and minimal education, express satisfaction with their current way of life), combined with an excessively boosteristic professional elite. The attitudinal picture for the South as a whole is not unlike the portrait of a small town writ large, where public controversy would only bring out bad feelings and make everybody mad. As long as most natives—especially educated natives— believe that their state and community are already ideal, the likelihood of regular challenges to southern ruling groups is dim indeed.

Implications for Politics

This review of the predispositions and attitudes of the general public reveals a South skewed toward the political right in many areas. On balance, most southerners are satisfied with life in their states and communities (at least as of 1968), opposed to additional changes in the intermediate color line, much more apt to think of themselves as conservative than liberal in their general outlook on politics, and more likely to emphasize the primary responsibility of individuals rather than of the national government to provide for employment and a good standard of living. Southerners possess a sense of warmth and affection for one another, and they still believe themselves to be different in important respects from nonsoutherners. Though most southerners do not think of themselves as strong or extreme conservatives, and some even classify themselves as liberal in their political views, conservatives outnumber liberals in the South on many, many political issues.

One key to understanding politics in the modern South is the recognition that the reentry of black southerners as voters did not fundamentally reshape the ideological balance within the region's mass public in favor of political liberalism. Because whites compose 80 percent of the southern population, their attitudes fix the basic shape of public opinion. The addition of blacks increases the proportion of southern liberals, but this change represents only a marginal variation on the essential design set by the much greater white population. When the conservatives' other major advantage, superior financial resources, is added to the general public's favorable views on conservatism, it is no mystery why the central tendency in southern politics is the selection of officeholders who neither campaign nor govern as overt liberals. We see an essential congruence in contemporary southern politics between a relatively conservative electorate and the election of politicians who bend over backwards to avoid being categorized as unqualified liberals.

The failure of southern liberalism is not simply a matter of well-financed conservative elites adroitly deploying multiple symbols and issues to manipulate, maneuver, and cajole an uninformed and credulous populace to vote against their own interests and preferences; the obdurate and unresolved dilemma of the liberal elites is that too many white voters welcome conservative positions and candidates and reject the symbols, policies, and beneficiaries of contemporary liberalism. There are simply not enough progressive whites to unite with blacks in most southern states to provide regular electoral majorities for unreservedly liberal candidates, though on occasion concatenations of unusual events, circumstances, and personalities may produce victories for politicians who campaign as fighting liberals. Barring dramatic shifts in the underlying ideological tendencies of the mass public, victories by conservatives (some unqualified, some qualified) remain the most likely outcome in the foreseeable future.

Reed's research stresses the continuing importance of southern regional identification, an identification that has always included a sense of being different from nonsoutherners, as well as an abiding sense of loyalty and affection toward the people, places, and heritage of the region. Stated another way, the symbol "southerner" still has a strong emotional appeal for most native southerners, white and black. The most striking interregional difference we have found concerns the perceived quality of life. Even in 1968, a year of exceptionally bitter political turmoil, majorities of whites *and* blacks in the South agreed that they were living in the best state and community.[24]

Widespread satisfaction with southern living reduces the likelihood of collective political action as a way of obtaining individual and group benefits. In a milieu of satisfaction, the tasks of political liberalism, let alone radicalism—criticism, reform, calls to prophetic justice—face formidable obstacles. In some locales rapid population growth and the costs of uncontrolled industrialization may be permanently altering perceptions of the South's advantages and creating conditions in which social and political criticism will find a more receptive audience than before. When and if most southerners begin to think that they are not living in the best state and best community, a nonsouthern sort of politics might emerge in Dixie. Thus far, most of the South does not seem to be Miami or Houston or even Atlanta scaled down, much less New York or Chicago or Los Angeles in miniature.

eleven

The Decline
of Southern
"Democracy"

THERE IS no majority party in the modern South. The Democratic party may still possess the loyalties of over half the electorate in a few (mainly Deep South) states, but in the mid-1980s only minorities of southerners explicitly claim to be Democrats or Republicans. Outcomes of most statewide elections now hinge upon whether Democratic or Republican candidates can attract sufficient numbers of independents to form winning coalitions. It is no news, of course, that Republicans constitute a regional minority. GOP politicians have long understood their weak strategic position and have learned to compete (and sometimes win) by assembling coalitions of Republicans, independents, and disaffected Democrats. For southern Democratic candidates long accustomed to overwhelmingly pro-Democratic electorates, however, it is a revolutionary (and often uncomfortable) experience to think of themselves as belonging to a minority party. In many parts of the region, especially in the Peripheral South, the immemorial Democratic strategy of simply uniting the party's adherents behind its nominees and turning them out on election day no longer suffices to generate victories. Democratic politicians and strategists will have to learn how to appeal both to the remaining loyalists *and* to voters who do not consider themselves Democrats, if they are to remain competitive in the emerging southern politics.

No institution was more central to the old southern politics than the Democratic party. The South, Cash concluded in 1941, having "so smashed the Republican party that . . . it either ceased altogether to exist or continued to exist only as a Federal-job-ring . . .was left as that curious anomaly, a so-called democratic country without an opposition party, a country in which, for practical purposes, there has been but one party from that day to this."[1] Although majorities of southerners with opinions on the matter have usually agreed that "the South would be better off, in general, if there were two political parties of about equal strength instead of one strong party,"[2] until very recently the Democratic party's nominees have won almost all state and local elections. But as the national Democratic party has become recognized as an instrument of racial, economic, and cultural liberalism, and as the region's urbanized white middle class has expanded, the Democratic party's primacy has been increasingly challenged by Republicans. Classic one-party politics is gone forever, and there is no better way to appreciate the new electoral politics of the contemporary South than to examine trends in partisan loyalties.

"Democracy" as a Fading Southern Imperative

Early in this century, most white southerners looked upon the rest of the nation—generally lumped together as Yankees—with abiding hostility and suspicion. Unable to forget or forgive the nightmare of war, defeat, and occupation, most whites shared the conviction that nonsoutherners must never again be allowed to interfere with southern racial practices. Acting almost as if it were an independent nation, the South pursued deterrence of outside intervention in race relations as the paramount objective of its "foreign" policy.[3] As a minority within the nation, white southerners needed a political organization capable of maximizing their leverage on national politics, and the Democratic party, of course, became that device.

From 1896 through 1932, the South usually constituted a "majority faction within a minority party,"[4] a strategic position of great influence within the national Democratic party. Whether measured by electoral college votes or by the composition of Senate and House Democratic caucuses, after 1896 the Democratic party was so weak outside the South that southerners formed either slim majorities (at best) or large minorities (at worst) of the national Democratic party. The vital legislative chamber was the Senate, where the tradition of unlimited debate enabled a determined minority of senators to kill undesired legislation. The southerners' well-known "revenge for Appomattox" was their ability to prevent the passage of civil rights legislation by the skillful use of party allies outside the South.[5] Not only was the Democratic party the party *of* the South, in Cash's sense of the term, but the national Democratic party was the region's voice in presidential and congressional politics.

Democracy gave southern whites something to love, honor, and glorify; Republicanism gave them something to hate, despise, and excoriate. Republicans were irredeemably identified with a long series of outrages against the white South—the Civil War, abolition of slavery, Reconstruction, threats of renewed federal intervention, and the exploitation of the South's vulnerable economic condition. Except in a few (mainly mountainous) areas, where grassroots Republicanism persisted, public support for the party of Lincoln entailed the stigma of providing aid and comfort to the region's historical enemy.

Before the Great Depression, most white southerners who pondered affairs of state held highly polarized images of the Democratic and Republican parties. The coincidence of Republican rule with the century's worst economic catastrophe reconfirmed and revitalized most southerners' suspicions of Republicans. Once again Republicanism was blamed for causing, and then failing to respond to, massive human suffering. President Franklin D. Roosevelt's emphasis on the "forgotten man," by comparison, reinforced the prevailing view of the Democrats as the party of the common whites.[6]

In their utter desperation, most southern whites welcomed the New Deal's activism, even though many New Deal programs went against the grain of conventional beliefs. Cash recognized numerous discrepancies and contradictions between traditional southern attitudes and the New Deal philosophy, but he argued that they often went unnoticed or were discounted in light of the practical urgencies of providing shelter, food, and work.[7] Democrats by birth and rearing before the New Deal, many southern whites who lived through the Great Depression also became Democrats by experience. For the rest of their lives most remained loyal to the Democratic party. Many might feel in recent times that the national party had deserted and betrayed *them,* but until the mid-1980s most survivors of the Solid South generation continued to think of themselves as "Democrats."[8]

Outside the South, James L. Sundquist has shown, the New Deal polarized the parties over the issue of governmental activism to promote economic well-being and instigated a prolonged process of partisan realignment, a process which frequently required more than two decades to complete.[9] Democratic advances in most northern and western states occurred in two distinct stages: the first surge coincided with the New Deal; the second did not appear until the late 1940s or early 1950s. There is no need to retrace the trends that Sundquist has identified, but it is important to emphasize the consequences of partisan realignment outside the South on southerners' strategic position within the Democratic party. Put simply, the waning of southern influence within the national Democratic party contributed dramatically to the erosion of mass loyalties to the Democratic party among white southerners.

The New Deal stimulated the first stage of Democratic increases beyond the South. As more northern and western Democrats entered Congress, southern Democrats suddenly became the "minority faction in a majority party."[10] The southerners' new vulnerability, however, did not result in significant policy defeats because Roosevelt deliberately avoided civil rights proposals.[11] Moreover, the South's numerical subjugation within the Democratic party was temporary. Nonsouthern Democrats began to be unseated in the late 1930s and early 1940s, and the relative size of the southern delegations again increased within the congressional Democratic parties. If Border State Democrats are grouped with southerners, as Havard has done, the "Greater South" produced absolute majorities of congressional Democrats as late as the mid-1950s.[12]

Both southern and nonsouthern Democrats realized the necessity of cooperation and compromise to ensure Democratic control of Congress. Southerners usually opposed new programs that would require large tax increases and mainly benefit nonsoutherners, but they often voted with the party's northern wing to support marginal changes in the original New Deal programs. David R. Mayhew has fittingly characterized the congressional Democrats as a party of "inclusive compromise,"[13] an intraparty politics that was rooted in the survival needs of each regional wing of the party. When issues were raised that could not be compromised—President Truman's civil rights proposals of 1948 furnish a fitting example—southerners sought and gained assistance from many conservative northern Republicans to kill the legislation.[14] Either through the politics of inclusive compromise with their fellow Democrats or through the politics of a conservative coalition with Republicans, southern Democrats could vote with the winning side on many roll calls and, more significantly, could continue to exercise a veto over proposed civil rights legislation. During the first stage of partisan realignment, the Democratic party remained an exceptionally useful vehicle for maintaining and enhancing the interests of southern conservatives in national politics.

This modus vivendi of congressional southern Democrats was still in effect in the early 1950s, when the SRC-CPS began its systematic sampling of the American electorate's partisan attachments. When respondents were asked in 1952, "Do you consider yourself to be a Democrat, Republican, Independent, or something else?" the answers demonstrated the South's uniqueness. Democrats outnumbered Republicans in the South by almost eight to one (76 percent to 10 percent). In the rest of the nation the partisan balance was much less lopsided, with Democrats enjoying only a moderate edge over Republicans (42 percent to 33 percent). Among white southerners native to the region, four-fifths claimed to be Democrats, giving the party a ten-to-one advantage over the 8 percent who acknowledged Republican identification. "White southerner" thus remained synonymous with "Democrat," while the label "Republican" still required considerable explanation and justification. As Shannon could plausibly observe of white southerners at midcentury, "One is born into the party as much as, or perhaps even more than, he is born within a church."[15]

In the second stage of partisan realignment outside the South, however, Democratic gains in the House and Senate in the late 1950s and early 1960s strengthened the party's liberal wing, once again converted southern congressmen into a minority within the Democratic party, and, this time, defeated white southern efforts to prevent federal intervention in race relations. Conservative southern Democrats confronted a permanent decline in their numerical strength within the party, as well as Democratic presidents willing to press aggressively for civil rights legislation. Passage of the Civil Rights Act of 1964 symbolized the defeat of conservative white southerners, and with programmatic liberals controlling the Democratic party, a broader agenda of economic and racial liberalism was enacted during the next two years. In the opinion of many southern conservatives, most Great Society legislation benefited the wrong groups and penalized (through taxes, inflation, or both) the "productive" groups in American society.[16]

What would happen to the Democratic party in the South if the liberal-labor wing of the national party actually took control and implemented a new agenda of domestic liberalism? In his final article about southern politics, "The Erosion of Sectionalism," Key argued that Democratic party unity "probably could not survive another New Deal,"[17] another round of economic liberalism. Lyndon Johnson's Great Society challenged regional orthodoxy even more fundamentally by including civil rights reforms. If southern Democratic solidarity could not withstand another New Deal, how could it possibly survive the Great Society? The short answer, of course, is that the Democratic party has ceased to attract the loyalties of a majority of southerners in the aftermath of the Great Society. In terms of self-professed partisan identification, Key's prediction of the collapse of southern Democratic solidarity has been fulfilled.

The Changing Partisanship of the Southern Electorate

In 1977 Beck published a classic analysis of the changing party loyalties of southerners. Using SRC-CPS party identification data from 1952 to 1972, and arguing that "realignment [in the South] requires pronounced growth in Republican affiliations," he showed that a partisan realignment of southerners had *not* occurred. Democratic party strength had clearly diminished, yet no commensurate gains had appeared in the ranks of self-labeled Republicans. Instead, independents were the main beneficiaries of Democratic decline. Accordingly, Beck concluded that the appropriate theoretical concept for understanding the South's modern party system was not realignment but "dealignment"—"a process in which traditional party coalitions dissolve without new party coalitions being formed to take their place."[18] Since 1976, however, self-identified Republicans have markedly increased in the region, raising the question of whether a genuine partisan realignment is under way.[19]

The notions of dealignment and realignment help clarify central features of the South's evolving party system.[20] As most practicing politicians would probably acknowledge, the present party system is splintered into *minorities* of Democrats, Republicans, and independents. The old Democratic majority has collapsed, but it has yet to be replaced by a Republican party that has attracted a new majority or even a new plurality of the electorate. Nonetheless, the process of realignment is under way and has recently accelerated; southern Republicans are indeed experiencing a "pronounced growth" in professed loyalties. As of the mid-1980s, the southern party system remains fundamentally dealigned, although the process of partisan realignment is moving forward.

Evidence for this interpretation is presented in table 11.1, showing the relevant SRC-CPS party identification data for the entire southern electorate and for southern whites from 1952 to 1984. The continuing disintegration of Democratic strength is apparent. Among all southerners, Democratic identification fell from three-fourths of the electorate in 1952 to two-fifths in 1984, an astonishing secular collapse of the former majority party's base of support. This massive decline was concentrated, of

Table 11.1. Party identification in the South, 1952–1984[a]

	Year								
Party identification	1952	1956	1960	1964	1968	1972	1976	1980	1984
All southerners									
Democrats	76	68	60	68	58	51	52	48	40
Independents	14	15	18	19	31	33	32	32	35
Republicans	10	17	22	13	11	15	16	20	25
Whites only									
Democrats	78	68	61	64	50	47	47	43	33
Independents	13	16	18	21	36	35	35	34	38
Republicans	9	15	21	15	14	18	19	23	29

Source: SRC-CPS presidential election year surveys. The 1984 results are based on a combination of cross-sectional and continuous-monitoring surveys.

a. Data are presented as percentages.

course, among white southerners. According to the CPS, by 1984 only a third of the region's racial majority still designated themselves Democrats. In addition, the CPS surveys report independents as constituting more than a third of the population, a finding consistent with dealignment. The beginning of partisan realignment is signaled by the rise in self-identified Republicans between 1976 and 1984, although, according to CPS, Republicans remained the smallest group of partisans in the South.

It is highly likely, however, that the 1984 CPS surveys understate southern Republicanism.[21] Other polls (see table 11.2) have reported much larger percentages of Republicans and smaller percentages of independents among southerners (especially among white southerners)— virtually the opposite of the CPS results. Using Gallup data, Thomas E.

Table 11.2. Comparing the polls: reported party identification of southerners and southern whites, 1984 and 1985[a]

Poll	All southerners			Whites only		
	Dem	Ind	Rep	Dem	Ind	Rep
CPS 1984[b]	43	38	19	35	41	24
CPS-CM 1984[c]	40	35	25	33	38	29
Gallup fall polls 1984[d]	40	24	36	—	—	—
Gallup final preelection poll 1984[e]	—	—	—	31	29	40
ABC/*Washington Post* exit poll 1984[f]	38	29	33	32	30	38
CBS/*New York Times* exit poll 1984[g]	—	—	—	33	28	39
New York Times/CBS November 1985 poll[h]	44	24	32	36	25	39

Sources: See footnotes b–h.
a. Data are presented as percentages.
b. CPS preelection survey, 1984.
c. CPS preelection survey combined with continuous-monitoring surveys, 1984. The regional results have been weighted to correspond to the 1980 racial composition of the South.
d. Gallup polls of September 7–October 29, 1984. *The Gallup Report,* no. 230 (November 1985), p. 25.
e. Thomas E. Cavanagh and James L. Sundquist, "The New Two-Party System," in John E. Chubb and Paul E. Peterson, eds., *The New Direction in American Politics* (Washington, D.C.: Brookings Institution, 1985), p. 59.
f. Peter Begans, "GOP Approaching Democrats as Nation's Top Party," ABC News Polling Unit, 1985, p. 3.
g. Cavanagh and Sundquist, "New Two-Party System," p. 46.
h. *New York Times*/CBS poll of November 18–19, 1985. Information helpfully provided by Barbara Farar of the *New York Times*.

Cavanagh and James L. Sundquist emphasize a phenomenal increase in Republicanism (28 to 40 percent in four months) among white southerners during the 1984 presidential campaign.[22] Election day exit polls of southern white voters by CBS/*New York Times* and ABC/*Washington Post* reported similar levels of Republican identification;[23] a *New York Times*/CBS Poll conducted in November 1985 found 39 percent of southern whites identifying as Republicans, 36 percent as Democrats, and 25 percent as independents.[24] In contrast in the CPS results, the Gallup polls and the news media polls reveal the strong gains in GOP identification for the region (and particularly for whites) that would be expected if a partisan realignment were in progress. Indeed, these other polls in table 11.2 show Republicans even outnumbering Democrats among white southerners.

As powerful as the trend toward Republicanism assuredly was among southern whites in 1984, it did not decisively shift the center of political gravity of the southern party system as a whole. Gallup's fall polls gave the Democrats a slim plurality over the Republicans (40 to 36 percent), as did an ABC/*Washington Post* exit poll of southern voters (38 to 33 percent).[25] According to the November 1985 *New York Times*/CBS Poll, 44 percent of southerners designated themselves as Democrats, 32 percent as Republicans, and 24 percent as independents. The most important area of agreement among the various polls is that the Democrats still constitute the largest group in the South, though largest now means a plurality rather than a majority. Republicans are currently enjoying their most favorable twentieth-century position with the southern electorate, but Republican identification still lags behind the Democrats. Despite the Democrats' fading advantage in party identification, the southern party system continues to be dealigned.

Because of the shortfall of self-identified Republicans in the 1984 CPS surveys, it seems prudent to set aside questions about the precise levels of Democrats, Republicans, and independents among various subgroups of southerners and to concentrate instead on detecting their partisan *tendencies*. The most practical way to gauge changes in the electorate's underlying partisan tendencies is to take into consideration the partisan leanings of self-described independents (see table 11.3). This procedure—adding to a given party's self-classified identifiers those independents who lean toward that party—should provide a fairly accurate indicator of the mass appeal of the Democratic party, though it may still underestimate Republican strength. For example, our calculation of 1984 Democratic party strength (Democratic identifiers plus independents who lean toward the Democrats) is 50 percent of the voting age population, which is identical with the results of both a February 1985 ABC/*Washington Post* poll (50 percent Democratic) and a November 1985 *New York Times*/

Table 11.3.   Changing partisan tendencies in the South, 1952–1984ᵃ

Partisan tendencyᵇ	1952	1956	1960	1964	1968	1972	1976	1980	1984
All southerners									
"Democrats"	83	72	64	73	68	60	61	58	50
"Republicans"	14	23	25	19	21	25	24	29	38
Whites only									
"Democrats"	85	72	65	70	62	56	56	53	43
"Republicans"	13	22	24	22	25	29	28	32	45

Source: SRC-CPS presidential election year surveys. The 1984 results are based on a combination of cross-sectional and continuous-monitoring samples.

a. Data are presented as percentages.

b. "Democrats," Democratic identifiers plus independents who lean toward the Democrats; "Republicans," Republican identifiers plus independents who lean toward the Republicans.

CBS poll (49 percent).[26] Yet our calculation of Republican party strength using the same procedure (38 percent) is four points lower than the ABC/*Washington Post* poll (42 percent) and five points below the *New York Times*/CBS poll (43 percent). In interpreting subsequent analyses this possible bias should be kept in mind.

In 1984 the Democratic party's lead over the Republicans narrowed appreciably. The Democrats' slight remaining advantage could easily disappear if the party were to suffer defections and be unable to attract sufficient support from pure independents. With a coalitional base in the neighborhood of 40 percent, the Republicans were moving up rapidly. They remained a minority, but a minority within striking distance of the Democrats whenever they could attract support from independents and nominal Democrats.

Among white southerners the 1984 CPS estimates show the Republicans with a slight edge. The November 1985 *New York Times*/CBS survey reported a wider gap among whites, 50 to 43, in favor of the Republicans. The Republican surge in the early 1980s, the sharpest ever observed among white southerners, doubtless reflected the success of the Reagan presidency in changing the image of the Republican party to conform to values and beliefs held by majorities of white southerners.[27] Apart from the federal deficit, Reagan's views and actions on the importance of military strength, the restoration of American influence in foreign policy, decreases in taxation, reduction in inflation, emphasis on economic growth, and his administration's efforts to change many civil rights policies were essentially consistent with the desires of most southern whites. Reagan's performance in office presumably revised the feelings of millions of southern whites about the Republican and Democratic parties.

The Demographic Basis of Modern Partisan Tendencies

The partisanship of the southern electorate is changing, but not all groups have displayed the same tendencies. Key placed considerable emphasis upon changes in the region's demography and social structure in creating two-party politics, themes subsequently pursued by a host of scholars.[28] We shall first examine the patterns of partisanship that have developed among the major demographic groups: native whites (as a whole and as partitioned into Solid South, post–World War II, and post–Voting Rights generations), migrant whites, and blacks (see table 11.4).[29]

Table 11.4.   Partisan tendencies of different demographic groups in the South, 1952–1984[a]

Partisan tendency[b]	1952	1956	1960	1964	1968	1972	1976	1980	1984
All native white southerners									
"Democrats"	86	77	73	75	64	62	63	59	45
"Republicans"	11	18	17	16	23	24	22	28	40
Democrats[c]	80	74	70	70	53	52	54	47	37
Solid South generation of native whites[d]									
"Democrats"	86	78	76	82	70	71	74	71	47
"Republicans"	12	17	17	11	19	20	18	16	37
Post–World War II generation of native whites									
"Democrats"	90	71	65	63	54	58	61	59	46
"Republicans"	7	23	19	25	28	24	17	29	38
Post–Voting Rights generation of native whites									
"Democrats"	—	—	—	—	—	49	49	48	43
"Republicans"	—	—	—	—	—	32	32	36	43
Migrant whites									
"Democrats"	—	—	—	52	56	39	37	39	35
"Republicans"	—	—	—	45	33	46	46	43	43
Blacks									
"Democrats"	—	—	—	87	96	75	82	80	76
"Republicans"	—	—	—	5	1	11	7	12	11

Source: SRC-CPS presidential election year surveys.
a. Data are presented as percentages.
b. "Democrats," Democratic identifiers plus independents who lean toward the Democrats; "Republicans," Republican identifiers plus independents who lean toward the Republicans.
c. Because of the historical importance of Democratic party identification among native whites, we have also included this time series.
d. Solid South generation, native whites who entered the electorate prior to 1946; Post–World War II generation, native whites who entered the electorate between 1946 and 1964; Post–Voting Rights generation, native whites who entered the electorate after 1964.

Because of the proportion of the electorate they constitute, whites native to the region still fundamentally shape the South's most important partisan tendencies. Historically, members of this group had been expected and required to exhibit loyalty to the Democratic party. For this reason, we have also included in table 11.4 the percentage of native white southerners who identified themselves as Democrats (that is, excluding independents who lean Democratic) from 1952 to 1984. Among native whites the most striking tendency is the collapse of Democracy as a cultural norm. The timing of the initial massive decline in Democratic strength—between 1964 and 1968—confirms Key's prediction of the corrosive impact upon traditional party loyalty of a decisive leftward shift by the Democratic party in national politics. At the conclusion of the Great Society years, barely half of the region's white natives explicitly considered themselves Democrats. It was still good politics to be a Democrat in the South—by our expanded definition of Democratic party support, over three-fifths of this group were still inclined toward the party—but something vital had gone out of the attachment between native whites and their traditional political party.

After 1976 support for the Democratic party again plummeted, in part because of Jimmy Carter's ineffectual presidency, but even more because of the performance of a popular and respected Republican chief executive. By 1984, only 37 percent of native white southerners labeled themselves Democrats. Even when leaning independents are added to the potential Democratic coalition, no more than a plurality of native whites were favorable disposed toward the Democratic party. Until recently native white southerners have been reluctant to align themselves with the Republican party. Counting self-identified Republicans and leaning independents, fewer than one in five expressed GOP inclinations in the 1950s and early 1960s, and fewer than one in four claimed such predispositions in the 1970s. This situation abruptly changed between 1976 and 1984, when the percentage of native whites favorably disposed toward the GOP nearly doubled, rising from 22 to 40 percent. Most of the upward surge occurred in response to the Reagan presidency.

The magnitude of the Democratic decline among native white southerners becomes even more apparent when recent partisan tendencies are traced among three age cohorts. Historically the Democratic monopoly of officeholding depended on the voting behavior of the Solid South generation, individuals who reached voting age before the end of World War II. Practically all of their formative political experiences predisposed them to stable Democratic identification and permanently alienated them from the Republican party.[30] Resolutely committed partisans of this generation were known and admired as "brass collar" or "yellow dog"

Democrats, southerners who would vote Democratic "even if Jesus Christ was the Republican candidate."

From 1952 through 1980 (see table 11.4) the Solid South generation remained tenaciously pro-Democratic. Democratic party loyalty eroded only modestly during the Eisenhower years and even revived briefly when Lyndon Johnson—a member and symbol of their political generation—headed the party ticket in 1964. Despite the Great Society, most members of the Solid South generation either continued to think of themselves as Democrats or were independents who still gave the benefit of their doubts to the region's traditional majority party. Reagan's presidency marked a critical turning point, inducing further defections from the Democrats and spectacularly increasing the ranks of older native white southerners who viewed the Republican party with favor. As of 1984, less than half of this generation professed any loyalty or leanings toward the Democratic party, while more than a third of them—at the least—were positively disposed toward the GOP. Yet, even as partisan change has finally begun to affect elderly native whites, their influence on regional politics has steadily waned as more and more of them have either died or become politically inactive. In 1952 the Solid South generation accounted for most of the southern electorate; in 1980 they constituted approximately one-seventh of the voters. The passage of time is rapidly decimating the generation whose politicians supplied much of the color and atmosphere—noble and ignoble—that permeated the old southern politics.

Among the post–World War II generation of native white southerners, those who began to vote between 1946 and 1964, a much more volatile pattern of shifting partisan tendencies has been evident. Democratic party strength declined continuously among this cohort between 1952 and 1968, recovered slightly in the early and middle 1970s, and then dropped again in the early 1980s. The attachments of this generation to the GOP have fluctuated markedly over the past three decades. Since 1976 the middle-aged white cohort has steadily increased its predisposition toward Republicanism, with gains probably due almost as much to disappointment with Carter as to satisfaction with Reagan.

Beck has offered several reasons why this particular cohort has been especially susceptible to partisan change. "It seems likely that the partisanship of the postwar cohorts was unusually fragile to begin with owing to weak childhood partisan socialization," he writes. These southerners "had not experienced directly the New Deal politics which gave meaning to and thus strengthened the partisanship of earlier cohorts. As a result, the affiliations of the postwar cohorts may have been more malleable. That the period after World War II was a time of changing party appeals to the southern electorate allowed this malleability to be exploited."[31] Though the 1984 CPS data show the Democrats with a slight lead over the Republicans, recent trends among middle-aged white southerners are clearly running in the Republicans' favor.

In assessing future prospects for genuinely competitive party politics in the South, the most interesting native whites are the members of the post–Voting Rights generation, those who became eligible to vote after 1964. CPS surveys report that this cohort was evenly divided between the two parties in 1984, a finding that probably understates the current Republican appeal among the young.[32] Nonetheless, the relative strength of the Republicans and the weakness of the Democrats among the post–Voting Rights generation is hardly surprising. Even more weakly attached to the Democratic party than their parents, this generation entered the system as voters during the period in which the Democratic party was becoming a leading instrument for destroying the outer color line and a spearhead for assaults against the intermediate color line. More recently, they have witnessed various attempts by the Reagan administration to redirect federal policies concerning the intermediate color line toward positions held by white majorities. Younger whites have further come to political awareness in an era in which the Democratic party has failed to produce a popular and successful chief executive, while the Republicans have overcome the Nixon debacle with a president whose popularity rivals that of Eisenhower and Roosevelt. Finally, as a group, the post–Voting Rights generation is much more highly educated than its predecessors and shares many of the aspirations toward middle-class values that the Republican party has come to represent. Whether these short-term factors will continue to undergird favorable sentiment for the Republican party cannot be predicted; but if the trends of the early 1980s do persist, the GOP will open a lead over the Democrats among the generation of white southerners that will provide most of the South's future political leaders.

Until very recently the partisan tendencies of native white southerners have varied substantially among the different political generations, with Republican strength inversely related to age. The most recent data, however, underscore the extraordinary impact of President Reagan's first term in reshaping attitudes toward political parties in the South. The favorable impact of the Reagan presidency was so widespread that older southern whites began to imitate younger southerners. As a consequence, in 1984 the differences in partisan tendencies among the three political generations of native white southerners were the smallest ever observed. According to the CPS results, Democrats and Republicans were exactly even among the youngest cohort, and the Democratic advantage had been severely reduced among middle-aged and elderly whites.[33]

The migration of millions of Yankees and midwesterners into the South has also helped undermine the Democratic party's predominance in party identification. Better educated, more prosperous, and not exposed in childhood to the cultural imperatives of Democracy, most white migrants to the South were unfamiliar with and unsympathetic toward one-party politics. Among this group a modest partisan advantage in favor of the GOP has stabilized since 1972. When the leaners are added to self-described partisans, the Republicans have maintained a slight plurality over the Democrats (43 percent compared to 35 percent in 1984, for example). About one-fifth of the migrants still describe themselves as pure independents.

Pro-Democratic loyalties of black southerners, the final major demographic group, are so familiar that little discussion is necessary. The policy shifts that alienated many white southerners from the national Democratic party simultaneously persuaded most black southerners to call themselves Democrats. By the end of the Great Society, perceptions of the two parties had generated such consensus among blacks that 96 percent of them identified with the Democrats or leaned in that direction. In subsequent surveys massive majorities of blacks have stayed Democratic. Republicanism had a modest appeal to some black southerners in the 1950s, but that party has never overcome the Democratic party's championship of civil rights in the 1960s. And as the Republican party has moved even more emphatically to the political right, it has essentially written off most black votes. In the early 1980s most blacks had ample cause to reject Republicanism, even if many were unenthusiastic about the Democratic party's response to their concerns.

Formal Education and the Modern Party System

Following the Second World War, perceptive observers began to notice the possibility of a two-party politics in the South that would divide the population along class lines over the New Deal agenda of governmental activism. Key believed that industrialization was deepening socioeconomic cleavages while creating new and stronger institutions that would represent the interests of middle-class and working-class southerners. Industrialization would increase the number of workers engaged in manufacturing and construction and would supposedly bolster—in due time—the traditionally weak position of organized labor. An organized working class, in turn, was expected to exert its strength behind the progressive wing of the southern Democratic party.

Key also argued that the changing economy was producing "industrial and financial interests that have a fellow feeling with northern Republicanism. A continuing growth of industry and a continued leftward veering of the Democratic party nationally would place a greater and greater strain on the Democratic loyalties of rising southern big business." And he predicted that "if and when Republicans make a real drive to gain strength in the South, they will find . . . a larger and larger group of prospects susceptible to their appeal."[34] A few years later Alexander Heard suggested that "the development in the South of an urban middle class . . . susceptible to the blandishments of both a liberal and a con- servative party would give the Republican party a potential source of votes in those states where it could achieve some kind of competitive equality."[35]

Middle- and upper-class white southerners broke with tradition and began to support the GOP in the 1952 presidential campaign. Analyses of precinct voting returns and survey data confirmed that Dwight Eisen- hower attracted disproportionate support among the more educated and affluent white southerners, while failing to win majority support among working-class whites. After documenting the Republican voting behavior of middle-class whites in 1952, Donald S. Strong was moved to exclaim, "They're acting like Yankees!"[36] Bartley and Graham emphasized that "the merchants, businessmen, and landowners of the black belt and the business-professional-white-collar residents of the cities and suburbs, all of whom were economically conservative and for the most part reason- ably prosperous, were seemingly being driven out of the Democratic party."[37]

Contrary to Key's scenario, however, the Democratic party also became less popular among working-class white southerners. The national party's identification with civil rights in particular and social change in general provoked enormous irritation, but strong economic grievances existed as well. "You can make any number of cases for what went wrong between the Democratic party and the working man," argued Halberstam. "My own favorite is the great failure of the party over the past twenty years to do anything about changing the tax burden placed on the working class and the middle class, while the very rich acquired smart tax lawyers to teach them how to escape responsibility. Thus the working people found themselves paying high taxes and getting very little in the way of services, since the money was going largely for defense and corollary needs."[38] Although the region's white workers did not ordinarily convert to Republicanism, they certainly became less Democratic between 1952 and 1984.

To determine the extent to which various socioeconomic classes of southern whites have differed in their fundamental party loyalties over the past three decades, we shall analyze trends in party identification among white southerners divided according to three broad categories of educational achievement—those who have attended college, high school graduates, and those who did not finish high school.[39] Even if most middle-class southerners were "acting like Yankees" in the 1952 presidential election, they were still thinking like traditional southerners in their basic partisanship (see figure 11.1). At midcentury staggering majorities of whites—regardless of their level of education—still called themselves Democrats or leaned toward the Democratic party. Three decades later, however, even when independents with Democratic leanings are added to the self-classified Democrats, the traditional majority party attracted only minorities of the better-educated whites and barely half of the least educated whites. Declining Democratic identification is apparent from the top to the bottom of white society.

The shifting partisan balance in the South has been led by college-educated whites, the "opinion-molding classes" who Phillips predicted would take the lead in supporting the Republican party.[40] Apart from two periods when Democratic strength dropped sharply (1964-1968 and 1980-1984), the trend data suggest that the massive collapse of Democratic party support has resulted from the accumulation of gradual changes over the past three decades. Moreover, among better-educated whites much of the Democratic loss has resulted in ever-increasing levels of Republican attractiveness. Prior to the Reagan presidency there were as many Republican identifiers and leaners among college-educated whites as there were Democratic, and by the conclusion of Reagan's first term the GOP had risen to a slight majority and had gained a decisive advantage over those educated white southerners who still favored the Democratic party. "Going Republican" has become the central tendency of educated whites, and the tremendous increase in sympathy and support for Republicanism among the region's most highly educated citizens provides firm support for competitive, two-party politics.

White high school graduates constitute a critically important partisan battleground in the modern South. Although whites with a high school education have experienced virtually continuous secular dealignment since the early 1950s, before 1984 the Democratic party maintained a fairly comfortable advantage among this group. In 1984 the partisan balance shifted dramatically toward convergence, as high school graduates began to approximate the pattern observed among college-educated whites four years earlier. The creation of a permanent Republican superiority in the partisan loyalties of southern whites will require converting or attracting huge numbers of whites whose education has stopped at high school. Shifts from 1976 to 1984 indicate that the Republicans are making enormous strides toward that goal.

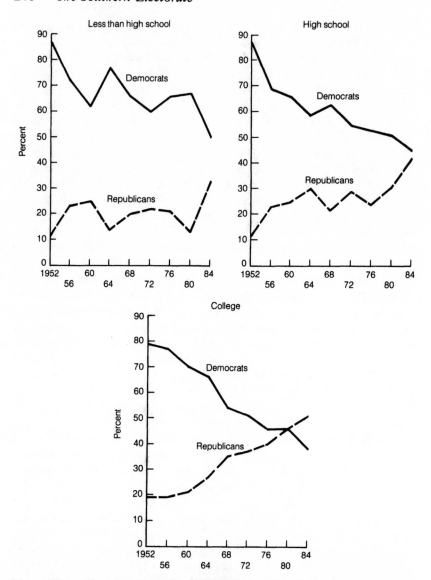

Figure 11.1. Changing partisan tendencies of white southerners, by level of education, 1952–1984. Democrats are Democratic identifiers plus independents who lean toward the Democrats; Republicans are Republican identifiers plus independents who lean toward the Republicans. Source: SRC-CPS presidential election year surveys.

Until quite recently whites without a high school education formed a substantially loyal corps of Democratic adherents. Dealignment has been their secular trend, but this process was periodically interrupted (in 1964, 1976, and 1980) by the reactivation of old Democratic party loyalties.[41] In 1984, however, for the first time in this century, only half of the region's poorly educated whites indicated any preference for the Democratic party. Much of the recent decline has been due to the relentless attacks on the Democratic party by President Reagan, who has often told the conservatives among this group exactly what they have wanted to hear. Though Republicanism did increase substantially in this group between 1980 and 1984, their partisanship is not crucial to Republican realignment. Minimally educated whites have evidenced about as much interest in joining the Republican party as most Republican leaders have expressed in converting them. The main Republican strategy among this group has been to target the religious fundamentalists using such social issues as school prayer, busing, and abortion.[42]

The southern party system in the mid-1980s was clearly linked to differences in educational achievement among whites. Democratic tendencies declined with increases in formal education, and Republican proclivities rose as education increased. Analyses of partisanship according to income levels and occupational status would probably show similar results, with attraction to the GOP increasingly common among whites at the top and in the middle of southern society.[43]

Political Ideology and the Modern Party System

Although American political parties in recent years have seldom exhibited extreme ideological cleavage between liberals and conservatives, beyond the South modest links have usually existed between political ideology and party identification. In the South, because citizens with different philosophies of government were confined within a single party, most politically active conservatives worked through (and usually dominated) the Democratic party. It is a matter of no small importance, therefore, that self-classified southern conservatives have increasingly identified themselves as Republicans or leaned toward Republicanism. This critical shift in the partisan affiliations of conservative southern whites is helping to create a more competitive, two-party politics, as well as a party system that is slightly more "rational" than in the past, at least in the sense that southerners with different political philosophies have begun to separate themselves into opposing political parties. In most southern states these changes have not yet culminated in sharply polarized conflict between a "liberal" or "progressive" Democratic party and a conservative Republican party, but they have engendered a partisan politics that is more similar to nonsouthern practices than before.

The potential partisan realignment of southern conservatives has been one of the most enduring topics in regional politics. Heard predicted in 1952 that "in the long run southern conservatives will find neither in a separatist group nor in the Democratic party an adequate vehicle of political expression. If this is true, they must turn to the Republican party."[44] Conservative southerners would be inclined to convert, he argued, if they lost control of the congressional Democratic party in making national policy *and* if liberal Democratic factions became sufficiently competitive to threaten continued conservative domination of southern state politics.[45] Heard developed a plausible scenario for conservative abandonment of the Democratic party:

> Competing for the large middle-class vote, it would appear that over a period of time the liberal factions might build a stable numerical superiority within the Democratic party. Should they achieve this goal, even in part, in the states where there are important numbers of traditional Republicans, they would give conservative southerners an incentive to seek refuge and allies in the Republican party. Conservative Democrats would carry with them to that party badly needed financial resources, energy, and impetus. . . Persons of wealth in and out of the South have the means to sustain the Republican party in a long struggle for victory.[46]

Few observers of Democratic politics in the South expected conservatives to abandon precipitously the semisacred and highly functional institution that they had controlled for generations. Key, Heard, and Sundquist have all stressed multiple practical barriers to the partisan realignment of southern conservatives.[47]

In fact, the customary regional differences in the association between ideology and partisanship still prevailed in 1968. Though the connection between ideology and party identification outside the South was hardly overpowering, majorities of liberals and conservatives did identify with rival political parties and moderates were split in their partisan leanings. In the South, though, only a trace of association linked ideology and partisanship. Majorities of self-classified liberals, moderates, *and* conservatives claimed to be Democrats. The South's few liberals, like liberals elsewhere in the nation, were already in their "natual" Democratic position. Yet southern middle-of-the-roaders were considerably more Democratic and less Republican than nonsouthern moderates, and the partisan affiliations of southern conservatives deviated profoundly from those of conservatives in the rest of the country. In 1968 only 22 percent of southern conservatives, compared with 48 percent of nonsouthern conservatives, identified themselves as Republicans. Among white southerners who classified themselves as conservatives, twice as many (50 percent) called themselves Democrats as Republicans (24 percent).

Why had so many southern conservatives remained Democratic after the Great Society? Although increased Democratic representation in Congress had destroyed the southern veto on national legislation, conservative southerners had much less reason to quarrel with the Democrats who occupied most of the region's elective offices. The conservative wing of the southern Democratic party remained formidable. If we add middle-of-the-roaders with conservative leanings to self-described conservatives, we find that the conservative wing accounted for 56 percent of southern Democrats, compared with only 27 percent who considered themselves liberals or leaned toward liberalism. In addition, the southern Republican party in 1968 included a substantial moderate wing (37 percent classified themselves as middle-of-the-road or liberal) and hence may not have appeared so attractive to southern conservatives. Moreover, far more southerners continued to think of themselves as Democrats rather than Republicans in *state* politics. According to CSEP state party identification results, 60 percent of southerners called themselves Democrats while only 18 percent labeled themselves Republicans in 1968. This three-to-one advantage in party identification meant that the conservative Democrats who won their party's nomination for statewide office could usually win the general election. In 1968, therefore, southern Democracy was not dominated by liberals; southern Republicanism was not totally monopolized by conservatives; and the Democrats possessed a decisive advantage in grassroots mass identification. For white conservatives to continue to wield decisive political influence in the region, it was both unnecessary and impractical to convert to Republicanism.

Since 1968 there has been a steady increase in the linkage between political ideology and party identification among southerners.[48] Southern liberals have basically remained loyal to the Democratic party, or they have at least leaned toward the Democrats (see figure 11.2). Southerners who think of themselves as middle-of-the-road have slowly weakened their attachments to the Democratic party, but most have thus far resisted the lure of Republicanism. Indeed, one-quarter of them classify themselves as independents with no partisan leanings. It is among southern conservatives that repudiation of the Democratic party has been most pronounced and that a secular realignment toward Republicanism is occurring. By 1980 white conservatives were more likely to identify themselves as Republicans than Democrats, and the gap between Republicans and Democrats widened again in 1984. Although Republicanism attracted less than a majority of self-classified conservatives, if independents

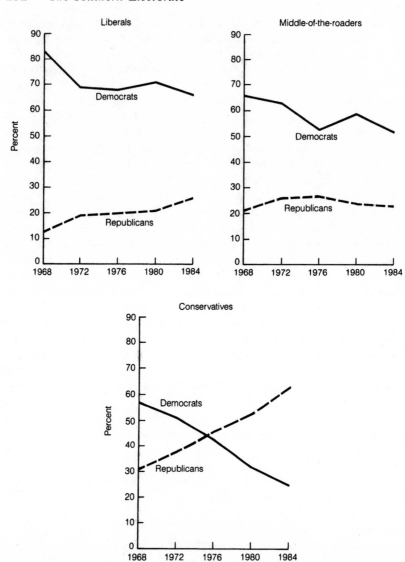

Figure 11.2. Changing partisan tendencies of white southerners, by political ideology, 1968–1984. Democrats are Democratic identifiers plus independents who lean toward the Democrats; Republicans are Republican identifiers plus independents who lean toward the Republicans. Sources: CSEP for 1968; SRC-CPS presidential election year surveys for other years.

who lean toward the Republicans are added to the totals (as they are in figure 11.2), profound secular changes are apparent in the party identifications of conservative white southerners.

The shifts among southern conservatives have altered the ideological composition of the Democratic and Republican parties (see table 11.5).[49] Conservative defections have obviously weakened the strategic position of the remaining conservative Democrats. In 1980-1984 conservatives fell to less than a third of the Democratic identifiers, surely the low point in this century for conservative influence within southern Democracy. These defections have strengthened the strategic position of grassroots middle-of-the-roaders (moderates) more than they have enhanced the clout of liberal Democrats. Whereas liberals have remained a minority among southern Democrats, ideological moderates were a slightly larger plurality of the Democratic electorate in 1980-1984 than they were in 1972. In the first decade after the Great Society, therefore, middle-of-the-roaders were the principal beneficiaries of the conservative exodus from the Democratic party.

Because of the persisting ideological diversity of southern Democrats, it is not surprising that most Democratic politicians have eschewed either undiluted liberalism or hard-line conservatism. "Given the continued presence of a traditional Democratic vote," Sundquist has argued, "the most successful Democratic candidates have been those who have retarded rather than stimulated the realignment process—in other words, the moderate centrists who are skilled in the political straddle, moving

Table 11.5. Changing ideological composition of southern parties, 1972 to 1980–1984[a]

Political ideology	Democrats		Independents		Republicans	
	72	80–84	72	80–84	72	80–84
All southerners						
Liberals	27	29	22	18	12	12
Moderates	37	40	35	33	33	20
Conservatives	36	32	43	48	56	67
White southerners						
Liberals	18	26	17	17	10	12
Moderates	38	43	38	32	32	21
Conservatives	45	32	46	52	58	68

Source: SRC-CPS presidential election year surveys.

a. Figures for 1980–1984 are averages of the 1980 and 1984 surveys. Data are presented as percentages. Because of rounding, totals may not sum to 100 percent.

just far enough to the center to attract strong black and liberal support but not so far as to drive a large bloc of moderate-conservative Democrats into the Republican ranks."[50] Such a "straddling" strategy may not prevail indefinitely among southern Democratic candidates. Sundquist continues:

> In the long run, however, the realignment appeared certain to continue to work its way steadily downward through the political levels—from presidential voting to statewide voting to local voting. . . Democratic strategists could not retard the process for long by holding their party to a moderately conservative course, no matter how clearly they might recognize the need to do so. For as the Republican party grew through the gradual accretion of conservatives, the Democratic party would automatically come under control of its liberal wing—strengthened in any case by the rapid growth in the number of black voters—and more liberals and neo-Populists would be among its candidates. And as that occurred, party lines would be sharpened and more and more moderates and conservatives would find their home among the Republicans, placing the Democratic party under even firmer liberal control. The cycle would continue until the realignment was complete at every level.[51]

The scenario presented by Sundquist is a future possibility; a more likely prospect over the near term is that conservative withdrawals will increase liberal influence within the Democratic party but that liberals will fall short of "dominating" or "controlling" the party. In most statewide contests Democrats are still competitive with Republicans, and they will not precipitously abandon a straddling strategy that has frequently succeeded. Thus far most southern Democratic parties seem firmly controlled by politicians who avoid unqualified liberalism, candidates who run as "progressive conservatives" or "conservative progressives" and who appeal to diverse ideological constituencies within the party. If attractive and well-financed centrist Democrats can also expand their appeal among different ideological groups within the entire electorate, such strategies may well produce many more Democratic victories in southern elections. On the basis of evidence presented in this book, a key question for future Democratic success concerns the relative importance of "liberals" and "moderates" in positions of authority within the Democratic party. In light of the severe and persisting obstacles facing southern liberals in statewide campaigns, we doubt that Democratic parties dominated by their liberal wings would be generally competitive in statewide contests. For the foreseeable future, liberals are unlikely to set the ideological tone for most of the South's Democratic parties.

Conservatives, though, have certainly become the dominant ideological force in southern Republican parties. Fifty-six percent of southern Republicans could be classified as conservatives in 1972, and in the early 1980s two-thirds could be so described. The so-called moderate wing of the GOP was in decline,[52] just as it was in the rest of the nation. And if conservative southern whites continue to shift into the Republican party, it could become the undisputed modern outlet for political influence among the region's most conservative whites.

Conservatives also increased in relative size among the region's critically important group of political independents, those individuals who have reservations about calling themselves either Democrats or Republicans. By 1980-1984 half the independents were self-described conservatives, a proportion several times larger than that of the liberal independents.

As a result of these changes, southerners can now sort themselves into political parties that reflect their own beliefs and values more clearly than in the past, and citizens who do not feel comfortable with either party can profess independence without violating cultural norms of respectability. On the one hand, conservatives, particularly younger conservatives anticipating future developments, can rally behind the Republican party. If their party's candidates still face difficult odds in many statewide races, conservatives can realistically believe that their numbers are growing within the Republican party and that the GOP is on its way to becoming the political voice of the South's preeminent models of success and wealth. On the other hand, liberals and moderates can identify with a contemporary Democratic party that is less crowded with white conservatives than before, despite the fact that southern Democratic parties are not ordinarily controlled or directed by their liberal wings.

The disintegration of southern one-party politics has transformed the role of the Democratic party. Southern Democracy no longer functions as the vehicle of white supremacy, and loyalty to the Democratic party has ceased to be an accepted test of regional orthodoxy. Thus far the decline of Democratic identification has not resulted in the wholesale triumph of Republicanism, since millions of southerners consider themselves political independents. When the partisan leanings of independents are taken into account, Democrats still retain a modest advantage over Republicans. Democratic victories in statewide contests can no longer be taken for granted, though the outcome of these campaigns often turns on the preference of the region's independents, and Democratic nominees need a much smaller share of these swing votes than do the Republicans to construct majority coalitions. For a southern politician who actually wants to hold state and local office, in most situations it is still safer, still more practical, to run as a Democrat. In most southern states, however, campaigning as a Republican is a diminishing liability, for the GOP is rapidly growing and has excellent future prospects. Our analysis has shown key sectors of the southern electorate—whites in general, but especially the conservatives, the college-educated, and the youngest generation—either realigning in favor of the Republican party or strongly moving in that direction. Given the right candidates, ample funds, and timely Democratic errors, it is increasingly possible for Republicans to exploit divisions within the Democratic party, to compete seriously for votes, and to win elections.

IV

The Revival of Party Competition

twelve

The Republican
Advantage in
Presidential Politics

THE POLITICAL reverberations of altered race relations, rapid socioeconomic and demographic change, and the expansion of an electorate much less attached to the Democratic party have laid the foundations for two-party politics in the South. Democratic monopolization of southern politics has ended, and Republicans now vigorously contest most major elections.[1] The dealignment of the old party system, coupled with the inception of partisan realignment, have entailed significant changes in partisan officeholding. Nonetheless, Republican candidates are not yet competitive for all types of offices, nor are they realistic contenders in all parts of the South.

Perhaps the best way to understand what has happened is to use Kevin Phillips's concept of "split-level realignment." As Cavanagh and Sundquist summarize Phillips's position, "the country now has a normal Republican majority at the presidential level, a competitive system in the Senate, and a system that favors the Democrats in the House of Representatives and below the federal level."[2] Split-level realignment, as we shall show, accurately describes the different central tendencies of partisan officeholding in the South (as well as in the entire nation). Republican candidates in the South have dominated presidential elections since 1968 and have won nearly half of the contests for the Senate in recent years, but they have made much less headway in capturing and retaining governorships. Because of these clear differences in GOP success according to the office sought, we shall provide separate analyses of southern two-party politics for the presidency, the Senate, and the governorships. This chapter demonstrates the evolution of a marked Republican advantage in presidential elections[3]; the next chapter will examine senatorial and gubernatorial elections.

The New Republican Superiority in Presidential Elections

Franklin Roosevelt's final campaign marked the termination of the Solid Democratic South so visible in presidential elections after 1876. Not since 1944 have all eleven states of the former Confederacy united behind a Democratic presidential candidate; indeed, the outcome of presidential elections in the South has changed radically over the past four decades. Although Democrats captured majorities of the region's electoral college vote in four of the five contests between 1948 and 1964, neither party carried the South's popular vote by a decisive margin. White dissatisfaction with the national Democratic party's agenda of economic and racial liberalism grew so intense during the 1960s, however, that Phillips correctly anticipated an "emerging Republican majority" in subsequent *presidential* elections in the South.[4] Within the region, campaigns since 1968 have produced two landslide popular vote victories (1972 and 1984) and three lopsided electoral college wins (1972, 1980, and 1984) for the Republicans, compared with no popular vote landslides and only one decisive electoral college victory (1976) for the Democrats. In the contemporary South the presidency has become the Republicans' office to lose rather than the Democrats' office to win.

To appreciate this momentous reversal in party fortunes, it is helpful to distinguish different levels of popular support for the two major parties and to apply these distinctions to the results of presidential elections. Key suggested five electoral settings along a continuum from "Strong Republican" to "Strong Democratic" but did not provide explicit criteria to differentiate each category.[5] David Olson has proposed a typology in which the percentages indicating different levels of two-party competition are explicitly defined.[6] The categories we shall employ essentially restate or extend distinctions made previously by Key or Olson, though in some instances their terminology has been modified.

Beginning with the least competitive situation for a political party, Olson suggested the phrase "electorally quiescent minority" to denote a party that either fails to contest general elections or conducts merely token campaigns.[7] We shall describe as quiescent any general election in which a party does not offer a candidate or in which the party receives less than 20.0 percent of the total general election vote. General elections in which a party draws between 20.0 and 44.9 percent of the vote reflect a more determined effort, one that can be labeled aspiring.[8] A genuinely competitive performance occurs when a party secures at least 45.0 percent but less than 55.0 percent of the vote. Victories on the order of 55.0 to 79.9 percent, a range of popularity encompassing most landslide elections, indicate a party's dominance. Finally, to distinguish the opposite

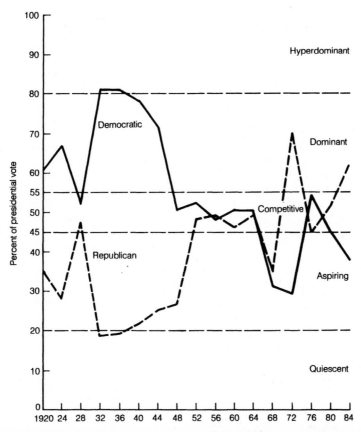

Figure 12.1. The transformation of presidential politics in the South: percent of total vote won by Democratic and Republican presidential candidates, 1920–1984. Sources: Richard M. Scammon, ed., *America at the Polls* (Pittsburgh: University of Pittsburgh Press, 1965); and appropriate volumes of Scammon's series, *America Votes*.

of a quiescent showing, we propose the term "hyperdominant" to designate a party attracting 80.0 percent or more of the vote.

The percentage distribution of the popular vote for Democratic and Republican presidential candidates between 1920 and 1984 is plotted in figure 12.1. Between 1920 and 1944, with the sole exception of the 1928 campaign, the Democratic party's presidential candidates enjoyed either dominant or hyperdominant status. By contrast, quiescence and marginal aspiration typified GOP presidential efforts through 1948.

Two dramatic turning points, the elections of 1948 and 1968, symbolize the decline and fall of presidential Democracy.[9] President Harry S. Truman was the first national Democrat widely perceived as favoring economic *and* racial liberalism, an ideological stance entirely repugnant to conservative white southerners. Truman's advocacy of civil rights legislation was by far the most important proximate stimulus for southern dissatisfaction with the Democrats in 1948. When the Democratic party also adopted civil rights proposals in its 1948 platform, dissident southerners bolted the Democratic convention and subsequently formed the States Rights party. The Dixiecrats, as they soon came to be known, nominated one Deep South governor for president (South Carolina's Strom Thurmond) and another for vice-president (Mississippi's Fielding Wright). After maneuvering successfully in four Deep South states (Mississippi, South Carolina, Alabama, and Louisiana) to keep Truman off the ballot and run Thurmond under the Democratic party label, the States Righters won 22 percent of the southern popular vote.[10] Under these extraordinary conditions, although the Dixiecrats failed to defeat Truman, his share of the southern vote plummeted to 51 percent, 21 percentage points below Roosevelt's final showing four years earlier. Moreover, Truman's reduced percentage was no temporary aberration, for over the next four presidential elections Democratic strength fluctuated closely around a thin majority of the popular vote. Landslide southern majorities for Democratic presidential nominees simply ceased to be attainable.

Although Truman's policies made his candidacy vulnerable among many white southerners in 1948 without substantially benefiting the Republicans, Dwight Eisenhower's 1952 campaign restored respectability to Republican presidential efforts.[11] In 1956 Eisenhower became the first Republican candidate in this century to win a plurality of the southern vote, and Richard Nixon and Barry Goldwater continued to attract comparable proportions of regional support. The 1952–1964 presidential contests were unusually close; in this transitional era, Democratic and Republican presidential nominees achieved roughly equal proportions of electoral support.

The second critical turning point in the decline of presidential Democracy, again signaled by the appearance of a robust protest movement—in this case George Wallace's American Independent party—occurred in 1968 at the conclusion of President Johnson's Great Society. The former Alabama governor attacked the Johnson administration's racial and economic liberalism while also contending that there was not "a dime's worth of difference" between the two major political parties. Wallace's appeal, like that of the Dixiecrats, was strongest in the Deep South, and he won a considerably larger share than Thurmond—34 percent—of the region's popular vote. Vice-President Hubert Humphrey, viewed by many southerners as the epitome of northern economic and racial liberalism, received only 31 percent of the southern vote, a performance that was 19 percentage points below Johnson's 1964 performance. Richard Nixon secured a slim plurality of the popular vote.[12]

Twenty years earlier a third party movement had ended the Democrats' long-standing dominance and relegated them to a merely competitive position in presidential elections; in 1968 another third party movement reduced the level of popular support for national liberal Democrats to proportions fairly similar to those achieved in the South by Republican nominees in the early 1920s. And when northern liberals—George McGovern in 1972 and Walter Mondale in 1984—subsequently won Democratic presidential nominations, the Democratic popular vote fell far short of the competitive range. Over the past four decades, in short, southern support for Democratic presidential candidates has descended from electoral domination through the competitive range to mere aspiration. Since 1964 Democratic competitiveness has been limited to the two occasions when a native southerner, Jimmy Carter, led the national ticket. Even Carter's original campaign produced no regional landslide in the popular vote, and a majority of his fellow southerners repudiated his leadership in 1980.[13]

During the second period of Democratic disintegration, after the Great Society had solidified the image of national Democrats as racial and economic liberals, and after the Wallace movement had played itself out, Republican campaigners came to enjoy distinct advantages over the Democrats. In every election since 1968 Republican presidential candidates have either beaten their rivals decisively or, at the very worst, remained competitive with them. The 1972 and 1984 Republican landslides occurred when the ideological differences between the major party candidates were most transparent, when conservative Republican presidents faced overtly liberal Democrats. In 1972 Nixon absorbed practically all of the Wallace voters. (Nixon's 70 percent of the popular vote was about the same as the combined percentages won by Nixon and Wallace in 1968.) Ronald Reagan's contest with Mondale in 1984 yielded another easy GOP victory, though the magnitude of Reagan's vote (62 percent) was smaller than Nixon's.[14] While remaining highly competitive, Republicans have run less spectacularly against the South's own Democratic nominees.

Southwide trends for the 1972–1984 presidential elections reveal patterns of electoral support that are vastly more beneficial to Republicans than to Democrats. The Republican advantage is not yet comparable in pervasiveness and stability to the Democrats' dominant position under

Roosevelt's leadership, but Republican presidential candidates averaged 57 percent of the vote in the four contests after 1968. Although the Democratic party is still capable of winning presidential contests in the South, it is unlikely to do so unless an array of powerful short-term factors, such as a charismatic Democratic candidate or egregious Republican misadventures concerning the economy or foreign policy, cumulate to the Democrats' advantage.

Viewed election by election, there has been considerable instability in the proportions of the popular vote won by Democratic and Republican candidates since the end of the Great Society. This volatility typically involves the *size* of the Republicans' victory margin, not the identity of the winning party. In fact, beneath the partisan flux that appears from one presidential campaign to the next, elements of grassroots stability exist that are extremely favorable to the Republicans.

The Grassroots Democratic Collapse

The disintegration of the Democratic Solid South in presidential elections is one of the most significant features of the new southern politics. An examination of presidential voting patterns in three periods of time from 1920 through 1980 for all eleven hundred southern counties reveals massive changes in the scope and location of consistent county-level support for Democratic and Republican presidential candidates, changes that have greatly strengthened Republican prospects. Taken in their entirety the eight presidential campaigns of 1920–1948 illustrate the reality of the Democratic Solid South, though the final election in this sequence marked a turning point in regional solidarity. Beginning with Dwight Eisenhower's 1952 campaign the southern Republican party experienced a great leap forward to political competitiveness, and the eight campaigns of 1952–1980 may be conveniently divided into the four elections that preceded (1952–1964) and that followed (1968–1980) the implementation of Lyndon Johnson's Great Society.

To compare central tendencies in county voting behavior all southern counties have been classified as Democratic, Republican, or mixed. A partisan county, whether Democratic or Republican, is defined as one that was carried by the same majority party in at least three-fourths of the contests within a given electoral period. Any county not qualifying as consistently Democratic or consistently Republican is described as mixed. Since county populations differ enormously, for each set of elections we have also calculated the average percentage of the total vote emanating from Democratic, Republican, and mixed counties. By comparing the proportion of stable partisan counties and the size of the vote cast by reliably Democratic and Republican counties over successive sets of elections, the magnitude of change in grassroots outcomes will become apparent.

Prior to 1952 the phrase "Solid South" accurately summarized the Democratic party's grassroots base in presidential elections. Democratic counties in the 1920–1948 elections outnumbered Republican counties by a factor of twenty-two (89 to 4 percent), a phenomenal Democratic advantage. Within the region Democratic supremacy was more pervasive in the Deep South than in the Peripheral South. The mountain sections of the Peripheral South constituted the sole geographic base hostile to the Democratic party.[15] Indeed, reliable presidential Republicanism through 1948 was essentially confined to Tennessee, and even there the Democrats maintained a much larger voter base.[16]

The progressive deterioration and collapse of the Solid South since midcentury is demonstrated in table 12.1. During the 1952–1964 presidential elections the Republican party achieved a genuinely competitive position at the county level in every Peripheral South state except Arkansas and began to create strongholds in the Deep South, most notably in South Carolina. Although all southern states save Virginia and South Carolina possessed more Democratic than Republican counties, the emerging centers of stable Republicanism were frequently the South's rapidly growing metropolitan counties. Even before the advent of the Great Society, Republican counties contained larger percentages of voters than did Democratic counties in a majority of states—Virginia, North Carolina, South Carolina, Florida, Tennessee, and Texas. Pronounced subregional differences existed. Although the Deep South counties remained far more Democratic than Republican, in the Peripheral South the average share of the total statewide vote produced in Republican counties (47 percent) substantially exceeded the size of the vote contributed by Democratic counties (32 percent).

In presidential elections after the Great Society, Republicans consolidated their 1952–1964 gains, and grassroots Democracy almost totally collapsed. The proportion of reliably Democratic counties fell from 55 percent in the pre–Great Society contests to 14 percent in 1968–1980 while the percentage of Republican counties increased from 26 to 30 percent. More important for practical politics, however, stable Democratic counties accounted for only 13 percent of the region's total vote compared with 48 percent for Republican counties. As is clearly shown in figure 12.2, huge Democratic losses occurred across the entire region. In no southern state did the Democratic party retain a voter base embracing more than a third of the counties or a fifth of the vote. By contrast, in nine states Republican counties outnumbered Democratic counties and

Table 12.1. Democratic devastation versus Republican consolidation in southern presidential elections: patterns of county-level partisanship before the Great Society (1952–1964) and after it (1968–1980), by state, subregion, and region[a]

	1952–1964 Elections						1968–1980 Elections					
	Percentage of counties[b]			Percentage of vote[c]			Percentage of counties			Percentage of vote		
Political unit[d]	Dem	Mix	Rep	Dem	Mix	Rep	Dem	Mix	Rep	Dem	Mix	Rep
Florida	51	13	36	14	38	48	1	61	37	1	36	62
Virginia	26	20	54	19	21	60	12	28	60	18	22	60
North Carolina	60	11	29	42	8	50	10	50	40	8	33	59
Texas	49	27	24	32	24	44	33	32	35	21	26	53
South Carolina	39	17	43	40	11	49	33	46	22	15	36	50
Louisiana	34	34	31	46	34	20	8	63	30	16	40	44
Mississippi	27	68	5	32	60	8	10	68	22	7	51	42
Tennessee	52	4	44	35	19	46	8	49	42	21	38	42
Alabama	84	7	9	60	14	26	9	81	10	3	58	39
Arkansas	77	4	19	75	2	24	8	71	21	18	56	25
Georgia	94	1	4	87	1	12	4	94	1	19	76	5
Deep South	64	22	14	58	20	22	10	77	13	12	54	33
Peripheral South	50	17	34	32	21	47	17	43	40	14	32	54
South	55	19	26	39	21	40	14	55	30	13	39	48

Source: Same as figure 12.1.

a. Democratic (Republican) counties are defined as counties that were carried by the Democratic (Republican) party in 75 percent or more of the elections within a given period. All counties not classified as Democratic or Republican are defined as mixed. Dem, Democratic county; Mix, mixed county; Rep, Republican county. Figures are rounded to the nearest whole percentage.

b. Percentage of counties classified as Democratic, Republican, or mixed.

c. Mean percentage of total vote emanating from Democratic, Republican, or mixed counties.

d. States are ranked (highest to lowest) according to the size of the Republican voter base in the 1968–1980 elections.

controlled either a majority of the vote (Florida, Virginia, North Carolina, Texas, and South Carolina) or a large plurality (Louisiana, Mississippi, Tennessee, and Alabama). Even before the Reagan administration began, the Republicans, especially in the Peripheral South, had established a marked superiority over the Democrats in the scope and vitality of their grassroots political bases.

The breadth of the Democratic collapse is staggering. It would be difficult to find comparable instances in American political history of such a rapid and comprehensive desertion of an established majority

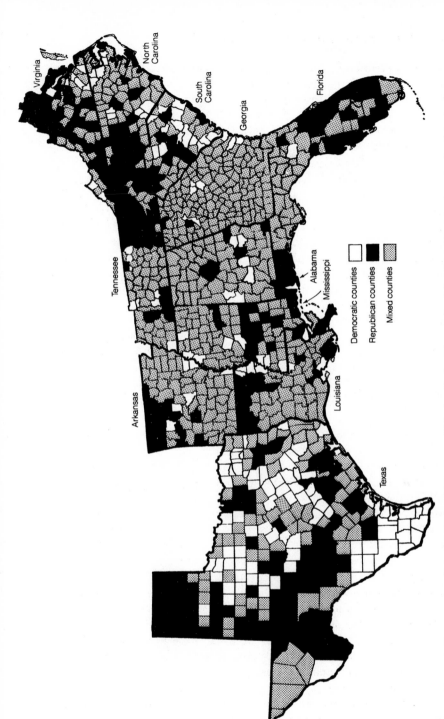

Figure 12.2. Democratic collapse and Republican consolidation in the aftermath of the Great Society: county-level voting patterns for 1968–1980 presidential elections in the South. Criterion for a partisan county: carried by the same party in at least three of four elections. Source: Scammon, *America Votes*.

party by an entire region.[17] In every state broad clusters of counties that were repeatedly Democratic in the 1952–1964 elections failed to be reliably Democratic in the 1968–1980 contests. These formerly Democratic counties included nearly half of all the southern counties, three-fifths of the Deep South counties, and more than a third of the Peripheral South counties. In the aftermath of the Great Society entire geographic sections with Democratic voting habits dating back to the end of Reconstruction—Southside Virginia, eastern North Carolina, the South Carolina piedmont, practically all of Georgia, the Florida panhandle, most of nonurban and non-black belt Alabama, Mississippi's northeastern hills, Middle Tennessee and much of West Tennessee, most of Arkansas outside the northwestern mountains, South Louisiana, and scattered portions of East, Central, and West Texas—ceased to be carried consistently by Democratic presidential candidates. With the exception of support won from a small number of urban areas with pronounced minority populations (Atlanta, Memphis, New Orleans, Durham, Richmond, Corpus Christi, Austin, and Little Rock), a larger group of rural and small-town counties with substantial minority concentrations (generally black but Hispanic in South Texas), and a few economically marginal rural counties (mainly in Texas), the Democratic party could not maintain its presidential base after 1964.

A completely different pattern emerges for the Republican party. Despite George Wallace's 1968 campaign and the presence of a southerner at the head of the Democratic ticket in 1976 and 1980 (factors that made the post–Great Society presidential elections a challenge to the Republicans), the Republican party retained and even extended its grassroots base over the 1968–1980 campaigns. One-fifth of the South's counties were consistently Republican both before and after the Great Society, and another tenth of the counties became Republican in the 1968–1980 elections. Prominent sources of persistent and emergent presidential Republicanism include Virginia's urban corridor and mountains, the piedmont and mountains of North Carolina, East Tennessee, urban South Carolina, the urban horseshoe of South Florida, urban Alabama, South Mississippi, North Louisiana, the mountains of northwestern Arkansas, and many of Texas's urban centers plus West Texas generally.

Presidential Republicanism in the mid-1980s encompasses three leading sources: mountain Republicanism, urban Republicanism, and interstate Republicanism. The party's original base, mountain Republicanism, has continued to be a reliable source of support. Urban Republicanism, rooted in the rapidly expanding white middle class, remains the key to Republican success. Since 1968 the Republican party has been repeatedly victorious in roughly half of the South's principal urban counties, compared with a Democratic success rate of only about 10 percent. In the typical southern state (Georgia and Arkansas are the only exceptions) the Republican party has become firmly established in several metropolitan settings. The most recent development, interstate Republicanism, refers to the proliferation of consistent Republican victories in numerous counties with smaller population centers, many of which are traversed by interstate highways and are therefore better situated to attract outside industry and possess a growing middle class than are the counties bypassed by the interstate highway system. Counties such as Cooke (Texas), Lincoln (Mississippi), Kershaw (South Carolina), and Henderson (Tennessee) illustrate the growing attractiveness of presidential Republicanism beyond metropolitan areas.

Thus patterns of Democratic collapse and Republican ascendancy underlie the volatility of recent presidential campaigns in the South. Especially in the Peripheral South, with its larger white urbanized middle class and its broader base of traditional Republicanism, the Republican party has developed a sufficiently extensive and stable base of support at the county level to make it not merely a competitive force but—barring stupendous Republican misrule—probably the dominant party in future presidential campaigns. Although the proportion of the vote controlled by Republican counties does not approach the Democratic party's advantage during the Solid South era, it provides a comfortable margin of error for Republican administrations. At the grassroots level the Democratic party has ceased to be a competitive institution. Had it not been for Carter's two campaigns and Wallace's presence in 1968, far more centers of consistent Republicanism would have emerged in the 1968–1980 elections. Since it cannot be assumed that the Democratic party will frequently nominate a southerner for the presidency, the unprecedented narrowness of the Democrats' grassroots base means that the party is heavily dependent upon spectacular Republican incompetence or misfortune for its future political success. For some time to come, Democratic presidential candidates are likely to be on the defensive in the South.

Group Voting Patterns in Presidential Elections

Given the history of southern racial divisions, it is hardly surprising that presidential elections commonly separate almost all blacks from most whites. As a rule, presidential candidates of the Democratic party are no longer competitive among white southern voters (see figure 12.3). Not since Johnson's campaign have a majority of white southerners voted Democratic, and only once since then—in Carter's 1976 candidacy—

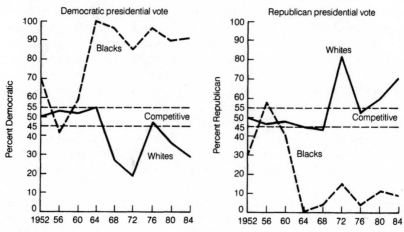

Figure 12.3. Race and presidential voting in the South, 1952–1984. Source: SRC-CPS presidential election year surveys.

has a Democratic nominee won as much as 45 percent of the white vote. Conspicuous northern liberals received the least white support, of course, but even Carter's reelection effort succeeded with little more than a third of southern white voters. Vastly different Democratic candidates, as well as vastly different socioeconomic conditions, would be required to make Democratic presidential candidates serious contenders again among most white southerners. By contrast, commencing in 1964 southern blacks have overwhelmingly cast their ballots in favor of Democratic nominees.

Republican presidential candidates became truly competitive with the Democrats among white southerners in 1952, and for the next three elections the white vote split fairly evenly between the major parties. In 1968 the Republicans opened a wide lead over the Democrats, but Wallace attracted many whites who otherwise would have much preferred Nixon to Humphrey. Republican ascendancy among southern whites began in 1972, after the demise of the Wallace movement, just as the previous era of Republican competitiveness followed the disbandment of the Dixiecrats. All subsequent Republican nominees have achieved majority white support, securing landslide white votes whenever conservative Republicans faced liberal northern Democrats. Among white southerners a reordering of presidential politics in favor of the Republicans is an accomplished fact.

Before Barry Goldwater's nomination, Republican presidential candidates could still draw respectable shares of the South's small black vote. Goldwater's frequently declared opposition to the 1964 Civil Rights Act, combined with Democratic championship of major civil rights legislation, ruined the GOP among southern blacks. None of the blacks surveyed by the Survey Research Center in 1964 reported voting for Goldwater, and later Republican candidates have never extracted more than miniscule shares of the southern black vote.

Racial division in partisan choices remains a cardinal feature of presidential politics in the South. The abiding racial cleavage, profound though it is, is by no means an unambiguous, straightforward manifestation of racism.[18] Racism—pure and simple—undoubtedly guides the presidential choices of some (unknown) percentage of white southerners; but, as we have argued throughout this book, interwoven economic, social, and cultural differences between most blacks and most whites are critically important in explaining the divergent central tendencies of white and black voters. W. Wayne Shannon expressed the realities well when he argued that white "southerners have been agitated by a wide range of specific policy disagreements with the northern wing of the Democratic party. These disagreements go far beyond the matter of civil rights. The evidence presented here suggests the development of a general revolt against the most basic policies of the northern party in recent years."[19]

Just as many white southerners left the Democratic party for reasons more complex than simple racism, so the Republican party's contemporary appeal to whites cannot be reduced to a modernized version of the Dixiecrats or the Wallace movement. There are, indeed, carefully calibrated and relatively subtle racial appeals, such as the Reagan administration's efforts to end or dismantle affirmative action programs in employment and to limit the use of busing to promote school desegregation, policies which gratify many conservative whites. But this is only part of the Republican party's broad appeal to white southerners. A partial list of the nonracial attractions would include promises to reduce rates of taxation on individuals and thus increase the real wages and salaries of the employed, to lessen the primacy of the federal government and return many programs to state and local governments, to reduce the federal government's regulatory activities, to manage the national government so that real economic growth can occur without high rates of inflation, to spend whatever it costs to provide a system of national defense second to none, and to restore patriotism, reinstitute school prayer, and restrict abortions. In the post-Great Society era Republican presidential candidates—most prominently Nixon and Reagan—have been far better positioned and far more inclined to tell white southern audiences exactly what they have wanted or hoped to hear from their national leaders than have Democratic nominees, who have mainly campaigned against the grain of conventional white wisdom.

Thus far we have treated whites and blacks as fairly monolithic groups in their political tendencies. This simplification is easily justified for black southerners: on grounds of practicality alone, there are so few "deviant" black southerners that exploration of differences among blacks would not take us far. Among whites the situation is different. Although central tendencies are clearly identifiable for southern whites, not all members of the region's racial majority have accepted Republicanism in presidential politics. An understanding of electoral trends can be advanced by showing how presidential voting behavior differs among whites according to their partisan identification and their degree of education.[20]

As we showed in the last chapter, the southern white electorate is increasingly composed of individuals who are not Democrats. Furthermore, among the dwindling number of whites who have thought of themselves as Democrats, a massive erosion of *strong* partisanship has occurred. Individuals willing to classify themselves as "strong" Democrats declined from an average of 39 percent of the whites in the four presidential election year surveys prior to the Great Society to an average of merely 18 percent of the southern white voters in the five presidential elections after the Great Society.[21] The growing preponderance of Republicans and independents, coupled with the decline of hard-core partisan Democrats, has created a southern white electorate that regards Democratic presidential candidates with suspicion, if not active hostility. Average votes for Democratic and Republican presidential candidates among southern whites in all categories of partisan identification before and after the Great Society are reported in table 12.2. The voting patterns so summarized speak volumes about the comparative prospects of Democratic and Republican presidential candidates among the South's white voters.

Even before the Great Society, strong Democrats were the only whites who contributed exceptionally cohesive support to Democratic presidential candidates. Almost half of the weak Democrats reversed themselves in the voting booth. Yet because seven-tenths of all white voters still thought of themselves as Democrats in the 1952–1964 era, Democratic presidential nominees could remain competitive despite heavy defections to the Republicans. During this period GOP presidential candidates developed an appeal that transcended Republican identification: in addition to winning the votes of practically all self-described Republicans and independents who leaned Republican, they carried most of the pure independents, made substantial inroads among independents who leaned toward the Democrats and among weak Democrats, and even gained some backing among strong Democrats. The breadth of support for Republicans far exceeded that for Democratic candidates. Nonetheless, because only 28 percent of the white voters in the 1952–1964 era clas-

Table 12.2. Breadth of presidential Republicanism among white southerners: presidential voting patterns before and after the Great Society, by party identification[a]

Party identification	1952–1964 Elections		1968–1984 Elections	
	Dem[b]	Rep[b]	Dem	Rep
Strong Democrats	82	18 (39)	75	19 (18)
Weak Democrats	52	48 (33)	45	47 (27)
Independents leaning Democratic	44	56 (5)	37	49 (8)
Independents	27	73 (4)	24	70 (12)
Independents leaning Republican	7	93 (4)	5	91 (12)
Weak Republicans	7	93 (8)	8	89 (13)
Strong Republicans	2	99 (8)	1	99 (10)

Source: SRC-CPS presidential election year surveys.

a. Data are presented as percentages. Each percentage reported is an average computed over the 1952–1964 and 1968–1984 presidential elections. Figures in parentheses report the average percentage of white southern adults with a specified party identification.

b. Dem, average Democratic vote; Rep, average Republican vote.

sified themselves as Republicans or independents, Republican presidential candidates could do no better than compete—more or less evenly—with the Democratic nominees.

Matters changed drastically after the Great Society. On the average, the *percentage* of the white vote achieved by Republican presidential candidates in the 1968–1984 campaigns remained about the same as in the 1950s and early 1960s among strong and weak Republicans, independents leaning toward the Republicans, and pure independents. But these groups, already preponderantly Republican in their presidential voting behavior, now amounted to 54 percent (on the average) of the white voters, virtually twice their share of the white electorate in the earlier period. In addition, Republican presidential nominees continued to attract almost half of the votes cast by independents who leaned toward the Democrats and by weak Democrats.

Since the Great Society, in short, Republican presidential candidates have consistently fared well across a wide spectrum of partisan identifiers. Republicans are almost always competitive among white southerners because they automatically draw huge majorities from self-identified Republicans, independents who lean toward the Republicans, and independents. With this secure base, runaway victories become possible when the Republicans nominate candidates—such as Nixon and Reagan—who are capable of running well among independents who lean toward the Democrats and among weak Democrats. Because Nixon's 1972 landslide was helped by McGovern's colossal weakness among white southerners, the more significant campaigns were those of Reagan, who began to transcend a purely partisan appeal in 1980 and who extended his strength in 1984 to include half of both the weak Democrats and the independents who lean Democratic.

By contrast, reliable and overwhelming support for the Democratic party's presidential ticket among southern whites has been reduced to a shrinking group of strong Democrats. The Democratic party has been especially vulnerable to white opposition whenever liberal nonsoutherners have faced conservative Republicans. When Humphrey, McGovern, and Mondale led the ticket, clear majorities were limited to strong Democrats.[22] Moderate nominees (Jimmy Carter in 1976 and 1980) broadened the party's appeal among southern whites, but only to the point of including majorities of weak Democrats and independents who leaned Democratic. To win presidential contests in the dealigned electorate of the modern South both parties require candidates who can rally independents and attract appreciable support from the opposition political party. On this imperative the Republicans have clearly bested the Democrats.

Finally, the realignment of southern presidential politics can be described in terms of the region's social structure. Among whites, Republican ascendancy is rooted in the upper and middle ranks of society, while Democratic strength is concentrated mainly among those whites who are not middle class—the have-nots and have-littles. College-educated whites—the heart of the new middle class—have led the Republican presidential realignment. According to SRC-CPS data, majorities of college-educated whites have voted Republican in eight of the past nine presidential elections. Especially since 1968, Republican presidential candidates have easily dominated their Democratic opposition among this important white group. As Strong observed in 1971, "The behavior of the more prosperous voters, particularly those of the Upper South, constitutes a party realignment. Persons with the highest incomes and most years of schooling have ceased to use the vote as an affirmation of regional loyalty and have come to vote Republican like the majority of their nonsouthern counterparts since the political reshuffling of the early New Deal era."[23]

A realignment of presidential voting in favor of the Republicans has also taken place among southern whites with a high school education. This group began to move toward the Republicans in the 1950s and early 1960s, was momentarily distracted by the Wallace movement in

1968, and has since voted Republican in every presidential election. Not even Carter's candidacies were sufficiently compelling to generate Democratic victories among whites with high school training.

Whites with scant formal education are the only group of southern whites who have displayed any loyalty to Democratic presidential candidates since 1964, and even among them there is no pattern of unwavering support. Poorly educated white southerners strongly repudiated Humphrey and McGovern (voting mainly for Wallace and Nixon in 1968 and overwhelmingly for Nixon in 1972); they returned to the party when a native southerner headed the national ticket; and they remained with the Democrats in 1984. In terms of the white electorate, therefore, Republican presidential victories have been grounded in those individuals with the greatest exposure to formal education, who are, presumably, those with superior access to resources of skill, money, and political experience. Republicans have built their successful presidential coalition from the apex of the social structure downwards; Democrats have attempted—usually without success—to maintain their coalition by building upwards.

Analyses of election returns and surveys reinforce the same fundamental conclusion: the manifest disintegration of the traditional Democratic Solid South and the ascendancy of the Republican party in presidential campaigns. The net result of the most recent presidential campaigns has been the establishment, for the first time in the South's history, of political bases for Republican presidential candidates that are far more impressive than the corresponding Democratic voter bases. Unless Republican presidents blunder in provocative and disastrous ways, and unless the national Democratic party begins to nominate presidential candidates acceptable to a much larger group of white southerners, presidential Republicanism in the South has advanced so far that the party can be expected to carry most, if not all, of the region's states in presidential politics in the foreseeable future.

thirteen

Partisan Competition for Senator and Governor

ALTHOUGH the Republican party has become firmly established as the dominant force in southern presidential elections, its nominees have faced more severe obstacles in winning the most important statewide contests. Because "the great issues of national politics drive the basic cleavages through the electorate and these divisions, in turn, project themselves into voting on state offices," Key argued that "powerful tendencies operate to induce voters to support both state and local candidates of the same party."[1] Nonetheless, he hardly expected identical outcomes in presidential and nonpresidential contests. "Sectionalism in national politics may very well be undergoing a decline yet its effects on the organization of state politics will long survive its demise," Key predicted. As a consequence, he suggested that "changes in the politics of a state government may lag considerably behind alterations in the presidential voting habits of the people of the state."[2]

Key's observations about American state politics accurately describe trends in the South. Scholars have variously referred to the growth of southern Republicanism as a "trickling down," "diffusion," or "translation" of GOP strength in presidential elections to nonpresidential campaigns.[3] As the effects of national candidates, issues, and events have diminished, Republican gains have been less spectacular. Republicans hold almost half of the South's seats in the U.S. Senate, but Democrats still win most governorships and other leading state offices, run the state legislatures and control most local offices.[4]

Trends in the Nonpresidential Party Battle

Regional trends in the party battle for senator and governor reveal significant gains by Republicans, yet nothing approaching their control of

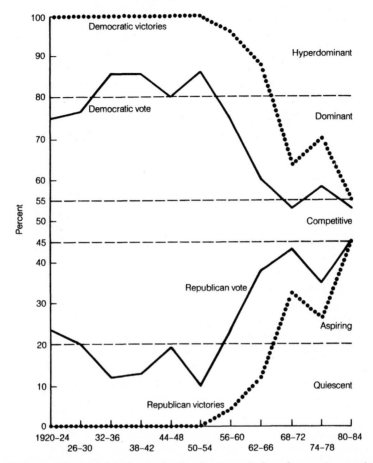

Figure 13.1. Senatorial voting in the South: percent of total vote compared with percent of elections won by Democratic and Republican candidates for senator, 1920–1984. Sources: *Congressional Quarterly's Guide to U.S. Elections* (Washington, D.C.: Congressional Quarterly, 1975); and appropriate volumes of Scammon, *America Votes.*

presidential elections. Both the size of the partisan vote and the proportion of partisan victories for eleven waves of senatorial elections from 1920 through 1984 are plotted in figure 13.1. The figure portrays the transformation of southern senatorships from total Democratic dominance (1920–1954) to a situation in which, aside from temporary gains in the wake of the Watergate scandals, the Democratic vote has dropped into the competitive range. By contrast, the Republican vote has either approached genuine competition (the Nixon wave) or actually entered the competitive zone (the Reagan wave). In the 1980–1984 elections Democratic senatorial candidates polled only 53 percent of the popular vote, their narrowest lead thus far. Growing Republican competitiveness in senatorial contests is reflected as well in the close fit between the size of the partisan vote in the 1980–1984 wave and the share of senate races actually won.

Because governorships are less likely to be directly affected by national issues, events, and personalities than senatorial campaigns, and because those national forces have generally hurt Democrats and helped Republicans, the governorship has been the greater challenge to Republican strategists. From the mid-thirties through the mid-fifties (see figure 13.2), Democratic gubernatorial candidates in the South enjoyed a hyperdominant status against an essentially quiescent Republican party. More aggressive Republican campaigns commenced in the early 1960s, but the Republican advance leveled off in subsequent waves of elections. Through the early 1980s the Democratic percentage of the popular vote hovered slightly above the zone of true competition, and most of the South's governors continued to be Democrats.

Thus far popular support for the South's Democratic senatorial and gubernatorial candidates has easily exceeded that for the Republicans. The traditional Democratic advantage is dissipating, however, especially in Senate elections. To understand more fully the Republicans' invigorated competitiveness in nonpresidential elections, it is important to reexamine SRC-CPS public opinion polls. Party identification data are highly useful in tracking the growth of Republican strength in the region. We shall show that increases in the aggregate level of the GOP popular vote in major statewide contests rest fundamentally upon durable changes in mass attitude toward the parties.

Precise estimates of an expected Republican vote in southern statewide elections are beyond our reach because we do not know whether a respondent is thinking about national or state-level politics when answering the standard SRC-CPS questions about party identification. Nonetheless, it is possible to use the survey data to make serviceable calculations of the *minimum* share of the vote that southern Republican candidates ought to poll in statewide contests.[5] We believe a reasonable definition of the "base," "hard-core," "bedrock," or "hip pocket" vote of the southern Republicans—the vote that party strategists can take for granted if they run experienced and well-financed candidates—is composed of *all* self-defined Republicans, *all* independents who lean toward the Republicans, and *half* of the "pure" independents.[6] In a region where the Democrats have continued to win most state and almost all local contests, those individuals claiming any identification with or leanings

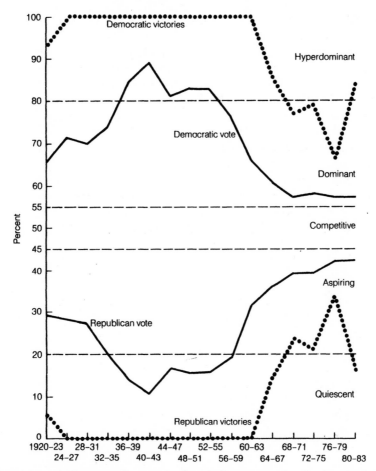

Figure 13.2. Gubernatorial voting in the South: percent of total vote compared with percent of elections won by Democratic and Republican candidates for governor, 1920–1983. Sources: Same as figure 13.1.

toward the Republican party have made a critical break with the South's ancestral party and should be expected to vote dependably for all GOP gubernatorial and senatorial nominees. It is unrealistic, however, to expect the Republicans to win consistent and full-fledged support for their statewide candidates from independents who have no party leanings. Although at least half of this group have voted Republican in every presidential contest since 1964, extensive ticket-splitting is likely among these individuals in state and local elections. Therefore it seems prudent to assume that the GOP can take for granted only half of the pure independents.

Using these criteria to identify hard-core Republican strength, the SRC-CPS party identification data reveal spectacular gains in the expected minimum vote for statewide Republican candidates in the South (see figure 13.3). The bedrock Republican vote has virtually tripled, rising from a mere 16 percent in 1952 to 44 percent in 1984. Indeed, the latter estimate may be slightly low. When the same procedure is applied to the sample of southerners in the *New York Times*/CBS Poll of November 1985, the Republican base is 47 percent, well within the range of genuine competition and only a few percentage points shy of an actual majority.

The utility of this approach becomes evident when estimates of the bedrock Republican vote in statewide elections are compared with the actual percentages of the total vote won by Republican nominees in waves

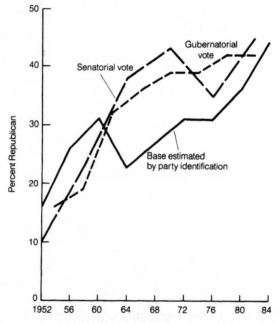

Figure 13.3. The rise of Republican strength in nonpresidential elections: bedrock Republican support compared with Republican shares of the senatorial and gubernatorial votes, 1952–1984. Estimated Republican base vote includes all self-identified Republicans, all independents who lean toward the Republicans, and half of the independents with no partisan inclinations. Sources: SRC-CPS presidential election year surveys for party identification data; appropriate volumes of Scammon, *America Votes,* for Republican popular vote for senators and governors.

of gubernatorial and senatorial elections. As figure 13.3 shows, the regional vote for Republican candidates actually *fell below* their supposed bedrock vote in the 1950s when Republican organizations generally did not field serious, well-financed candidates for these offices. GOP prospects improved in the 1960s, especially in the explosive and turbulent aftermath of the national Democratic party's championship of racial, economic, and social liberalism. The Republican vote for both offices began to *exceed* the minority party's bedrock vote as Republican candidates induced defections among traditionally Democratic voters. A handful of Republicans even won election, but for the most part the Democrats' partisan surplus was still so substantial that party disunity did not necessarily mean defeat for its candidates.

In the 1970s the hard-core Republican vote advanced to almost a third of the electorate and then stalled as the citizenry endured an era of muddled national politics in which neither Republicans nor Democrats governed satisfactorily. Republican successes chiefly occurred when conservative candidates managed to unite the Republican base with sufficient numbers of conservative Democrats, as in the case of the election of North Carolina's Jesse Helms to the Senate in 1972. By and large, however, Republican candidates for governor and senator were still unable to count on enough support from nominal Democrats to be truly competitive.[7]

The bedrock Republican vote rose again in 1980 and expanded even more impressively in 1984. Southern Republicans have the potential to be truly competitive with the Democrats in terms of mass loyalties, and prospective Republican candidates have abundant incentives to compete for the region's highest offices. If the party loyalties of the mid-1980s prove durable, and if the GOP can find enough attractive, experienced, and well-financed candidates, Republican nominees for major statewide offices should make impressive gains during the next wave of elections. Whether 1984 is the precursor of a period of evenly matched competition between the parties, a way station pointing toward eventual Republican hegemony over the most significant offices, or a temporary deviation from the usual Democratic ascendancy obviously depends upon future events. Whatever the future holds, the massive transformation of party loyalties has created the strongest foundation yet seen in the region for satisfying the ambitions of aspiring Republican officeholders.

Eroding Barriers to Senatorial and Gubernatorial Republicanism

Evaluated according to the ultimate concern of most politicians—electability—the Republican party has clearly overcome its historical decrepitude in southern campaigns for senator and governor. Even though changes in party identification currently under way may ultimately work to the Republicans' advantage, it is important to ask why the Democratic party continued to win most governorships and senatorial campaigns in the two decades following federal intervention in southern affairs. In view of the opportunities for Republican competitiveness presented by the region's urbanization, economic development, and expanding middle class, by the sharpening of ideological differences between the parties in national politics, and by federal intervention under Democratic guidance into southern race relations, it is essential to understand why southern Republicans were not *more* successful in elections below the presidency.

Democratic superiority in party identification has been the principal impediment to Republican success in nonpresidential elections. The sheer number of Democrats, along with independents who sympathized with them, in the southern electorate has often made Republican hopes for statewide office unrealistic. In turn, the strong probability of defeat made the tasks of recruiting able candidates and raising money to finance them difficult. Nevertheless, Republican prospects have varied greatly within the region. Analysts have long expected Republicans to perform much better in the Peripheral South than in the Deep South.[8] Because it possesses more traditional Republicans, a larger urbanized white middle class, more migrants from the Northeast and Midwest, and fewer black Democrats, the Peripheral South should contain considerably more potential Republican voters than the Deep South.

Reliable survey data for the southern subregions are normally impossible to obtain, but through the generosity of Gerald C. Wright, Jr., such data for 1976–1982 are at our disposal. Wright and his colleagues have adapted an extensive set of national telephone polls for the purpose of sampling political attitudes in the American states. The data "come from the CBS/*New York Times* Polls, 1976 through 1982. There are 52 polls that we use in all. Each is based on a national sample using random digit dialing. We simply aggregate the results by state for our state measures of partisanship."[9] In turn, we have aggregated results from the appropriate states to produce estimates of Republican strength in the Peripheral South and the Deep South. Respondents identifying themselves as "independents" have been assigned to the expected Republican vote based on the regional distribution of such identifiers in the 1976–1980 SRC-CPS polls.

The CBS/*New York Times* data reveal Republican candidates at a disadvantage in both subregions but with decidedly more favorable prospects in the Peripheral South than in the Deep South (see table 13.1). According to our estimates, the hypothetical bedrock Republican vote in the Peripheral South was 40 percent. When factors specific to particular

Table 13.1. Subregional differences in Republican strength: comparisons of average Republican popular vote in major statewide contests and size of the bedrock GOP base expected from party identification data, 1976–1982[a]

Category	Peripheral South	Deep South
Partisan vote actually won[b]	43	34
Expected Republican base[c]		
All southerners	40	33
White southerners	44	37
Black southerners	16	13

Sources: For CBS/*New York Times* polls, 1976–1982, personal communication from Gerald C. Wright, Jr.; for popular votes, appropriate volumes of *America Votes*.

a. Data are presented as percentages.

b. Mean share of subregional popular vote won in 1976–1982 gubernatorial and senatorial elections.

c. Republican base comprises all self-identified Republicans, all independents leaning toward the Republicans, and half of pure independents. The last two categories have been estimated in the subregions from the regional distribution of such identifiers in the 1976–1980 SRC-CPS polls.

elections have assisted the Republicans, their Peripheral South nominees have been well positioned to win major statewide offices. Since the Great Society, Peripheral South Republicans have frequently converted their impressive grassroots base into actual officeholding, winning 43 percent of the Senate contests and 35 percent of the gubernatorial races. Republican candidates in the Deep South, however, have lacked the mass support they needed to become consistently competitive with Democratic nominees. The Deep South's hard-core Republican vote was no more than a third of the electorate. With Democratic candidates for governor and senator expected to poll landslide majorities, Deep South Republicans could win only when the Democrats failed to unite behind a nominee. In view of the underlying division of partisan attitudes, it is not surprising that Republicans in the Deep South managed to win only 22 percent of the 1965–1984 Senate campaigns and a mere 8 percent of the governorships.

An additional obstacle to Republican advances in nonpresidential elections has been the insulation of many offices from the direct impact of presidential campaigns. Since conservative trends in national politics are among the most powerful stimulants of southern Republicanism, GOP victories below the presidency should decline as offices become removed in time from the immediate effects of presidential politics. In this respect southern gubernatorial elections are far more "protected" from the conservative contagion of national politics than are contests for the Senate.

Because of the six-year senatorial term, every other senatorial election coincides with a presidential campaign. But only North Carolina still selects its governor exclusively in presidential years, and the scheduling of southern governorships in nonpresidential years effectively protects most Democratic nominees from the "contamination" produced by popular Republican presidential nominees, unpopular Democratic presidential candidates, or both. Furthermore, whereas gubernatorial campaigns cover a fairly small range of issues and hence expose a more limited number of potential Democratic liabilities to Republican attack, senatorial elections are based upon the entire domestic and foreign policy agenda and thus invite conservative Republican attacks on a broad array of controversial topics. In general it has been much easier for Republican candidates to force Democrats into a defensive crouch in senatorial than in gubernatorial contests. Other factors being equal, southern Republicans should win higher percentages of Senate seats than of governorships.

Other factors are frequently *unequal,* however, and GOP success in both offices should also be affected by the presence or absence of an incumbent officeholder.[10] Unseating a Democratic incumbent is obviously the most difficult task for a Republican nominee, for only under abnormal circumstances should sitting Democratic senators or governors be vulnerable to defeat. Open-seat elections, those in which no incumbent is involved, offer much better odds for Republican success. For Republican officeholders the value of incumbency is more problematic. Although Republican senators should certainly benefit from the traditional advantages of incumbency, the South's Republican governors are in a much more exposed and frustrating position, since they must attempt to govern in concert with Democratic legislatures. By calculating rates of Republican victories according to office and type of election, it is possible to clarify the electoral context of modern southern Republicanism.

The anticipated difference in Republican victories between senatorial and gubernatorial campaigns is reflected in table 13.2, with Republicans capturing a third of the senate races versus a fourth of the governorships held between 1965 and 1985. Democratic incumbency frustrated Republican hopes in both senatorial and gubernatorial races. Only four Democratic senators and one Democratic governor have been upset by Republicans. Better Republican performances in Senate than in gubernatorial contests appeared in open-seat elections. Republicans won almost two-fifths of the open-seat Senate races, as compared with three-tenths of the open-seat governorships. The starkest contrast in successful Republicanism concerns the Republican incumbents. All but one of the South's incumbent Republican senators have won reelection, while only two of the seven Republican governors have retained their office. Re-

Table 13.2.   Southern Republicanism in context: percentage of Republican victories by office and type of election, 1965–1985

Type of election	Senators		Governors	
Democratic incumbent	10	(51)[a]	6	(25)
Open-seat	38	(31)	30	(64)
Republican incumbent	93	(18)	29	(11)
Totals	34	(100%)	24	(100%)

Sources: Congressional Quarterly's Guide to U.S. Elections (Washington, D.C.: Congressional Quarterly, 1975); and appropriate volumes of *America Votes.*
   a. Figures in parentheses report the percentage distribution of all elections.

publican governors have inevitably confronted Democratic legislatures, a situation that often vitiates successful leadership. It is much easier for Republican senators than for governors to establish reputations as effective officeholders.

Since higher rates of Republican senatorial victories prevailed in each type of election, why haven't more Republican senators been elected? The figures in parentheses in table 13.2 provide the central explanation: Democratic incumbency constrained Republican senatorial gains between 1966 and 1984. Half of all the Senate campaigns involved incumbent Democrats, very few of whom could be believably attacked as liberals. Among southern governorships the predominant type of campaign was the open-seat election (64 percent). The irony of nonpresidential southern Republicanism has been that the setting most conducive to Republican gains has appeared more often in the office that is comparatively isolated from national political influences, while the office that is more susceptible to pro-Republican national influences has frequently been immunized through Democratic incumbency.

The perils of open-seat gubernatorial elections did not escape the attention of southern Democrats, who responded by importing into the governorship the political advantages long obvious from senatorial incumbency. Since the possibility of continuous reelection to the Senate gave Democratic senators an enormous advantage over Republican competitors, why not retard and obstruct gubernatorial Republicanism by changing the rules to the Democrats' advantage? Between 1966 and 1984 nine southern states revised their constitutions to permit governors to serve a second consecutive four-year term. Though there are many "good government" reasons to allow for the possibility of succession, this change has had obvious consequences for partisan politics. By reducing the frequency of open-seat governorships, where Democrats are more vulnerable, and increasing the number of elections involving Democratic incumbents, its practical effect has been to discourage aggressive, well-financed Republican opposition whenever a Democratic governor seeks reelection. The competitiveness of the South's traditional minority party is certainly not advanced, in terms of building mass loyalty or sustaining elite interest, when open-seat governorships occur no more frequently than once every eight years.

Consistent with expectations, subregional differences in mass partisanship further qualify the proportions of Republican victories for Senate and governor in different types of electoral settings. As is evident in table 13.3, Republican success rates diminish steadily from Peripheral South senatorial campaigns to Deep South governorships for all elections, for contests involving Democratic incumbents, and (apart from Peripheral South governorships) for open-seat elections. Only among Republican incumbents is the anticipated subregional pattern disrupted, due to the vulnerabilities of incumbency for Peripheral South Republican governors and to the perfect reelection record established by the Deep South's incumbent Republican senators.

Democratic and Republican Campaign Strategies

To conclude this discussion of nonpresidential politics we shall examine the different campaign strategies of Democrats and Republicans. By the early 1970s virtually all serious Democratic senatorial and gubernatorial candidates understood that black participation was an irreversible reality of southern electoral politics and that Democratic nominees needed solid black support to win general elections. Whether or not a particular Democratic politician was strongly preferred by blacks in the Democratic primaries, a "new South" style of campaigning, one in which nominees deliberately refrained from antiblack rhetoric, became standard across

Table 13.3. Southern Republicanism in subregional context: percentage of Republican victories by office and type of election, 1965–1985, by subregion

Type of election	Peripheral South		Deep South	
	Senators	Governors	Senators	Governors
Democratic incumbent	20	10	4	0
Open-seat	44	45	25	11
Republican incumbent	89	33	100	0
Totals	45	34	22	8

Sources: Same as table 13.2.

the region. Even George Wallace, the most obvious exception to this characterization of Democratic office seekers, came to rely heavily upon black support in his successful 1982 campaign. As long as an overwhelming proportion of black voters (nine-tenths or better) supports Democratic candidates in southern general elections, the size of the black electorate means that Democratic victories require no more than roughly 40 percent of the white vote in the Deep South and 45 percent of the white vote in the Peripheral South, rates of white support than can ordinarily be exceeded by Democratic incumbents and frequently obtained by Democratic candidates (especially in the Deep South) in open-seat elections.

At the same time that Democratic nominees for statewide office have vigorously solicited black support, they have purposely distanced themselves from such liberal national Democrats as Hubert Humphrey, George McGovern, Walter Mondale, and Edward Kennedy. Most victorious southern Democrats have waged campaigns that skillfully intertwine conservative postures (budgetary restraint, opposition to increased taxation, enthusiasm for school prayer and the death penalty) with progressive themes (support for equal opportunities, educational advancement, environmental protection). If it has often been difficult to decide whether specific Democrats could be more accurately described as progressive conservatives or conservative progressives, the common denominator of the new South generation of Democratic nominees has been their refusal to present themselves unambiguously as either national liberal Democrats or unreconstructed southern Democrats.

The southern Democratic imperative (the propensity of Democratic campaigners to modify any strong impulse toward a consistently conservative or consistently progressive image) has reflected in the most fundamental and compelling way the political constraints inherent in any effort to unite at the polls mainly working-class blacks and blue-collar to middle-class whites—the indispensable components of Democratic majorities in the South. By deliberately blurring distinctions between conservatism and progressivism Democratic politicians have been able to appeal on different grounds to black (and liberal white) Democrats and to moderate and conservative white Democrats. When executed with imagination and finesse, the Democratic strategy has frequently resulted in victory because Democratic nominees have offered something of value to substantial majorities of the potential electorate.

Whether the Democratic strategy endures obviously hinges upon whether or not Democrats remain a majority of the electorate. This situation appears to be a realistic assumption for some Deep South states; indeed, majorities of the Deep South's whites *and* blacks still consider themselves

Democrats or lean in that direction. Given these favorable conditions, the main task of Democratic candidates is simply to unify the party for the general elections. In the most recent set of senatorial and gubernatorial elections in the Deep South, 1978–1984, Democrats won 73 percent of the open seats. Republicans prevailed only when the candidacies of their Democratic rivals were compromised by irreconcilable divisions within their own party.[11] If Deep South Democrats can unite—a problematic assumption—they will still have the votes to prevail in most open-seat contests in the foreseeable future.

In the Peripheral South a different pattern of party loyalties prevails. Whites in this subregion no longer prefer Democrats to Republicans, and Republicans may even have opened a clear lead over Democrats among the white majority. Because Democrats are a subregional minority, party unity is necessary but far from sufficient to secure Democratic victories in major statewide elections. A campaign strategy that does no more than unite the party faithful while more or less ignoring other voters will not often succeed with an electorate in which non-Democrats constitute the majority. Democratic candidates for senator and governor in the Peripheral South won only half of the open-seat campaigns between 1978 and 1985, capturing four of six governorships but merely two of six senatorial elections. Though severe intraparty conflicts usually contributed to the Democrats' losses, the problem for Peripheral South Democrats is more fundamental than preventing party disunity. If they are to remain competitive, Democratic candidates and strategists in the Peripheral South will have to look beyond the party and pay more attention to the wishes and preferences of some of the non-Democrats.

Unlike the Democratic strategy, the Republican approach to southern governorships and senatorships has often lacked the indispensable advantage of being directed toward broad majorities of voters. As Strong itemized Republican weaknesses in the early 1970s, "Southern Republicans have a rigid ideology: clean government, sympathy for big business, low taxes, a minimum of concern for poor people, and a genteel type of racism. Moreover, they take their ideology seriously. This seriousness prevents them from being flexible enough to broaden their basis of support."[12]

Though few Republican nominees in recent times have run overtly antiblack campaigns and though some Republicans may strive diligently to win black support, the opposition of such prominent national Republicans as Barry Goldwater, Richard Nixon, and Ronald Reagan to the racial and economic policies favored by most blacks has prevented Republican candidates for statewide offices from establishing credibility with most black voters. The net result is that Republican candidates—some eagerly, some reluctantly—concede the vast majority of black voters to the Democrats. Having thus written off about one-fifth of the entire Deep South electorate and slightly more than a tenth of the total vote in the Peripheral South, Republican politicians must compensate by winning substantial white majorities—on the order of 60 percent in the Deep South and 55 percent in the Peripheral South—if they are to defeat the Democrats.

Such white majorities have easily been achieved by Republican presidential candidates, present less of an obstacle to Peripheral South than to Deep South Republicans, and are certainly attainable by incumbent Republican senators thoughout the region. It is a different matter, however, to win consistently the votes of three-fifths of the Deep South whites or five-ninths of the Peripheral South whites against incumbent Democrats or in open-seat contests. Precisely because most Democratic candidates have spent years avoiding any political stances that would invite Republicans to attack them convincingly as national liberal Democrats, many Republican candidates for senator or governor have been severely damaged by their inability or unwillingness to attract significant black support.

In recent years, though, Republican parties in many southern states have been rejuvenated by a new generation of candidates and strategists. These party activists (of whom South Carolina's Lee Atwater is the best example) have refocused the Republican party's goals to the task of winning statewide elections, and they have brought to their work energy, imagination, and skill. Recognizing that the Republicans constituted only a minority of the electorate, they were nonetheless convinced that their party had a message that could appeal to hundreds of thousands of conservative and moderate-to-conservative whites who did not ordinarily think of themselves as Republican. With ample financing, ideal candidates, and campaign strategies designed to attract disaffected Democrats and independents, Republican strategists believed that the natural appeal of conservatism among white southerners could be redirected toward GOP nominees. Republican candidates could thus win statewide elections without a majority of the voters thinking of themselves as "Republicans." There are various ways to describe what happened; in practical terms it has usually amounted to combining the Nixon voters and the Wallace voters, the educated conservatives and the uneducated conservatives, the uptown church members and the fundamentalists, the middle-class conservatives and the working-class conservatives.[13] In the process non-Republicans have been given ample reasons to abandon the Democrats in specific elections and "go Republican." Republican strategists have seen the opportunities for electoral change and have increasingly constructed majority voting coalitions.

These Republican advances have been most prominent in the Peripheral South. Even before President Reagan's first term, whites in this subregion were splitting almost evenly between Democratic and Republican predispositions. Republican candidates needed only marginal increases in their share of the white vote to win statewide elections, and in many instances they matched or exceeded the target of 55 percent of the white vote needed for victory. We suspect that among whites in the Peripheral South the Republicans hold an edge over the Democrats. It is no longer difficult to elect Republican senators and governors in open-seat situations, and incumbent Republican senators easily win reelection. If Republican strategists can learn how to reelect Republican *governors* in the Peripheral South (essentially by blaming Democratic legislatures rather than the Republican governors for deadlock, indecision, or the failure to enact popular measures), the Republican party will be in an excellent position to expand its presence at lower levels of state and local offices.

According to Phillips, "The gathering Republicanism of the Outer South virtually dictates the coming alignment of the Deep South."[14] This may well come to pass, but the general Republican strategy in nonpresidential elections will be harder to execute in the Deep South than in the Peripheral South. In the Deep South the gap is still too wide between the share of the white vote that Republicans can reasonably expect to poll and the proportion they need for statewide victories. GOP presidential candidates can more than close the gap, but Deep South Democrats— Joe Frank Harris, Dick Riley, George Wallace, Sam Nunn, and others— cannot be credibly attacked as liberal Democrats. As a consequence, many Republican candidates have foundered on their party's negative image among blacks. Republican campaigners in the Deep South must accordingly depend more on Democratic mistakes, miscalculations, malfeasance, and factionalism than on anything they can do for themselves. When Republicans do win, it is through their ability to split the tickets of independents and Democrats.

Part of the explanation for recent Republican successes in southern nonpresidential elections is that the party's strategists and campaigners have clearly understood their minority standing and have been compelled to discover how to appeal to voters who do not share the Republican faith in all respects.[15] There may be a lesson here for southern Democrats, especially in the Peripheral South, who must face their own minority status. Peripheral South Democrats need to learn to think like Republicans, not by shifting to the right and imitating Republican policies, but by acknowledging the reality of their actual or impending minority position and revising their campaign strategies to match new circumstances. Democratic candidates and strategists will have to confront the twin problems of all minority parties that wish to win elections: the need to unify the party stalwarts and the need to broaden the party's appeal among voters not formally disposed to vote for its nominees. Peripheral South Democrats will increasingly have to devise ways to attract the growing number of middle-class southerners, the independents, and perhaps even some Republicans. Thinking beyond the wishes and interests of Democratic partisans amounts to a radically different way of perceiving political reality for southern Democrats. At issue for Peripheral South Democrats is their party's survival as a competitive institution. And if Peripheral South developments anticipate future Deep South patterns, Deep South Democrats may soon need to learn how to interest voters who are not party loyalists.

The traditional Democratic domination of statewide elections in the South has vanished. Although GOP gains in senatorial and gubernatorial contests have not yet matched the degree of success that Republican presidential candidates have enjoyed, genuine party competition for the most visible and powerful statewide offices has become commonplace. Republicans have made giant strides in races for the U.S. Senate, and, once elected, almost all Republican senators have managed to stay in office. Governorships have been harder for the Republicans to win, and most Republican incumbents have been unable to win reelection. If Republican strategists can solve the problem of reelecting their governors, the party will be in much stronger position to wrest additional gains in state and local contests.

In the altered electoral environment of the contemporary South the outcomes of senatorial and gubernatorial races will depend upon many short-term forces—the presence or absence of an incumbent, the perceived leadership and personal qualities of the candidates, the effectiveness of rival mass-media strategies, the salient issues of the day, the presence or absence of powerful national forces, advantages in financial resources, the quality of the competing grassroots organizations. In the Peripheral South, where Republican strength is more advanced, the cumulative impact of short-term factors will be especially important. In the Deep South, the Democratic edge in party identification remains a factor, and there most serious Republican candidates still need both Democratic disarray and their own short-term advantages in order to secure victories.

fourteen

The Reshaping
of Southern
Politics

IMMENSE socioeconomic, demographic, and political forces have reshaped the South in the twentieth century, sometimes shattering, sometimes simply modifying traditional institutions, practices, and beliefs. We shall conclude this book by developing several themes that link the past with the future of southern politics: the strikingly different but still tangential position of blacks; the increasing prominence of middle-class southerners embracing entrepreneurial individualism as their political creed; the diminished presence of black belt whites in leadership roles; the rise of urban leaders; changing elite perspectives on race and economic development; the gradual modification of one-party Democratic rule; and, in a growing number of states, the establishment of sustained two-party competition for major offices.

The Politics of Race

Key concluded *Southern Politics* by urging the necessity of resolving the South's racial dilemma. "The way is hard and progress is slow," he conceded. "Yet until greater emancipation of the white from the Negro is achieved, the southern political and economic system will labor under formidable handicaps."[1] Prospects for immediate reform were so bleak and unpromising that Key could imagine such an "emancipation" occurring only after secular socioeconomic forces (withdrawal from the region by dissatisfied black southerners, as well as huge increases in urbanization and industrialization) had fashioned a more permissive environment, one in which "progressive" white southerners could slowly assimilate "qualified" blacks into active political involvement.

Although these trends certainly contributed to the eventual dissolution of the Jim Crow South, Key's scenario for racial change profoundly underestimated political developments. Key failed to anticipate the civil rights movement, the "revolt from below" by black southerners, and he largely discounted the possibility of effective national intervention to reform southern race relations. Much of the fierce racial conflict that suffused southern politics from the *Brown* decision and the Montgomery bus boycott through the heyday of George Wallace and the black power movement—conflict that in the broadest sense represented an historical reckoning with the traditional caste system—was initiated by small numbers of black southerners determined to protest the injustices and irrationalities of southern racism. Southern race relations now lies somewhere between old-fashioned strict segregation, on the one hand, and complete racial integration, on the other. The entrenched and pervasive racism that victimized practically all black southerners through the early 1960s has been ameliorated, and many white southerners have been released from the obligation to practice white supremacy. No longer does the white South differ radically from the rest of the nation in its treatment of black people.[2]

Visible changes have occurred concerning the outer color line. Abolishing racial segregation in public accommodations removed a tremendous source of interracial friction and tension, and the return of black southerners to the polls almost completely ended overt racism in political campaigns. From a vantage point two decades removed from the climactic period of federal intervention, the southern political system is considerably more democratic, considerably more open to minority involvement and participation, than it was during the first six decades of this century.

Yet even these obvious improvements warrant qualification and perspective. In terms of the leverage that they can realistically expect to exert in southern politics, blacks have made substantial gains but still face enduring limitations (see table 14.1). If systematic black disfranchisement magnified the numerical advantage of the South's large white majority in the past, to what extent have white advantages diminished in recent decades? Ratios of white voter registration rates to black voter registration rates indicate how evenly or unevenly the races are mobilized, and the results show that traditional white advantages in relative mobilization diminished considerably—due to federal intervention and extensive organization within black communities—between 1960 and 1970 and hovered around unity in 1980. Thus the long-standing white superiority in rates of voter registration, an area where rapid change *was* possible, has essentially vanished.

The more fundamental and permanent white advantage, however, flows from the vastly different sizes of the white and black populations. Because

Table 14.1.   Race and voter registration: diminishing white advantage in voter registration rates versus continuing white advantage in number of registered voters, by state, subregion, and region, 1960–1980

	White advantage in					
	Rate of voter registration[b]			Number of registered voters[c]		
Political unit[a]	1960	1970	1980	1960	1970	1980
Texas	1.2	0.9	1.1	9.2	6.5	9.9
Arkansas	1.6	0.9	1.1	7.1	4.8	6.9
Florida	1.8	1.2	1.1	9.9	8.3	6.3
Virginia	2.0	1.1	1.3	8.7	5.6	6.1
Tennessee	1.2	1.1	1.0	7.0	6.6	5.5
Georgia	1.9	1.3	1.1	5.7	4.1	4.7
North Carolina	2.4	1.3	1.3	8.9	5.4	4.5
Alabama	4.5	1.3	1.2	13.0	4.2	3.3
Louisiana	2.5	1.3	1.1	6.2	3.6	3.0
Mississippi	12.3	1.2	1.2	21.7	2.4	2.8
South Carolina	4.2	1.1	0.9	8.3	3.0	2.3
Deep South	3.2	1.2	1.1	7.9	3.5	3.2
Peripheral South	1.6	1.1	1.1	8.6	6.3	6.7
South	2.1	1.1	1.1	8.4	5.1	5.1

Sources: Calculated from U.S. Bureau of the Census, *Statistical Abstract of the United States: 1982–83* (Washington, D.C.: Government Printing Office, 1982), p. 488; *Voting and Registration in the Election of November 1980,* Current Population Reports, series P-20, no. 370 (Washington, D.C.: Government Printing Office, 1982), pp. 31–32.

a. States are ranked (highest to lowest) according to the white advantage in the number of registered voters for 1980.

b. Ratio of white voter registration rate to black voter registration rate.

c. Ratio of number of white registered voters to number of black registered voters.

blacks are nowhere near a majority of any state's population, whites invariably cast most of the votes in general elections. Although ratios of white registered voters to black registered voters have declined, once blacks became effectively mobilized these ratios have been inherently much more resistant to rapid change. When white registrants outnumber black registrants by two to one or three to one in the Deep South states with the largest black populations (South Carolina, Mississippi, Louisiana, and Alabama) and hold an advantage of more than six to one in the Peripheral South states with the smallest black populations (Texas, Arkansas, Florida, and Virginia), the population-based limitations on black political leverage are manifest. Minority status ineluctably constrains and limits black political influence in the modern South.

Much more mixed results have followed the assault on the intermediate color line. The enormous historical disparities between the races in jobs, schooling, and housing could hardly be overcome in less than a generation. It is not surprising, therefore, that in the 1980s, despite progress, whites are more educated, are more likely to work in middle-class employment, and earn substantially higher incomes than blacks as a group. Only recently have southern schools even attempted to provide equal educational opportunities for blacks. Future generations of black southerners will be better educated than their predecessors, and gains in formal education will be translated into an expanded black middle class.

Nearly one-quarter of southern black families already have incomes higher than the median southern white family. At the same time, a large fraction of black families possess incomes that are above poverty but well below affluence, and a considerable minority remain trapped in poverty. Until very recently impoverishment was the central tendency of the black experience in the South, and nearly one-third of the South's black families, versus only one-fourteenth of its white families, continued to experience poverty in the late 1970s.[3] Egregious differences in rates of poverty not only illustrate a broad range of racially based socioeconomic disparities but powerfully reinforce political cleavages—cleavages appearing more distinctly in national than in state elections—between most blacks and most whites.

Because poverty and marginal economic status affect the two racial groups so differently, the economic priorities of most southern whites and most southern blacks commonly diverge rather than converge. Most whites believe in the primacy of individual rather than governmental responsibility for family economic well-being; nearly half of southern blacks, according to the opinion surveys, place central reliance upon government rather than upon themselves for good jobs and wages. Politicians who advocate massive governmental assistance programs for the impoverished are viewed as radical by most southern whites, who perceive themselves as being overtaxed to pay for programs they detest on behalf of recipients whom they do not esteem. Furthermore, blacks and whites usually differ strongly on most current civil rights controversies, especially on matters involving affirmative action to compensate for past discrimination.

When persistent interracial differences on these types of issues are combined with the whites' vastly superior political leverage, the inescapable conclusion for southern politics is that, even under the most favorable circumstances imaginable, black political influence will operate at the margins rather than the center of decisionmaking. Only when whites sharply divide will blacks be positioned to affect electoral outcomes, and then the result will be more to assist the winning white group than to secure immediate, substantial benefits for blacks. Joel Williamson aptly summarizes the fundamental racial situation in this way:

> After their momentary fright in the 1950s and 1960s, the Conservative elite in the South has come to realize that the civil-rights movement has resulted in no great revolution in race relations . . . Things are better, and blacks are more free in this last quarter of the twentieth century; but while the white elite might not have everything just the way they want it all the time in relations with black people, they generally have them so. On the other hand, over time they virtually always get exactly what they want from the mass of white people. The self-conscious all-white communion is still in place in the South, and, sadly, it is spreading to cover the nation.[4]

Whites totally monopolized the electorate of the old southern politics, and they remain predominant in the electorate underlying the new southern politics. This is especially true in the Peripheral South, where whites contributed 85 percent of the registered voters in 1984, and it is still the case in the Deep South, where the majority group formed 76 percent of the electorate. On matters involving the races, outcomes in modern southern politics depend more upon the whites' continuing numerical supremacy in the electorate than upon the significant increases that blacks have achieved in their proportion of the total electorate.

White priorities and preferences still fundamentally define southern political agendas, and blacks are usually placed in the position of reacting to the prevailing white views. To understand why biracial politics directed toward liberal goals faces long odds, why most Democratic officeholders blend conservative and progressive themes, and why conservative Republicanism is on the rise, it is crucial to focus on the values, beliefs, and predilections of the white majority, and particularly on the urban middle-class sector of white opinion.

The Political Leverage of the Growing Middle Class

Since World War II the southern social order has been remarkably transformed. Like Americans generally, practically all employed southerners inhabit the new middle class or the working class, and, even more important, by 1980 the South's new middle class outnumbered its working class. The contrast between 1940, when less than a quarter of southern jobholders performed white-collar duties, and 1980, when a majority of them did so, points to the establishment of a far more complex and diversified socioeconomic setting than ever before. It also signifies the replacement of the agrarian middle class's traditionalists by the entrepreneurial individualists of the new middle class as the central source of regional leadership. Significant features of the old South persist, of course, as illustrated by the heavy concentration of blacks (especially men) in the working class and the prominence of whites (particularly women) in the new middle class.

The reigning political philosophy of the new southern middle class is the entrepreneurial version of the individualistic political culture, a blend of conservative and progressive themes. In its emphasis on low rates of taxation, minimal regulation of business, and resolute opposition to unions and redistributive welfare programs for have-nots and have-littles, the current political ideology retains important continuities with the traditionalistic political culture. Its progressive element consists in its willingness to use governmental resources to construct the public infrastructure—highways, airports, harbors, colleges and universities, research parks, health complexes—that in turn stimulates and makes possible additional economic growth. The critical transition occurred in the aftermath of federal intervention, as southern states began to spend much larger amounts of money on public education. In due course the social payoff will be a significant reduction in the waste of human talent that had been one of the worst outcomes of traditional southern politics.

For a region accustomed to economic stagnation, the prospect of actually making and keeping big money is an incredibly powerful stimulant. Visions of material abundance obviously excite those with realistic prospects of achieving wealth, and a growing economy at least offers steady employment for the vast majority of southerners who will never attain affluence. Furthermore, because southern state governments collect lower taxes, wealthy southerners can keep more of their earnings than is possible elsewhere, and those with smaller incomes pay less tax than their nonsouthern counterparts. The southern business creed, which has reminded more than one observer of a new "McKinley era,"[5] exerts a compelling popular appeal extending far beyond its direct and most obvious beneficiaries.

In the evolving struggle for power and advantage in southern politics, the new middle class enjoys impressive advantages. It is the most conspicuously successful segment of the society, and its numbers expand yearly. Through personal ownership or institutional control, its members command far more financial resources than any other part of the society, and the new middle class furnishes almost all of the region's managerial and entrepreneurial leadership. Yet the political domination of the middle class occurs also because many of its core values and beliefs are widely shared elsewhere in the society. Though most southerners are not militant conservatives, conservatism's attraction far outstrips liberalism's appeal among the region's working class as well as its middle class. The South has many uncritical loyalists but few loyal critics, and southern politics generally involves narrow ranges of public controversies. Whatever their educational achievement or social position, most white southerners appear satisfied with the region's quality of life and hostile to movements advocating or implying radical political changes.

Not the least of the middle class's assets is the common ground it shares with the white working class and (to a lesser extent) with blacks in terms of emotional predispositions to particular political symbols. When the reactions of middle-class whites, working-class whites, and blacks to relevant political terms are divided into three categories—symbols toward which a majority of a given group felt "warm," those toward which a majority of a particular group felt "cold," and those toward which no majority sentiment existed—the results help explain the persistent absence of effective have-not coalitions and the enduring success of middle-class whites.

Successful campaigns against the haves (the upper-middle class) presuppose this group's isolation, an isolation not at all supported by the facts (see table 14.2). To the contrary, the evidence of political symbols suggests numerous ties binding the white middle class and white working class (for example, warmth toward conservatives and Republicans and coldness toward radical students and black militants), as well as important opinions shared by both of the white classes and the blacks, including attitudes toward southerners, police, whites, military, Democrats, blacks, marijuana users, and gays/lesbians.

In contrast, black southerners were completely distinct, completely separated from white workers and the white middle class. Nothing unites blacks and working-class whites that is not equally approved and disapproved by the white middle class. Many realities—white middle-class invulnerability compared with multiple black vulnerabilities, the absence of symbols uniquely joining blacks to working-class whites versus the many commonalities uniting the white middle and working classes, and the conservative nature of the views shared by all three groups—contribute significantly to the thoroughly middle-class orientation of electoral politics in the region.

Beyond Black Belt Control

The predominance of the middle class also influences the types of politicians who can prevail in statewide races and the policies they pursue

Table 14.2.   Class, race, and political symbols: the white middle-class advantage in southern politics, 1972–1984[a]

Central tendencies shared by	Group reactions to particular symbols		
	Majority feels "warm"	No majority tendency	Majority feels "cold"
Middle-class whites, working-class whites, and blacks	Police, whites, southerners, military, Democrats, blacks	—	Marijuana users, gays and lesbians
Middle-class whites and working-class whites only	Conservatives, Republicans	Big business, women's liberation, unions, people on welfare, liberals, evangelicals, civil rights leaders	Radical students, black militants
Middle-class whites and blacks only	—	—	—
Working-class whites and blacks only	—	—	—
Middle-class whites only	—	—	—
Working-class whites only	—	—	—
Blacks only	Civil rights leaders, people on welfare, unions, liberals, women's liberation, evangelicals, big business	Conservatives, Republicans, black militants, radical students	

Sources: 1972–1984 SRC-CPS presidential election year surveys.
a. Classifications are based on the mean thermometer ratings presented in figures 3.3 and 3.4.

once elected. One of the most crucial differences between the old and new southern politics is the collapse of the black belt as a central source of leadership in state and national politics. In every southern state long-term population shifts have reduced substantially the proportion of whites residing in high-black rural counties. This secular change has loosened the grip of tradition upon southern politics, for it has undermined the prospects of most politicians currently residing in black belt areas to create followings capable of winning either U.S. Senate seats or governorships.

Over the decades precipitous losses have occurred in the de facto representation of the black belt in the U.S. Senate.[6] In the 1920s nearly three-fourths of all southern senators had been born in a high-black rural county, and two-fifths of them still resided there when elected (or reelected) to the Senate. Even if most senators no longer lived in the black belt, all could be depended upon to support the racial policies espoused by their colleagues from the most conservative part of the region. When the civil rights movement commenced its offensive against southern racism in the 1960s, almost 90 percent of the region's population resided outside the high-black rural counties, and only three of the South's twenty-two senators still lived in a high-black rural county. Though nearly all southern senators voted against the major civil rights legislation, the hard-core southerners were so isolated from the rest of the Senate that they were unable to sustain filibusters against the Civil Rights Act and Voting Rights Act.

The decline and fall of black belt influence has meant the end of the most transparent forms of southern racism in the U.S. Senate. Because most southern senators take conservative positions on many controversies of the intermediate color line, however, the demise of the black belt has by no means resulted in the triumph of racial liberalism within the delegation. To the contrary, a few southerners still vote as though they were living in the 1920s and a smaller number sometimes talk that way for the record. On the whole, though, the region's senatorial delegation has been emancipated from its former unquestioning subservience to the racial views of the black belt whites.

Diminishing black belt control over southern governorships also represents a major change in *state* racial policies. Unlike the situation around the turn of the century, in most states unregenerate black belt conservatives failed to dominate the governorship during the racial crises of the 1950s and 1960s. After the *Brown* decision black belt whites again succeeded for a time in rallying non–black belt whites to the common cause of massive resistance. Nonetheless, despite the fact that most white southerners vastly preferred segregation to integration, they did not usually elect totally unreconstructed black belt politicians to implement segregationist policies. No more than nine of the fifty-four governors elected (or reelected) between 1950 and 1965 had been born and were still living in high-black rural counties when chosen governor.

Moreover, even before federal intervention, black belt whites were losing their ability to persuade white politicians from other parts of the region to maintain without deviation the black belt line on race relations (see table 14.3). On the crucial issue of racial segregation, politicians can be classified as strong or militant segregationists, moderate segregation-

Table 14.3. Beyond the conservative black belt position on race: campaign stances on racial segregation of successful candidates for governor, before federal intervention (1950–1965) and after (1966–1980), by place of socialization and current residence

Relationship to high-black rural sector[a]	Campaign racial stance prior to federal intervention					Campaign racial stance after federal intervention				
	SS[b]	MS[b]	NS[b]	N[b]	All[c]	SS	MS	NS	N	All
Born and still living in the high-black rural sector	67	22	11	(9)	17	14	0	86	(7)	15
Born in the high-black rural sector but living elsewhere	45	50	5	(20)	38	13	7	80	(15)	33
Neither born nor currently living in the high-black rural sector	33	54	13	(24)	45	4	8	88	(24)	52
All governors[d]	43	47	9		100	9	7	85		100
Number of cases	(23)	(25)	(5)	(53)		(4)	(3)	(39)	(46)	

Sources: Demographic classifications are based upon information presented in Samuel R. Solomon, *The Governors of the American States, Commonwealths, and Territories, 1900–1980* (Lexington, Ky.: Council of State Governments, 1980). For racial classifications based on 1950–1973 campaigns, see Earl Black, *Southern Governors and Civil Rights* (Cambridge, Mass.: Harvard University Press, 1976), pp. 347–352. Classifications of 1974–1980 campaigns were made by the authors following procedures discussed in *Southern Governors*, pp. 11–22.

a. Because of the paucity of cases, the category "born outside the high-black rural sector but currently residing in it" has been omitted. No governors met these criteria for the 1966–1980 elections, and only one satisfied them for the 1950–1965 elections.

b. SS, strong segregationist; MS, moderate segregationist; NS, nonsegregationist; N, number of cases. See text for definition of terms. Data, except for N, are presented as percentages.

c. Percentage of all governors with specified relationship to the high-black rural sector.

d. Percentage of all governors classified as strong segregationists, moderate segregationists, or nonsegregationists.

ists, and nonsegregationists.[7] Segregationists, whether militants or moderates, all accepted the principle of racial segregation. But whereas strong segregationists emphatically and enthusiastically defended the South's racial traditions, moderate segregationists were less preoccupied with race, less zealous in their commitment to preserve racial segregation. Nonsegregationists, who ranged from racially liberal politicians to candidates who simply chose not to use the language of segregation, did not publicly campaign as segregationists.

Militant support for segregation, the stance typical of black belt governors, was *not* the central tendency among governors who resided outside the high-black rural section. Unqualified support for segregation was advocated by only 45 percent of the successful candidates who were born in the black belt but resided elsewhere at the time of their election, and by merely one-third of the governors who had no ties to the most conservative part of the region.

Black protest and federal intervention, not any gradual tendency toward racial liberalism among southern politicians themselves, liberated white politicians from the explicit defense of Jim Crow. Following federal intervention, most successful southern politicians finally abandoned segregationist postures.[8] Politicians with interests and constituencies outside the high-black rural counties began to run as nonsegregationists, and, after a flurry of last-ditch resistance, even candidates with ties to the black belt jettisoned segregation. No better symbol of the change exists than George Wallace, who did so much to obstruct the civil rights movement (in his come-from-behind victory in 1970, Wallace galvanized white voters by warning, "If I don't win, them niggers are going to control this state"), but who began to solicit black votes in 1974 in order to fashion "a new image to improve his national standing."[9] When Wallace returned to campaigning in 1982 after four years of retirement, he apologized to black Alabamians for his past behavior and asked for their support in another successful gubernatorial campaign. As a result of federal intervention, state racial policies were no longer held hostage to the obsessive concerns of conservative black belt whites. Led by the Peripheral South, the southern states could begin the long and difficult process of adjusting to desegregation.

The traditionalistic state policies fashioned and maintained by the black belt elite included not only the preservation of white supremacy in all forms and the constriction of state electorates to safe and sound voters, but also antipathy to taxation, very limited notions of state responsibility for public services, the primacy of local elite control over economic development at the expense of more rapid growth, and firm reliance upon the Democratic party as the only legitimate instrument for the control of state government. In light of the black belt elite's historical success in shaping public policy, the waning of black belt governors has been of no small consequence in shifting the region away from policies and practices that failed to nurture and encourage the talents and skills of colossal numbers of its citizens.[10]

The Rise of Urban Leaders

Attention to the fate of political leaders from the high-black rural counties charts the decline of pristine rural conservatism but does not identify the emerging demographic sources of state leadership. The broader transformation of southern politics involves a shift from an almost completely rural politics in the 1920s to a mixed urban and rural politics in the

1970s and 1980s. Most southern governors in the 1920s were unmistakable products of rural culture, individuals who had been born in the country or in small towns and who were still living in similar settings when elected to high office. Even in the 1970s, the rural and small town *origins* of most of the region's political elite were still plainly visible.

In plotting the gradual rise of urban and big city politicians, we have found that in the 1970s majorities of southern senators and governors claimed either a medium-sized city or a large metropolitan area as their place of residence (see figure 14.1). The combination of a rural or small-town childhood with adult experiences in larger cities has become advantageous in statewide campaigns, allowing candidates to bridge different sectors of the electorate. Though southern politicians with exclusively big city backgrounds have occasionally won their states' highest offices, complete identification with a large metropolitan area is generally a liability in statewide contests.

The main political significance of these secular changes again consists in the weakening of the traditionalistic political culture, for the admixture of politicians from medium-urban and large metropolitan areas frequently produces governors and senators whose connections, interests, and priorities differ from those characteristic of purely rural politicians. During this transformation the values associated with entrepreneurial

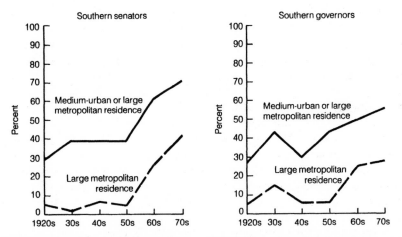

Figure 14.1. The changing southern political elite: rise of U.S. senators and governors with urban residence, 1920s–1970s. Sources: Calculated from Samuel R. Solomon, *The Governors of the American States, Commonwealth, and Territories, 1900–1980* (Lexington, Ky.: Council of State Governments, 1980); and appropriate volumes of *Congressional Directory* (Washington, D.C.: Government Printing Office).

individualism have gained strength, though it helps a politician to be perceived as someone who can simultaneously appeal to the "dynamic" *and* the "static" South, someone who stands both for "progress" (usually understood as economic growth) and for preserving some of the more civilizing norms of the older rural culture.

Changing Attitudes of Southern Elites

Over the past six decades the basic goals and objectives of southern political elites have changed. By circumscribing southern white control over race relations, federal intervention in the mid-1960s constituted a watershed which shifted the structure and dynamics of southern politics in the general direction of political democracy. Moreover, the once dominant pattern of conservative modernization has increasingly been challenged and superseded by the expansion of entrepreneurial individualism; and, as a secondary development, the older strain of agrarian radicalism has gradually given way to a neo-Populist protest less connected to agriculture. Investigation of the Democratic governors' campaign rhetoric reveals critical modifications over time in white elite attitudes concerning racial segregation and the achievement of economic development.[11]

Measured against the white South's historical determination to maintain white supremacy, the regional trends charted in figure 14.2 document exceedingly significant changes in the politics of race. Southern racial orientations fall into three periods, those dominated successively by moderate segregationists, militant segregationists, and nonsegregationists. Although a willingness to protect and preserve white supremacy was the cardinal "given" of the old southern politics, the finality of white political control meant that it was frequently unnecessary for candidates to flaunt their racial conservatism. From the 1920s through the 1940s the vast majority of Democratic governors, in the Deep South as well as the Peripheral South, campaigned as moderate rather than strong segregationists. During these decades racial themes in gubernatorial campaigns were comparatively subdued and sometimes completely ignored. Nonetheless, if a politician's good faith concerning segregation was challenged, he immediately denounced his accusers and affirmed his allegiance to Jim Crow.

After the Supreme Court decisively shattered the racial status quo by declaring segregated public schools unconstitutional, many victorious gubernatorial candidates responded as Key predicted they would, by becoming obstreperous defenders of racial segregation.[12] During the era of massive resistance, white public opinion was overwhelmingly opposed even to token school desegregation; neither the executive nor the legis-

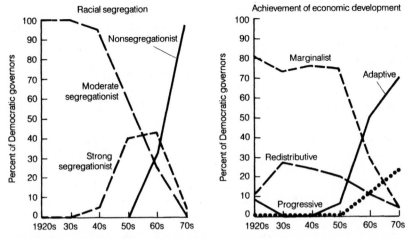

Figure 14.2. The transformation of southern elite views: Democratic governors' campaign stances on racial segregation and achievement of economic development, 1920s–1970s. See text for definition of categories. Sources: For classifications based on 1950–1973 campaigns, Earl Black, *Southern Governors and Civil Rights* (Cambridge, Mass.: Harvard University Press, 1976), pp. 347–352. Classifications of 1920–1949 and 1974–1979 campaigns were made by the authors following the procedures described ibid., pp. 11–22.

lative branch of the national government reinforced the Court's position; and blacks remained a small fraction of southern electorates. In this contentious milieu militant segregationists enjoyed a signal advantage in electoral politics, particularly in second primaries where the more restrained of the two participants was typically isolated as "weak" or "soft" on maintaining segregation, ridiculed as the "bloc vote" candidate, and soundly defeated. Strong segregationists won the governorship of every southern state at least once after 1954, but frenzied insistence on white supremacy was far more characteristic of the Deep South than of the Peripheral South. Almost two-thirds of the Deep South governors in the 1950s and 1960s, compared with roughly one-fourth of the Peripheral South chief executives, campaigned as militant segregationists. Across the South more strong segregationists were elected governors in the 1960s than were any other types of politicians.

Ultimately the South's strong segregationists could not withstand the pressures of federal intervention, and the years of massive resistance gave way to a new political era increasingly dominated by successful nonsegregationists. Responding in large measure to the demands of the civil rights movement, President Johnson persuaded Congress to enact a series of laws which, in their totality, redefined the working assumptions of southern electoral politics. Passage and implementation of these laws eventually led to the decline of overtly segregationist campaigning and to the rise of a new generation of white politicians more or less publicly reconciled to desegregation and black political participation.[13] This momentous transition was accomplished with much less strife, commotion, and hesitation in the Peripheral South than in the Deep South. During a decade in which nonsegregationist governors were barely visible in the Deep South (9 percent), they accounted for nearly half (47 percent) of the Democratic governors elected in the Peripheral South. Yet by the early 1970s, with much larger black electorates and with the desegregation of schools and public accommodations a fait accompli, nonsegregationist campaigning became commonplace in the Deep South as well as the Peripheral South.

In view of the South's historical impoverishment it is important also to analyze changing elite attitudes toward the achievement of economic development. Again employing a typology developed to analyze elite attitudes during the Second Reconstruction, we shall use information concerning the politicians' campaign stances on increased support for public education and class politics in order to group Democratic governors as marginalists, redistributives, adaptives, or progressives.[14] These terms, which are meant to symbolize alternative paths to economic development, have been created by cross-classifying two dimensions: whether or not a politician favors substantially increased expenditures for public education as a means to facilitate long-term economic development; and whether or not a candidate champions the cause of have-nots. Politicians who neither favor substantially increased funding for public education nor champion the interests of have-nots are defined as marginalists, while campaigners who champion have-nots but do not advocate significantly greater educational expenditures are called redistributives. Adaptives are candidates who want increased educational funding but avoid class politics; progressives both support more money for public education and promote the interests of have-nots.

Each of these perspectives on the achievement of economic development is closely related to the more general elite orientations previously discussed. Thus marginalists fall within the tradition of conservative modernization in their relative unwillingness to create an educational infrastructure conducive to economic development, and adaptives may be subsumed under the broader category of entrepreneurial individualism in their readiness to justify increased spending for public education as an investment in economic development. Redistributives correspond to the tradition of agrarian radicalism in being less committed to economic development than to winning immediate benefits and services for their have-not constituents. Progressives represent a more sophisticated variety of neo-Populism, one highly sensitive to the need to expand educational opportunities in order to increase the job skills of southerners.

Significant changes appear when elite attitudes on economic development are plotted decade by decade (see figure 14.2). The old southern politics produced Democratic governors who were more concerned to limit state expenditures or to redistribute modest resources than to develop an educational infrastructure that might eventually allow larger percentages of southerners to qualify for better jobs and induce more attractive industries to settle in the region. From the 1920s through the 1950s most southern governors—and especially Peripheral South governors—campaigned as marginalists. Though not necessarily opposed to incremental increases in educational expenditures, the marginalists were basically standpatters. During these decades redistributives were the main alternative to marginalists, and they were prominent only in the Deep South. Neither marginalists nor redistributives entertained bold and innovative thoughts about achieving economic development.

Since the 1950s adaptives have emerged as the most common type of Democratic governor. Forced to compete within and beyond the region for new industry, southern governors have increasingly advocated higher expenditures for education as a means of strengthening economic development. The critical transformation has involved the displacement of conservative modernization by entrepreneurial individualism as the "typical" route to the governor's mansion. Just as redistributives constituted the main challenge to marginalists in the old southern politics, by the 1970s progressives were the leading alternative to adaptives. Whether adaptive or progressive, southern Democratic governors have become far more persuaded that economic development necessitates greater investment in public education than they were in the past.

Finally, the changing attitudes of southern elites may be brought into clearer focus by examining the two policy areas together.[15] To simplify the presentation of trends and heighten the contrast between politicians who explicitly upheld racial segregation and those who did not, militant segregationists and moderate segregationists have been combined into a single category. The percentage distribution of eight combinations of racial and economic development positions over time, reported in table 14.4, summarizes (from the standpoint of victorious white politicians) the transition from the old to the new southern politics.

The pivotal change in the nature of southern state leadership has been *the decline of segregationist marginalists and the rise of nonsegregationist adaptives*. Representing an exceedingly traditional mix of racial and eco-

Table 14.4. From segregationist marginalists to nonsegregationist adaptives: southern Democratic governors' campaign stances on racial segregation and achievement of economic development, 1920–1979[a]

Campaign stances	1920s	1930s	1940s	1950s	1960s	1970s
Segregationist marginalists	81	73	76	74	21	0
Segregationist redistributives	11	27	24	20	11	0
Segregationist adaptives	8	0	0	6	25	0
Segregationist progressives	0	0	0	0	11	4
Nonsegregationist marginalists	0	0	0	0	7	4
Nonsegregationist redistributives	0	0	0	0	0	4
Nonsegregationist adaptives	0	0	0	0	25	69
Nonsegregationist progressives	0	0	0	0	0	19
Number of governors	(37)	(37)	(37)	(35)	(28)	(26)

Source: Same as figure 14.2.
a. Data are presented as percentages.

nomic views, segregationist marginalists contributed between three-quarters and four-fifths of the South's Democratic governors in each decade from the 1920s through the 1950s. The old South pattern disintegrated in the 1960s under the weight of federal intervention. During this stormy period there was no unmistakable "winning combination" of stances on segregation, investing in public education, and the use of "class" appeals. In the following decade, though, the comparatively innovative nonsegregationist adaptives emerged as the typical winners in the new southern politics. Peripheral South Democrats, less mesmerized by Jim Crow and more committed to rapid economic development, initiated the conversion to nonsegregationist adaptives a decade before the Deep South did so. In the 1970s majorities of Democratic chief executives in both subregions campaigned as nonsegregationist adaptives. By settling the principle of racial segregation, federal intervention indirectly encouraged the region's politicians to concentrate more single-mindedly on stimulating economic development, an endeavor that was of paramount importance to the growing middle class.

Beyond Pure One-Party Politics

The traditional hegemony of southern Democracy has ended. Millions of southerners, of course, still think of themselves as Democrats, and many of them continue to vote for their party's candidates. In the past two decades, however, millions of other southerners have come to feel that the policies and candidates associated with the national Democratic party serve neither their interests nor their ambitions, and these negative perceptions have begun to affect many state and local candidates of southern Democracy. As yet many of the Democrats who have lost their political faith have not fully converted to Republicanism. But even though self-identified Republicans remain a minority of the electorate, the region now contains so many independents that Democratic candidates can be defeated whenever non-Democrats (Republicans and independents) join forces.

To appreciate how thoroughly the old one-party politics has been modified, it is useful to compare the Republican party's potential for winning elections with its actual performance after the Voting Rights Act of 1965. Though the rise of an urban new middle class provides a firm social grounding for the diffusion of Republican loyalties across the South, the size of that white middle class varies considerably from one state to another. Disregarding other factors, the larger the white urbanized new middle class, the greater the potential for Republican advances.

Republican efforts to create electoral majorities are also more likely to succeed if the party can tap a traditional Republican vote, one concentrated in geographical areas that for historical reasons have long been predisposed toward Republicanism. To the extent that the Republican party remained a live option for voters even during the era of the Democratic Solid South, GOP campaigners would be less dependent upon extensive social change to provide a foundation for durable Republicanism. Again setting aside other considerations, the greater the size of the traditional Republican vote, the easier the task of winning elections.[16]

Using the South itself as a point of reference, we have arrayed the southern states according to their presumed readiness for Republican advances (see figure 14.3). In the figure the percentage of the 1980 labor force contributed by the white urbanized new middle class is plotted against the traditional Republican base, estimated by averaging the mean Republican vote in presidential, senatorial, and gubernatorial campaigns for 1920–1949. Because they exhibit strength on both dimensions, Florida, Virginia, and the Peripheral South as a whole appear exceptionally receptive to Republican gains. Texas, despite a white urban middle class second only to Florida's, seems moderately less poised for Republican gains because of its smaller base of traditional Republicanism. Tennessee and North Carolina share the region's broadest traditions of grassroots Republicanism (mountain Republicanism, especially in East Tennessee) but do not possess large urbanized white middle classes comparable to those of Florida, Texas, and Virginia. Arkansas and all five Deep South states appear least ready for broad Republican gains. With smaller tra-

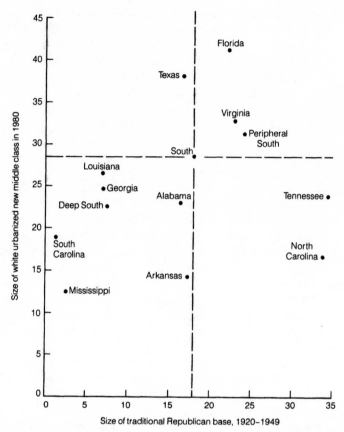

Figure 14.3. Variations in readiness for southern Republicanism: size of traditional Republican base in 1920–1949 presidential, senatorial, and gubernatorial elections compared with size of 1980 white new middle class in urbanized areas, by state, subregion, and region. Sources: Calculated from U.S. Bureau of the Census, *1980 Census of Population,* I, *Characteristics of the Population,* appropriate state reports, table 78; Richard M. Scammon, ed., *America at the Polls* (Pittsburgh: University of Pittsburgh Press, 1965); and *Congressional Quarterly's Guide to U.S. Elections* (Washington, D.C., Congressional Quarterly, 1975).

ditional bases and smaller white urbanized new middle classes, they would need other factors, such as dynamic candidates or compelling events and issues, to overcome inherent Republican weaknesses.

The ultimate test of southern Republicanism is the electability of its candidates. Have the southern states with the greatest potential for Republican advances actually produced more Republican victories than states with less potential? Have the states with the least potential for Republican success experienced substantially fewer Republican victories than states with greater potential? By and large, the proportion of Republican victories since 1965 in presidential, senatorial, and gubernatorial races, as well as the average percentage of state legislative seats won by GOP candidates, has corresponded to the underlying Republican potential (see table 14.5). Southern Republicanism in the two decades after federal intervention was especially advanced in Virginia and Tennessee, where the party won at least half of all contests for all three leading offices and attained substantial minority blocs in the state legislatures. In North Carolina, South Carolina, and Texas, the GOP did well in presidential and senatorial contests. With the exception of South Carolina, the states in which Republicans won 50 percent or more of

Table 14.5. Southern Republicanism after federal intervention: percentage of Republican victories for selected offices, 1965–1985, by state, subregion, and region

Political unit	Percentage of Republican victories			
	President	Senator	Governor	State legislator[a]
Virginia	100	50	50	22
Tennessee	80	57	60	39
North Carolina	80	57	40	18
South Carolina	80	50	20	12
Texas	60	57	14	14
Florida	80	33	20	29
Arkansas	60	0	30	4
Mississippi	60	29	0	3
Louisiana	60	0	20	5
Alabama	60	13	0	3
Georgia	40	14	0	13
Deep South	60	22	8	8
Peripheral South	77	43	34	21
South	69	33	24	14

Sources: For presidential, senatorial, and gubernatorial data, same as table 13.2; for state legislators, calculated from appropriate volumes of U.S. Bureau of the Census, *Statistical Abstract of the United States* (Washington, D.C.: Government Printing Office).

a. For state legislators the figure is the average percentage of Republican state legislators elected to the 1966–1984 legislatures.

the contests for at least two major offices ranked high on one (and sometimes both) of the dimensions presumably conducive to Republican success.

Florida stands alone in its uneven pattern of Republican growth. In spite of its exceptional potential for Republican gains, Florida was the most prominent GOP disappointment in the period 1965–1984. Republican candidates have done extremely well at the top of the ballot (winning four of the last five presidential elections) and at the bottom (possessing the region's second largest delegation of Republican state legislators), but the party's nominees for the most significant statewide races have failed to fulfill expectations. The Florida Republicans who won early victories for governor (Claude Kirk in 1966) and senator (Edward Gurney in 1968) proved to be political embarrassments, and Republican activists engaged in such fierce intraparty rivalries that the minority party was frequently divided in general elections.

Another set of states—Arkansas, Mississippi, Louisiana, and Alabama—favored Republican candidates in presidential elections but usually elected Democrats in senatorial, gubernatorial, and state legislative campaigns. Because of Jimmy Carter's two races, Georgia was the least Republican state, the only southern state in which Republicans failed to win a majority of the post-1965 presidential campaigns. In all these states the scattered Republican victories were roughly consistent with their poor showing vis-à-vis the white urban middle class and the traditional GOP base.

Republican prospects are clearly brighter in Peripheral South states with traditional Republican bases or rapidly urbanizing middle classes than they are elsewhere in the region. In most southern states the governorship remains the Democrats' office to lose rather than one that the Republicans can win without Democratic disarray. Coupled with the almost automatic election of Democratic majorities in the region's legislatures, *state* politics in the South will probably remain under partial or complete Democratic control in the foreseeable future.

Future Partisan Balance

The Democratic party in the South is now composed of whites and blacks, and in some quarters it is doubtless perceived as a "black" political party. In fact, although most politically active blacks are Democrats, most southern Democrats are whites. Indeed, a majority of the modern Democratic party's southern identifiers are whites born and raised in the region. The racial, social, and ideological diversity of the Democratic party explains both its strengths and its weaknesses. Though much of the party's leadership and financial support derives from affluent whites, the vast majority of white and black southern Democrats did not attend college, belong to the working class, and are modestly housed. Robust differences in political philosophy further complicate the party's racial and socioeconomic diversity.

Under imaginative and skillful leadership, it is still possible for liberals, moderates, and conservatives to unite in the task of electing Democrats. Most Democratic candidates for state office prevail by assembling virtually all of the black vote and a sufficiently large minority of the white vote. Whenever party unity *is* achieved, Democratic nominees can be truly formidable in most of the Deep South and truly competitive in most of the Peripheral South. Because Democrats still constitute majorities of the electorate in the Deep South, party unity is usually sufficient for victory. In much of the Peripheral South, though, even a united Democratic party may no longer be large enough to win general elections. To achieve victory Democrats have to appeal to many political independents as well.

Nevertheless, the Democratic party is acutely vulnerable to racial, social, and ideological cleavages that have no easy solutions; and it is not always possible to present a cohesive party in general elections. When Democrats divide, whether over critical issues of public policy or simply over the conflicting ambitions of rival politicians, Republicans are strategically positioned to construct winning ad hoc coalitions of real Republicans, independents, and disaffected Democrats. Unless there is a profound revitalization and remobilization of Democratic support in the lower two-thirds of the South's social structure, as time goes on Democratic majorities will become even harder to achieve in statewide elections.

Southern Republicanism increasingly epitomizes the values and beliefs of the most affluent white southerners, as well as those who aspire to such status and rewards. Though its mass base includes some working-class southerners, in terms of real influence and control the GOP is preeminently the vehicle of upper-middle-class, well-educated, conservative whites. Southern Republicanism is the party of *Southern Living,* if that magazine could be imagined to possess an explicit political philosophy. The appeal of the southern version of the American Dream is palpable, but the party's firm grounding in the upper middle class also entails serious risks and liabilities for southern Republicanism as a potential majority party.

The Republican party has practically no attraction, of course, to the region's black voters. Although some white southerners find the absence of blacks a compelling argument in favor of Republicanism ("Why don't you leave the niggers behind and come join us?" was the friendly invitation to one of the authors after he had addressed a gathering of South Carolina Republicans), others decry the party's limited appeal to blacks and rationalize it as the regrettable but predictable consequence of a misguided and underdeveloped black middle class. The practical effect of microscopic black support is that Republicans can win two-candidate elections only by capturing landslide majorities of the white vote.

Unlike the case with the Democrats, substantial portions of the mass base of many southern Republican parties consist of transplanted Yankees and midwesterners. Migration gives the GOP an expanding membership, yet makes some state Republican parties appear "foreign" to many native southerners. Furthermore, while the Democratic party's roots lie in the middle and lower portions of the South's social structure, southern Republicans look upward for their core support. The apex of the social order is a better place to acquire leaders, ideology, and finance than to find votes. If the Republican party is ever to capture the partisan loyalties of a majority of all southerners, its working vision of who is politically important, who really counts in the society, will have to be dramatically broadened. Country clubs and magnificent resorts, the natural habitats of the Republican elite, do not provide the best vantage points for "seeing" the millions of southerners in the lower-middle and working classes.

Democrats will probably continue to win most southern state and local offices for some time to come. But the shift of conservatives from the Democratic to the Republican party and the GOP's popularity among college-educated whites portend a brighter Republican future. Educated white conservatives have already realigned their party identifications. Including the partisan leanings of independents, 65 percent of educated conservatives were sympathetic to the Republicans, while merely 28 percent found the Democrats attractive in 1980. On the eve of Ronald Reagan's first term, highly educated white conservatives were clearly embracing Republicanism. Reagan's performance in office presumably accelerated the realignment: by 1984, 75 percent of the white conservatives with some exposure to college leaned toward or identified with the Republicans, compared with only 18 percent who favored the Democrats. This stratum of southern society contributes most of the Republican party's officeholders, candidates, organizers, and fund raisers.

Throughout southern history economic achievement and political conservatism have not ordinarily been long separated from actual political power. As a group, conservatives—educated and uneducated—used the Democratic party as their main political instrument in the past. Partisan realignment of the most highly educated sector of southern conservatives probably signifies a fundamental shift in the party affiliations of conservative southerners generally, a shift that may eventually make the Republicans the South's leading party.

Nonetheless, despite the obvious political assets enjoyed by educated white conservatives, a comprehensive Republican realignment in southern politics is not inevitable. In the dealigned electorate Republican success depends upon creating *and* sustaining favorable impressions of the GOP as well as negative images of the Democrats among white voters, perceptions that are influenced by the performance of Republican and Democratic officeholders in the South and also by the tides of national partisan politics, which cannot always favor the GOP. Continued economic growth is crucial to Republican success, for it is through the expansion of jobs that Republicans can appeal to the region's common whites. Fluctuations in the business cycle will doubtless provide political opportunities for the Democrats in the future.

Shifts in party strength since the Great Society have been most convincingly expressed in the outcomes of presidential elections. The symbols and issues associated with Republican presidential candidates have generally been far closer to the interests, beliefs, wishes, and expectations of the white middle class than have those identified with Democratic presidential candidates. In recent times no politician has exploited the mismatch in party symbols more skillfully than Ronald Reagan, who is much more conventionally "southern" in his style and practice of politics than either Lyndon Johnson or Jimmy Carter. Shrewdly blending themes from the entrepreneurial individualistic culture and the traditionalist heritage, Reagan's positions on most issues—with the glaring exception of his administration's massive federal deficits—appear eminently reasonable to most middle-class southern whites. If Reagan's performance in office during his second term continues to meet with white voter approval, Reagan will have done more to weaken the Democratic party's standing among white southerners than any president since Johnson.

The Democrats who have won office since federal intervention have usually done so by deliberately mixing presentable features of the traditionalistic culture with dynamic aspects of the entrepreneurial culture. A judicious fusion of conservative and progressive themes expresses the essence of modern southern Democracy and constitutes an operational definition of political "moderation" in the South. At best it is a winning formula; at worst it allows most Democrats to remain competitive. Democratic nominees are unlikely to abandon this style of campaigning.

All southern Republicans embrace conservatism, but some are more militantly right-wing than others. Because the national political agenda provides the Republican far right with more targets and symbols to deploy against their opponents than do the more mundane and practical agendas of state politics, the far right has done much better in contests for the U.S. Senate than for the governorships. Senate races are more likely to involve distinct ideological contrasts than are gubernatorial campaigns. In Senate contests "progressive-conservative" Democrats will sometimes fight conservative or right-wing Republicans, and voters may find it fairly easy to pick the candidate nearest to their own views.

The situation will be somewhat different in most gubernatorial contests. In state politics there is no reliable demand for an unadulterated conservative Republicanism. Although most Republican gubernatorial candidates will emphasize conservative themes more than their Democratic opponents, they will not ordinarily win southern governorships by marketing themselves as uptown Dixiecrats. Far more likely to succeed are those Republican contenders who imitate the winning Democrats by combining elements of conservatism with dynamic, progressive appeals. Voters in future elections for governor may have difficulty perceiving striking issue differences between Democratic and Republican nominees. Frequently their effective choices will lie between the "progressive conservatives" or "conservative progressives" of the Democratic party and the "conservatives" or "moderate conservatives" of the Republican party.

Statewide elections in the new southern politics will typically determine which segments of the white middle class will rule, that is, whether the self-described "moderates" or the "conservatives" of the educated middle class will hold the key offices, command the public institutions, make the policies, and distribute the patronage and perquisites of a rapidly growing region. Though elected officials will differ in agendas, priorities, and style, the middle-class politicians of both parties will normally strive to maintain a friendly climate for economic development, will tax individuals and corporations at comparatively low rates, will spend substantial sums only for purposes that unmistakably serve the self-interest of the expanding middle class, and will generally minimize transfer payments that would mainly benefit have-not and have-little southerners. Southern elections will not ordinarily focus on explicit differences between whites and blacks, nor will they usually feature overt conflicts between middle-class and working-class southerners. By and large, open political conflict will involve differences within the white middle class itself. Whether the moderates rule through the Democratic party or the conservatives govern through the Republican party, southern politics can be expected to perpetuate much of the past even as a different future beckons.

Notes

1. Old Politics, New People

1. V. O. Key, Jr., *Southern Politics in State and Nation* (New York: Knopf, 1949), p. 4.

2. J. Morgan Kousser, *The Shaping of Southern Politics* (New Haven: Yale University Press, 1974), p. 224.

3. Ibid., esp. pp. 45–82, 246–250. See also Key, *Southern Politics*, pp. 531–663; and Jerrold G. Rusk and John J. Stucker, "The Effect of the Southern System of Election Laws on Voting Participation: A Reply to V. O. Key, Jr.," in Joel H. Sibley, Allan G. Bogue, and William H. Flanigan, eds., *The History of American Electoral Behavior* (Princeton: Princeton University Press, 1978), pp. 198–250. For a vivid depiction of black belt whites in action, see Lawrence C. Goodwyn, "Populist Dreams and Negro Rights: East Texas as a Case Study," *American Historical Review*, 76 (December 1971), 1435–56.

4. Kousser, *Shaping of Southern Politics*, pp. 224, 236.

5. Ibid., pp. 224–225. "Broadly based oligarchy" is Walter Dean Burnham's apt phrase for the American polity after 1896, quoted ibid. See his "Changing Shape of the American Political Universe," *American Political Science Review*, 59 (March 1965), 23.

6. Kousser, *Shaping of Southern Politics*, and Goodwyn, "Populist Dreams and Negro Rights."

7. W. J. Cash, *The Mind of the South* (New York: Knopf, 1941), pp. 128–129.

8. Jasper Berry Shannon, *Toward a New Politics in the South* (Knoxville: University of Tennessee Press, 1949), p. 9.

9. These generalizations are derived from Key, *Southern Politics*; Cash, *Mind of the South*; and Shannon, *Toward a New Politics*.

10. William C. Havard, "From Past to Future: An Overview of Southern Politics," in William C. Havard, ed., *The Changing Politics of the South* (Baton Rouge: Louisiana State University Press, 1972), pp. 701–710. For an authori-

tative history of the achievements and limitations of the progressive movement in the South, see Dewey W. Grantham, *Southern Progressivism* (Knoxville: University of Tennessee Press, 1983).

11. Key, *Southern Politics,* pp. 11–12.

12. In 1924, for example, Republican presidential candidate Calvin Coolidge received 1,100 votes in South Carolina. This paltry sum prompted Cole Blease, a rip-roaring Democratic demagogue, to comment as follows: "I do not know where he got them. I was astonished to know that they were cast and shocked to know that they were counted." Quoted in George B. Tindall, *The Emergence of the New South, 1913–1945* (Baton Rouge: Louisiana State University Press, 1967), p. 166.

13. Kousser, *Shaping of Southern Politics,* pp. 72–82. Our discussion of this topic is based primarily on Kousser's analysis.

14. C. Vann Woodward, *Origins of the New South, 1877–1913* (Baton Rouge: Louisiana State University Press, 1951), p. 372.

15. Kousser, *Shaping of Southern Politics,* pp. 72–82.

16. Cash, *Mind of the South,* p. 130. See also Albert D. Kirwan, *Revolt of the Rednecks* (Lexington: University of Kentucky Press, 1951), p. 132.

17. Kousser, *Shaping of Southern Politics,* p. 80.

18. The state chapters of Key, *Southern Politics,* provide numerous illustrations of conservative domination of state government and politics. For an excellent analysis of rural control in a southern state legislature, see William C. Havard and Loren P. Beth, *The Politics of Mis-Representation: Rural-Urban Conflict in the Florida Legislature* (Baton Rouge: Louisiana State University Press, 1962).

19. Key, *Southern Politics.*

20. Turner Catledge, *My Life and The Times* (New York: Harper & Row, 1971), p. 104.

21. Kousser, *Shaping of Southern Politics,* p. 262.

22. Cash, *Mind of the South,* p. 129.

23. Key, *Southern Politics,* p. 309. See also pp. 298–311, 489–528.

24. Ibid., p. 523.

25. Hugh Douglas Price, "Southern Politics in the Sixties: Notes on Economic Development and Political Modernization" (Paper delivered at the 1964 annual meeting of the American Political Science Association, Chicago, Ill.), p. 10.

26. Key, *Southern Politics,* p. 5.

27. Ibid.

28. Ibid., p. 11.

29. Ibid., pp. 5, 9.

30. Paul B. Sheatsley, "White Attitudes toward the Negro," *Daedalus,* 91 (Winter 1966), 219–222.

31. Cash, *Mind of the South;* Lillian Smith, *Killers of the Dream* (New York: Norton, 1949); Larry L. King, *Confessions of a White Racist* (New York: Viking Press, 1971); and, among many possibilities, "The Artificial Nigger," in Flannery O'Connor, *The Complete Stories* (New York: Farrar Straus Giroux, 1971), pp. 249–270.

32. Personal observation of one of the authors in the early 1960s.

33. Key, *Southern Politics*, p. 6.

34. Kousser, *Shaping of Southern Politics*.

35. See Numan V. Bartley, *The Rise of Massive Resistance* (Baton Rouge: Louisiana State University Press, 1969); Francis M. Wilhoit, *The Politics of Massive Resistance* (New York: George Braziller, 1973); Neil R. McMillen, *The Citizens' Council* (Urbana: University of Illinois Press, 1971); and Earl Black, *Southern Governors and Civil Rights* (Cambridge, Mass.: Harvard University Press, 1976).

36. Key, *Southern Politics*, pp. 664, 672, 674–675.

37. Ibid., pp. 670, 672–675.

38. Ibid., p. 669.

39. Books incorporating systematic comparisons of the Deep South and the Peripheral South include Donald R. Matthews and James W. Prothro, *Negroes and the New Southern Politics* (New York: Harcourt, Brace & World, 1966), esp. pp. 169–173, 355–357; Bernard Cosman, *Five States for Goldwater* (University, Ala.: University of Alabama Press, 1966); Louis M. Seagull, *Southern Republicanism* (Cambridge, Mass.: Schenkman, 1975); and Black, *Southern Governors*. For an alternative categorization in which Virginia, Florida, Tennessee, and Texas are termed "evolving states," Arkansas, Georgia, and North Carolina are called "wavering states," and Alabama, Mississippi, Louisiana, and South Carolina are designated "protest states," see Havard, *Changing Politics of the South*.

40. Key, *Southern Politics*, p. 5.

41. See Philip E. Converse, "A Major Political Realignment in the South?" in Allan P. Sindler, ed., *Change in the Contemporary South* (Durham: Duke University Press, 1963), pp. 195–222.

42. The most recent comprehensive discussion of the region's changing population is Dudley L. Poston, Jr., and Robert H. Weller, eds., *The Population of the South* (Austin: University of Texas Press, 1982). Migration patterns are intensively examined in Jeanne C. Biggar, "The Sunning of America: Migration to the Sunbelt," *Population Bulletin*, 34 (March 1979), 1–42.

43. Rand McNally, *1982 Commercial Atlas and Marketing Guide* (Chicago: Rand McNally, 1982), pp. 46–47.

44. Paul Allen Beck and Paul Lopatto, "The End of Southern Distinctiveness," in Laurence W. Moreland, Tod A. Baker, and Robert P. Steed, eds., *Contemporary Southern Political Attitudes and Behavior* (New York: Praeger, 1982), pp. 160–182; and Paul Allen Beck, "Partisan Dealignment in the Postwar South," *American Political Science Review*, 71 (June 1977), 477–496.

2. Industrialization and Urbanization

1. V. O. Key, Jr., *Southern Politics in State and Nation* (New York: Knopf, 1949), p. 673. We do not assume that such power structures are necessarily monolithic and unitary, though they may well be tightly organized and highly consensual in their goals.

2. Edward C. Banfield, *Political Influence* (New York: Free Press, 1961), p. 263.

3. Key, *Southern Politics*, pp. 673–674. Key thought that, even controlling for racial composition, blacks were more likely to face rigid barriers to political participation in rural areas. The most perceptive and prescient analysis of race relations in the metropolitan South is still Lewis Killian and Charles Grigg, "Race Relations in an Urbanized South," *Journal of Social Issues*, 22 (January 1966), 20–29.

4. T. Harry Williams, *Huey Long* (New York: Knopf, 1969), pp. 182, 185. The entire chapter, "Blood on the Moon," pp. 181–213, is worth reading.

5. Williams's biography of Long is a superb example. See also William F. Holmes, *The White Chief: James Kimble Vardaman* (Baton Rouge: Louisiana State University Press, 1970); J. Harvie Wilkinson III, *Harry Byrd and the Changing Face of Virginia Politics* (Charlottesville: University Press of Virginia, 1968); and William Anderson, *The Wild Man from Sugar Creek* (Baton Rouge: Louisiana State University Press, 1975). For a fascinating theoretical discussion of interest groups and state power structures, see Thomas B. Edsall, "Money and Morality in Maryland," *Society*, 11 (May-June 1974), 74–81.

6. The state chapters in Key's *Southern Politics* contain varying amounts of information on power structures up to midcentury. More recent characterizations may be found in the relevant state chapters in William C. Havard, ed., *The Changing Politics of the South* (Baton Rouge: Louisiana State University Press, 1972); in Neal R. Peirce's *The Megastates of America* (New York: Norton, 1972), *The Deep South States of America* (New York: Norton, 1974), and *The Border South States* (New York: Norton, 1975); in Jack Bass and Walter DeVries, *The Transformation of Southern Politics* (New York: Basic Books, 1976); and in Robert Sherrill, *Gothic Politics in the Deep South* (New York: Grossman, 1968).

7. Richard Hofstadter, *The Age of Reform* (New York: Knopf, 1955), p. 23. For a comprehensive study, see Gilbert C. Fite, *Cotton Fields No More* (Lexington: University Press of Kentucky, 1984).

8. Jasper Berry Shannon, *Toward a New Politics in the South* (Knoxville, University of Tennessee Press, 1949), pp. 41–44, 48. Shannon also added the local newspaper editor to the governing class.

9. Key, *Southern Politics*, p. 662.

10. Daniel J. Elazar, *American Federalism*, 2nd ed. (New York: Thomas Y. Crowell, 1972), p. 99.

11. Ibid., pp. 99–102.

12. See Barrington Moore, Jr., *Social Origins of Dictatorship and Democracy* (Boston: Beacon Press, 1966), pp. xi–xvii and 111–155; Dwight B. Billings, Jr., *Planters and the Making of a "New South"* (Chapel Hill: University of North Carolina Press, 1979); Jonathan M. Wiener, *Social Origins of the New South* (Baton Rouge: Louisiana State University Press, 1978); and Numan V. Bartley, "Beyond *Southern Politics:* Some Suggestions for Research," in Merle Black and John Shelton Reed, eds., *Perspectives on the American South*, II (New York: Gordon and Breach, 1984), 35–47.

13. W. J. Cash, *The Mind of the South* (New York: Knopf, 1941), pp. 179–185.

14. Billings, *Planters.*

15. James C. Cobb, *The Selling of the South* (Baton Rouge: Louisiana State University Press, 1982), p. 267. See also James C. Cobb, *Industrialization and Southern Society* (Lexington: University Press of Kentucky, 1984).

16. Williams, *Huey Long,* p. 187.

17. George B. Tindall emphasizes "business progressivism" in his interpretation of southern state governments in the 1920s and argues that "expansion and efficiency became by and large the norm of Southern statecraft in the decades that followed." See his *Emergence of the New South* (Baton Rouge: Louisiana State University Press, 1967), p. 233 and, more generally, pp. 219–284.

18. Williams, *Huey Long,* p. 187.

19. Elazar, *American Federalism,* p. 94.

20. There is a vast literature on Populism; obviously we cannot do justice to the topic in the space available. See Lawrence C. Goodwyn, *Democratic Promise* (New York: Oxford University Press, 1976).

21. Shannon, *Toward a New Politics,* p. 50.

22. Key, *Southern Politics,* p. 307.

23. Williams, *Huey Long;* Allan P. Sindler, *Huey Long's Louisiana* (Baltimore: Johns Hopkins Press, 1956); Key, *Southern Politics,* pp. 156–182; and Cash, *Mind of the South,* pp. 284–287.

24. Peirce, *Deep South States,* p. 208.

25. Key, *Southern Politics,* p. 254.

26. Elazar, *American Federalism,* p. 94.

27. On the prodigious wheeling and dealing of LBJ, see Robert A. Caro, *The Path to Power* (New York: Knopf, 1982); Ronnie Dugger, *The Politician* (New York: Norton, 1982); and Alfred Steinberg, *Sam Johnson's Boy* (New York: Macmillan, 1968). There is no satisfactory biography of Connally.

28. Our discussion of the geography of southern manufacturing is based on maps prepared from Census Bureau data. Detailed descriptions of the economies of groups of southern counties may be found in Donald J. Bogue and Calvin C. Beale, *Economic Areas of the United States* (New York: Free Press, 1961).

29. See Tindall, *Emergence of the New South,* pp. 318–353 and 391–472. The southern blend of industry and small-town setting is celebrated in Hamilton C. Horton, Jr., "The Enduring Soil," in Fifteen Southerners, *Why the South Will Survive* (Athens: University of Georgia Press, 1981), pp. 57–67.

30. At least two qualifications must be attached to the proposition that the South and the non-South have increasingly resembled each other in the size of their industrial sectors. The most significant interregional difference is the much lower rates of union membership in the South, which will be discussed in the next chapter. The second notable qualification is that specific jobs and skills may vary within particular industrial sectors. For example, southern manufacturing has been far more devoted than nonsouthern manufacturing to the production of nondurable goods.

31. David C. Perry and Alfred J. Watkins, eds., *The Rise of the Sunbelt Cities*

(Beverly Hills: Sage Publications, 1977); and Kirkpatrick Sale, *Power Shift* (New York: Random House, 1975).

32. Alfred J. Watkins and David C. Perry, "Three Theories of American Urban Development," in Perry and Watkins, eds., *Sunbelt Cities,* p. 42.

33. Ibid., p. 95.

34. Sale, *Power Shift,* pp. 17–88.

35. Watkins and Perry, "Three Theories," pp. 46–51.

36. Major studies of the southern city include Rupert Vance and Nicholas Demerath, eds., *The Urban South* (Chapel Hill: University of North Carolina Press, 1954); Perry and Watkins, eds., *Sunbelt Cities;* Carl Abbott, *The New Urban America* (Chapel Hill: University of North Carolina Press, 1981); Blaine Brownell, *The Urban Ethos in the New South* (Baton Rouge: Louisiana State University Press, 1976); Blaine Brownell and David Goldfield, eds., *The City in Southern History* (Port Washington, N.Y.: Kennikat Press, 1977); Patricia Dusenberry and Thad L. Beyle, *Southern Urban Trends* (Research Triangle Park, N.C.: Southern Growth Policies Board, 1978); and David R. Goldfield, *Cotton Fields and Skyscrapers* (Baton Rouge: Louisiana State University Press, 1982).

37. See Peirce, *Megastates of America,* pp. 450–563.

38. Earl Black, *Southern Governors and Civil Rights* (Cambridge, Mass.: Harvard University Press, 1976), pp. 22–26. These criteria were used to classify every county in every census year from 1920 through 1980. For the justification for setting the threshold of high-black counties at 30 percent, see Donald R. Matthews and James W. Prothro, *Negroes and the New Southern Politics* (New York: Harcourt, Brace & World, 1966), pp. 115–120.

39. Key, *Southern Politics,* p. 666.

40. The census closest in time to a particular election was used to classify counties as large metropolitan, medium urban, low-black rural, or high-black rural. For example, classifications based on the 1950 census were used to determine the distribution of the presidential vote in 1948 and 1952, and the 1960 census was applied to the 1956, 1960, and 1964 elections.

41. Key, *Southern Politics,* p. 145. Key used the term as a partial explanation for the willingness of some farmers turned mill hands to vote for politicians who did nothing to further their interests.

42. Shannon, *Toward a New Politics,* p. 50.

43. Key, *Southern Politics,* p. 471.

44. Ibid., pp. 463–485. Key's state chapters also suggest such links.

45. Interview with the legislator in the early 1970s.

46. Peter A. Lupsha and William J. Siembieda, "The Poverty of Public Services in the Land of Plenty: An Analysis and Interpretation," in Perry and Watkins, eds., *Sunbelt Cities,* pp. 182, 185–187. See also Chandler Davidson and George Korbel, "At-Large Elections and Minority-Group Representation: A Re-Examination of Historical and Contemporary Evidence," *Journal of Politics,* 43 (November 1981), 982–1005.

47. Key, *Southern Politics,* pp. 528, 673–674.

48. See, for example, the interesting discussion of Houston entrepreneurs in William D. Angell, Jr., "To Make a City: Entrepreneurship on the Sunbelt Frontier," in Perry and Watkins, eds., *Sunbelt Cities,* pp. 109–128.

49. At the state level, the politicians generally conform to the "adaptive" type discussed in Black, *Southern Governors*, pp. 16–19, 283–298.

50. Elazar, *American Federalism*, pp. 106–107.

51. Lupsha and Siembieda, "Poverty of Public Services," p. 188.

52. For a thorough discussion of "high-tech" campaigning, see Larry J. Sabato, *The Rise of Political Consultants* (New York: Basic Books, 1981).

3. The Rise of Middle-Class Society

1. V. O. Key, Jr., "The Erosion of Sectionalism," *Virginia Quarterly Review*, 31 (Spring 1955), 163–164.

2. Ibid., p. 164.

3. Allison Davis, Burleigh B. Gardner, and Mary R. Gardner, *Deep South* (Chicago: University of Chicago Press, 1941), p. 15. Other valuable studies of the traditional South's social structure include Charles S. Johnson, *Shadow of the Plantation* (Chicago: University of Chicago Press, 1934); Arthur F. Raper, *Preface to Peasantry* (Chapel Hill: University of North Carolina Press, 1936); John Dollard, *Caste and Class in a Southern Town* (New Haven: Yale University Press, 1937); Hortense Powdermaker, *After Freedom* (New York: Viking Press, 1939); and Gunnar Mrydal, *An American Dilemma* (New York: Harper & Row, 1944).

4. Davis, Gardner, and Gardner, *Deep South*, p. 59.

5. Leonard Reissman, "Social Development and the American South," *Journal of Social Issues*, 22 (January 1966), 105–109.

6. Because the U.S. Census of Population does not distinguish farm owners from farm tenants but rather combines them as farm managers, the percentage of farm owners has been estimated by multiplying the number of farm managers by the rate of farm ownership reported in the U.S. Census of Agriculture for the year closest to a given census year. Farm tenants are then determined by subtracting farm owners from farm managers.

7. The irony of this situation is elaborated in Henry Allen Bullock, *A History of Negro Education in the South* (Cambridge, Mass.: Harvard University Press, 1967).

8. See Joseph L. Bernd, "Georgia: Static and Dynamic," in William C. Havard, ed., *The Changing Politics of the South* (Baton Rouge: Louisiana State University Press, 1972), pp. 304–311.

9. See John C. McKinney and Linda Brookover Borque, "The Changing South: National Incorporation of a Region," *American Sociological Review*, 36 (June 1971), 399–412.

10. Reissman, "Social Development," p. 107.

11. More precisely, the most successful southerners are drawn from the upper middle class. The most popular and accessible self-image of the new middle class is displayed monthly in the pages of *Southern Living* magazine, which provides a running education on how to be simultaneously southern and upper middle class. To live in the style celebrated by *Southern Living* requires either genuine affluence or massive indebtedness and is far beyond the reach of most southerners who consider themselves "middle class." For a perceptive and appreciative essay

on the sociological functions of *Southern Living,* see John Shelton Reed, *One South* (Baton Rouge: Louisiana State University Press, 1982), pp. 119–126.

12. The Comparative State Elections Project was organized by James W. Prothro and David M. Kovenock of the University of North Carolina at Chapel Hill. It surveyed 7,673 Americans in 1968 and includes one of the largest samples of southern respondents ever collected.

13. In the following analysis "middle class" is based on the self-placement of respondents and includes those who considered themselves either "average middle class" or "upper middle class." Separate analyses were performed for the upper middle class, which was slightly more conservative than the entire middle class on most of the survey data we examined.

Although these results support the conventional wisdom regarding the conservatism of the southern middle class, it should be emphasized that only a minority of these 1968 respondents (23 percent) identified themselves as *strong* conservatives. The southern middle class has a right wing, but that segment of opinion should not be taken as representative of the entire middle class.

14. On the average, 18 percent of the white middle-class respondents in the 1972–1984 surveys took the position that individuals were exclusively responsible for their own economic situation.

15. A few symbols were used only once ("marijuana users" and "gays/lesbians") and some only twice ("police," "evangelicals," and "radical students").

16. The concepts of valence and position issues are discussed in Donald E. Stokes, "Spatial Models of Party Competition," *American Political Science Review,* 57 (June 1963), 372–374.

17. Data on southern unionization have been taken from F. Ray Marshall, *Labor in the South* (Cambridge, Mass.: Harvard University Press, 1967), p. 299; and U.S. Bureau of the Census, *State and Metropolitan Area Data Book: 1982* (Washington, D.C., 1982), p. 502.

18. For a useful discussion of labor union activity across the South in the mid-1970s, see "State-by-State Profiles," *Southern Exposure,* 4, nos. 1–2 (1976), 170–202. This special issue of *Southern Exposure* contains many interesting articles on the southern labor movement.

19. Far and away the best study of southern labor unions is Marshall, *Labor in the South.* "Of all the factors influencing the structure of union organization in the South," Marshall concluded, "the most decisive are the economic, or . . . technological-budgetary constraints, market forces, and the degree of competition. These economic factors influence the ideological, political and social contexts which in turn affect union membership, but . . . the influence of noneconomic forces usually is more indirect." Ibid., p. 312. At the same time, Marshall did not reduce the question of union growth to purely economic considerations. Ibid, p. 309. In addition to the special issue of *Southern Exposure* cited in the previous note, see Cliff Stone and Bob Hall, "It's Good to Be Home in Greenville . . . But It's Better if You Hate Unions," and Michael B. Russell, "Greenville's Experiment: The Non-Union Culture," in *Southern Exposure,* 7 (Spring 1979), 82–93 and 94–97, 100.

The individualistic traits of southern workers were stressed by W. J. Cash, *The*

Mind of the South (New York: Knopf, 1941) and, more recently, by Robert E. Botsch in an intensive study of fifteen North Carolina furniture workers. See Botsch, " 'You Can't Have It Both Ways': The Difficulties of Unionization in the South," in Merle Black and John Shelton Reed, eds., *Perspectives on the American South*, I (New York: Gordon and Breach, 1981), 173–186. Although the biracial character of the southern working class creates obvious opportunities for dividing workers, racial splits are not inevitable. Chandler Davidson emphasizes the common interests of black and white workers and provides numerous examples of interracial cooperation in *Biracial Politics* (Baton Rouge: Louisiana State University Press, 1972), pp. 233–244. Labor's "unrealized potential" in southern politics is succinctly discussed in Jack Bass and Walter DeVries, *The Transformation of Southern Politics* (New York: Basic Books, 1976), pp. 392–396.

20. For an analysis of organized labor's political role outside the South, see J. David Greenstone, *Labor in American Politics* (New York: Knopf, 1969).

21. George B. Rabinowitz, "On the Nature of Political Issues: Insights from a Spatial Analysis," *American Journal of Political Science*, 22 (November 1978), 793–817.

22. The most elaborate case for the possibility of working-class alliances across racial lines in the modern South has been made by Davidson in *Biracial Politics*, pp. 220–276. We find his argument challenging but unpersuasive. See also Paul Luebke, "The Social and Political Bases of a Black Candidate's Coalition: Race, Class, and Ideology in the 1976 North Carolina Primary Election," *Politics and Society*, 9, no. 2 (1979), 239–261. In our opinion sporadic coalitions of southern working-class whites and blacks are possible, but such alliances have been far from the central tendency in the past and will not become central in the future. Our findings are much more consistent with the pessimistic conclusions of Numan V. Bartley and Hugh D. Graham, *Southern Politics and the Second Reconstruction* (Baltimore: Johns Hopkins University Press, 1975), pp. 136–200; and Robert E. Botsch, *We Shall Not Overcome* (Chapel Hill: University of North Carolina Press, 1980).

23. Botsch, " 'You Can't Have It Both Ways.' "

24. John Shelton Reed, "The *Prevailing* South?" in National Humanities Center, *Newsletter*, 5 (Summer 1984), 6.

4. The Old Order

1. For comparative analyses of race relations in the South and South Africa, see especially George M. Fredrickson, *White Supremacy* (New York: Oxford University Press, 1981); and John W. Cell, *The Highest Stage of White Supremacy* (Cambridge: Cambridge University Press, 1982).

2. V. O. Key, Jr., *Southern Politics in State and Nation* (New York: Knopf, 1949), pp. 665, 675.

3. Gunnar Myrdal, *An American Dilemma* (New York: Harper & Row, 1944), p. 219.

4. Herbert Blumer, "The Future of the Color Line," in John C. McKinney

and Edgar T. Thompson, eds., *The South in Continuity and Change* (Durham: Duke University Press, 1965), p. 323.

5. Marion D. Irish, "The Southern One-Party System and National Politics," *Journal of Politics,* 4 (February 1942), 80.

6. John Dollard provides an extended discussion of white gains from southern-style racism in *Caste and Class in a Southern Town* (New Haven: Yale University Press, 1937), pp. 97–219. A particularly thoughtful analysis of black-white relations is Lillian Smith, *Killers of the Dream* (New York: Norton, 1949). For a more recent treatment of segregationist values and practices, see the fascinating work of James W. Loewen, *The Mississippi Chinese: Between Black and White* (Cambridge, Mass.: Harvard University Press, 1971), esp. pp. 1–72.

7. Key, *Southern Politics,* p. 665.

8. Blumer, "Color Line," pp. 322–323.

9. Ibid., pp. 328, 330, 335.

10. Ibid., p. 328.

11. Ibid., pp. 329–330.

12. Ibid., pp. 330–335. (quotation on p. 330).

13. See, for example, Charles S. Bullock III and Charles M. Lamb, eds., *Implementation of Civil Rights Policy* (Monterey, Calif.: Brooks-Cole, 1984); Harrell R. Rodgers, Jr., and Charles S. Bullock III, *Law and Social Change* (New York: McGraw-Hill, 1972); Gary Orfield, *Must We Bus?* (Washington, D.C.: Brookings, 1978); and J. Harvie Wilkinson III, *From Brown to Baake* (New York: Oxford University Press, 1979).

14. Blumer, "Color Line," p. 331.

15. Ibid., p. 335.

16. Horace Mann Bond, *The Education of the Negro in the American Social Order* (New York: Octagon Books, 1966), p. x.

17. W. J. Cash, *The Mind of the South* (New York: Knopf, 1941), p. 428.

18. Ibid., pp. 428–429.

19. See Henry Allen Bullock, *A History of Negro Education in the South* (Cambridge, Mass.: Harvard University Press, 1967).

20. Benjamin E. Mays, *Born to Rebel* (New York: Charles Scribner's Sons, 1971), p. 1.

21. Mays, *Born to Rebel,* pp. 22–23, 25.

22. Ibid., pp. 33–34, 49.

23. The problem of overcoming intimidation and economic dependence is a recurrent theme in studies of the civil rights movement. See especially Anne Moody, *Coming of Age in Mississippi* (New York: Dial Press, 1968); James W. Silver, *Mississippi: The Closed Society* (New York: Harcourt, Brace & World, 1964); and Pat Watters and Reese Cleghorn, *Climbing Jacob's Ladder* (New York: Harcourt, Brace & World, 1967). Mississippi's barriers of intimidation and economic dependence were especially high. See Lester M. Salamon and Stephen Van Evera, "Fear, Apathy, and Discrimination: A Test of Three Explanations of Political Participation," *American Political Science Review,* 67 (December 1973), 1288–1306.

24. Mays, *Born to Rebel,* p. 49.

25. Key's analysis of black politics, for example, did not anticipate the civil rights movement. Myrdal more successfully captured many of the undercurrents of protest among black southerners; see *American Dilemma,* pp. 518–520.

26. Mays, *Born to Rebel,* p. 49.

27. Ibid., p. 35.

28. Myrdal, *American Dilemma,* pp. 720–721, 770 (italics in the original have been omitted). See generally pp. 720–735.

29. Ibid., pp. 721, 770.

30. Ibid., pp. 721, 769–771.

31. Ibid., pp. 776, 824.

32. Howell Raines, *My Soul Is Rested* (New York: G. P. Putnam's Sons, 1977), p. 34.

33. See Key, *Southern Politics,* pp. 619–643; Steven F. Lawson, *Black Ballots* (New York: Columbia University Press, 1976), pp. 23–54; and Richard Kluger, *Simple Justice* (New York: Knopf, 1976), pp. 234–237. Innumerable examples of obstacles to black political participation in the late 1930s and early 1940s are presented in Ralph J. Bunche, *The Political Status of the Negro in the Age of FDR* (Chicago: University of Chicago Press, 1973), pp. 253–571.

34. 321 U.S. 649 (1944).

35. Key, *Southern Politics,* p. 643.

36. Donald R. Matthews and James W. Prothro, *Negroes and the New Southern Politics* (New York: Harcourt, Brace & World, 1966), p. 17.

37. David J. Garrow, *Protest at Selma* (New Haven: Yale University Press, 1978), p. 7.

38. Key, *Southern Politics,* p. 650. See also pp. 5, 661.

39. Ibid., p. 649.

40. Ibid., p. 650.

41. Ibid., pp. 555–598.

42. Ibid., pp. 560, 576.

43. Garrow, *Protest at Selma,* pp. 31–77, 179–211.

44. Key, *Southern Politics,* pp. 579, 617–618.

45. U.S. Bureau of the Census, *The Social and Economic Status of the Black Population in the United States: An Historical View, 1790–1978,* Current Population Reports, Special Studies, series P-23, no. 80 (Washington, D.C.: Government Printing Office, 1979), p. 93.

46. Bond, *Education of the Negro,* pp. 102–103. Inconsistencies in capitalizing "Negro" were in the original quotation.

47. Ibid., pp. 84–115. See also Louis R. Harlan, *Separate and Unequal* (Chapel Hill: University of North Carolina Press, 1958); and Bullock, *History of Negro Education,* pp. 1–166.

48. Bond, *Education of the Negro,* p. 257.

49. Ibid., pp. 151–366; and Bullock, *History of Negro Education,* 167–193.

50. Kluger, *Simple Justice,* pp. 131–137.

51. Ibid., pp. 136–137.

52. Ibid., p. 193. See also Bullock, *History of Negro Education,* pp. 216–219; and Doxey A. Wilkerson, "The Negro School Movement in Virginia: From

'Equalization' to 'Integration,' " *Journal of Negro Education,* 29 (Winter 1960), 17–29.

53. Kluger, *Simple Justice,* pp. 186–194, 202–213.

54. Bullock, *History of Negro Education,* p. 230.

55. Ibid.

56. Wilkerson, "Negro School Movement in Virginia," p.18.

57. Bullock, *History of Negro Education,* p. 219.

58. Data on educational expenditures are presented in Harry S. Ashmore, *The Negro and the Schools* (Chapel Hill: University of North Carolina Press, 1954), pp. 153, 156.

59. Ibid., p. 109.

60. Kluger, *Simple Justice,* p. 302.

61. Ashmore, *Negro and the Schools,* pp. 131–132.

62. Kluger, *Simple Justice,* pp. 293–294.

63. For the basis of the preceding two paragraphs, see ibid., pp. 290–294.

64. Ibid., pp. 3–26, 294–366, 451–507.

65. Ibid., pp. 3–4, 294–305, 365–366.

66. Ibid., pp. 365–366.

67. Ibid., p. 506.

68. 347 U.S. 483 (1954). For an engrossing account of the Supreme Court's handling of the school desegregation cases, see Kluger, *Simple Justice,* pp. 543–747.

69. J. W. Peltason, *Fifty-Eight Lonely Men* (New York: Harcourt, Brace & World, 1961).

70. Kluger, *Simple Justice,* pp. 751–752. This important opinion is also discussed in Jack Bass, *Unlikely Heroes* (New York: Simon and Schuster, 1981), pp. 123–125.

71. Expositions of white segregationist opinion are presented in John Bartlow Martin, *The Deep South Says "Never"* (New York: Ballantine Books, 1957); William D. Workman, Jr., *The Case for the South* (New York: Devin-Adair, 1960); and James J. Kilpatrick, *The Southern Case for School Segregation* (New York: Crowell-Collier, 1962).

72. Numan V. Bartley, *The Rise of Massive Resistance* (Baton Rouge: Louisiana State University Press, 1969), is the leading study. See also Francis M. Wilhoit, *The Politics of Massive Resistance* (New York: Braziller, 1973); Robbins L. Gates, *The Making of Massive Resistance* (Chapel Hill: University of North Carolina Press, 1964); and Benjamin Muse, *Virginia's Massive Resistance* (Bloomington: Indiana University Press, 1961).

73. Ernest Q. Campbell, *When a City Closes Its Schools* (Chapel Hill: Institute for Research in Social Science, 1961).

74. Bartley, *Rise of Massive Resistance,* pp. 77–78.

75. Southern Education Reporting Service, *A Statistical Summary, State by State, of School Segregation-Desegregation in the Southern and Border Area from 1954 to the Present* (Nashville: Southern Education Reporting Service, 1967), pp. 2, 43–44. See also Rodgers and Bullock, *Law and Social Change,* p. 75.

76. Key, *Southern Politics,* p. 650.

77. The classic portrait of black students crossing the color line in elementary education is Robert Coles, *Children of Crisis* (Boston: Atlantic–Little, Brown, 1967).

5. Penetrating the Outer Color Line

1. David J. Garrow integrates the theoretical literature concerning civil rights protest in the final chapter of *Protest at Selma* (New Haven: Yale University Press, 1978), pp. 212–236. See also E. E. Schattschneider, *The Semisovereign People* (New York: Holt, Rinehart & Winston, 1960); and Michael Lipsky, "Protest as a Political Resource," *American Political Science Review*, 62 (December 1968), 1144–58.

2. The protest is discussed in David J. Garrow, *Bearing the Cross: Martin Luther King, Jr., and the Southern Christian Leadership Conference, 1955–1968* (New York: Morrow, 1986); J. Mills Thornton III, "Challenge and Response in the Montgomery Bus Boycott of 1955–1956," *Alabama Review*, 33 (July 1980), 163–235; David L. Lewis, *King: A Critical Biography* (Baltimore: Penguin Books, 1970), pp. 46–84; and Stephen B. Oates, *Let the Trumpet Sound: The Life of Martin Luther King, Jr.* (New York: Harper & Row, 1982), pp. 55–112.

3. Martin Luther King, Jr., *Stride toward Freedom* (New York: Harper & Brothers, 1958) pp. 63–64, 112.

4. Ibid., pp. 53–180; Lewis, *King*, pp. 58–84; and Thornton, "Challenge and Response," p. 211.

5. Thornton, "Challenge and Response," p. 215.

6. King, *Stride*, p. 151.

7. August Meier, "On the Role of Martin Luther King," in August Meier and Elliott Rudwick, eds., *The Making of Black America*, II (New York: Atheneum, 1971), 353–361 (quotation on 354–355). The article originally appeared in *New Politics*, 4 (Winter 1965), 52–59.

8. King, *Stride*, pp. 59–60.

9. The definitive study of King and SCLC is Garrow, *Bearing the Cross*.

10. King, *Stride*, pp. 87, 102.

11. Ibid. pp. 85, 190.

12. Garrow, *Protest at Selma*, p. 221.

13. William C. Havard suggests that Key's thought could be classified in the "Scottish Common Sense School" of philosophy, observing that "throughout his work Key exhibits an openness to the plain meaning of experience, a tendency to accept metaphysical dualism, a rejection of determinism, and a critical moral sense that are characteristic of a developed philosophy of common sense." See "Building on the 'Key' Stone," in Merle Black and John Shelton Reed, eds., *Perspectives on the American South*, II (New York: Gordon and Breach, 1984), 28. One of the blind spots of common sense, of course, is the difficulty of imagining radically different patterns of behavior.

14. Numan V. Bartley and Hugh D. Graham, *Southern Politics and the Second Reconstruction* (Baltimore: Johns Hopkins University Press, 1975), pp. 184–187.

15. Harrell R. Rodgers, Jr., and Charles S. Bullock III, *Law and Social Change* (New York: McGraw-Hill, 1972), pp. 58–59.

16. Clayborne Carson, *In Struggle: SNCC and the Black Awakening of the 1960s* (Cambridge, Mass.: Harvard University Press, 1981), pp. 9–11. The most comprehensive treatment of the Greensboro sit-ins is William H. Chafe, *Civilities and Civil Rights* (New York: Oxford University Press, 1980).

17. Carson, *In Struggle*, pp. 14, 17. See also Donald R. Matthews and James W. Prothro, *Negroes and the New Southern Politics* (New York: Harcourt, Brace & World, 1966), pp. 407–466.

18. Chafe, *Civilities*, p. 99.

19. Carson, *In Struggle*, p. 14.

20. Chafe, *Civilities*, p. 71.

21. See Harvard Sitkoff, *The Struggle for Black Equality* (New York: Hill and Wang, 1981), pp. 76–82.

22. Carson, *In Struggle*, p. 30.

23. August Meier and Elliott Rudwick, *CORE* (New York: Oxford University Press, 1973), p. 135.

24. Pat Watters and Reese Cleghorn, *Climbing Jacob's Ladder* (New York: Harcourt, Brace & World, 1967), p. 45.

25. Meier and Rudwick, *CORE*, p. 136.

26. Ibid., pp. 135–138.

27. Pat Watters, *Down to Now* (New York: Pantheon, 1971), p. 91.

28. Ibid., p. 92.

29. Allison Davis, Burleigh B. Gardner, and Mary R. Gardner, *Deep South*, abridged ed. (Chicago: University of Chicago Press, 1965), p. 344.

30. Meier and Rudwick, *CORE*, pp. 139–143.

31. Carson, *In Struggle*, pp. 35–37; and Victor S. Navasky, *Kennedy Justice* (New York: Atheneum, 1971), pp. 20–24, 96–99.

32. Meier and Rudwick, *CORE*, p. 139.

33. Watters and Cleghorn, *Climbing*, p. 44–45.

34. Ibid., p. 45. See also Howell Raines, *My Soul Is Rested* (New York: G. P. Putnam's Sons, 1977), pp. 123–129.

35. Navasky, *Kennedy Justice*, pp. 23–24.

36. Meier and Rudwick, *CORE*, pp. 143–144.

37. Carson, *In Struggle*, p. 37.

38. Sitkoff, *Struggle for Black Equality*, p. 113.

39. Garrow, *Protest at Selma*, p. 221.

40. Ibid.

41. Ibid., pp. 221–222.

42. Ibid., p. 222.

43. Watters, *Down to Now*, pp. 265–266. This experienced journalist also stressed that "the Birmingham police were, on balance, no worse than most the movement was up against in the South and tamer than the average constabulary encountered by the movement in Mississippi and across the rural black belt." Ibid. See also Garrow, *Protest at Selma*, pp. 2–3.

44. Accounts of the Birmingham protests are contained in Garrow, *Protest*

at Selma, pp. 136–144; Watters, *Down to Now,* pp. 261–270; and Raines, *My Soul is Rested,* pp. 139–185. The leading study of President Kennedy's changing position on and commitment to the civil rights cause is Carl M. Brauer, *John F. Kennedy and the Second Reconstruction* (New York: Columbia University Press, 1977).

45. Meier and Rudwick, *CORE,* p. 214.

46. Garrow, *Protest at Selma,* p. 3.

47. Bayard Rustin, *Down the Line* (Chicago: Quadrangle Books, 1971), pp. 112, 115. See also James Q. Wilson, "The Negro in Politics," *Daedalus,* 94 (Fall 1965), 949–973.

48. Garrow, *Protest at Selma,* pp. 148–149; and Sitkoff, *Struggle for Black Equality,* pp. 136–143.

49. Sitkoff, *Struggle for Black Equality,* p. 149.

50. Chafe, *Civilities,* p. 146.

51. Sitkoff, *Struggle for Black Equality,* p. 149.

52. Rodgers and Bullock, *Law and Social Change,* p. 62. See pp. 63–66 for a discussion of compliance with the public accommodations provisions.

53. George H. Gallup, *The Gallup Poll: Public Opinion, 1935–1971* (New York: Random House, 1972), vols. I–III.

54. Harold C. Fleming, "The Federal Executive and Civil Rights: 1961–1965," *Daedalus,* 94 (Fall 1965), 941–942.

55. Gallup, *The Gallup Poll,* III, 1812, 1842, 1881, 1883–84, 1894–95, 1898, 1905, 1908, 1934, 1939, 1944, 1957, 1966, 1973–74, and 1979.

56. Sitkoff, *Struggle for Black Equality,* pp. 164–165.

57. Gallup, *The Gallup Poll,* III, 1837–38, 1933.

58. Fleming, "The Executive and Civil Rights," pp. 940–945; and Brauer, *Kennedy and the Second Reconstruction,* pp. 230–320.

59. See, for example, Rowland Evans and Robert Novak, *Lyndon B. Johnson: The Exercise of Power* (New York: New American Library, 1966), pp. 31–33, 65, 287–288.

60. Rustin, *Down the Line,* p. 111.

61. Rodgers and Bullock, *Law and Social Change,* pp. 63–64.

62. Data reported in this paragraph are based on tables in Garrow, *Protest at Selma,* pp. 7, 11. For a detailed discussion of the struggle for voting rights during this period, see Steven F. Lawson, *Black Ballots* (New York: Columbia University Press, 1976).

63. *Report of the U.S. Commission on Civil Rights, 1959* (Washington, D.C.: Government Printing Office, 1959); and *1961 U.S. Commission on Civil Rights Report* (Washington, D.C.: Government Printing Office, 1961). The best discussion of the reliability of the registration estimates is Donald R. Matthews and James W. Prothro, "Social and Economic Factors and Negro Voter Registration in the South," *American Political Science Review,* 62 (March 1963), 26.

64. Matthews and Prothro, *New Southern Politics,* pp. 115, 118, 120.

65. Ibid., p. 126.

66. Previous studies of black registration during the 1950s in specific states had discovered higher registration rates among blacks in some rural counties

than in the largest metropolitan counties. See H.D. Price, *The Negro and Southern Politics* (New York: New York University Press, 1957), esp. pp. 44–45; and John H. Fenton and Kenneth N. Vines, "Negro Registration in Louisiana," *American Political Science Review*, 51 (September 1957), 710–711. Fenton and Vines also pointed out (p. 711): "Even though the urban centers do not provide favorable environments for securing a high proportion of Negro registration, the 'pilot' role of activities in urban centers toward launching Negro registration is important. In all parishes studied the registration of Negroes was initiated by business and professional Negroes residing in the major urban center of the parish. In the event resistance to Negro registration made it necessary to resort to legal and political action, the city provided the resources and locus for suits against the registrar, for requests to the F.B.I. to investigate reluctant registrars, and for bargains which might be negotiated with courthouse politicians."

67. V. O. Key, Jr., *Southern Politics in State and Nation* (New York: Knopf, 1949), p. 651. Based on his investigation of black politics in urban Florida, Price argued that "intensive efforts to register Negro voters without reaching a *modus vivendi* with local white candidates and without producing tangible results are likely to have little permanent effect." See his *Negro and Southern Politics*, p. 56.

68. Matthews and Prothro, *New Southern Politics*, pp. 115–116.

69. Price, *The Negro and Southern Politics*, p. 55, stressed the encouragement that white Democratic politicians gave to blacks in Jacksonville. He also observed that areas of extensive Republican growth in Florida were generally poor sites for increased black registration (p. 56). In 1960 Orange County, Florida, and Fairfax County, Virginia, two areas of unusually pronounced Yankee in-migration, had fewer than one-fifth of their eligible blacks registered.

70. For discussions of Memphis, see Key, *Southern Politics*, pp. 58–75; and Harry Holloway, *The Politics of the Southern Negro* (New York: Random House, 1969), pp. 272–309.

71. Watters and Cleghorn, *Climbing*, p. 76. Other valuable studies of black politics in southern cities include Chandler Davidson, *Biracial Politics* (Baton Rouge: Louisiana State University Press, 1972); Holloway, *Politics of the Southern Negro*; Everett Carll Ladd, Jr., *Negro Political Leadership in the South* (Ithaca: Cornell University Press, 1966); Daniel C. Thompson, *The Negro Leadership Class* (Englewood Cliffs, N.J.: Prentice-Hall, 1963); William R. Keech, *The Impact of Negro Voting* (Chicago: Rand McNally, 1968); and Chafe, *Civilities*.

72. Harry Holloway, "The Negro and the Vote: The Case of Texas," *Journal of Politics*, 23 (August 1961), 541.

73. Chafe, *Civilities*, p. 18.

74. Watters and Cleghorn, *Climbing*, p. 82.

75. Holloway, "Negro and the Vote," p. 541.

76. Ibid., p. 527.

77. Key, *Southern Politics*, p. 655.

78. Holloway, "Negro and the Vote," pp. 542–556; and Alfred B. Clubok, John M. DeGrove, and Charles D. Farris, "The Manipulated Negro Vote: Some

Pre-Conditions and Consequences," *Journal of Politics*, 26 (February 1964), 112–129.

79. Holloway, "Negro and the Vote," p. 527.

80. Clubok, DeGrove, and Farris, "Manipulated Negro Vote," p. 117.

81. Holloway, "Negro and the Vote," pp. 541–556.

82. Ibid., pp. 553–554.

83. Watters and Cleghorn, *Climbing*, pp. 41–279, esp. pp. 55–59; Navasky, *Kennedy Justice*, pp. 96–155; Carson, *In Struggle*, pp. 38–39; and Brauer, *Kennedy and the Second Reconstruction*, pp. 112–116.

84. Watters and Cleghorn, *Climbing*, p. 48.

85. Ibid., pp. 114–115.

86. Ibid., pp. 113–143; and Garrow, *Protest at Selma*, p. 20.

87. These generalizations draw upon Watters and Cleghorn, *Climbing*, pp. 113–209.

88. See Lester M. Salamon and Stephen Van Evera, "Fear, Apathy, and Discrimination: A Test of Three Explanations of Political Participation," *American Political Science Review*, 67 (December 1973), 1288–1306; Anne Moody, *Coming of Age in Mississippi* (New York: Dial Press, 1968); and Raines, *My Soul Is Rested*, pp. 233–290.

89. Carson, *In Struggle*, pp. 45–129; Watters and Cleghorn, *Climbing*, pp. 210–243; Moody, *Coming of Age in Mississippi;* and Howard Zinn, *SNCC: The New Abolitionists* (Boston: Beacon Press, 1965), pp. 190–215.

90. Watters and Cleghorn, *Climbing*, p. 101. Their discussion of the black middle class (pp. 92–107) is especially interesting.

91. This theme is discussed in Lester M. Salamon, "Leadership and Modernization: The Emerging Black Political Elite in the American South," *Journal of Politics*, 35 (August 1973), 622–627.

92. Watters and Cleghorn, *Climbing*, pp. 124–127.

93. Ibid., pp. 64–65.

94. U.S. Commission on Civil Rights, *Political Participation* (Washington, D.C.: Government Printing Office, 1968), pp. 224–253.

95. Garrow, *Protest at Selma*, p. 19.

96. Laughlin McDonald, *Voting Rights in the South* (New York: American Civil Liberties Union, 1982), p. 15.

97. Garrow, *Protest at Selma*, esp. pp. 31–132, 212–236.

98. Ibid., pp. 222–223.

99. McDonald, *Voting Rights,* p. 16.

100. Merle Black, "Racial Composition of Congressional Districts and Support for Federal Voting Rights in the American South," *Social Science Quarterly*, 59 (December 1978), 442.

6. The Limited Leverage of a Franchised Minority

1. Donald R. Matthews and James W. Prothro, *Negroes and the New Southern Politics* (New York: Harcourt, Brace & World, 1966), pp. 478, 481. See

also Joe R. Feagin and Harlan Hahn, "The Second Reconstruction: Black Political Strength in the South," *Social Science Quarterly,* 51 (June 1970), 42–56; and Charles S. Bullock III, "The Election of Blacks in the South: Preconditions and Consequences," *American Journal of Political Science,* 19 (November 1975), 727–739.

2. See William R. Keech, *The Impact of Negro Voting* (Chicago: Rand McNally, 1968); and Earl Black, *Southern Governors and Civil Rights* (Cambridge, Mass.: Harvard University Press, 1976, pp. 342–344.

3. James Q. Wilson, "The Negro in Politics," *Daedalus,* 94 (Fall 1965), 949.

4. Matthews and Prothro, *New Southern Politics,* p. 478.

5. For analyses of the social and economic conditions affecting blacks in the 1960s, see, for example, St. Clair Drake, "The Social and Economic Status of the Negro in the United States," *Daedalus,* 94 (Fall 1965), 771–814; Kenneth Clark, *Dark Ghetto* (New York: Harper & Row, 1965); and Sar A. Levitan, William B. Johnston, and Robert Taggart, *Still a Dream: The Changing Status of Blacks since 1960* (Cambridge, Mass.: Harvard University Press, 1975).

6. SRC-CPS national survey of 1968; respondents giving "don't know" answers have been excluded.

7. Harvard Sitkoff, *The Struggle for Black Equality* (New York: Hill and Wang, 1981), p. 200.

8. Ibid., p. 209.

9. On this transition, see Clayborne Carson, *In Struggle: SNCC and the Black Awakening of the 1960s* (Cambridge, Mass.: Harvard University Press, 1981), pp. 111–190; August Meier and Elliott Rudwick, *CORE* (New York: Oxford University Press, 1973), pp. 259–357; and Sitkoff, *Struggle for Black Equality,* pp. 167–212.

10. See Stokely Carmichael and Charles V. Hamilton, *Black Power* (New York: Vintage Books, 1967), esp. pp. 58–84.

11. Carson, *In Struggle,* pp. 190–206; and Meier and Rudwick, *CORE,* pp. 374–431.

12. Carson, *In Struggle,* p. 208.

13. Ibid., p. 209.

14. Ibid., pp. 209–210.

15. Martin Luther King, Jr., *Where Do We Go from Here: Chaos or Community?* (New York: Bantam Books, 1967), pp. 27–77.

16. Carson, *In Struggle,* pp. 216, 218–219. See Carmichael and Hamilton, *Black Power,* for the most widely publicized exposition of the ideology.

17. Samuel DuBois Cook, "The Tragic Myth of Black Power," *New South,* 21 (Summer 1966), 58–59.

18. Ibid., p. 62. See Joel D. Aberbach and Jack L. Walker, "The Meanings of Black Power: A Comparison of White and Black Interpretations of a Political Slogan," *American Political Science Review,* 64 (June 1970), 367–388.

19. Cook, "Myth of Black Power," pp. 58, 60.

20. See, for example, Meier and Rudwick, *CORE,* pp. 429–430. Carson chronicles the collapse of SNCC in *In Struggle,* pp. 215–303.

21. Sitkoff, *Struggle for Black Equality,* pp. 219–220. See David J. Garrow, *The FBI and Martin Luther King, Jr.* (New York: Norton, 1981).

22. Carson, *In Struggle,* p. 288.

23. Sitkoff, *Struggle for Black Equality,* pp. 221–222.

24. Data for 1968 have been taken from Voter Education Project, *Voter Registration in the South: Summer, 1968* (Atlanta: Southern Regional Council, 1968). According to Mack Jones, "Political activists in many jurisdictions question the reliability of the estimates available. Estimates of black registration are thought to be inflated." See Jones, "Black Officeholding and Political Development in the Rural South," *Review of Black Political Economy,* 6 (Summer 1976), 383.

25. Our discussion is based primarily on David J. Garrow, *Protest at Selma* (New Haven: Yale University Press, 1978), pp. 179–211. Excellent studies of the enforcement of the Voting Rights Act include Howard Ball, Dale Krane, and Thomas P. Lauth, *Compromised Compliance: Implementation of the 1965 Voting Rights Act* (Westport, Conn.: Greenwood Press, 1982); and Richard Scher and James Button, "Voting Rights Act: Implementation and Impact," in Charles S. Bullock III and Charles M. Lamb, eds., *Implementation of Civil Rights Policy* (Monterey, Calif.: Brooks-Cole, 1983), pp. 20–54.

26. Scher and Button, "Voting Rights Act," p. 49.

27. Garrow, *Protest at Selma,* p. 181.

28. Ibid. The calculation is based on information contained in Jones, "Black Officeholding," pp. 384–385.

29. Garrow, *Protest at Selma,* p. 186; these data are also discussed in Harrell R. Rodgers, Jr., and Charles S. Bullock III, *Law and Social Change* (New York: McGraw-Hill, 1972), p. 34. See also U.S. Commission on Civil Rights, *Political Participation* (Washington, D.C.: Government Printing Office, 1968), p. 155.

30. The number of covered counties is given in Jones, "Black Officeholding," p. 384. Counties to which examiners have been sent are listed in U.S. Commission on Civil Rights, *The Voting Rights Act: Unfulfilled Goals* (Washington, D.C.: Government Printing Office, 1981), pp. 101–104.

31. Jones, "Black Officeholding," pp. 384–385. "As late as mid-1968," Scher and Button observed, "examiners functioned in only 58 of 185 counties in which fewer than 50 percent of adult blacks were registered." See their "Voting Rights Act," p. 32.

32. Jones, "Black Officeholding," p. 384.

33. Ibid., p. 376.

34. Scher and Button, "Voting Rights Act," pp. 41–43.

35. U.S. Bureau of the Census, *Statistical Abstract of the United States: 1982–83* (Washington, D.C.: Government Printing Office, 1982), p. 488.

36. Matthews and Prothro, *New Southern Politics,* pp. 115–120; Johnnie Daniel, "Negro Political Behavior and Community Political and Socioeconomic Structural Factors," *Social Forces,* 47 (March 1969), 274–279; and Merle Black, "Racial Composition of Congressional Districts and Support for Federal Voting

Rights in the American South," *Social Science Quarterly,* 59 (December 1978), 435–450.

37. U.S. Commission on Civil Rights, *Political Participation,* pp. 224–256.

38. Richard Murray and Arnold Vedlitz, "Race, Socioeconomic Status, and Voting Participation in Large Southern Cities," *Journal of Politics,* 39 (November 1977), 1064–72, and "Racial Voting Patterns in the South: An Analysis of Major Elections from 1960 to 1977 in Five Cities," *The Annals,* 439 (September 1978), 29–39.

39. Murray and Vedlitz, "Race," p. 1070.

40. Sidney Verba, Bashiruddin Ahmed, and Anit Bhatt, *Caste, Race, and Politics* (Beverly Hills: Sage, 1971), p. 243.

41. Black, *Southern Governors,* pp. 326–334.

42. For similar observations on the 1960s, see Numan V. Bartley, *From Thurmond to Wallace* (Baltimore: Johns Hopkins University Press, 1970), p. 9; and Numan V. Bartley and Hugh D. Graham, *Southern Politics and the Second Reconstruction* (Baltimore: Johns Hopkins University Press), p. 188.

43. See Earl Black and Merle Black, "The Changing Setting of Minority Politics in the American Deep South," in Tinsley E. Yarbrough, John P. East and Sandra Hough, eds., *Politics 73: Minorities in Politics* (Greenville, N.C.: East Carolina University Publications, 1973), pp. 35–50.

44. See Harold W. Stanley, "Explaining Electoral Mobilization: White Southerners and Racial Backlash, 1952–1980" (Paper presented at the 1981 meeting of the Southern Political Science Association, Memphis, Tennessee).

45. Black, *Southern Governors,* pp. 330–334; Earl Black, "Competing Responses to the 'New Southern Politics': Republican and Democratic Southern Strategies, 1964–1976," in Merle Black and John Shelton Reed, eds., *Perspectives on the American South,* I (New York: Gordon and Breach, 1981), 151–164.

46. Wilson, "Negro in Politics," p. 951.

47. Senator Jesse Helms of North Carolina, one of a small number of southern politicians who keep alive the tradition of race-baiting, began a televised debate with Governor Jim Hunt in 1984 by attacking the governor's support among North Carolina blacks. Helms was reelected, but with the lowest percentage of any incumbent Republican senator in the South.

48. Wilson, "Negro in Politics," p. 950.

49. Scher and Button, "Voting Rights Act," p. 44.

50. The 1982 results were compiled from data in Joint Center for Political Studies, *National Roster of Black Elected Officials,* XII (Washington, D.C.: JCPS, 1982), xvi-xvii.

51. Jones, "Black Officeholding," p. 405.

52. Ibid., pp. 376 (quotation), 385–386.

53. Chandler Davidson, "Minority Vote Dilution," in Chandler Davidson, ed., *Minority Vote Dilution* (Washington, D.C.: Howard University Press, 1984), p. 20.

54. Garrow, *Protest at Selma,* p. 192.

55. J. Morgan Kousser, "The Undermining of the First Reconstruction," in Davidson, ed., *Minority Vote Dilution,* pp. 31–32.

56. We are not arguing that the purpose or consequence of these techniques or practices is necessarily to weaken the voting strength of blacks, but that these devices might be so used. As Davidson acknowledges, it is not easy to define the concept of dilution: "The essential characteristics of vote dilution are difficult to specify. In spite of two decades of vote dilution litigation and a number of articles on the subject in law reviews and other scholarly journals, no concise and comprehensive definition has emerged." He concludes that "what seems to be common to the various types of vote discrimination dealt with . . . under the label *dilution* is a process whereby election laws or practices, either singly or in concert, combine with systematic bloc voting among an identifiable group to diminish the voting strength of at least one other group." See *Minority Vote Dilution*, p. 4.

For an interesting discussion of the problems and dilemmas in assessing the consequences of various techniques and practices, see Susan A. MacManus and Charles S. Bullock III, "Racial Representation Issues: The Role of Experts in Determining Dilution of Minority Influence," *PS,* 18 (Fall 1985), 759–769. See also Alexander P. Lamis, "The Runoff Controversy: Implications for Southern Politics," *PS,* 17 (Fall 1984), 782–787; and Harold W. Stanley, "The Runoff: The Case for Retention," *PS,* 18 (Spring 1985), 231–236.

57. Davidson, ed., *Minority Vote Dilution;* Steven F. Lawson, *In Pursuit of Power* (New York: Columbia University Press, 1985), p. xii; and Scher and Button, "Voting Rights Act," p. 34.

58. Kousser, "Undermining the First Reconstruction," p. 36.

59. Wilson, "Negro in Politics," pp. 951–958.

60. Joint Center for Political Studies, *National Roster of Black Elected Officials,* pp. xvi-xvii.

61. Thomas R. Dye, "State Legislative Politics," in Herbert Jacob and Kenneth N. Vines, eds., *Politics in the American States,* 2nd ed. (Boston: Little, Brown, 1971), p. 177.

62. Chandler Davidson and George Korbel, "At-Large Elections and Minority-Group Representation: A Re-Examination of Historical and Contemporary Evidence," *Journal of Politics,* 43 (November 1981), 982–1005; and U.S. Commission on Civil Rights, *The Voting Rights Act: Unfulfilled Goals,* pp. 38–63.

63. Dye, "State Legislative Politics," p. 177.

64. Jones, "Black Officeholding," p. 386.

65. For a stimulating comparative analysis, see Peter K. Eisinger, *The Politics of Displacement: Racial and Ethnic Transition in Three American Cities* (New York: Academic Press, 1980).

7. Confronting the Intermediate Color Line

1. The stages identified here are similar to distinctions made by A. B. Cochran, "Desegregating Public Education in North Carolina," in Thad L. Beyle and Merle Black, eds., *Politics and Policy in North Carolina* (New York: MSS Information Corp., 1975), pp. 198–213; and by Michael R. Fitzgerald and Robert F. Durant, "Southern Schools Twenty-Five Years after *Brown:* White Flight and

Urban Public School Desegregation" (Paper delivered at the 1980 Citadel Symposium on Southern Politics, Charleston, S.C., March 27–29, 1980), pp. 1–8. See also Harrell R. Rodgers, Jr., and Charles S. Bullock III, *Law and Social Change* (New York: McGraw-Hill, 1972), pp. 69–111; Harrell R. Rodgers, Jr., and Charles S. Bullock III, *Coercion to Compliance* (Lexington, Mass.: Heath, 1976); Charles S. Bullock III, "Equal Education Opportunity," in Charles S. Bullock III and Charles M. Lamb, eds., *Implementation of Civil Rights Policy* (Monterey, Calif.: Brooks-Cole, 1983), pp. 55–92; Benjamin Muse, *Ten Years of Prelude* (New York: Viking, 1964); Gary Orfield, *The Reconstruction of Southern Education* (New York: Wiley-Interscience, 1969), and *Must We Bus?* Washington, D.C.: Brookings, 1978); J. Harvie Wilkinson III, *From Brown to Baake* (New York: Oxford University Press, 1979); U.S. Commission on Civil Rights, *Twenty Years after Brown* (Washington, D.C., n.d.); Thomas F. Pettigrew and M. Richard Cramer, "The Demography of Desegregation," *Journal of Social Issues,* 15 (October 1959), 61–71; Donald R. Matthews and James W. Prothro, "Stateways versus Folkways: Critical Factors in Southern Reactions to *Brown v. Board of Education,*" in Gottfried Dietze, ed., *Essays on the American Constitution* (Englewood Cliffs: Prentice-Hall, 1964), pp. 130–156; James W. Prothro, "Stateways versus Folkways Revisited: An Error in Prediction," *Journal of Politics,* 34 (May 1972), 352–364; Beth E. Vanfossen, "Variables Related to Resistance to Desegregation in the South," *Social Forces,* 47 (September 1968), 39–44; Michael W. Giles, "H.E.W. versus the Federal Courts: A Comparison of School Desegregation Enforcement," *American Politics Quarterly,* 3 (January 1975), 81–90; and Michael W. Giles, "Black Concentration and School District Size as Predictors of School Segregation: The Impact of Federal Enforcement," *Sociology of Education,* 48 (Fall 1975), 411–419.

2. See chapter 4 for a discussion of the consequences of *Briggs v. Elliot.*

3. J.W. Peltason, *Fifty-Eight Lonely Men* (New York: Harcourt, Brace & World, 1961); and Jack Bass, *Unlikely Heroes* (New York: Simon and Schuster, 1981).

4. Orfield, *Reconstruction of Southern Education;* and Bullock, "Equal Education Opportunity."

5. Orfield, *Reconstruction of Southern Education,* p. 1.

6. See *Green v. County School Board of New Kent County,* 391 U.S. 430 (1968); and *Alexander v. Holmes County Board of Education,* 396 U.S. 19 (1969).

7. Orfield, *Must We Bus?* pp. 285–297; and Leon Panetta and Peter Gall, *Bring Us Together* (New York: Lippincott, 1971).

8. U.S. Civil Rights Commission, *Twenty Years,* p. 49.

9. We have defined blacks as isolated from whites if whites constitute less than 10 percent of a school's total enrollment. By this criterion, 22 percent of southern black students attended racially isolated schools in 1976–1977. If we had used a 20 percent ceiling on whites to indicate isolation, the percentage of "racially isolated" blacks would obviously have increased, though it would probably not have exceeded 30 percent of the region's black students. The Civil Rights Commission reported that 30 percent of southern blacks in 1972 attended "pre-

dominantly minority" schools, defined as 80 to 100 percent black in total enrollment. Ibid.

10. Department of Health, Education, and Welfare, Office for Civil Rights, *Directory of Elementary and Secondary School Districts, and Schools in Selected School Districts: School Year 1976–1977* (Washington, D.C.: HEW, n.d.), vols. I–II.

11. Our indicator, which defines desegregation for blacks in terms of a particular percentage of whites enrolled in a school, is similar to Prothro's measure in "Stateways versus Folkways Revisited," p. 356. "Our focus is on the percentage of blacks in integrated schools," Prothro observed. "In order not to count a school as integrated if several hundred blacks are attending a school that has only three or four white pupils, we have used a 20 percent cut-off point. If 20 percent or more of the pupils in a school are white, then the blacks attending that school are counted as attending a desegregated school." Since we wished to distinguish blacks who attended all-black or virtually all-black schools from blacks who did not, we used a lower ceiling on the percentage of whites.

Other studies have defined isolation or segregation in terms of a percentage of blacks in a public school. The U.S. Commission on Civil Rights originally defined a racially isolated school as one composed of 90 to 100 percent Negroes. See *Racial Isolation in the Public Schools* (Washington, D.C.: 1967), pp. 2–7. Thomas R. Dye used the same indicator in his reanalysis of public school segregation in 1965–66. See his "Urban School Segregation: A Comparative Analysis," *Urban Affairs Quarterly*, 4 (December 1968), 142.

It should be noted that we are not measuring the degree of racial balance within a given school system, i.e., the extent to which all schools within a particular system reflect the racial composition of the school system as a whole. This is a different question, for which Michael W. Giles has developed an appropriate indicator. See his "Measuring School Desegregation," *Journal of Negro Education*, 43 (Fall 1974), 517–523.

12. See Orfield, *Must We Bus?* esp. pp. 391–420.

13. 418 U.S. 717 (1974).

14. Orfield, *Must We Bus?* p. 417.

15. See, for example, *Swann v. Charlotte-Mecklenburg Board of Education*, 402 U.S. 1 (1971).

16. Orfield, *Must We Bus?* pp. 400–402.

17. Mark Lowry II, "Schools in Transition," *Annals of the Association of American Geographers*, 63 (June 1973), 178. The available data do not permit precise knowledge, but our estimates suggest that the most common patterns of school attendance in the black belt counties in 1976–77 were biracial public schools coexisting with private schools servicing a large minority of whites. Considering the long-standing resistance of black belt whites to any racial change, it is rather surprising that more than half of the white students in these majority black rural counties appeared to be enrolled in the public schools.

18. George H. Gallup, *The Gallup Poll: Public Opinion, 1972–1977*, I (Wilmington, Del.: Scholarly Resources, Inc., 1978), 370–371.

19. Ibid., pp. 178–179.

20. Donald R. Matthews and James W. Prothro, *Negroes and the New Southern Politics* (New York: Harcourt, Brace & World, 1966), pp. 351–358.

21. Bullock, "Equal Education Opportunity," p. 55. For analyses of desegregation in southern higher education, see Q. Whitfield Ayres, "Racial Desegregation in Higher Education," in Bullock and Lamb, eds., *Implementation of Civil Rights Policy,* pp. 118–147; and Q. Whitfield Ayres, "Racial Desegregation, Higher Education, and Student Achievement," *Journal of Politics,* 44 (May 1982), 337–364.

22. Robert J. Steamer, "Southern Disaffection with the National Democratic Party," in Allan P. Sindler, ed., *Change in the Contemporary South* (Durham: Duke University Press, 1963), p. 152.

23. William Julius Wilson, *The Declining Significance of Race,* 2nd ed. (Chicago: University of Chicago Press, 1980). For a good discussion of equal employment opportunities, see Harrell R. Rodgers, Jr., "Fair Employment Laws for Minorities: An Evaluation of Federal Implementation," in Bullock and Lamb, eds., *Implementation of Civil Rights Policy,* pp. 93–117.

24. Thomas J. Naylor and James Clotfelter, *Strategies for Change in the South* (Chapel Hill: University of North Carolina Press, 1975), p. 10. The discussion is based on data reported in the Census of Population for 1960 and for 1980.

25. Virginia and Texas had much higher patterns of white family income than the other southern states, patterns that placed them in proximity to Massachusetts, New York, and Pennsylvania.

26. Naylor and Clotfelter, *Strategies for Change,* p. 10.

27. For a convenient review of the problem, see Paul E. Mertz, *New Deal Policy and Southern Rural Poverty* (Baton Rouge: Louisiana State University Press, 1978).

28. Nick Kotz provides a revealing account in *Let Them Eat Promises* (Englewood Cliffs: Prentice-Hall, 1969).

29. Southern poverty rates have been calculated from the U.S. Bureau of the Census, *1970 Census of Population,* I, *Characteristics of the Population* (Washington, D.C.: Government Printing Office, 1973), appropriate state reports, table 58; and *1980 Census of Population,* I, *Characteristics of the Population* (Washington D.C.: Government Printing Office, 1983), appropriate state reports, tables 82 and 92.

30. For example, although large majorities of whites and blacks expressed warmth toward the symbol "poor people" in the CPS surveys, only 41 percent of white southerners felt warm toward "people on welfare," compared with 80 percent of southern blacks. The other whites and blacks were either cold or indifferent toward the symbol "people on welfare." This is one of the reasons why it is quite difficult to organize southern whites successfully on the issue of assisting poor people through governmental programs.

31. Robert E. Botsch, *We Shall Not Overcome* (Chapel Hill: University of North Carolina Press, 1980), p. 160.

32. George H. Gallup, *The Gallup Poll: Public Opinion 1935–1971* (New York: Random House, 1972), II, 1059.

33. SRC-CPS presidential election year survey.

8. The Changing Electorate

1. V. O. Key, Jr., *Southern Politics in State and Nation* (New York: Knopf, 1949), p. 526.

2. Ibid., pp. 489, 508.

3. Walter Dean Burnham, "The Changing Shape of the American Political Universe," *American Political Science Review*, 59 (March 1965), 23.

4. In estimating turnout rates, we have used a variety of U.S. Census reports as sources of the voting age population and have taken the popular votes from *Congressional Quarterly's Guide to U.S. Elections* (Washington, D.C.: Congressional Quarterly, 1975), and various volumes of Richard M. Scammon's indispensable series, *America Votes*.

5. Key, *Southern Politics*, p. 523.

6. George B. Tindall, *The Disruption of the Solid South* (Athens: University of Georgia Press, 1972), pp. 51–52.

7. According to estimates by Walter Dean Burnham, turnout in the 1980 presidential election in the South was 50.0 percent, compared to 56.9 percent in the non-South. See Burnham, "The 1980 Earthquake: Realignment, Reaction, or What?" in Thomas Ferguson and Joel Rogers, eds., *The Hidden Election* (New York: Pantheon, 1981), p. 101.

8. Key, *Southern Politics*, p. 407.

9. See, for example, Larry Sabato, *The Democratic Party Primary in Virginia* (Charlottesville: University Press of Virginia, 1977).

10. Key gave particular attention to the isolation of southern state politics from the battle for the presidency. See *Southern Politics*, pp. 506–508. For a recent analysis that emphasizes higher levels of gubernatorial turnout in presidential than nonpresidential years, see Samuel C. Patterson and Gregory A. Caldeira, "Getting Out the Vote: Participation in Gubernatorial Elections," *American Political Science Review*, 77 (September 1983), 675–689.

11. See, for example, Lawrence C. Goodwyn, "Populist Dreams and Negro Rights: East Texas as a Case Study," *American Historical Review*, 76 (December 1971), 1435–56; Theodore Rosengarten, *All God's Dangers: The Life of Nate Shaw* (New York: Knopf, 1974); T. Harry Williams, *Huey Long* (New York: Knopf, 1969); and Nell Irvin Painter, *The Narrative of Hosea Hudson: His Life as a Negro Communist in the South* (Cambridge, Mass.: Harvard University Press, 1979).

12. Self-reports of turnout are notoriously unreliable, and the absolute levels calculated for various subgroups appear to be highly exaggerated. The leading analyses of the accuracy of SRC-CPS turnout data are Aage R. Clausen, "Response Validity: Vote Report," *Public Opinion Quarterly*, 32 (Winter 1968–69), 588–606; Steven Rosenstone and Raymond Wolfinger, "The Effect of Registration Laws on Voter Turnout," *American Political Science Review*, 72 (March 1978), 41–43; and Paul R. Abramson and William Claggett, "Race-Related Differences in Self-Reported and Validated Turnout," *Journal of Politics*, 46 (August 1984), 719–738.

13. Donald R. Matthews and James W. Prothro, *Negroes and the New South-*

ern Politics (New York: Harcourt, Brace & World, 1966), pp. 65–70; and Carol A. Cassel, "Change in Electoral Participation in the South," *Journal of Politics,* 41 (August 1979), 907–917.

14. Cassel, "Change in Electoral Participation," p. 917.

15. These generalizations are based on SRC-CPS and Census Bureau surveys.

16. Cassel, "Change in Electoral Participation," stresses this conclusion.

17. Harold W. Stanley emphasizes increases in formal education as a major explanation of rising southern turnout in presidential elections. See his "Explaining Electoral Mobilization: White Southerners and Racial Backlash, 1952–1980" (Paper presented at the 1981 meeting of the Southern Political Science Association, Memphis, Tennessee).

18. Paul Allen Beck and Paul Lopatto, "The End of Southern Distinctiveness," in Laurence W. Moreland, Tod A. Baker, and Robert P. Steed, eds., *Contemporary Southern Political Attitudes and Behavior* (New York: Praeger, 1982), pp. 160–182; and Paul Allen Beck, "Partisan Dealignment in the Postwar South," *American Political Science Review,* 71 (June 1977), 477–496.

19. Key, *Southern Politics,* pp. 526–528. One of Key's greatest strengths as a student of politics was his lack of embarrassment in emphasizing the obvious when important consequences for the functioning of a political system were at stake.

9. Contemporary Racial Attitudes

1. C. Vann Woodward, *The Burden of Southern History* (Baton Rouge: Louisiana State University Press, 1960), p. 16.

2. John Shelton Reed, "Southerners," in Stephan Thernstrom, ed., *Harvard Encyclopedia of American Ethnic Groups* (Cambridge, Mass.: Harvard University Press, 1980), p. 944.

3. See Merle Black and John Shelton Reed, "Blacks and Southerners: A Research Note," *Journal of Politics,* 44 (February 1982), 165–171.

4. Reed, "Southerners," pp. 945, 948.

5. As did Daniel Elazar in his pioneering work, *American Federalism,* 2nd ed. (New York: Thomas Y. Crowell, 1972), Samuel C. Patterson has stressed the importance of comparing subjective orientations to politics in the American states. See "The Political Cultures of the American States," *Journal of Politics,* 30 (February 1968), 187–209. Frequency distributions for regions and thirteen states, covering more than 200 questions asked in the Comparative State Elections Project, are presented in Merle Black, David M. Kovenock, and William C. Reynolds, *Political Attitudes in the Nation and States* (Chapel Hill: Institute for Research in Social Science, 1974). The topics we have chosen to analyze in this chapter and the next obviously do not exhaust all the aspects of southern culture that are helpful in understanding southern political behavior. John Shelton Reed's creative scholarship has been particularly instructive: *The Enduring South* (Chapel Hill: University of North Carolina Press, 1974), *One South* (Baton Rouge: Louisiana State University Press, 1982), and *Southerners* (Chapel Hill: University of North Carolina Press, 1983) describe and analyze the core cultural values of

white southerners and emphasize the importance of religion, family ties, and attachments to persons, places, and things in the region. See also W. J. Cash, *The Mind of the South* (New York: Knopf, 1941); George Brown Tindall, *The Ethnic Southerners* (Baton Rouge: Louisiana State University Press, 1976); Louis D. Rubin, Jr., ed., *The American South: Portrait of a Culture* (Washington, D.C.: Voice of America Forum Series, 1979); and Charles Grier Sellers, Jr., ed., *The Southerner as American* (New York: Dutton, 1960). Key's marvelous sketches of different political cultures in southern states capture variations in the style, tone, and content of politics in the 1940s; see the state chapters in V. O. Key, Jr., *Southern Politics in State and Nation* (New York: Knopf, 1949).

6. Thomas F. Pettigrew, *Racially Separate or Together?* (New York: McGraw-Hill, 1971), pp. 187–188.

7. In some aspects of politics, especially those involving *national* political stimuli, the South has clearly become much more similar to the rest of the nation, as Paul Allen Beck and Paul Lopatto have shown; see "The End of Southern Distinctiveness," in Laurence W. Moreland, Tod A. Baker, and Robert P. Steed, eds., *Contemporary Southern Political Attitudes and Behavior* (New York: Praeger, 1982), pp. 183–196. Nevertheless, it is well to recall Reed's observation that while "many of the most dramatic and visible" of the South's cultural differences from the non-South have been "diminishing," "an accumulating body of literature demonstrates that many, more subtle, regional cultural differences not only remain but show no sign of disappearing." Reed, *One South*, p. 78. For a study that emphasizes continuing regional differences in political attitudes, see Harry Holloway and Ted Robinson, "The Abiding South: White Attitudes and Regionalism Reexamined," in Merle Black and John Shelton Reed, eds., *Perspectives on the American South*, I (New York: Gordon and Breach, 1981), 227–252.

8. Ulrich B. Phillips, "The Central Theme of Southern History," *American Historical Review*, 34 (October 1928), 31.

9. George Brown Tindall, "The Central Theme Revisited," in Sellers, ed., *Southerner as American*, p. 123.

10. Thomas F. Pettigrew, "Regional Differences in Anti-Negro Prejudice," in John C. Brigham and Theodore A. Weissbach, eds., *Racial Attitudes in America* (New York: Harper & Row, 1972), p. 162.

11. Donald R. Matthews and James W. Prothro, *Negroes and the New Southern Politics* (New York: Harcourt, Brace & World, 1966), pp. 331–366. Though the terms "integration" and "desegregation" are not identical in meaning, for the study of mass attitudes it is reasonable to treat them as synonyms. Other studies of the racial beliefs of white southerners using survey data include Mildred A. Schwartz, *Trends in White Attitudes toward Negroes* (Chicago: National Opinion Research Center, 1967); Andrew M. Greeley and Paul B. Sheatsley, "Attitudes toward Racial Integration," *Scientific American*, December 1971, pp. 13–19; Angus Campbell, *White Attitudes toward Black People* (Ann Arbor: Institute for Social Research, 1971); and D. Garth Taylor, Paul B. Sheatsley, and Andrew M. Greeley, "Attitudes toward Racial Integration," *Scientific American*, June 1978, pp. 42–49.

12. Paul B. Sheatsley, "White Attitudes toward the Negro," *Daedalus*, 91 (Winter 1966), 219–222.

13. Matthews and Prothro, *New Southern Politics*, pp. 332–335.

14. Ibid., pp. 361–366. See also Fred Powledge, *Black Power—White Resistance* (Cleveland: World, 1967), pp. 97–127.

15. Matthews and Prothro concluded from their examination of 1961 data that "education decreases dedication to strict segregation, but extremely high levels of education are apparently necessary to produce actual acceptance of integration," See *New Southern Politics*, p. 343.

16. The pattern of black initiative and white response is illustrated time after time in William H. Chafe, *Civilities and Civil Rights* (New York: Oxford University Press, 1980).

17. Matthews and Prothro, *New Southern Politics*, p. 365.

18. Earl Black, *Southern Governors and Civil Rights* (Cambridge, Mass.: Harvard University Press, 1976), p. 342.

19. On the use of quotas see George H. Gallup, *The Gallup Poll: Public Opinion 1935–1971* (New York: Random House, 1972), II, 1059.

20. See Black and Reed, "Blacks and Southerners."

21. Ibid., 171.

10. The Conservative Advantage in Public Opinion

1. In a subtle and provocative analysis of the impact of religion on American politics, Walter Dean Burnham argues that "our electoral politics will continue to be suffused with a religious dimension closely interwoven with patriotism and the Protestant ethic." See "The 1980 Earthquake: Realignment, Reaction, or What?" in Thomas Ferguson and Joel Rogers, eds., *The Hidden Election* (New York: Pantheon, 1981), p. 139. Since the South is the most Protestant section of a largely Protestant nation, the importance of individual rather than collective responsibility for economic success might be even more salient there than in the nation as a whole. For a recent study, see Tod A. Baker, Robert P. Steed, and Laurence W. Moreland, eds., *Religion and Politics in the South* (New York: Praeger, 1983).

2. W. J. Cash, *The Mind of the South* (New York: Knopf, 1941), pp. 362, 364.

3. Ibid., pp. 364–365.

4. David Halberstam, "The End of a Populist," *Harper's*, January 1971, p. 40.

5. Ibid.

6. These patterns were not unique to the South. See, for example, Arthur H. Miller, "Political Issues and Trust in Government, 1964–1970," *American Political Science Review*, 68 (September 1974), 951–972.

7. John Shelton Reed, "Southerners," in Stephan Thernstrom, ed., *Harvard Encyclopedia of American Ethnic Groups* (Cambridge, Mass.: Harvard University Press, 1980), p. 945.

8. Charles Angoff and H. L. Mencken, "The Worst American State," *Amer-*

ican Mercury, 24 (September, October, and November 1931), 1–16, 177–188, 355–371, reprinted in Charles Press and Oliver P. Williams, eds., *Democracy in the Fifty States* (Chicago: Rand McNally, 1966), pp. 7–32.

9. H. L. Mencken, *Prejudices: Second Series* (New York: Knopf, 1920), pp. 136–154.

10. For instructive comparative analyses of the fifty states, see Virginia Gray, Herbert Jacob, and Kenneth N. Vines, eds., *Politics in the American States*, 4th ed. (Boston: Little, Brown, 1983); and Ann O'M. Bowman and Richard C. Kearney, *The Resurgence of the States* (Englewood Cliffs: Prentice-Hall, 1986).

11. Ben-Chieh Liu, *The Quality of Life in the United States* (Kansas City: Midwest Research Institute, 1973).

12. John Shelton Reed, *One South* (Baton Rouge: Louisiana State University Press, 1982), pp. 154–156.

13. Ibid., pp. 156–157.

14. Merle Black, David M. Kovenock, and William C. Reynolds, *Political Attitudes in the Nation and States* (Chapel Hill: Institute for Research in Social Science, 1974), p. 197.

15. Reed, *One South*, p. 156.

16. Ibid., p. 161.

17. John L. Sullivan, "Political Correlates of Social, Economic, and Religious Diversity in the American States," *Journal of Politics*, 35 (February 1973), 70–84.

18. Since the CSEP survey Florida has become even more heterogeneous, and we would be surprised if the percentage of Floridians now believing they inhabited the best community of the best state had not sharply declined from its 1968 level. "As immigrants from the North and South have flooded in, the state has lost, save in a few counties hard up against the Georgia and Alabama borders, whatever tenuous ties it had with its Deep South neighbors. Perhaps, in racial matters, that was good riddance," observed Neal R. Peirce and Jerry Hagstrom. "But what has developed on the Florida peninsula is a deeply disjointed society, one that has yet to develop a coherent sense of itself and perhaps never will. Anglo factory workers, elderly fresh in from the Frostbelt, Latin Americans—all may call themselves Floridians. But many do not; they and all their Floridian neighbors know their roots are elsewhere and that they have a quite limited commitment to their new 'home.' Florida, in short, is not so much beneficiary as victim of its widely heralded growth. The Floridian experience proves that tumultuous, rapid growth is as destructive to a society and natural environment as the more feared processes of population decline and economic stagnation." Neil R. Peirce and Jerry Hagstrom, *The Book of America* (New York: Norton, 1983), p. 515. Florida is an extreme case, of course, but it suggests that diversification of the population may reduce perceptions of the "quality of life" in other southern states.

19. Reed, *One South*, pp. 159–160.

20. John Shelton Reed, *The Enduring South* (Chapel Hill: University of North Carolina Press, 1974), p. 35.

21. Reed, *One South*, pp. 157, 160–161.

22. Black, Kovenock, and Reynolds, *Political Attitudes*, p. 21.

23. V. O. Key, Jr., *Southern Politics in State and Nation* (New York: Knopf, 1949), p. 310.

24. In a telephone survey conducted by the Carolina poll in November 1985, 78 percent of North Carolinians agreed that they were living in the "best state." Among those respondents with opinions, 82 percent expressed satisfaction.

11. The Decline of Southern "Democracy"

1. W. J. Cash, *The Mind of the South* (New York: Knopf, 1941), p. 129.

2. The Gallup poll occasionally asked this question of southerners from 1939 through 1966. Of those who had opinions, majorities always preferred two-party politics. See George H. Gallup, *The Gallup Poll: Public Opinion, 1935–1971* (New York: Random House, 1972), I, 182, 398, 585, II, 985, and III, 1728–29, 1822, 1900, 2036.

3. V. O. Key, Jr., *Southern Politics in State and Nation* (New York: Knopf, 1949), pp. 315–382.

4. David M. Potter, *The South and the Concurrent Majority* (Baton Rouge: Louisiana State University Press, 1972), p. 59.

5. Key, *Southern Politics*, pp. 9, 345–368; and William S. White, *Citadel*, (New York: Harper and Brothers, 1957). The autobiography of former Illinois Senator Paul H. Douglas contains a remarkably candid analysis of the South's role in the Senate. See his *In the Fullness of Time* (New York: Harcourt Brace Jovanovich, 1972), pp. 196–221.

6. The most succinct analysis of President Roosevelt's treatment of the South is Frank Freidel, *F.D.R. and the South* (Baton Rouge: Louisiana State University Press, 1965).

7. Cash, *Mind of the South*, pp. 343–371.

8. For the term "Solid South generation," see Paul Allen Beck, "Partisan Dealignment in the Postwar South," *American Political Science Review*, 71 (June 1977), 484–487.

9. James L. Sundquist, *Dynamics of the Party System*, rev. ed. (Washington, D.C.: Brookings Institution, 1983), pp. 198–268, 332–351.

10. Potter, *South and Concurrent Majority*, p. 60.

11. Freidel, *F.D.R. and the South*, pp. 71–102.

12. William C. Havard, "From Past to Future: An Overview of Southern Politics," in William C. Havard, ed., *The Changing Politics of the South* (Baton Rouge: Louisiana State University Press, 1972), p. 716.

13. David R. Mayhew, *Party Loyalty among Congressmen* (Cambridge, Mass.: Harvard University Press, 1966), pp. 146–168.

14. Douglas, *In the Fullness of Time*, pp. 202–204. On the origins of the conservative coalition, see James T. Patterson, *Congressional Conservatism and the New Deal* (Lexington: University of Kentucky Press, 1967); and John T. Manley, "The Conservative Coalition in Congress," *American Behavioral Scientist*, 17 (November-December 1973), 223–247.

15. Jasper Berry Shannon, *Toward a New Politics in the South* (Knoxville: University of Tennessee Press, 1949), p. 10.

16. For a penetrating analysis of the growth of severe conflict within the Democratic party, see Sundquist, *Dynamics,* pp. 269–297, 352–375.

17. V. O. Key, Jr., "The Erosion of Sectionalism," *Virginia Quarterly Review,* 31 (Spring 1955), 165.

18. Beck, "Partisan Dealignment in the Postwar South," p. 480. See also E. M. Schreiber, "Where the Ducks Are: Southern Strategy versus Fourth Party," *Public Opinion Quarterly,* 35 (Summer 1971), 157–169; Bruce A. Campbell, "Change in the Southern Electorate," *American Journal of Political Science,* 21 (February 1977), 37–64, and "Patterns of Change in the Partisan Loyalties of Native Southerners, 1952–1972," *Journal of Politics,* 39 (August 1977), 730–761; Philip E. Converse, "A Major Political Realignment in the South?" in Allan P. Sindler, ed., *Change in the Contemporary South* (Durham: Duke University Press, 1963), pp. 195–222; Douglas S. Gatlin, "Party Identification, Status, and Race in the South, 1952–1972," *Public Opinion Quarterly,* 39 (Spring 1975), 39–51; Charles D. Hadley, "Survey Research and Southern Politics: The Implications of Data Management," *Public Opinion Quarterly,* 45 (Fall 1981), 393–401; Raymond Wolfinger and Robert B. Arseneau, "Partisan Change in the South, 1952–1976," in Louis Maisel and Joseph Cooper, eds., *Political Parties: Development and Decay* (Beverly Hills: Sage Publications, 1978), pp. 179–210; Everett Carll Ladd, Jr., with Charles D. Hadley, *Transformations of the American Party System,* 2nd ed. (New York: Norton, 1978); and John R. Petrocik, *Party Coalitions: Realignments and the Decline of the New Deal Party System* (Chicago: University of Chicago Press, 1981), pp. 82–87.

19. Beck has analyzed a recent shift in the direction of partisan realignment in Florida. See Paul Allen Beck, "Realignment Begins? The Republican Surge in Florida," *American Politics Quarterly,* 10 (October 1982), 421–438.

20. Several scholars have suggested that the processes of dealignment and realignment may be simultaneously present. For especially helpful analyses, see William Schneider, "Realignment: The Eternal Question," *PS,* 15 (Summer 1982), 449–457; Harold W. Stanley, "Southern Partisan Changes: Dealignment, Realignment, or Both" (MS, Political Science Department, University of Rochester, January 1986); and Robert H. Swansbrough and David M. Brodsky, "Partisan Realignment in Tennessee" (Paper presented at the 1985 annual meeting of the Southern Political Science Association, Nashville, Tennessee).

21. For the ten-state South, self-identified Republicans constituted only 19 percent of the sample, virtually the same as four years earlier. This result is not realistic. The paucity of Republicans is not the result of using the Solid South sample of states; when the border states and the District of Columbia are added to create the Border South, only 20 percent identify themselves as Republicans. In correspondence with one of the authors of this book, Martin P. Wattenberg pointed out an additional reason to think that the strength of Republicans is underestimated: "The fact that the reported vote was only 54% for Reagan whereas the actual Southern returns were 62% immediately led me to the conclusion that it would be misleading to go with these data." Wattenberg then suggested that "more believable figures" could be obtained by combining the usual cross-sectional survey with the continuous-monitoring surveys that CPS conducted throughout 1984.

We have followed Wattenberg's helpful advice in using the 1984 CPS surveys. Except for groups for which the relevant information did not appear in the continuous-monitoring surveys (native whites, migrant whites, and the ideological groups of whites), the results we report arise from combining the cross-sectional and continuous-monitoring surveys. See table 11.2 for comparisons of the original CPS results and the results based on the combined data sets.

22. Thomas E. Cavanagh and James L. Sundquist, "The New Two-Party System," in John E. Chubb and Paul E. Peterson, eds., *The New Direction in American Politics* (Washington, D. C.: Brookings Institution, 1985), pp. 54–59. See also Everett Carll Ladd, "On Mandates, Realignments, and the 1984 Presidential Election," *Political Science Quarterly,* 100 (Spring 1985), 19–22.

23. Cavanagh and Sundquist, "New Two-Party System," p. 46; and Peter Begans, "GOP Approaching Democrats as Nation's Top Party," ABC News Polling Unit, 1985, p. 3.

24. Results supplied by Barbara Farar of the *New York Times.*

25. See *The Gallup Report,* no. 230 (November 1984), p. 25; and Begans, "GOP Approaching Democrats," p. 3.

26. For the ABC/*Washington Post* poll, see Begans, "GOP Approaching Democrats," p. 3. See note 24 for the *New York Times*/CBS poll.

27. See Cavanagh and Sundquist, "New Two-Party System," pp. 50–54.

28. Key, *Southern Politics,* pp. 664–675. In addition to the works cited in note 18, see Alexander Heard, *A Two-Party South?* (Chapel Hill: University of North Carolina Press, 1952); Donald S. Strong, *The 1952 Presidential Election in the South* (University, Ala.: Bureau of Public Administration, 1955); Donald S. Strong, *Urban Republicanism in the South* (University, Ala.: Bureau of Public Administration, 1960); Donald S. Strong, "Durable Republicanism in the South," in Sindler, ed., *Change in the Contemporary South,* pp. 174–194; Donald S. Strong, "Further Reflections on Southern Politics," *Journal of Politics,* 33 (May 1971), 239–256; Bernard Cosman, *Five States for Goldwater* (University, Ala.: University of Alabama Press, 1966); James W. Prothro, Ernest Q. Campbell, and Charles M. Grigg, "Two-Party Voting in the South: Class vs. Party Identification," *American Political Science Review,* 52 (March 1958), 131–139; Carol A. Cassel, "Class Bases of Southern Politics among Whites, 1952–1972," *Social Science Quarterly,* 58 (March 1978), 700–707; Louis M. Seagull, *Southern Republicanism* (Cambridge, Mass.: Schenkman, 1975); and Norman H. Nie, Sidney Verba, and John R. Petrocik, *The Changing American Voter* (Cambridge, Mass.: Harvard University Press, 1976), pp. 221–223.

29. See Beck, "Partisan Dealignment in the Postwar South," 480–489; and Paul Allen Beck and Paul Lopatto, "The End of Southern Distinctiveness," in Laurence W. Moreland, Tod A. Baker, and Robert P. Steed, *Contemporary Southern Political Attitudes and Behavior* (New York: Praeger, 1982), pp. 163–169.

30. Beck, "Partisan Dealignment in the Postwar South," pp. 484–487.

31. Ibid., p. 486.

32. See, for example, Cavanagh and Sundquist, "New Two-Party System," pp. 48–49, for a discussion of "the GOP's youth movement."

33. Because the CPS cross-sectional survey in 1984 may have underestimated southern Republicans, it is instructive to consider generational differences among all members of the South's racial majority. Examining partisanship among all southern whites allows us to use the combined cross-sectional and continuous-monitoring surveys, thus greatly enlarging the number of cases for analysis.

When native and migrant whites are combined, the expected generational differences in partisan attachments and leanings indeed appear. The Democrats held a clear lead (48 to 40 percent) only among whites of the Solid South generation, while the Republicans had wrested a similar advantage (49 to 39 percent) among the youngest generation of southern whites. Middle-aged southern whites were more evenly split in their partisan inclinations, with Democrats marginally higher (45 to 42 percent).

34. Key, *Southern Politics*, pp. 673–674.

35. Heard, *A Two-Party South?* p. 248.

36. Donald S. Strong, "The Presidential Election in the South, 1952," *Journal of Politics*, 17 (August 1955), 382.

37. Numan V. Bartley and Hugh D. Graham, *Southern Politics and the Second Reconstruction* (Baltimore: Johns Hopkins University Press, 1975), p. 185.

38. David Halberstam, "The End of a Populist," *Harper's*, January 1971, p. 40.

39. We also used perceived social class to determine the extent to which various socioeconomic classes of southerners have differed in party identification. Since sharper divisions appeared when southerners were classified by formal education than by perceived social class, results with the former indicator have been reported. There are other useful ways to classify individuals. Wolfinger and Arseneau found substantial increases in Republican identification among professional and managerial workers, as well as sales and clerical employees, between the 1950s and 1975. See "Partisan Change in the South," p. 205. See also Nie, Verba, and Petrocik, *Changing American Voter*, pp. 221–223, for a discussion of party identification and status in the South.

40. Kevin P. Phillips, *The Emerging Republican Majority* (New York: Anchor Books, 1970), p. 232.

41. Sundquist provides a very interesting discussion of the revitalization of old partisan attachments as one theoretical possibility. See *Dynamics*, pp. 444–449.

42. See Tod A. Baker, Robert P. Steed, and Laurence W. Moreland, eds., *Religion and Politics in the South: Mass and Elite Perspectives* (New York: Praeger, 1983); and James L. Guth, "The Christian Right Revisited: Partisan Realignment among Southern Baptist Ministers" (Paper presented at the annual meeting of the Midwest Political Science Association, Chicago, Illinois, April 19–20, 1985.

43. Alexander P. Lamis, for example, reported a strong relationship in 1980 between family income and party identification in *The Two-Party South* (New York: Oxford University Press, 1984), p. 216.

44. Heard, *A Two-Party South?* p. 247.

45. Ibid., pp. 247–248.

46. Ibid., p. 248.
47. Key, *Southern Politics*, pp. 277–297; Heard, *A Two-Party South?* p. 245; and Sundquist, *Dynamics*, pp. 269–297, 352–375.
48. Sundquist argues that "the evidence . . . points to a continuing realignment of the electorate along liberal-conservative lines." *Dynamics*, p. 438.
49. For an excellent analysis of ideological differences in the composition of Democratic and Republican elites in a southern state, see Alan I. Abramowitz, "Ideological Realignment and the Nationalization of Southern Politics: Party Activists and Candidates in Virginia," in Merle Black and John Shelton Reed, eds., *Perspectives on the American South*, I (New York: Gordon and Breach, 1981), 83–106.
50. Sundquist, *Dynamics*, p. 374.
51. Ibid., p. 375.
52. This intraparty cleavage was visible in North Carolina between the right-wing conservative faction headed by Senator Jesse Helms and a group of moderate conservatives associated with Governor James Martin.

12. The Republican Advantage in Presidential Politics

1. See Alexander P. Lamis, *The Two-Party South* (New York: Oxford University Press, 1984).
2. See Thomas E. Cavanagh and James L. Sundquist, "The New Two-Party System," in John E. Chubb and Paul E. Peterson, eds., *The New Direction in American Politics* (Washington, D.C.: Brookings Institution, 1985), p. 40. They cite Kevin Phillip's biweekly newsletter, *The American Political Report*, January 11, 1985.
3. For analyses of southern presidential politics, in addition to the studies cited in chapter 11, note 20, see James L. Sundquist, *Dynamics of the Party System*, rev. ed. (Washington, D.C.: Brookings Institution, 1983), pp. 269–297, 352–375; Numan V. Bartley and Hugh D. Graham, *Southern Politics and the Second Reconstruction* (Baltimore: Johns Hopkins University Press, 1975); Kevin P. Phillips, *The Emerging Republican Majority* (Garden City: Anchor Books, 1970), pp. 187–289; Lamis, *Two-Party South*, pp. 7–43; Robert P. Steed, Laurence W. Moreland, and Tod A. Baker, eds., *The 1984 Presidential Election in the South* (New York: Praeger, 1985); and Earl Black, "Competing Responses to the 'New Southern Politics': Republican and Democratic Southern Strategies, 1964–1976," in Merle Black and John Shelton Reed, eds., *Perspectives on the American South*, I (New York: Gordon and Breach, 1981), 151–164.
4. Phillips, *Emerging Republican Majority*, pp. 187, 286–289.
5. V. O. Key, Jr., *American State Politics* (New York: Knopf, 1956), pp. 97–100.
6. David M. Olson, "Attributes of State Political Parties: An Exploration of Theory and Data," in James A. Riedel, ed., *New Perspectives in State and Local Politics* (Waltham, Mass.: Xerox College Publishing, 1971), pp. 127–129.
7. Ibid., pp. 128–129.

8. Ibid., p. 128.

9. Sundquist, *Dynamics*, pp. 272–277, 363–364; Phillips, *Emerging Republican Majority*, pp. 187–289.

10. On the Dixiecrats, see V. O. Key, Jr., *Southern Politics in State and Nation* (New York: Knopf, 1949), pp. 329–344; Alexander Heard, *A Two-Party South?* (Chapel Hill: University of North Carolina Press, 1952), pp. 20–33, 160–168; Robert A. Garson, *The Democratic Party and the Politics of Sectionalism, 1941–1948* (Baton Rouge: Louisiana State University Press, 1974), esp pp. 232–321; and Emile B. Ader, "Why the Dixiecrats Failed," *Journal of Politics*, 15 (August 1953), 356–369.

11. Donald S. Strong, *The 1952 Presidential Election in the South* (University, Ala.: Bureau of Public Administration, 1955); Bartley and Graham, *Southern Politics and the Second Reconstruction*, p. 86; and George B. Tindall, *The Disruption of the Solid South* (Athens: University of Georgia Press, 1972), pp. 49–53.

12. See Philip E. Converse et al., "Continuity and Change in American Politics: Parties and Issues in the 1968 Election," *American Political Science Review*, 63 (December 1969), 1083–1105; and David M. Kovenock, James W. Prothro, and Associates, *Explaining the Vote: Presidential Choices in the Nation and the States, 1968*, part II (Chapel Hill: Institute for Research in Social Science, 1973).

13. See Walter Dean Burnham, "The 1980 Earthquake: Realignment, Reaction, or What?" in Thomas Ferguson and Joel Rogers, eds., *The Hidden Election* (New York: Pantheon, 1981), pp. 98–140.

14. See Harold W. Stanley, "The 1984 Presidential Election in the South: Race and Realignment," in Steed, Moreland, and Baker, *1984 Presidential Election in the South*.

15. Key, *Southern Politics*, pp. 280–285.

16. Ibid., pp. 75–81.

17. Phillips stressed "the extraordinary 1968 debacle of the Democratic party—a collapse never before experienced by the Democrats throughout the *entire* region." (Emphasis in original). *Emerging Republican Majority*, p. 187.

18. See Stanley, "1984 Presidential Election," for a cogent discussion of the racial cleavage in presidential voting.

19. W. Wayne Shannon, "Revolt in Washington: The South in Congress," in William C. Havard, ed., *The Changing Politics of the South* (Baton Rouge: Louisiana State University Press, 1972), p. 664.

20. Wolfinger and Arseneau have previously examined presidential voting behavior among different groups of partisans in the South. See Raymond Wolfinger and Robert B. Arseneau, "Partisan Change in the South, 1952–1976," in Louis Maisel and Joseph Cooper, eds., *Political Parties: Development and Decay* (Beverly Hills: Sage Publications, 1978), pp. 188–192.

21. In 1984 only 14 percent of white southerners identified themselves as strong Democrats.

22. Only a thin majority (57 percent) of strong Democrats supported Humphrey and McGovern. By contrast, Walter Mondale received 86 percent of the

vote among a much smaller group of strong Democrats in 1984. As Wolfinger and Arseneau have observed, "those Southerners who remain Democrats are less and less prone to defect." "Partisan Change in the South," p. 192.

23. Donald S. Strong, "Further Reflections on Southern Politics," *Journal of Politics,* 33 (May 1971), 254.

13. Partisan Competition for Senator and Governor

1. V. O. Key, Jr., *American State Politics* (New York: Knopf, 1956), p. 34.

2. Ibid., p. 27.

3. James L. Sundquist, *Dynamics of the Party System,* rev. ed. (Washington, D. C.: Brookings Institution, 1983), p. 392; Douglas S. Gatlin, "Socio-Economic Bases of Party Competition: A Case Study of North Carolina" (Ph. D. diss. University of North Carolina, 1963), p. 92, as quoted in Thad L. Beyle and Peter B. Harkins, "North Carolina," in David M. Kovenock, James W. Prothro, and Associates, *Explaining the Vote: Presidential Choices in the Nation and the States, 1968,* part II (Chapel Hill: Institute for Research in Social Science, 1973), pp. 379–380; and Louis M. Seagull, *Southern Republicanism* (Cambridge, Mass.: Schenkman, 1975), pp. 83–146.

4. For accounts of particular senatorial and gubernatorial elections in the modern South, see Numan V. Bartley and Hugh D. Graham, *Southern Politics and the Second Reconstruction* (Baltimore: Johns Hopkins University Press, 1975); Seagull, *Southern Republicanism;* Earl Black, *Southern Governors and Civil Rights* (Cambridge, Mass.: Harvard University Press, 1976); and Alexander P. Lamis, *The Two-Party South* (New York: Oxford University Press, 1984). Excellent succinct analyses of Senate and gubernatorial politics may be found in the biennial editions of *The Almanac of American Politics,* written by Michael Barone and various associates. Several books provide overviews of the major statewide political tendencies in southern states: see William C. Havard, ed., *The Changing Politics of the South* (Baton Rouge: Louisiana State University Press, 1972); Neal R. Peirce, *The Deep South States of America* (New York: Norton, 1974), and *The Border South States* (New York: Norton, 1975); and Jack Bass and Walter DeVries, *The Transformation of Southern Politics* (New York: Basic Books, 1976).

5. For an interesting discussion of different patterns of national party identification and state party identification in the region, see Charles D. Hadley, "Dual Partisan Identification in the South," *Journal of Politics,* 47 (February 1985), 254–268. He sensibly urges (p. 266) "the importance of including state and national partisan identification questions on state and national surveys for a future series of national and state elections to facilitate further analysis of the phenomenon of dual party identification and partisanship change." For an earlier analysis of this topic, see Philip E. Converse, "A Major Political Realignment in the South?" in Allan P. Sindler, ed., *Change in the Contemporary South* (Durham: Duke University Press, 1963), pp. 198–202.

6. For the voting behavior of southern white independents in presidential elections, see Raymond Wolfinger and Robert B. Arseneau, "Partisan Change in

the South, 1952–1976," in Louis Maisel and Joseph Cooper, eds., *Political Parties: Development and Decay* (Beverly Hills: Sage Publications, 1978), p. 189. The conservatism of many independents may propel them toward Republican candidates.

7. Occasionally Republican candidates—Winthrop Rockefeller and Linwood Holton are the best examples—won by mobilizing blacks rather than conservative white Democrats, but this was not the usual route to success.

8. For example, see V. O. Key, Jr., *Southern Politics in State and Nation* (New York: Knopf, 1949), pp. 277–296, 668–675; Alexander Heard, *A Two-Party South?* (Chapel Hill: University of North Carolina Press, 1952); and Seagull, *Southern Republicanism*.

9. Personal communication from Gerald C. Wright, Jr. See Gerald C. Wright, Robert S. Erikson, and John P. McIver, "Measuring State Partisanship and Ideology with Survey Data," *Journal of Politics*, 47 (May 1985), 469–489.

10. The importance of incumbency is discussed in Richard G. Hutcheson III, "The Inertial Effect of Incumbency and Two-Party Politics: Elections to the House of Representatives from the South, 1952–1974," *American Political Science Review*, 69 (December 1975), 1399–1401. See also Wolfinger and Arseneau, "Partisan Change in the South," pp. 183–185.

11. Examples of Democratic intraparty conflict that greatly assisted Republican victories are the gubernatorial contests in South Carolina (1974) and Louisiana (1979) and the senatorial campaigns in Mississippi (1978), Georgia (1980), and Alabama (1980).

12. Donald S. Strong, "Further Reflections on Southern Politics," *Journal of Politics*, 33 (May 1971), 254.

13. See, for example, Kevin P. Phillips, *The Emerging Republican Majority* (Garden City: Anchor Books, 1970), pp. 228–239, 286–289. Bartley and Graham argue that "in the 1968 presidential election, Wallace, Humphrey, and Nixon each received approximately one-third of the votes cast in the southern states . . . How these three voting groups will fit into a two-party system is, in a simplified sort of way, the basic question of contemporary southern politics." *Southern Politics and the Second Reconstruction*, p. 192. Relatively uneducated white conservatives are the main targets of organizational efforts by prominent right-wing religious organizations.

14. Phillips, *Emerging Republican Majority*, p. 287.

15. For an extended discussion of campaign strategy, see Walter DeVries and V. Lance Tarrance, *The Ticket-Splitter: A New Force in American Politics* (Grand Rapids, Mich.: William B. Eerdmans Publishing Co., 1972). Sundquist observes that "some of the most phenomenal ticket-splitting in history" occurred in southern elections during the 1960s and 1970s. *Dynamics*, p. 373.

14. The Reshaping of Southern Politics

1. V. O. Key, Jr., *Southern Politics in State and Nation* (New York, Knopf, 1949), p. 675.

2. For an optimistic appraisal of contemporary race relations in the South,

see John Shelton Reed, "Up from Segregation," *Virginia Quarterly Review,* 60 (Summer 1984), 377–393.

3. Regional poverty rates have been calculated by the authors from the following publications of the U.S. Bureau of the Census: *1970 Census of Population,* I, *Characteristics of the Population,* appropriate state reports, table 58; and *1980 Census of Population,* I, *Characteristics of the Population,* appropriate state reports, tables 82 and 92.

4. Joel Williamson, *The Crucible of Race* (New York: Oxford University Press, 1984), p. 521.

5. See Hugh Douglas Price, "Southern Politics in the Sixties: Notes on Economic Development and Political Modernization" (Paper presented at the annual meeting of the American Political Science Association, Chicago, September 1964); and William C. Havard, "From Past to Future: An Overview of Southern Politics," in William C. Havard, ed., *The Changing Politics of the South* (Baton Rouge: Louisiana State University Press), p. 726.

6. Our demographic analysis is based on information collected from the following sources: Samuel R. Solomon, *The Governors of the American States, Commonwealths, and Territories, 1900–1980* (Lexington, Ky.: Council of State Governments, 1980); and appropriate volumes of *Congressional Directory* (Washington, D.C.: Government Printing Office).

7. These terms are discussed in Earl Black, *Southern Governors and Civil Rights* (Cambridge, Mass.: Harvard University Press, 1976), pp. 11–16.

8. This development is examined in Black, *Southern Governors.*

9. *New York Times,* June 3, 1970; and Jack Bass and Walter DeVries, *The Transformation of Southern Politics* (New York: Basic Books, 1976), p. 68. (Bass and DeVries discuss Wallace's initial overtures to blacks on pp. 68–69.)

10. Not every governor residing in the black belt hewed to every aspect of traditionalistic orthodoxy, of course; several, especially after the Voting Rights Act, won black support. But most of the black belt governors were grounded in the traditionalistic political culture.

11. Because so few Republican governors were elected during the decades under consideration, they have been excluded from the analysis.

12. "It is chiefly when the equilibrium in race relations is threatened that the issue of the Negro comes to the fore in political discussion." Key, *Southern Politics,* p. 665.

13. Black, *Southern Governors,* pp. 162–243, 309–344.

14. Ibid., pp. 16–21.

15. For a discussion of changing elite views during the Second Reconstruction, see Black, *Southern Governors,* pp. 281–305.

16. Louis M. Seagull emphasized both factors in his study of presidential and gubernatorial Republicanism in the region. See *Southern Republicanism* (Cambridge, Mass.: Schenkman, 1975). The classic statement of the analytical significance of traditional partisan loyalties is V. O. Key, Jr., and Frank Munger, "Social Determinism and Electoral Decision: The Case of Indiana," in Eugene Burdick and Arthur J. Brodbeck, eds., *American Voting Behavior* (New York: Free Press, 1959, pp. 281–299.

Index